Psychology and Educational Inclusion

Psychology and Educational Inclusion

Identifying and Supporting Learners with SEN

Edited by

Georgia Niolaki, Kate Carr-Fanning and Aris R. Terzopoulos

Open University Press

Open University Press
McGraw Hill
Unit 4
Foundation Park
Roxborough Way
Maidenhead
SL6 3UD

email: emea_uk_ireland@mheducation.com
world wide web: www.mheducation.co.uk

First edition published 2024

Copyright © Open International Publishing Limited, 2024

All rights reserved. Except for the quotation of short passages for the purposes of criticism and review, no part of this publication may be reproduced, stored in a retrieval system, or transmitted, in any form or by any means, electronic, mechanical, photocopying, recording or otherwise, without the prior written permission of the publisher or a licence from the Copyright Licensing Agency Limited. Details of such licences (for reprographic reproduction) may be obtained from the Copyright Licensing Agency Ltd of Saffron House, 6–10 Kirby Street, London EC1N 8TS.

Executive Editor: Eleanor Christie
Editorial Assistant: Phoebe Hills
Content Product Manager: Graham Jones

British Library Cataloguing in Publication Data
A catalogue record of this book is available from the British Library

ISBN-13: 978-0-3352-5178-0
ISBN-10: 0335251781
eISBN: 978-0-3352-5179-7

Typeset by Transforma Pvt. Ltd., Chennai, India

Fictitious names of companies, products, people, characters and/or data that may be used herein (in case studies or in examples) are not intended to represent any real individual, company, product or event.

Praise page

"A truly inspiring and skilfully crafted text. Niolaki, Carr-Fanning and Terzopoulos have achieved an excellent balance of interweaving theory, research, and practice. Complex and contemporary issues are addressed in an accessible way, making it an absolute 'must-read' for all those studying, working or planning to work in either special or inclusive education."
  Dr Paula Hamilton, School of Education, University of Chester, UK

"This book is highly recommended for psychologists and educators alike, whether currently practising or in training. Confidently marrying psychological and educational theory, research and practice, the book guides the reader through important factors in special and inclusive education. The book covers a diverse range of topics and the reflection points really make the reader think about the influence of different perspectives on teaching and support."
  Lynn Lovell, Head of Professional Standards,
  British Dyslexia Association, UK

"This is an invaluable resource which will appeal to a wide target audience including undergraduate, postgraduate education and psychology students and professional development courses in the UK and further afield.
The book actively encourages a critical approach to gain a deeper understanding of the differing elements which may contribute to the realities, constraints and tensions of inclusive practice. The breadth and depth of knowledge and experience of the authors and contributors provides a wealth of material which is contextualised in cultural, economic, social perspectives.
Each chapter is clearly laid out so the busy student/practitioner is easily able to see the aim and scope, while the reflective and practical activities aid focus.
A great strength of the book is the promotion of a balanced approach which acknowledges differing viewpoints from psychology and inclusive educational practice and promotes an integrated approach."
  Julia Kender, Independent Consultant in SpLD and
  Adaptive Teaching and Learning, UK

Contents

List of contributors x
Acknowledgements xvi
Introduction: the book in a snapshot! xvii

PART I THEORETICAL PERSPECTIVES AND PRACTICAL CONTEXTS 1

1 THE SPECIAL AND INCLUSIVE EDUCATIONAL CONTINUUM: UNDERSTANDING SPECIAL EDUCATIONAL NEEDS AND APPROACHES TO PRACTICE 3

   Kate Carr-Fanning and Helen Curran

2 THE SPECIAL AND INCLUSIVE EDUCATIONAL CONTINUUM: TRANSLATING THEORY INTO POLICY AND PRACTICE 20

   Helen Curran and Kate Carr-Fanning

3 BRONFENBRENNER AND UNIVERSAL DESIGN: A TALE OF TWO THEORIES FOR INCLUSION 32

   Mary Quirke, Ke Ren and Conor Mc Guckin

4 MIGRANT CHILDREN WITH SPECIAL EDUCATIONAL NEEDS: DYNAMIC AND COMPLEX ECOLOGIES AND THEIR IMPLICATIONS FOR EDUCATIONAL PRACTICE 47

   Clara Rübner Jørgensen and Graeme Dobson

PART II SPECIFIC AREAS OF NEED 61

5 AUTISM AND INCLUSIVE PRACTICE 63

   Rachael Davis, Margaret Laurie and Laura Crane

6   UNDERSTANDING AND RESPONDING TO SOCIAL, EMOTIONAL AND
    MENTAL HEALTH NEEDS   79

    Kate Carr-Fanning

7   SOCIAL INEQUALITY IN THE CLASSROOM: EXPLORING THE EFFECTS OF
    SOCIAL INEQUALITY ON CHILD DEVELOPMENT AND MENTAL HEALTH   99

    Patrycja J. Piotrowska and Richard Rowe

8   THE PSYCHOLOGY OF INCLUDING LEARNERS WITH ATTENTION DEFICIT
    HYPERACTIVITY DISORDER   113

    Kate Carr-Fanning

9   DYSLEXIA: RECOGNITION OF NEEDS AND OVERCOMING LITERACY
    BARRIERS THROUGH EVIDENCE-BASED PRACTICES   133

    Georgia Niolaki, Aris Terzopoulos, Jennifer Donovan and
    Jackie Masterson

10 WHY ARE CIRCLES SO SMART? BECAUSE THEY HAVE 360 DEGREES!   151

    Donna-Lynn Shepherd

PART III PHYSICAL AND SENSORY NEEDS   177

11 DEVELOPMENTAL COORDINATION DISORDER: 'I'M FALLING …
    THROUGH THE CRACKS'   179

    Tanya Rihtman and Susan Allen

12 PSYCHO-EDUCATIONAL ASSESSMENT AND INSTRUCTION FOR
    STUDENTS WHO HAVE VISUAL IMPAIRMENTS   204

    Vassilios Papadimitriou and Ayse Dolunay Sarica

13 AUDITORY PROCESSING AND ITS IMPLICATIONS FOR LEARNERS:
    'MY EARS WORK FINE, IT IS THE WAY I PROCESS SOUND'   217

    Carmel Capewell

PART IV BILINGUALISM AND EXCEPTIONAL COGNITIVE ABILITIES 229

14 BILINGUALISM, SECOND LANGUAGE LEARNING AND DEVELOPMENTAL
    DIFFERENCES 231
    Aris Terzopoulos, Georgia Niolaki and Jackie Masterson

15 WHY IT IS IMPORTANT TO GIVE ADDITIONAL SUPPORT TO CHILDREN
    AND YOUNG PEOPLE OF EXCEPTIONAL COGNITIVE ABILITY 246
    Lyn Kendall

Epilogue: A journey at the end! Is it truly the end or the beginning? 261
Index 262

List of contributors

Georgia Niolaki has a BA (Hons) in Education and completed her MA in Literacy Learning and Literacy Difficulties and her PhD at the Institute of Education, University College London. Georgia is a Senior Lecturer in SpLD/Dyslexia at Bath Spa University where she is Award Leader for the SpLD (dyslexia) programme. She is also a Visiting Research Associate at the UCL Institute of Education. In 2016, Georgia completed the PGCert in Language, Literacies and Dyslexia at the University of Birmingham, and she is an Associate Member of the British Dyslexia Association (AMBDA) and a Trustee of the BDA. In January 2018, she became a member of the Experimental Psychological Society. Georgia is the principal investigator for the development of a new spelling test for primary school children, a project that is funded by the British Academy BA/Leverhulme Senior Research Fellowships (2017–19) and Bath Spa Seed funding (2021–23). This demonstrates Georgia's interest in spelling research and in supporting individuals with spelling and reading difficulties.

Kate Carr-Fanning is an Assistant Professor in Psychology of Education in the School of Education at the University of Bristol. She completed her BA (Hons) in Psychology before commencing her PhD in Psychology and Education at Trinity College Dublin, where she explored stress, emotion and coping with learners with ADHD. Kate has over 10 years of experience of teaching and leadership within higher education, on programmes focused on special and inclusive education, teacher education, psychology of education, childhood and youth and education studies. Her research interests centre on social, emotional and/or mental health difficulties, with a particular focus on attention deficit hyperactivity disorder (ADHD), children/learner voice, participatory research and practice, and school-based programmes of inclusion. Kate has almost 20 years of experience working and researching 'with' schools and charities in the area of inclusion across Europe and in the USA. At present, she sits on the Board of Governors for Herewood Academy, Coventry. She is also on the Board of Directors of ADHD Ireland and on the Professional Advisory Board of ADHD Europe. Kate is a Chartered Psychologist (CPsychol) with the British Psychological Society (BPS) and a Fellow of the Higher Education Academy (FHEA).

Aris Terzopoulos has a BA (Hons) in Education and completed his MA in Literacy Learning and Literacy Difficulties at the Institute of Education, University College London. He started his PhD with a European Scholarship at UCL with Professor Jackie Masterson and then moved to the University of Dundee with a fully-funded scholarship under the supervision of Lynne Duncan. Aris's PhD is on word representations in the mental lexicon of bilingual adults and children and on construction of psycholinguistic databases for researchers, teachers and pupils. Aris is a Lecturer in Psychology and is currently involved in research projects involving electroencephalographic measurements of word representations of bilingual adults, construction of the first bilingual word database for children (Bilex-kids), and experimental case studies of bilingual and monolingual children with developmental language difficulties.

Helen Curran is a Senior Lecturer in SEN at Bath Spa University. She trained as a primary school teacher, later becoming a SENCO, assistant head teacher and local authority advisory and dyslexia consultant. Helen's research focuses on SEN policy and the role of the SENCO. She leads on the National SENCO Workforce survey, alongside NASEN, now in its third year.

Mary Quirke is currently a PhD researcher in the School of Education at Trinity College Dublin, and a guidance practitioner. She has a passion and knowledge about guidance and inclusion in education due to her active engagement with learners, teachers and employers in Ireland and across Europe. Mary's primary research interests include UD(L), career guidance/educational guidance and counselling, professional practice development, and inclusion practices. ORCID iD: https://orcid.org/0000-0001-5848-2709

Conor Mc Guckin PhD is an Associate Professor of Educational Psychology in the School of Education at Trinity College Dublin. He convenes the Inclusion in Education and Society Research Group. Conor's research interests include psychology applied to educational policy and practices, bully/victim problems among children and adults, and inclusive education. He is an Associate Fellow of both the British Psychological Society (BPS) and the Psychological Society of Ireland (PSI). Conor is a Chartered Psychologist with both the BPS and PSI and a Chartered Scientist with the UK Science Council.

Ke Ren has a BA (Hons) in Early Childhood Education, an MEd in Early Intervention and a PhD from Trinity College Dublin. Her research interests focus on early intervention and creating inclusive education environments for all children and young people. As a lecturer, Ke leads Dissertation and Special Education modules at St. Nicholas Montessori College. Furthermore, she serves as a postgraduate research supervisor at Dublin City University, the University of East London and Trinity College Dublin. Her extensive background as an early intervention specialist focuses on supporting families of children with complex needs. Ke's dedication to her work and evidence-based practices drives her research, which she hopes will help children and their families achieve their full potential.

Clara Rübner Jörgensen is Assistant Professor in the Department for Disability Inclusion and Special Needs at the School of Education, University of Birmingham. She has extensive experience of conducting qualitative and ethnographic research in schools and educational settings in Europe and Central

America, exploring educational inequalities, school policies and practices, inclusive teaching strategies, and the experiences of children and young people from migrant and minority ethnic backgrounds. Her current research interests include the education of migrant children with special educational needs, pupil school mobility, and the transitions and pathways of young carers.

Graeme J. Dobson is Associate Professor in the School of Education, University of Birmingham. He is a qualified teacher and former SENCO, school leader and local authority advisor. He is an Associate Member of the British Dyslexia Association and Senior Fellow of the Higher Education Academy. His research interests include the leadership of inclusion in schools, the allocation of resources for vulnerable groups, and the experiences of migrant children with special educational needs.

Rachael Davis is a Lecturer and Researcher in Psychology & Education at Queen Margaret University. Previously a Research Fellow at the University of Edinburgh, Rachael is a Developmental Psychologist whose research focuses on autism, cognition and education; she co-designs novel and inclusive methods for children frequently excluded from research. Central to her work is a commitment to involving the communities that she works with in the research process, ensuring this research has a strong participatory ethos and has real-world relevance to the people that matter.

Margaret Laurie is a research specialist who focuses on learning through play, manipulatives and neurodiversity. She completed her PhD at the University of Edinburgh, looking at how digital toys can support socially interactive play for autistic children, and then worked at the LEGO Foundation building tools to measure learning through play from children's perspectives. She currently spends most of her time working for Play Included, and some of her time as an honorary Research Fellow at the Faculty of Education at the University of Cambridge, as part of the Play, Education, Learning And Development (PEDAL) team.

Laura Crane is an Associate Professor at the Institute of Education (IoE), UCL's Faculty of Education and Society, where she is Deputy Director of the Centre for Research in Autism and Education (CRAE). At IoE, Laura leads the Special and Inclusive Education (Autism) MA, where she supports a broad range of practitioners to embed neurodiversity-affirmative approaches within their practice. Laura is committed to supporting schools to be more research-engaged, and chairs the innovative Pan London Autism Schools Network, which brings together academic researchers and school staff to share expertise and to co-create research that positively impacts schools and pupils.

Patrycja Piotrowska has a BSc (Hons) in Psychology & Criminology and completed her PhD in Psychology at the University of Sheffield. Her PhD focused on examining the relationship between socio-economic status and broadly conceptualised behavioural problems among children and adolescents. She worked in a research and policy team for a mental health charity, as a Postdoctoral Fellow at the University of Sydney and for Neuroscience Research Australia (NeuRA). Patrycja has completed several large-scale research projects, and her main areas of interest include factors underlying emotional and behavioural difficulties in children and young people, particularly the role of social inequality. She has written numerous papers on social inequalities and conduct problems, parenting programmes, and children's socio-emotional development. Patrycja is a Co-Investigator on the Nuffield Foundation Grant that is exploring the mechanisms linking socio-economic status and child antisocial behaviour.

Richard Rowe holds a BSc (Hons) in Psychology from the University of Manchester and completed an MSc and PhD in Applied Cognitive Psychology at the University of Reading. Richard then became a post-doctoral researcher at the Institute of Psychiatry working on behavioural, genetic and epidemiological approaches to developmental psychopathology. Professor Rowe has been an academic at the University of Sheffield for more than 15 years, working on projects addressing the development of antisocial behaviour and the role of social inequalities. He is a Principal Investigator on the Nuffield Foundation Grant that is exploring the mechanisms linking socio-economic status and child antisocial behaviour.

Jennifer Donovan completed her MA in Special and Inclusive Education and her PhD at the Institute of Education, University College London where she was also Programme Leader for the MA in Specific Learning Difficulties (dyslexia). Jennifer is a member of the Accreditation Board for the British Dyslexia Association and the Education Panel for the Dyspraxia Foundation. Her research interests include the assessment and support of literacy difficulties with learners of all ages, with a particular interest in spelling assessment and intervention. Her current research involves working with specialist teachers to investigate the effectiveness of a dynamic assessment approach to spelling. She is an active practitioner assessing and supporting children, young people and adults with literacy difficulties.

Jackie Masterson's main research interests are in the areas of literacy development and literacy difficulties. Professor Masterson has used models of skilled reading to provide a context for thinking about the set of cognitive processes that are required for competent reading and spelling. She has investigated potential sensory difficulties as underlying causes of literacy problems and looked at relationships with verbal memory processes. Jackie has also carried out research into object and action naming in children and adults.

Donna-Lynn Shepherd is a Lecturer at the Institute of Education, UCL's Faculty of Education and Society, and a maths and psychology teacher at Lord Williams's School, a very large secondary comprehensive. She has more than 20 years of international classroom experience across mainstream and specialist settings, from nursery to postgraduate levels. Her research interests include maths education (particularly affective aspects and inclusive pedagogy) and autism, and she is the co-author of *Teaching in Effective Primary Schools: Research into Pedagogy and Children's Learning* (Trentham Books, 2019).

Tanya Rihtman has a PhD in Occupational Therapy awarded by the Hebrew University, Jerusalem. As an academic and paediatric occupational therapy clinician, her research interests focus on the assessment and support of early motor and sensory development in childhood, factors that facilitate and hinder occupational participation in childhood, and cultural influences on childhood development. Tanya has published peer-reviewed papers and book chapters across a range of subjects related to early childhood development, is the Occupational Therapy Programme Lead at Oxford Brookes University, and is chair of the Royal College of Occupational Therapists' Play and Occupational Therapy guideline development group.

Susan Allen is an academic and children's occupational therapy clinician. Her research interests include the impact of sensory and motor difficulties on everyday life for children and their families at home, at school and within the community. Susan's current PhD research is on optimising support for mothers of children with sensory processing differences to support mother and child participation in daily occupations. Sue is a Senior Lecturer at Oxford Brookes University and provides consultancy services worldwide.

Ayse Dolunay Sarica has a BS degree in Psychology, MS degrees in Special Education and Forensic Psychology, and a PhD in Special Education. She has been working in the field of early childhood special education since 2004 with an extra focus on infants and toddlers with visual impairments. Dolunay has served in three Turkish universities and also joined the Department of Early Childhood at Teachers College, Columbia University (USA) as a visiting scholar during the 2016–17 academic year. She also led the early intervention programme at the Special Education Research Centre at Ankara University (2004–14). Dolunay is currently an Associate Professor at Buca Faculty of Education, Department of Special Education, Dokuz Eylül University (Izmir) and is the head of the Unit of Intellectual Disabilities. Dolunay's professional interests include early childhood special education, early intervention, visual impairments, family studies, child and adult attachment, and adult-child interaction. She has written more than 30 journal articles, books and book chapters in her fields of interest. She is an associate editor of the *Eurasian Journal of Educational Research* and *Western Anatolian Journal of Educational Sciences*. Dolunay has worked on four national projects, one sponsored by WHO. She teaches many undergraduate and graduate courses in her department and has and still is advising masters and doctoral theses at the Institute of Educational Sciences, Dokuz Eylül University.

Vassilios Papadimitriou is a post-doctoral researcher in the Department of Special Education at the University of Thessaly. He holds a bachelor degree in Greek Philology (2004) from the University of Athens. In 2008, he obtained a postgraduate diploma in Special Education and Psychology from the University of Athens and in 2016 received his PhD degree from the University of Thessaly. His thesis examined the effect of handedness on braille reading and spelling accuracy of students with severe visual impairments. He has participated in the project 'Handedness and Braille Literacy in Individuals with Severe Visual Impairments', which was implemented under the 'ARISTEIA' Action of the 'Operational Program Education and Lifelong Learning'. Finally, he has been an Adjunct Lecturer in the Hellenic Open University for the last four years.

Carmel Capewell is a Senior Lecturer in the School of Education at Oxford Brookes University. She is a module lead for undergraduate and postgraduate modules for Early Years Education, Special Education Needs, Educational Psychology and Research Methods. She is the dissertation supervisor for students at all levels from undergraduate to DPhil students. Her main research interests are on developing research methods to encourage the active involvement of young people of all ages to provide their perspective of educational and health issues that are central to their lives. She has adapted the Photovoice methodology for both individuals and groups. She is the co-convenor for the BERA Research Methodology SIG where she has organised a number of online events. She is an active member of the ECER Network 25, running workshops with international members to develop understanding of the ethics and practicalities of researching with children.

Lyn Kendall is a Psychologist and Educator who serves as British Mensa's Gifted Child Consultant. During her 45-year career, she has worked with children of all ages and intellects, focusing mainly on the fields of Special Educational Needs and Gifted and Talented Education. Lyn holds a master's degree in Special Needs and Inclusion, is a member of the British Psychological Society and is a CBT practitioner. Lyn's book, *A Brilliant IQ, Gift or Challenge?* was published in 2020. She provides support for parents and professionals alike and undertakes media work for programmes like 'Victoria Derbyshire' and 'This Morning'. She appeared regularly on Channel 4's hit TV show 'Child Genius'. Lyn retired from full-time teaching in 2017 to focus on her private consultancy work, and now provides assessment and support services under the banner of Kendall Tuition. Among other services, she lectures and provides teacher training programmes. She was recently appointed a national 'gifted child' expert for the STEAM STARS project.

Acknowledgements

We would like to thank all the contributors for dedicating time to writing their chapters. We would also like to thank those staff members at Open University Press, McGraw-Hill Education, who have supported us patiently and wisely – especially Eleanor Christie, who has been with us for many years and has always supported us tirelessly, passionately and with dedication. Our heartfelt thanks need to go to Phoebe Hills, who worked with us diligently up to the end. It was not always an easy journey, and in between hectic schedules, we all worked with passion. I am sure we would like to thank our families, students and friends, for believing that we could bring all these diverse people, ideas and disciplines together to write this handbook.

Introduction: the book in a snapshot!

By the end of this introduction, you will be able to:
- explain the approach we adopted in this book
- identify who this book is for and how it came about
- break down the four different parts to the book.

Psychology and educational inclusion: the perspective of this book

Inclusion is the reinvention of the learning environment for each learner based on their unique strengths, difficulties and differences. National and international policy and legislation advocate the inclusion, alongside their peers, of children with special or additional – or *different* – learning needs, which (for ease of communication) we refer to in this book as special educational needs (SEN). Psychology and special education have a dominant and, one could argue, essential role within the current inclusive process, but these approaches must be understood and adopted critically and reflectively in ways that do not contribute to exclusion. This book explores the contributions psychology can make to inclusive practice and is comprised of chapters which present different methods and approaches along the special and inclusive education continuum, drawing on theory and research from psychology.

Psychology can make a significant and substantial contribution to the inclusion agenda; its current dominance (particularly more deficit-based approaches) can be problematic when adopted and used uncritically. This book will enable the reader to identify the approach (special versus inclusive), understand its contributions and limitations, and so apply it critically and effectively while striving to work inclusively. We also hope that the book will help you to evaluate inclusive practices through the range of different needs and proposed responses, such as accommodations or interventions. We look in particular at special needs, difficulties and differences, and strive to work within the confines of the realities of current inclusive practices and the neurodivergence and neuro-affirmative frameworks. These frameworks have been gaining prominence recently, and (like all things inclusive) are in the process of being negotiated within current practices, which can be associated with tensions and inconsistencies. The aim is to develop readers' understanding of holistic and inclusive approaches in recognising the individual's strengths, differences and difficulties, while trying to promote inclusion and create opportunities for empowerment.

Anyone who has ever worked in a classroom will know what a lofty goal this is – but it's definitely one worth pursuing! Essentially, we are suggesting that the process of inclusion should adopt evidence-informed practices (a particular strength of psychology) in the planning, delivery and evaluation of responses that are tailored to the unique strengths, needs and circumstances of learners identified as having SEN. Although we acknowledge that sometimes existing evidence bases may veer towards special educational approaches, which may be what certain learners need and want, it is also something that future research needs to consider and rectify.

Understanding these different areas in psychology and education and key contemporary, national and international issues, is essential for pre- and in-service professionals working with children with SEN. Many books in this area adopt very psychological approaches, perhaps (but not always) targeting psychological audiences, without a full consideration for education, especially inclusive educational practice. Others do not look critically at the approach(es) inherent in the methods they present or propose. Books about inclusion, on the other hand, can take a very critical look at psychology, which can sometimes obscure the current realities of this area of practice. This book strives to bridge this gap by integrating psychological and inclusive educational perspectives with a user-inspired, evidence-informed approach.

Who is this book for?

The idea of this book stems from our teaching and research expertise in psychological and educational programmes in higher education in the UK and elsewhere. We all have academic and/or practical backgrounds in psychology, but we teach in applied areas. We have struggled to find appropriate books to support our students. We have tried to create a theoretical and activity-based handbook for future psychologists and educators to provide insight into psychology-informed educational inclusion. We hope the book will be an essential resource for undergraduate and postgraduate courses in teacher education, psychology, educational psychology, other education programmes, and CPD courses in higher education.

Overview of the book

We hope this book will enable educators and psychologists to develop their understanding of special and inclusive educational practice more generally, while also considering in depth certain areas of need (e.g. autism or dyslexia), along with key issues within this area of practice, such as co-occurrence, labelling, recognition of needs and appropriate responses. At times, we will focus on inclusive practice entirely and at other times, due to the area of need or what the current evidence base suggests, we will explore more inclusive approaches to special education. We would argue that a key part of this book is for the reader to think critically about the different approaches taken within individual chapters. The book also looks at cases of bilingualism, exceptionally able children and children who experience socio-economic disadvantage, topics that frequently affect learners with SEN, but are rarely included in books which consider special and inclusive educational practice.

Overview of Parts I–IV

We adopted a holistic and systemic approach (i.e. interactions between various biological, cognitive, behavioural, emotional, social and environmental factors) to understanding and responding to SEN in this book.

Part I focuses on the theoretical and practical context of the book. In Chapter 1, we begin with the theoretical framework for the book and for this area of practice, which is the special and inclusive educational continuum, and how psychology contributes to the different approaches along this continuum. It also critically considers ways to understand and respond to SEN, drawing on different models (e.g. medical/individual, social, systemic ecological, and neuro-affirmative) and explores issues with terminology. Chapter 2 provides the policy, legislative and practical context of special and inclusive educational practice in England. In Chapter 3, the dynamic theories of Universal Design for Learning (UDL) and Bronfenbrenner's ecological systems theory are considered and applied in a practical way to inclusive education. This book considers SEN to be the result of demands beyond the learner's capacity, which can encompass needs beyond those commonly identified, such as English as an additional language (EAL) and immigration. In Chapter 4, the authors apply ecological systems theory to understand the needs of migrant children with SEN and demonstrate the need for cultural sensitivity and an appreciation for the many complex and intersecting contexts and factors involved when working with such children and their families.

In Part II, Chapters 5 through 10 explore specific areas of need, which are among the most common, to illustrate the complexities involved in different areas of need. The section begins with a chapter on the needs of autistic learners (Chapter 5) and learners with social, emotional and mental health (SEMH) needs (Chapter 6–8). The chapters on SEMH begin with an overview of this diverse area of need (Chapter 6) and then move on to draw on specific examples of social inequalities (Chapter 7) and attention deficit hyperactivity disorder (ADHD) (Chapter 8). Finally, specific learning differences (SpLD) are considered, in the chapters on developmental dyslexia (Chapter 9), developmental dyscalculia and difficulties with mathematics (Chapter 10).

In Part III, the book moves on to explore more physical- and sensory-based learning differences and needs, with chapters on developmental coordinate disorder (DCD) and dyspraxia (Chapter 11), visual impairments (Chapter 12) and auditory processing disorder (APD) (Chapter 13).

Each of the chapters in Parts II and III have two main aims, to enable psychologists and educators to (a) identify, assess and/or understand differences, difficulties and needs, and (b) develop and evaluate responses, such as interventions, educational programmes, accommodations or differentiation to enable the learner to be included and to flourish. A core part of the book is for the reader to critically reflect on the different approaches presented in the different chapters. As you read, consider where on the special and inclusive educational continuum the approaches discussed fall, and it will become clear why there is a need to adopt a 'pick-and-mix' approach, given the current realities of inclusive practices and the unique needs, wishes and strengths of individual learners.

In Part IV, the final two chapters, the authors focus on common and often overlooked issues in the field of educational needs and challenges, namely bilingual children's literacy challenges (Chapter 14) and exceptionally able children's needs (Chapter 15). While these types of learners and many others would not be identified as learners with SEN, especially if we think about the SEND Code of Practice (2014), they do have additional needs, which require support so that they can engage with the curriculum, be included within their school communities and achieve their full potential. Like the chapters in Parts II and III, these chapters provide evidence-informed practices that can equip teachers with inclusive tools to understand the needs of these learners and develop appropriate responses.

Part I

Theoretical Perspectives and Practical Contexts

In this part of the book, we provide a theoretical framework addressing the 'special and inclusive educational continuum'. We also impart an overview of policy and legislation, and as we shall see, theory and practice in inclusive education do not always align. The authors in the two follow-up chapters (3 and 4) explore ecological systems theory and Universal Design for Learning (UDL), and social inequality perspectives via the lens of migrant children, respectively. The aim is to provide teachers and psychologists with useful thinking tools, to enable them to understand, design and evaluate their practice to be as inclusive as possible for diverse learners and needs.

1 The special and inclusive educational continuum: understanding special educational needs and approaches to practice

Kate Carr-Fanning and Helen Curran

By the end of this chapter, you will be able to:

- critically consider the concept of special educational needs (SEN)
- critically consider and apply models of disability to educational practice
- compare and contrast different educational approaches (along the special and inclusive education continuum) to working with learners with SEN
- reflect on your own practice and identify and critically consider the approaches and methods you use in your practice.

This chapter provides the theoretical framework for the book. It begins by critically exploring and applying different theoretical models to understanding and working with learners with special educational needs (SEN) along the 'special and inclusive educational continuum'. As the book focuses on psychology and educational inclusion, we will consider the contributions and limitations of psychology to special and inclusive education.

Models of disability: how do we understand SEN?

This section will begin with a critical reflection on needs, before moving on to critically consider models of disability; each model provides a different way of understanding (and responding to) SEN.

What are SEN?

When we begin to think about working with learners with SEN, we need first to reflect on what we mean by the term, what exactly the 'needs' are that such learners have and how they might be different from students without SEN.

> *Free writing exercise*
> Spend three minutes addressing the following question: 'I think SEN are …'

In theory, we can define 'needs' in a number of ways. We could, for instance, see needs in terms of impairments, as something lacking in the person and giving rise to their difficulties; for example, we could think of a child's learning difficulty as being due to a memory deficiency. We could also view need as what the person requires in order to reduce or overcome their learning difficulty. Accordingly, we could remove the demands on memory or provide the learner with opportunities to develop strategies, such as using memory aids. In school, we can also understand 'needs' as educational. For example, a learner with difficulties reading might need Braille, 'talking books' or one-to-one support. As we see in Chapter 2, policy and legislation can define SEN in ways that may not always align with theory of educational inclusion.

Individual model: disability is impairment

The individual model, also known as the medical model, views disability as personal deficits, defects or psychological dysfunction – that is, impairments. The individual model dominates current educational practice for learners with SEN. The individual model, according to Priestley (1998), has two components: the psy-medical and the bio-medical (see Table 1.1), each identifying 'the problem' or need as different types of personal impairments.

Disability as a deficit is conceptualised in terms of diagnosis and treatment. Psy-medical professionals identify the deficit through medical and/or psychological (standardised or normative) testing. They then provide the appropriate treatment or 'cure' for the deficit. The advantage of this approach is that formal assessments, diagnostic systems and tools can contribute to more reliable

Table 1.1 Individual model

Individual model	
Bio-medical model	*Psy-medical model*
Neurobiology and physiology impairments (e.g. visual or neurological impairment)	Psychological impairments (e.g. cognitive processes, emotions and behaviours)

identification of impairments. It provides a common language (Lilienfeld and Landfield 2008), which enables researchers to develop knowledge and tools that can then be used by psychologists and educators, and practice is based on the best available evidence.

The difficulty is that 'the problem' is assumed to be located solely within the child. This focus on identifying impairments means that the social and environmental context (e.g. what is happening in the classroom or at home) is neglected during assessment and intervention (Wright, Lopez and Magyar 2021). This is why psychology and the individual model is so often criticised. A significant issue with this approach is the use and consequences of SEN labels (discussed further below). For example, due to fears around children, teachers may not want to refer a child for assessment (Carr-Fanning 2015). Fuchs and Fuchs (2007) criticised delays in identification where educators adopt the 'Wait to Fail Approach', giving learners the opportunity to fail multiple times, possibly developing secondary difficulties (e.g. anxiety, low self-esteem), before stepping in and assessing needs and intervening. In contrast, early intervention should be about identifying and supporting children early to avoid long-term negative outcomes. Conversely, parents may willingly adopt or even 'fight' for medicalised labels, and advocacy groups may emphasise biological underpinnings seeking to reduce stigma and promote acceptance (Schnittker 2017).

This approach, and its focus on impairments, is about finding and 'fixing' the problem with the learner, which is disempowering for the individual, because it positions them as tragic victims. This positioning is evident in representations in the media through the language used to describe and discuss children with SEN (e.g. as sufferers or patients), by the perceptions and expectations held by professionals and families, and the negative self-perceptions such children hold about themselves (Swain and French 2000).

> Reflection
> In what ways have you observed the individual model in practice, and what were its advantages and disadvantages?

Social model: disability is socially constructed

The social model emerged in reaction to the limitations in the 'medicalisation' of disability, specifically the emphasis on impairments. The social model is based on human rights and a respect for human dignity, and so it is about social justice. It shifted the focus away from personal impairments to the disabling effects of the social, political and environmental contexts (Reindal 2009) by claiming that difficulty/disability is not the 'natural' consequence of an impairment, but rather is the effects of social oppression, unfair expectations and rejection.

Disability is viewed as socially constructed, based largely on the idea that there is no such thing as 'reality' or 'normal'. Normative expectations are viewed as social structures created by people and groups (Shakespeare and

Watson 2001). For example, in a world created for people in wheelchairs, people who walked would be disabled; they would have to stoop to reach countertops or enter doorways. The problem is that environments are created on normative standards, thus people who are different cannot participate in the same way. Normative standards vary across and within contexts and are based on social values and contextual rules for behaviour.

Foucault (1994) believed that certain practices represent efforts to medicalise (and so control) socially undesirable behaviours. He suggested that as science progressed, education systems changed their methods of control, with 'treatment' replacing more traditional forms of punishment. The power to define someone as 'in need' or 'disabled' and then treat, fix or 'help' them, attempts to normalise people to realities that may be oppressive or non-existent. We can think about this in terms of individualised education: a child is assessed and then set targets, these targets are consistently reviewed, and interventions are put in place to achieve these targets. As the child achieves these targets, they progress towards an ever more socially and academically 'normal' outcome (Thomas and Loxley 2007).

> *Reflection*
> What norms exist in your school/classroom? What happens (what would you and others do) when a learner does not fit in with these norms?

According to the social model, 'the problem' is located within the social and environmental context. Such problems are known as barriers-to-participation. Barriers are anything that prevents the learner from participating in education or society. While these barriers are, as Thomas (2007: 73) suggested, initially external 'barriers-to-doing', they become internalised 'barriers-to-being' through the 'socially engendered undermining of [people's with impairments] psycho-emotional wellbeing'. Table 1.2 provides some examples of barriers-to-participation; take a look at it first and then identify the barriers in the Activity below and consider how you might remove them.

> *Activity*
> Identify and remove the barriers-to-participation
> - A teacher thinks a student would be better off in a special school because they don't have the resources or expertise to support the student's needs.
> - The main pedestrian entrance to a school with several learners with visual impairments has a large ice patch.
> - An employer implements a new recruitment procedure where all applicants need to read and sign a form on the spot.

- A young person believes that they should not work in a shop because of their difficulties with numbers.
- A community home for young adults with SEN is built on cheap land outside of town.
- A young man with autism spectrum disorder (ASD) asked to stop volunteering at a charity shop because customers found his behaviour rude.
- A teacher delivers all information for her science class verbally.
- A school is reluctant to admit learners with SEN, owing to the potential impact on SAT scores and league tables.

Notwithstanding its influence, especially in advocating for the rights of people with disabilities, the social model has been criticised for being nothing more than a 'buzzword'. Insofar as the individual model over-focuses on the person, the social model over-emphasises social forces, ignoring the impairment (Terzi 2004). Even if all barriers were identified and removed, the person would still experience this impairment and without some sort of difference, there would be no social reaction.

Thomas (2007) developed a social relational understanding of disability, which views disability as something imposed on top of the effects of impairments. People still experience impairments, and they experience oppression because of those impairments. This still shifts the agenda to being about 'emancipation' from this 'oppression' because disability is still social, and environmental factors that create barriers deny opportunities and 'dis-able' people. This relational approach is like the metaphor of the square peg in the round hole. The problem is not the peg or the hole, it is about the fit, and the goal is getting the right person-environment fit (P-E fit).

Reflection
Can you think of an example of where there was a good P-E fit in your classroom? Can you identify an example of where there was a bad P-E fit?

Neuro-affirmative models: diversity, not disability

Problem-focused approaches, like the individual and social models, dominate modern psychology (Wright, Lopez and Magyar 2021) and inclusive education (Terzi 2004). They provide a fractured and disempowering perspective of people and socio-environmental contexts. In contrast, affirmative models and neurodivergence perspectives, sometimes referred to in combination as neuro-affirmative models, fall within a strengths-based framework.

Table 1.2 Barriers-to-participation

Barrier	Example barrier	Suggested removal of barrier
Real barriers *Anything in the physical environment*	Stairs to access a building or a classroom	Put in a ramp or a lift to enable access
Attitudinal barriers *Negative attitudes, assumptions, expectations or stigma towards a learner based on their impairment or label. Attitudes are developed and maintained within social groups (e.g. families, communities, cultures, the media)*	Children with challenging behaviour viewed as 'mad, sad or bad'	A classroom where mental health that underlies the behaviour is understood and supported, so that the child feels accepted and a sense of belonging
Political or systemic barriers *Lack of legislation or policy within a school or country protecting learners' with SEN rights to access education, support or intervention, either directly or indirectly*	A school might be reluctant to admit and include a learner with SEN due to concerns about the impact on the school's achievement and league table results	School adopts a formal and informal policy of accepting learners with SEN
Economic barriers *A lack of financial assistance to enable people with impairments to access goods and services*	No disability benefits. No access to reasonable accommodations or necessary treatment. No ability to take up paid employment	Provide disability benefit in terms of money or access to free treatment. Remove barriers to employment
Psycho-emotional barriers *The effects of experiencing other barriers. These external barriers become internalised and undermine psycho-emotional well-being (e.g. negative self-perceptions)*	Learners with dyslexia have low academic self-esteem and view themselves as 'stupid' and 'slow' because of their experiences in school and when they compare themselves with their peers	Remove the barriers to learning that developed these self-perceptions in the first place (e.g. provide learners with audiobooks, spellchecker, multisensory teaching, a computer to take exams) Try to develop learners' self-esteem, such as providing opportunities for success and feedback about their strengths and encourage them to feel proud of their diversity. Teachers can educate children, their peers, parents and others to accept and celebrate these learners' diversity

Strengths

A strengths-based approach is based on the idea that every person, group and environment has strengths and resources, and these are the focus of assessment and intervention. A strengths-based approach is optimistic about people; it assumes people are capable, adaptive and self-determining, with access to personal and social resources. In practice, a strengths-based approach champions collaborative relationships, preventative and promotive approaches, developing competencies, personal and social resources, and the resilience of all learners (Wright, Lopez and Magyar 2021).

Neurodiversity

Neurodiversity, neurodivergence and the neuro-affirmative model have a lot in common with the social model, in that there is an emphasis on social justice, changing the environment to accommodate difference, and the acceptance and celebration of difference.

The term 'neurodiversity' has for most of its short history been strongly associated with the autism community; it was coined by Harvey Blume, an Australian social scientist with autism and popularised by Steve Silberman's book *NeuroTribes* (2015). The idea of neurodiversity was put forward in response to oppression and stigmatisation, with advocates championing the rights of people who are different to be respected and accepted with dignity.

Judy Singer, an Australian sociologist, coined the term neurodiversity to promote equality and inclusion of 'neurological minorities'. Neurodiversity is premised on the assertion that there is no such thing as a 'normal' brain – or person. Differences in learning, development or behaviour are examples of diversity; one type of brain or way of being among the many possible brains and ways of being, none of which are 'normal', and all are just a little different. Neurodiversity refers to diversity (or neuro-differences) in the human brain and cognition (e.g. sociability, learning, communication, attention, mood and other mental processes). It is a term that encompasses all brain types.

Like the social model, neurodiversity insists that differences (sometimes called disorders or disabilities) should be afforded the same respect and acceptance as other aspects of diversity (e.g. ethnicity/race, gender or religion). For example, people who are left-handed are a neurodiverse group, living in a majority right-hand world; they do not have to be medically labelled and cured.

The theory is known as neurodiversity, but there is a distinction between neurodiversity and neurodivergent. Originally, the term 'neurotypical' was used to refer to people with the majority brain. However, in recognition that everyone is diverse, neurodiversity is now used for everyone, with the term 'neurodivergent' applied to those who share specific types of differences, such as people with dyslexia or autism. In this way, everyone is neurodiverse, and as well as being neurodiverse, some may also be neurodivergent.

In contrast to approaches that focus on accommodating difficulties, notions of diversity view differences as a resource and an opportunity (Norwich 2014). As such, neurodiversity provides a more empowering framework, which focuses on the strengths of the individual, creating inclusive environments characterised by an acceptance and a celebration of difference, and a respect for human dignity (Carr-Fanning 2020). However, it has been criticised for ignoring impairments and the experience of those impairments.

Affirmative models

Due to this recognition and celebration of strengths and diversity, neurodiversity shares similarities with the affirmative model of disability, which according to French and Swain (2004: 150) is:

> ... a non-tragic view of disability and impairment which encompasses positive social identities, both individual and collective, for disabled people grounded in the benefits of lifestyles and life experiences of being impaired and disabled.

This model is not only about neurodiversity, but about the celebration of diversity more broadly, and so includes aspects like ethnicity/race, gender, age, sexual orientation and social class. There are intersections between characteristics that need to be considered; for example, in Chapter 4, we consider the intersection of SEN and migrant children and in Chapter 8, we consider the role of gender and ADHD.

As French and Swain (2004) suggest, people without a disability might not readily accept neuro-affirmative approaches. They might struggle to accept that a person could feel positive or proud of their impairment. However, people with a disability tend to rate themselves as more fortunate than outsiders (Marini 2012). As illustrated by the 'mine-thine problem', when a person lives with an impairment, they adapt and learn to cope and so will consistently choose their own impairment over any other (Wright, Lopez and Magyar 2021). Educators and psychologists have a role to play when it comes to educating children and families about their strengths (Glazzard et al. 2015). One study found that children with ADHD reported more positive beliefs when their parents and teachers also did so (Carr-Fanning 2015).

There is a need to be critical when applying strengths-based approaches to learners with SEN. We need to be mindful that we are not imposing normative standards on a diverse group. Runswick-Cole and Goodley's (2013) review of the resiliency and disability literature suggested that how resilience (or positive outcomes) is defined and measured is done so based on narrow ableist norms; and they suggested that we allow the person to decide what it means to 'live well'.

Reflection
What strengths have you observed in your learners with SEN?

Holistic models: an integrated approach

The final means of understanding disability is through more holistic approaches, based on the work of theorists such as Bronfenbrenner and his bio-ecological model (2005), and Engel and his biopsychosocial model (2005). These frameworks are essentially integrated approaches, which consider the factors present within other models and how they *interact* to produce learning, behaviour and inclusion (or exclusion). That includes all learning, development and behaviour as determined by the interaction between a range of factors (e.g. biological, psychological, social, cultural, political and environmental). For example, a young person with ADHD may smoke cigarettes due to the personality trait extraversion, a tendency towards risk-taking and impulsivity, media portrayals of smoking as 'cool', a desire to fit in with their social group and they might have a parent who smokes. We cannot assume their behaviour is entirely attributable to risk-taking or their social world.

A comprehensive account of Bronfenbrenner's (2005) model is provided in Chapter 3, where it is applied to inclusive education and Chapter 4, where it is used to understand the needs of refugees with SEN. In Chapter 9, another holistic model, the *hybrid model*, is considered for the identification of SENs (Niolaki et al. 2020). As Shakespeare and Watson suggest, 'Disability is a complex dialectic of biological, psychological, cultural and socio-political factors, which cannot be extricated except with imprecision' (2001: 22).

Identifying, labelling and language

Labels are not inherently negative; they are functional. We would struggle to navigate the world without the use of labels and schemas. The purpose of disability or SEN labels and categories has multiple purposes. Labels provide a common language and are useful for administrative purposes (e.g. resource allocation) and provide that shared language discussed earlier. The problem with labels is that they impact the perceptions, expectations and responses of the learner and of other people.

Stigma refers to any attribute or behaviour that causes a person to be labelled as unacceptably different from the norm. Differences are not universally stigmatised. For example, Mozart's ability to play the piano and compose is and was an accepted, valued and respected difference. It is the 'unacceptable' difference or 'deviance' that causes stigmatisation. The effects of stigma may be significant, as Howard Becker (1963) asserted; the deviant label has consequences not only for self-image, but also for all future social participation. A learner's identity or self-image has a significant impact on how the learner feels and what they do. For example, if a child does not believe they are 'smart', they may not put in the effort at school. Indeed, labels can be disempowering, as people with labels have been found to present with learnt helplessness (Kerr 2001) and we know that teachers' expectations have a significant impact on learners (Rosenthal and Jacobson 1968).

According to Norwich's (2007) 'dilemma of difference', a dilemma exists about whether or not to recognise difference – that is, diagnose/label children. On one hand, identification and intervention may be necessary to provide appropriate support and avoid negative outcomes. On the other hand, labelling may result in social oppression and exclusionary practices, which can harm psychological well-being, especially the person's sense-of-self. As a result, Thomas and Loxley (2007) argued that SEN labels and medicalised knowledge require deconstruction. However, as Carr-Fanning, Mc Guckin and Shevlin (2013) suggest, there is no dilemma regarding whether people *should* recognise difference. Recognition is inevitable; people will inevitably construct stories to cope with difference. For example, learners with SEN often acquire additional labels (e.g. weird, stupid, lazy). If medical knowledge was deconstructed, then practice could end up reliant on teachers' implicit beliefs, which are potentially more detrimental and less subject to change.

The impact of implicit beliefs and assumptions is demonstrated in the 'Double Empathy Problem', which states that there is no objective reason to believe that the communication methods used by people with autism spectrum disorders (ASDs) are deficient. Difficulties in communication and understanding between people with and without ASD do not stem from autism-related deficits, but from inherent difficulties in empathising with people with different ways of communicating (Milton 2012). Advocacy movements were historically focused on 'awareness'-raising; more recently, the focus has shifted to 'acceptance' – creating a society where people feel valued and respected for their differences.

Another important shift in terminology in the field is around the use of person-first language (e.g. using child with autism rather than autistic child), the so-called Lancet convention. It emerged due to concerns around labelling and stigmatisation, and efforts to make sure the learner was recognised as a person first and foremost. More recently, due to the impact of the social and neuro-affirmative models, there has been a shift back, a 'reclaiming' of identity, where people and advocacy groups reject person-first terminology, preferring to identify as an autistic person or an ADD-er. There are other preferences that ought to be considered, such as whether someone wishes to identify as 'having' or 'being' dyslexic. We mainly adopt person-first terminology in this book, because we believe that it is up the individual to decide how they want to identify.

We have endeavoured to use more respectful language throughout this book, with a focus on difference and difficulties, rather than deficits, disorders, suffering or other medicalised language. However, it is important to acknowledge that there is potentially problematic language used in this book, like the term 'special' educational needs or SEN. If we are celebrating diversity (e.g. differences in how someone processes mathematical concepts or responds socially), then being identified or talked about as 'special' is at odds with these respectful stances. We have adopted this language for ease of communication because it's the most commonly used language within the literature and within practice, for now.

Figure 1.1 Special and inclusive educational continuum

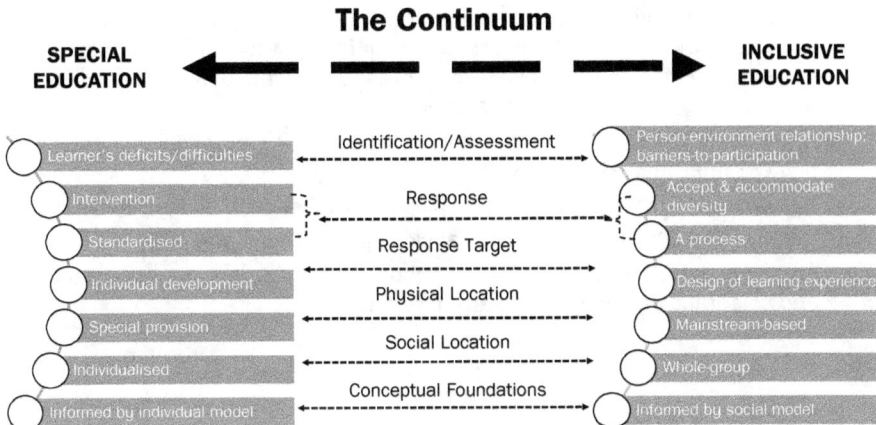

The special and inclusive education continuum

There are two dominant approaches to practice: special and inclusive education, usually considered separately. There are some key distinctions: they consider different characteristics, and the responses, target and locations can be different (see Figure 1.1). However, special and inclusive education is better understood in practice as a continuum. Practice usually is not one or the other, but rather varying combinations of the two. A given response typically uses methods from both approaches. For ethical and research-informed practice, educators need to adopt and apply principles and practices critically and reflectively. It is important to be able to identify the approach you are using, its strengths and limitations, and when adopting special education approaches to also work inclusively. Psychology can make contributions to both approaches and so we consider this field of science first.

> *Activity*
> Are the following special or inclusive education?
> - A young person struggling to get out of bed in the morning is prescribed antidepressants.
> - Changing the seating arrangements in a classroom, so that the child who processes auditory stimuli in a different way and sometimes feels overwhelmed and struggles to listen to the teacher moves to sit at the front of the class.
> - Adopting a multisensory approach to teaching a student with dyslexia.

- Developing emotional literacy and emotional-regulation skills in a student who feels and deals with emotions in a different way, and also reducing the number of social demands by providing a quiet room in the school which they can use during class or break.
- A learner with learning differences associated with dyslexia presents a poster rather than sitting a written exam.
- A learner with ADHD sits on a bouncing ball (rather than a chair) in class.
- Using Social Stories to teach social skills in a student with ASD.
- An anti-bullying campaign within a school, which focuses on acceptance and celebration of people who are different.

Psychology as a science and a practice

Psychology is the study of the mind and behaviour (APA 2022). Psychology is a diverse scientific discipline that explores different aspects of, and factors affecting, learning and development (e.g. biological, cognitive, emotional, personal and social processes). The practice of psychology involves using psychological knowledge (especially evidence-based/research-informed practice) to understand and support mental, emotional, physical and/or social development and learning, including differences and difficulties. Psychology provides the tools, developed through scientific research, to identify and understand needs and design interventions and educational accommodations to include learners with SEN.

Evidence-based interventions are educational practices or programmes that possess evidence to show that they are effective for a specific group of learners in a particular setting. Interventions are often applied in a uniformed (standardised) way. Similarly, research-informed practice is educational experiences, designed based on the best available evidence, although there is more flexibility in how knowledge is applied. Practice is based on the best available evidence and the needs and background of the child/children in a particular context. The evidence is produced through research, enabling educators to better understand learners' needs, provide quality teaching and work inclusively.

The special and inclusive continuum

We can understand education for learners with SEN as existing along a continuum. At one end of the spectrum, *full inclusion* means that the learner receives quality teaching, appropriately designed educational experiences, and can participate fully in the classroom and access the curriculum alongside their peers. For some learners, all of their needs will not be met in this way, and they may benefit from more individually tailored educational experiences, which includes – but is not limited to – interventions. These educational experiences can be in a class setting or be more individualised, such as one-to-one or in small groups in mainstream education. They may be conducted in a mainstream classroom for some or all of the learners' educational experiences. For example, they may receive the support of an assistant in the classroom, they could have a specific intervention once or twice a week in the resource room, or they may attend a special class within a mainstream environment. At the other end of the continuum, the learner may need more specialised educational experiences, and they might attend a special school or further still have specialist (one-to-one or small-group intervention) within that special school.

Psychology of special education

Perhaps the main distinction between 'special' and 'inclusive' education is how individualised it is. The more individualised an approach is, the more towards the special education side of the spectrum you are working. That said, you can have an individualised approach that is inclusive – it just depends on the educational experience.

Special education is the provision of individualised support and intervention for learners with difficulties where the knowledge, tools and skills are associated with the individual model (see p. 4). Special education is designed to be needs-based and individualised, which means that each student should have an education plan that is tailored to their specific needs, which arise from a specific area of difficulty. However, such individualised education should also include learner voice and their strengths, which aligns with the neuro-affirmative model. Traditionally, special education is associated with special schools and other forms of segregation, such as special classes within mainstream schooling. The aim of special education is to provide support to the learner, and it is not necessarily about teaching content per se, but rather to support the learner develop the skills (e.g. academic, social, emotional, behaviour) to be able to be successful and to learn independently.

There is an important role for psychology in terms of clearly identifying and developing the evidence base for effective practice to meet the needs of learners with SEN (i.e. what works and what works well) using an individualised approach. For example:

- Identifying and understanding difficulties (e.g. standardised assessment, aetiology, risk factors, mental health difficulties that underlie challenging behaviours).
- Conducting psychological research and developing evidence bases that can be applied to meet SEN and support children's development.

Psychology of inclusive education

Educational inclusion

Inclusion goes beyond education, encompassing society and beyond SEN, embracing all forms of diversity. Educational inclusion is about education 'for all' learners (Ainscow, Booth and Dyson 2006), where regardless of diversity each person has a right to participate in and benefit from education.

> Inclusive education is about the why, how, when and the consequences of educating all learners. It involves the politics of recognition, and it is concerned with the serious issue of who in included and who is excluded within education and society in general.
>
> (Barton 2003: 10)

> Inclusive education is an unabashed announcement, a public and political declaration and celebration of difference. It requires continual proactive responsiveness to foster an inclusive educational culture.
>
> (Corbett and Slee 2000: 134)

While educational inclusion is supposed to happen alongside peers, it is more than location or mainstreaming, as Warnock observed: 'Inclusion is not a matter of where you are geographically, but of where you feel you belong' (2005: 38). Educational inclusion's conceptual foundations is the social mode; so it is not about the learner adapting to 'fit in' with the education system, it is about removing barriers, facilitating participation and a sense of belonging (Ainscow 2000). In a practical sense, the idea underlying inclusion is one that 'reinvents' the learning experience for each child. Chapter 3 provides a model – Universal Design for Learning – to enable this reinvention. Importantly, inclusion and working inclusively is a *process*; it is constantly changing and adapting, it is pursued by critically reflective educators, and it is never an 'endpoint' (Norwich 2007).

Psychology and educational inclusion

Within educational inclusion, psychologists may be seen as the source of the problem, rather than its solution, because research and practice are dominated by the individual model – where needs are attributed to psychobiological impairments (Hick, Kershner and Farrell 2009). One-size-fits-all additive approaches, proffered by some forms of psychology, do not align well with inclusion, which advocates systemic change. However, psychology and education are interdependent. Historically, the psychological approaches that have been adopted have focused on deficits. However, these principles can be used to study diversity and optimal learning experiences. Positive psychology, for example, has shown how the field can shift focus to studying different characteristics. Indeed, diversity has been central to the field since its inception. For over a century, personality traits have been studied, traits that are not viewed as 'good' or 'bad', but different ways of interacting with social and learning opportunities. As there are so many forms and approaches within psychology, some have not been as influential within special and inclusive education. A significant critique of psychology for educational inclusion is the role of power – the power to diagnose and treat (or fix) someone. Conversely, if psychology can shift the paradigm, then this power imbalance shifts from diagnosis and treatment to understanding and acceptance. Furthermore, there are a range of ways in which we can use psychologically informed knowledge and tools to promote that systemic change. For example, psychology can contribute to educational inclusion through:

- Understanding the psycho-emotional experience of learners with SEN, teachers and other stakeholders (e.g. children's voice).
- Understanding the conditions and processes (e.g. attitudes, group dynamics) that contribute to inclusion and exclusion.
- Identifying and understanding neurodivergences, differences or diversity in learning and behaviour.
- Developing and systematically testing tools, practices and principles that support quality teaching, empowering and transformative educational experiences, differentiated teaching and learning, accommodations and neuro-affirmative/strengths-based education.

Conclusion

This chapter presents the theoretical framework for the book, namely the social and inclusive educational continuum. We have critically considered the construct of SEN through the lenses of the models of disability, as arising from individual-level deficits (medical/individual model) or the results of barriers-to-participation (social, physical, psycho-emotional forces) within educational environments that prevent participation (social model). We also explored an alternative strengths-based approach known as the neuro-affirmative model where learners are recognised, valued and celebrated for their neuro-differences and affirmed for the strengths in those differences. We also explored the role of language and labels within this area of practice, including their contributions (e.g. share language) and limitations (e.g. stigma), and the need to be careful in the terms we use, and always go with the preferences of the individual learner and their family. We outlined the contributions that psychology can make to inclusive education, with a particular focus on evidence-based practice and the need for critical reflection. A significant part of this is being able to identify where on the special and inclusive educational continuum an approach falls and any potential problems that may pose in terms of the leaner's inclusion and their development. Psychology has an important role within the inclusive process, but it must be used appropriately, critically and reflectively, with the ultimate goal of promoting inclusion and providing opportunities for empowerment.

References

Ainscow, M. (2000) The next step for special education, *British Journal of Special Education*, 27 (2): 76–80.

Ainscow, M., Booth, T. and Dyson, A. (2006) *Improving Schools, Developing Inclusion*. London: Routledge.

American Psychological Association (APA) (2022) *Definition of psychology*. Available at: https://dictionary.apa.org/psychology (accessed 14 December 2022).

Barton, L. (2003) *Inclusive Education and Teacher Education*. London: Institute of Education, UCL.

Becker, H.S. (1963) *Outsider: Studies in the Sociology of Deviance*. New York: Free Press.

Bronfenbrenner, U. (2005) *Making Human Beings Human: Bio-ecological Perspectives on Human Development*. Thousand Oaks, CA: Sage.

Carr-Fanning, K. (2015) *There's nothing so wrong with you that what's right with you couldn't fix: a study of stress, emotion, and coping in students with ADHD*. PhD thesis, Trinity College Dublin.

Carr-Fanning, K. (2020) The right to dignity or disorder? The case for attention deficit hyperactivity diversity, *Studies in Arts and Humanities*, 6 (1): 14–30.

Carr-Fanning, K., Mc Guckin, C. and Shevlin, M. (2013) Using student voice to escape the spider's web: a methodological approach to de-victimizing students with ADHD, *Trinity Education Papers*, 2: 85–111.

Corbett, J. and Slee, R. (2000) An international conversation on inclusive education, in F. Armstrong, D. Armstrong and L. Barton (ed.), *Inclusive Education: Policy, Contexts, and Comparative Perspectives*. London: David Fulton.

Engel, G.L. (1977) The need for a new medical model: a challenge for biomedicine, *Science*, 196 (4286): 129–136.

Foucault, M. (1994) Two lectures, in N. Dirks and S.B. Ortner (eds.), *Culture, Power, History*. Princeton, NJ: Princeton University Press.

French, S. and Swain, J. (2004) *Whose Tragedy? Towards a Personal Non-tragedy View of Disability*. London: Sage.

Fuchs, L.S. and Fuchs, D. (2007) A model for implementing responsiveness to intervention, *Teaching Exceptional Children*, 39 (5): 14–20.

Glazzard, J., Stokoe, J., Huges, A., Netherwood, A. and Neve, L. (2015) *Teaching and Supporting Children with Special Educational Needs and Disabilities in Primary Schools*, 2nd edition. London: Sage.

Hick, P., Kershner, R. and Farrell, T. (2009) *Psychology for Inclusive Education*. New York: Routledge.

Kerr, H. (2001) Learned helplessness and dyslexia: a carts and horses issue?, *Reading*, 35 (2): 82–85.

Lilienfeld, S.O. and Landfield, K. (2008) Issues in diagnosis: categorical vs. dimensional, in W.E. Craighead, D.J. Miklowitz and L.W. Craighead (eds.), *Psychopathology: History, Diagnosis, and Empirical Foundations*. Chichester: Wiley.

Marini, I. (2012) What we counsel, teach, and research regarding the needs of persons with disabilities: what have we been missing?, in I. Marini, N.M. Glover-Graf and M. Millington (eds.), *Psychosocial Aspects of Disability: Insider Perspectives and Strategies for Counselors*. New York: Springer.

Milton, D.E.M. (2012) On the ontological status of autism: the 'double empathy problem', *Disability & Society*, 27 (6): 883–887.

Niolaki, G., Taylor, L.M., Terzopoulos, A. and Davies, R. (2020) Literacy difficulties in higher education: identifying students' needs with a hybrid model, *Educational & Child Psychology*, 37 (2): 80–92.

Norwich, B. (2007) *Dilemmas of Difference, Inclusion and Disability: International Perspectives and Future Directions*. London: Routledge.

Norwich, B. (2014) Recognising value tensions that underlie problems in inclusive education, *Cambridge Journal of Education*, 44 (4): 495–510.

Priestley, M. (1998) Constructions and creations: idealism, materialism and disability theory, *Disability & Society*, 13 (1): 75–94.

Reindal, S.M. (2009) Disability, capability, and special education: towards a capability-based theory, *European Journal of Special Needs Education*, 24 (2): 155–168.

Rosenthal, R. and Jacobson, L. (1968) Pygmalion in the classroom, *The Urban Review*, 3 (1): 16–20.

Runswick-Cole, K. and Goodley, D. (2013) Resilience: a disability studies and community psychology approach, *Social and Personality Psychology Compass*, 7 (2): 67–78.

Schnittker, J. (2017) *The Diagnostic System: Why the Classification of Psychiatric Disorders is Necessary, Difficult, and Never Settled*. New York: Columbia University Press.

Shakespeare, T. and Watson, N. (2001) The social model of disability: an outdated ideology?, in S.N. Barnartt and B.M. Altman (eds.), *Exploring Theories and Expanding Methodologies: Where We Are and Where We Need to Go* (vol. 2). Berlin: Elsevier.

Silberman, S. (2015) *NeuroTribes: The Legacy of Autism and the Future of Neuodiversity*. New York: Avery

Swain, J. and French, S. (2000) Towards an affirmation model of disability, *Disability & Society*, 15 (4): 569–582.

Terzi, L. (2004) The social model of disability: a philosophical critique, *Journal of Applied Philosophy*, 21 (2): 141–157.

Thomas, C. (2007) *Sociologies of Disability and Illness: Contested Ideas in Disability Studies and Medical Sociology*. Basingstoke: Palgrave Macmillan.

Thomas, G. and Loxley, A. (2007) *Deconstructing Special Education and Constructing Inclusion*, 2nd edition. Maidenhead: Open University Press.

Warnock, M. (2005) *Special Educational Needs: A New Look*. London: Philosophy of Education Society of Great Britain.

Wright, B.A., Lopez, S.J. and Magyar, J.L. (2021) Widening the diagnostic focus: a case for including human strengths and environmental resources, in C.R. Snyder, S.J. Lopez, L.M. Edwards and S.C. Marques (eds.), *The Oxford Handbook of Positive Psychology*, 3rd edition. New York: Oxford University Press.

2 The special and inclusive educational continuum: translating theory into policy and practice

Helen Curran and Kate Carr-Fanning

By the end of this chapter, you will be able to:

- identify and understand key legislation in relation to SEN and inclusive provision in schools and settings
- understand the process by which the legal definition of SEN is applied in schools and settings
- understand the four broad areas of need in terms of special educational provision
- understand the varying roles within the process of making special educational provision, and the responsibilities of these roles
- critically consider the potential challenges in making special educational provision.

Special and inclusive education: policy and legislation

A brief history of inclusive education

When concepts of inclusion are discussed, it is often in relation to educational contexts (Armstrong et al. 2010; Graham-Matheson 2012) and frequently the debate is concerned with the inclusion of children with special educational needs and difficulties (SEN) within mainstream educational provision (Lewis and Norwich 2005; Evans 2007; Gibson 2009). However, to understand the current inclusive education landscape for children with SEN, it is important to consider how historical policy has influenced present-day practice. While the history of special, integrated and inclusive education is long, for the purposes of this chapter, the Warnock Report (DES 1978) to the present day will be briefly explored before examining current educational policy in England.

It could be argued that the Warnock Report (DES 1978) was instrumental regarding the inclusive schooling movement. To an extent, the report's significance lies not only with the introduction of the term 'special educational needs' (Sewell and Smith 2021), but also in the way it positioned the notion of SEN. Many of the recommendations from the report became law in the 1981 Education Act, including that children with SEN should be predominantly educated within mainstream schools. However, it is notable that, as Glazzard and colleagues (2015) would argue, this did not place requirements on schools to adapt learning or the environment; consequently, this led to the integration, rather than inclusion, of children with SEN. Yet this is not to dispute the report's significance, with Hornby describing the Warnock Report as central to the speeding up of inclusive schooling, stating it 'led to acceleration in the move to implement inclusion education in the United Kingdom and other parts of the world' (2011: 321).

Certainly since 1978, a plethora of legislation has followed that has sought to further the inclusive schooling agenda. The current, central legislation that pertains to the education of children with SEN is the Children and Families Act 2014. The Children and Families Act 2014 was the resulting legislation from the consultative Green Paper 'Support and Aspiration, a new approach to SEND' (DfE 2012), which sought to address the weakness within the SEN system, identified by the House of Commons Education and Skills Committee (2006), the Lamb Inquiry (DCFS 2009) and Ofsted (2010). Issues included a lack of clarity regarding strategic direction for SEN, poor outcomes for children and young people, and parental dissatisfaction, which were all in part due to a lack of consistency and an adversarial experience of the system.

The Children and Families Act 2014, described by the government as the most significant reforms for 30 years (DfE 2014), set out the new approach to SEN provision, which included an integrated system, replacing statements with Education, Health and Care plans (EHCPs) and a new SEN Support category, with the aim that children would be identified early through a new graduated approach. The Special Educational Needs and Disabilities Code of Practice (DfE/DoH 2015), the statutory guidance detailing the operational and strategic elements of the SEN reforms, states the vision of the reforms as being 'the same as for all children and young people – that they achieve well in their early years, at school and in college, and lead happy and fulfilled lives' (DfE/DoH 2015: 11). The SEND Code of Practice also states that all pupils should 'have access to a broad and balanced curriculum' and crucially, expectations should be 'high … for every pupil' (DfE/DoH 2015: 94). Person-centred planning, collaboration with parents and families, and a focus on aspirational outcomes are central to the guidance.

The Children and Families Act 2014 in practice: provision in schools

When considering the application of the Children and Families Act 2014 and the SEND Code of Practice (DfE/DoH 2015), it is worth considering to whom this refers. Currently, approximately 16.6 per cent of the school population has been identified as having SEN, with 12.6 per cent of children and young people at SEN Support and the remaining 4 per cent having an EHCP (DfE 2022). To determine whether a child has SEN, the legal definition should be considered. Therefore, this means that the children or young person with SEN:

> (a) has a significantly greater difficulty in learning than the majority of others of the same age, or
>
> (b) has a disability which prevents or hinders him or her from making use of facilities of a kind generally provided for others of the same age in mainstream schools or mainstream post-16 institutions.
>
> (Children and Families Act 2014: 19)

It should be noted that the above legal definition of SEN is the same definition which was introduced in the 1981 Education Act, and this is potentially one of the criticisms levelled at the Children and Families Act 2014. The use of the definition was retained despite the findings of an Ofsted report in 2010, which found that the term SEN was used too widely and that it did not represent children accurately. The report also suggested that in terms of identification, the assessment of special educational needs was inconsistent, not only between different areas, but also within local areas. Yet it is not just the accuracy with which the term is applied that is the issue. Glazzard (2013) argues that the term SEN is pathological regarding the individual and creates division, thus working against the notion of inclusion and, as a consequence, fails the child. Norwich (2010), in agreement, has further identified a range of issues with the term SEN, including negative labelling, issues with defining the category and the creation of a separatist field. However, as Petersen (cited in Williams et al. 2009) argues, the definition is enshrined within law, which in turn is cited in a raft of educational policy. To change the terminology, Petersen believes, could create an even more disjointed system and further dent confidence, particularly that of parents, a good argument for the continued retention of the term in the current statutory guidance.

Reflection
Do you feel confident *in how you understand and apply* the definition of SEN? Referring to the legal definition, what would you consider to be the challenges associated with its application in a practical context?

Applying the definition of SEN: current guidance

The SEND Code of Practice (DfE/DoH 2015), the statutory guidance for schools and settings who work with children with SEN, provides detail regarding the process of identifying SEN in schools, noting the importance of schools and settings to have a 'clear approach' to identification (2015: 94). This process is called the 'graduated approach' and is a four-part cycle incorporating assess, plan, do and review, with each element seeking to further understand the needs as well as the strengths of the individual, with regular monitoring and revision of provision to further understand what is supporting good progress and a move towards securing positive outcomes. A key element of this process is the child at the centre and the importance of family involvement. This echoes the ecological systems theory proposed by Bronfenbrenner, which suggests how child development is impacted by many factors, at different levels; in this instance, transactions between the child and different 'systems' such as the teacher, the school, the local authority and beyond (Tahir et al. 2019).

> *Reflection*
> Consider the graduated approach and how this may work in a school or setting? Would you consider it to be a process through which barriers are identified and adjustments made? Or a process through which a child's needs are identified and targeted?

To support this revisiting process, the SEND Code of Practice outlines four broad areas of need, with the guidance suggesting that schools should 'review how well equipped they are to provide support across these areas' (DfE/DoH 2015: 96). The Code of Practice is clear that the purpose is to support in developing the wider understanding of the child and how their needs should be planned for, rather than seek to attribute a category to a pupil. Equally, needs may present across several areas, hence the importance of a detailed assessment to develop a holistic understanding of the child's profile, including strengths and areas for support.

The four broad areas of need, as detailed by the SEND Code of Practice (DfE/DoH 2015) are:

1. *Communication and interaction*: speech, language and communication needs. The guidance notes that 'children and young people with Autism Spectrum Disorder ... are likely to have particular difficulties with social interaction' (2015: 97).
2. *Cognition and learning*: learning difficulties. The guidance covers a wide range of needs, including moderate learning difficulties, severe learning difficulties, profound and multiple learning difficulties, as well as specific learning difficulties (e.g. dyslexia, dyscalculia and dyspraxia).

3 *Social, emotional and/or mental health difficulties*: includes a wide range of social and emotional difficulties with the guidance highlighting that individuals may become withdrawn or isolated, as well as display 'challenging, disruptive or disturbing behaviour' (2015: 98) (e.g. anxiety, depression, self-harm, substance misuse, ADHD, attachment disorders).
4 *Physical and/or sensory needs*: the guidance refers to a range of needs that require specific educational support to access educational facilities (e.g. vision, hearing or multisensory impairments).

In terms of policy, a change was made to the Introduction to the Code in relation to the four broad areas of need. Whereas the 2001 SEN Code of Practice (DfES 2001) referred to Behaviour, Emotional and Social Development (BESD), the current version (DfE/DoH 2015) has replaced this with Social, Emotional and Mental Health (SEMH) needs. The purpose of this change was to move the focus away from the behaviour and to consider the behaviour as a symptom or a 'possible unmet SEN' (DfE/DoH 2015: 4). Tutt and Williams agree and propose that SEMH is a 'more helpful label' (2015: 115) due to the focus on the underlying cause rather than the specific behaviour, as well as providing greater recognition of mental health issues.

> Reflection
> How useful do you think it is to have four broad areas of need? Are there any specifically helpful elements of adopting this approach as a practitioner? What hindrances, if any, might there be?

The challenge of enacting SEN and inclusive practice in policy

The overarching principles of the SEND Code of Practice (DfE/DoH 2015) highlighted by Hellawell (2019) suggest the guidance is based on the social model of disability, meaning that the barriers to educational provision are located within the environment; barriers that should be addressed by changes enacted through the four-part cycle of the graduated approach. However, it could equally be argued that the medical model of disability is also prevalent within the statutory guidance. The categories of SEN with the focus on within-child deficits and the needs assessment process could be considered examples of this. Certainly, the graduated approach, the system for determining and providing support for children with SEN, could be viewed as both – a process to evaluate and adapt the environment, and an assessment-based process to identify deficits within the child that is based on teacher assessment (Hodkinson 2019).

Armstrong (2017) outlines several problems with this. The bureaucratic reliance on categorical labels to access resources (e.g. for support or intervention) and increased occupational pressure on educators, mean they have less time to understand and support students, creating real challenges for developing the individualised needs-based approach. These factors create similar problems for constructing an inclusive classroom. Also, when students have needs that require individualised support, time out of class to attend special provision will mean that they miss out on some parts of the curriculum, falling behind or missing out on opportunities to achieve.

The mixed picture of inclusion within the SEND Code of Practice (DfE/DoH 2015) presents a further challenge to the development of inclusive practices. Such a challenge lies with the language used and the lack of definitions within the Code (DfE/DoH 2015). The Code refers to schools and colleges using their 'best endeavours to ensure that such provision is made for those who need it. Special Education provision is underpinned by high-quality teaching and is compromised by anything less' (2015: 25). Certainly, high-quality teaching is the first response to SEN, yet this has not been defined. Equally, the term 'best endeavours' is open to interpretation, with variation not only between schools but also between classes.

While inclusion is implicit within the SEND Code of Practice, with Ekins stating it is 'essential that the needs of pupils with SEN and/or disability are being met as part of their legal entitlement in schools' (2012: 47), there is no one singular definition of what this might look like, leaving the term open to interpretation. The way in which inclusion is defined, and enacted, varies enormously, and as Warnes, Done and Knowler suggest, this 'raises questions as to the extent to which the goal of inclusive education can be comprehensively realised or functions as a political rhetoric' (2022: 40). The lack of definition consequently places the responsibility for not only providing, but determining, an inclusive environment with the school. While the complexity of how needs are met effectively should not be underestimated (Ekins 2012), the indication here is that it is the adults enacting inclusion within the school who are responsible (Ainscow and Sandill 2010). This infers that those setting the inclusive ethos in their schools need to have a good understanding of SEN and inclusion. Yet Williams-Brown and Hodkinson (2021) found that there is confusion among educational professionals as to not only how inclusion is defined, but how this links with the standards agenda. This echoes the work of Ball, Maguire and Braun (2012), who suggest that the inclusive agenda sits outside of the main educational policy agenda. Despite such confusion, this highlights the importance that those working with children with SEN have a clear professional and contextual understanding of inclusion, and what this looks like in both an environmental and pedagogical sense.

The first response to provision

High-quality teaching

From a practical perspective, the SEND Code of Practice states that 'high quality teaching that is differentiated and personalised will meet the individual needs of the majority of children and young people' (DfE/DoH 2015: 25).

High-quality teaching should be the first response to addressing the child's needs. Yet, a challenge for practitioners is that although it is suggested that schools should keep the quality of teaching under review, the notion of high-quality teaching is not defined; further complicating this are the various factors associated with the design of a teaching environment, both from a physical and pedagogical perspective (Zhang et al. 2022).

While the SEND Code of Practice (DfE/DoH 2015) may not provide a complete definition of high-quality teaching, the notion of high-quality, universal provision for all is not a new approach. Historically, there have been many models of and approaches to the idea of reinventing the learning experience of children; one of these approaches to quality teaching is Universal Design (UD). Universal Design originated in the field of architecture but was applied to education, culminating in a framework known as Universal Design for Learning (UDL) (CAST 2022).

UDL supports high-quality teaching and offers a framework through which learning, and teaching, can be optimised, based on an understanding of the way humans learn (CAST 2022). The idea is not an add-on approach to students with SEN, but rather the teacher takes into consideration the diversity of learner approaches and the strengths of all leaners within the group. It provides a useful framework because it focuses on multiple dimensions to learning experiences, such as what the learner brings, what skills could be developed or needed, and how the educational experience can be redesigned to create space for learning and development (Zhang et al. 2022).

UDL provides a framework through a series of guidelines (see also Chapter 4 for a more detailed description of the model). These include:

1. Multiple means of engagement – the 'why' of learning.
2. Multiple means of representation – the 'what' of learning.
3. Multiple means of action and expression: the 'how' of learning (CAST 2022).

> Reflection
> Consider the last lesson you observed. Can you identify and adapt the 'why', 'what' and 'how' of the learning experience and make some suggestions for how these could be improved upon?

Not only can UDL help us to understand the notion of high-quality teaching, it also links with the graduated approach (DfE/DoH 2015), which highlights the importance of understanding the strengths and needs of the individual through revisiting the four-part cycle of assess, plan, do and review. However, central to this understanding is the individual and the importance of involving the individual, and their family, at all stages; ensuring that they have a clear voice within the process.

Learner voice

Learner voice is about rights and capacity. According to the UN Convention on the Rights of the Child (United Nations 1989), young people have the right to express their views on matters affecting them, in line with their age and maturity (Article 12). In an educational context, voice refers to the process of eliciting learner perceptions and experiences and is central to the notion of UDL. Voice is not just about the right to participate. It can have a range of positive outcomes, such as citizenship education, teacher/learner development, learner engagement, and improving educational structures and practices. Within legislation, the Children and Families Act 2014 states that a local authority in England must have regard to the specific matters which concern children, young people and their families. This means that their views and wishes must be taken into account. Equally, the importance of proactively engaging and collaborating with children, young people and families is stated, particularly in relation to decision-making. Finally, such decision-making should not be made in isolation and children, young people and families should be supported in this aspect (Children and Families Act 2014).

Within the SEND Code of Practice (DfE/DoH 2015), learner voice is defined as the individual being involved at every stage of the graduated approach, with opportunities for them to *meaningfully* take part in the process. So, inclusion needs to be meaningful and authentic, not tokenistic. Sharma (2021) suggests that eliciting pupil voice should not be considered as an activity on its own; instead, there needs to be frequent, genuine opportunities, which should be recorded from the start of the process. The inclusion of all voices, within the graduated approach, should be both operationally and strategically considered by senior leaders both in and outside of educational settings, and specific consideration should be given not only to how and when opportunities to engage are provided, but also by whom. This shows how an understanding of the roles and responsibility not only within this process, but the wider provision of support for SEN, is crucial.

Supporting children in schools: roles and responsibilities

The SEND Code of Practice states that the special educational needs coordinator (SENCO) has 'an important role to play with the headteacher and governing body in determining the strategic development of SEN policy and provision in the school' (DfE/DoH 2015: 108). The SENCO is often the person to whom people turn when they have concerns about children and young people, with Griffiths and Dubsky (2012) highlighting the significant responsibility of the role in relation to SEN provision. Despite this responsibility, in practice it is the class/subject teacher who has overall responsibility and accountability for the progress and development of all children in their class, including those with SEN. Throughout, the 2015 Code is emphatic that the teacher should take the lead when working alongside parents and pupils.

From a policy perspective, this means that the responsibility of the graduated approach, including the assessment and provision of support, is located with the teacher, with the 2015 Code stating that this includes 'where pupils access support from teaching assistants or specialist staff' (2015: 99). However, as highlighted by Lehane, 'it is hard to have any picture of what this might mean or look like' (2017: 63). This issue is further compounded not only by the urgent need to improve the minimum requirements for teachers' SEN training within initial teacher training (Carter 2015), but also the enduring perception of who should be supporting children with SEN. As highlighted by Webster (2014), the teaching assistant has long been assumed the main support for children with SEN, yet, as Radford and colleagues (2015) suggest, there must be an effective partnership between the teacher and teacher assistant roles, with the teacher retaining responsibility.

> *Reflection*
> Reflect on the teaching assistant deployment you have observed. Who develops and delivers the teaching plans for children with SEN?

While the understanding and performance of roles may provide challenges, it should be noted that it is through the enactment of these roles that a truly inclusive environment can be derived. From a practical perspective, inclusion can be defined as a school making a radical set of changes, through a systematic review, to ensure all children are embraced (Frederickson and Cline 2009; Liasidou 2012). This highlights the importance of the SENCO having the opportunity to not only effectively lead and support colleagues, but to create an inclusive ethos and expectation. Application of the graduated approach in a more medicalised fashion suggests that teachers will continue to look externally for support regarding SEN, rather than considering their own practice (Hodkinson 2019), a move which is detrimental to developing inclusive learning environments.

Summary: the challenges for special and inclusive education

The SEND Code of Practice is clear that the vision for children with SEN is the same as for all children: 'that they achieve well in the early years, at school and in college, and lead happy and fulfilled lives' (DfE/DoH 2015: 11). This chapter has illustrated that one of the biggest challenges for special and inclusive education is to avoid the dilemma of difference, and identify and meet the unique needs of learners with SEN when concepts of inclusion in policy and practice are open to interpretation.

Equally, it is clear that high-quality support, led by the teacher, should be the first response to SEN. However, it is evident that high-quality teaching and inclusive education rely heavily on the knowledge and skills of practitioners, which may vary depending on their own experiences and training. Teacher education in SEN has been found to be ad hoc and inadequate given the demand. Increased pressures on educators and reductions in resources mean they have less time to work with learners and create differentiated learning experiences for all the diversities present within their classrooms (Armstrong 2017). One particularly marginalised group are learners with challenging behaviours, whose behaviour is often misunderstood and more subject to exclusion (Armstrong 2017). Therefore, despite policy and legislation calling for educational inclusion, there are significant systemic challenges to its realisation at both a cultural and environmental level.

References

Ainscow, M. and Sandill, A. (2010) Developing inclusive education systems: the role of organisational cultures and leadership, *International Journal of Inclusive Education*, 14 (4): 401–416.

Armstrong, D. (2017) Wicked problems in special and inclusive education, *Journal of Research in Special Educational Needs*, 17 (4): 229–236.

Armstrong, A., Armstrong, D. and Spandagou, I. (2010) *Inclusive Education: International Policy & Practice*. London: Sage.

Ball, S., Maguire, M. and Braun, A. (2012) *How Schools Do Policy: Policy Enactments in Secondary Schools*. Abingdon: Routledge.

Carter, A. (2015) *Carter Review of Initial Teacher Training (ITT)*. Available at: https://www.gov.uk/government/uploads/system/uploads/attachment_data/file/399957/Carter_Review.pdf (accessed 5 May 2016).

CAST (2022) *The UDL Guidelines*. Available at: https://udlguidelines.cast.org/ (accessed 3 August 2022).

Children and Families Act (2014) c. 6. London: The Stationery Office. Available at: http://www.legislation.gov.uk/ukpga/2014/6/pdfs/ukpga_20140006_en.pdf (accessed 1 August 2014).

Department for Children, Schools and Families (DCFS) (2009) *The Lamb Inquiry: Special Educational Needs and Parental Confidence*. London: DCSF. Available at: https://webarchive.nationalarchives.gov.uk/ukgwa/20130401151715/https:/www.education.gov.uk/publications/eOrderingDownload/01143-2009DOM-EN.pdf (accessed 2 February 2013).

Department for Education (DfE) (2012) *Support and Aspiration: A New Approach to Special Educational Needs and Disability*, Cm 8027. London: The Stationery Office. Available at: https://www.gov.uk/government/uploads/system/uploads/attachment_data/file/198141/Support_and_Aspiration_Green-Paper-SEN.pdf (accessed 15 March 2015).

Department for Education (DfE) (2014) *Parents feel more supported ahead of radical SEND reforms* [Press Release], 15 August 2014. Available at: https://www.gov.uk/government/news/parents-feel-more-supported-ahead-of-radical-send-reforms (accessed 1 September 2014).

Department for Education (2022) *Special Educational Needs in England*. London: DfE. Available at: https://explore-education-statistics.service.gov.uk/find-statistics/special-educational-needs-in-england/2021-22 (accessed 2 August 2022).

Department for Education and Department of Health (DfE/DoH) (2015) *Special Educational Needs and Disability Code of Practice: 0 to 25 years*. London: DfE. Available at: https://www.gov.uk/government/uploads/system/uploads/attachment_data/file/398815/SEND_Code_of_Practice_January_2015.pdf (accessed 1 February 2015).

Department for Education and Skills (DfES) (2001) *Special Educational Needs Code of Practice*. London: DfES. Available at: https://assets.publishing.service.gov.uk/government/uploads/system/uploads/attachment_data/file/273877/special_educational_needs_code_of_practice.pdf.

Department of Education and Science (DES) (1978) *Special Educational Needs: Report of the Committee of Enquiry into the Education of Handicapped Children and Young People*. London: HMSO. Available at: http://www.educationengland.org.uk/documents/warnock/warnock1978.html (accessed 30 September 2014).

Education Act (1981) c. 60. London: HMSO. Available at: http://www.legislation.gov.uk/ukpga/1981/60/pdfs/ukpga_19810060_en.pdf (accessed 5 July 2016).

Ekins, A. (2012) *The Changing Face of Special Educational Needs: Impact and Implications for SENCos and Their Schools*. Abingdon: Routledge.

Evans, L. (2007) *Inclusion*. Abingdon: Routledge.

Frederickson, N. and Cline, T. (2009) *Special Education Needs, Inclusion and Diversity*, 2nd edition. Maidenhead: Open University Press.

Gibson, S. (2009) Inclusion versus neo-liberalism: empowering the 'other', in S. Gibson and J. Haynes (eds.), *Perspectives on Participation and Inclusion: Engaging Education*. London: Continuum.

Glazzard, J. (2013) A critical interrogation of the contemporary discourses associated with inclusive education in England, *Journal of Research in Special Educational Needs*, 13 (3): 182–188.

Glazzard, J., Stokoe, J., Hughes, A., Netherwood, A. and Neve, L. (2015) *Teaching and Supporting Children with Special Educational Needs and Disabilities in Primary Schools*. London: Learning Matters.

Graham-Matheson, L. (2012) Leading on inclusion', in J. Cornwall and L. Graham-Matheson (eds.), *Leading on Inclusion: Dilemmas, Debates and New Perspectives*. London: Routledge.

Griffiths, D. and Dubsky, R. (2012) Evaluating the impact of the new National Award for SENCos: transforming landscapes or gardening in a gale?, *British Journal of Special Education*, 39 (4): 164–172.

Hellawell, B. (2019) *Understanding and Challenging the SEND Code of Practice*. London: Sage.

Hodkinson, A. (2019) *Key Issues in Special Education Needs, Disability and Inclusion*, 3rd edition. London: Sage.

Hornby, G. (2011) Inclusive education for children with special educational needs: a critique, *International Journal of Disability, Development & Education*, 58 (3): 321–329.

House of Commons Education and Skills Committee (2006) *Special Education Needs: Third Report of the Session 2005–6*, HC 478-1. London: The Stationery Office. Available at: https://publications.parliament.uk/pa/cm200506/cmselect/cmeduski/478/47802.htm.

Lehane, T. (2017) 'SEN's completely different now': critical discourse analysis of three 'Codes of Practice for Special Educational Needs' (1994, 2001, 2015), *Educational Review*, 69 (1): 51–67.

Lewis, A. and Norwich, B. (2005) *Special Teaching for Special Children? Pedagogies for Inclusion*. Maidenhead: Open University Press.

Liasidou, A. (2012) Inclusive education and critical pedagogy at the intersections of disability, race, gender and class, *Journal for Critical Education Policy Studies*, 10 (1): 168–184.

Norwich, B. (2010) Can we envisage the end of special educational needs? Has special educational needs outlived its usefulness?, *Psychology of Education Review*, 34 (2): 13–21.

Office for Standards in Education (Ofsted) (2010) *The Special Educational Needs and Disability Review: A Statement is Not Enough*. Manchester: Ofsted. Available at: https://www.gov.uk/government/uploads/system/uploads/attachment_data/file/413814/Special_education_needs_and_disability_review.pdf (accessed 5 October 2015).

Radford, J., Bosanquet, P., Webster, R. and Blatchford, P. (2015) Scaffolding learning for independence: clarifying teacher and teaching assistant roles for children with special educational needs, *Learning and Instruction*, 36: 1–10.

Sewell, A. and Smith, J. (2021) *Introduction to Special Educational Needs, Disability and Inclusion*. London: Sage.

Sharma, P. (2021) Barriers faced when eliciting the voice of children and young people with special educational needs and disabilities for their Education, Health and Care Plans and Annual Reviews, *British Journal of Special Education*, 48 (4): 455–476.

Tahir, K., Doelger, B. and Hynes, M. (2019) A case study on the ecology of inclusive education in the United States, *Journal for Leadership and Instruction*, 18 (1): 17–24.

Tutt, R. and Williams, P. (2015) *The SEND Code of Practice 0–25 Years: Policy, Provision and Practice*. London: Sage.

United Nations (1989) *United Nations Convention on the Rights of the Child*. Available at: https://www.unicef.org.uk/wp-content/uploads/2016/08/unicef-convention-rights-child-uncrc.pdf.

Warnes, E., Done, E.J. and Knowler, H. (2022) Mainstream teachers' concerns about inclusive education for children with special educational needs and disability in England under pre-pandemic conditions, *Journal of Research in Special Educational Needs*, 22 (1): 31–43.

Webster, R. (2014) 2014 Code of Practice: how research evidence on the role and impact of teaching assistants can inform professional practice, *Educational Psychology in Practice*, 30 (3): 232–237.

Williams, T., Lamb, B., Norwich, B. and Peterson, L. (2009) Special Educational Needs has outlived its usefulness: a debate, *Journal of Research in Special Educational Needs*, 9 (3): 199–217.

Williams-Brown, Z. and Hodkinson, A. (2021) What is considered good for everyone may not be good for children with special educational needs and disabilities: teacher's [sic] perspectives on inclusion in England, *Education 3–13*, 49 (6): 688–702.

Zhang, L., Jackson, H., Yang, S., Basham, J., Williams, C. and Carter, R. (2022) Codesigning learning environments guided by the framework of Universal Design for Learning: a case study, *Learning Environments Research*, 25 (2): 379–397.

3 Bronfenbrenner and Universal Design: a tale of two theories for inclusion

Mary Quirke, Ke Ren and Conor Mc Guckin

> By the end of this chapter, you will be able to:
> - understand how Bronfenbrenner's theory fits with your work compared with other psychological theories
> - understand the terms 'Universal Design' and 'Universal Design for Learning' and how they relate to inclusion and your practice
> - demonstrate the value of combining 'Bronfenbrenner' and 'Universal Design' when designing and conducting your practice to be as inclusive as it can for a diversity of learners.

Introduction

Let's be honest! Your job as an educator is multifaceted – from having to know about numeracy and literacy, assessment of learning (A*o*L) and assessment for learning (A*f*L), to other important things you probably have not been taught about in your initial education course, including how to deal with a myriad of issues such as bereavement, bullying and tiredness. But at the heart of your work is the important question posed by Sapon-Shevin: 'what kind of a world do we want to create, and how should we educate students for that world?' (2003: 26).

In this chapter, we encourage you to be a reflexive and inclusive reader. So, as you read, first reflect upon your own experience of educational inclusion – either from your own experience as a learner, or with the role you now have in education. Second, as you reflect upon your own experiences, think about how the content of this chapter can help you to become a more inclusive practitioner. We will show you that theories are, simply put, just a collection of good ideas that can help your practice.

We will first introduce you to the great thinking tool Urie Bronfenbrenner (1979, 1986) provided us with to consider the learner, not just in terms of their physical, intellectual, emotional and social development but, importantly, how the learner is influential in – and by – people and the social structures around them (e.g. friends, family, neighbourhood, government, world issues). That is, Bronfenbrenner's work helps us to see the learner 'in context'. The second thinking tool is framed by Universal Design (UD) (Story, Mueller and Mace 1998) and Universal Design for Learning (UDL) (Rose and Meyer 2002), approaches that support future development of inclusive practice. These approaches help our work to be as inclusive as possible for the great variety of learners we encounter.

Psychology and education: understanding the developing person using theory

Theory allows us to understand the developing person while appreciating the role of psychology in education. Table 3.1 provides a short overview of the key thinking about the development of children and young people that we have gained from great thinkers in the field of developmental psychology. The combined understanding that we get from each of these small reviews enables us to begin to develop a more holistic perspective of how the individual develops and learns.

Bronfenbrenner classically declared that, 'it can be said that much of contemporary developmental psychology is *the science of the strange behavior of children in strange situations with strange adults for the briefest possible periods of time*' (1977: 317, emphasis in original), and correctly identified a central weakness in all these classic theories. They largely ignored the important symbiotic relationships between children and their 'ecologies' – that is, the very real situations and influences that we all encounter in daily life. Observing the rich relationships, both proximal (e.g. dyadic relationships in the family home) and distal (e.g. influence of world politics, national policies) can be influential and enables us to understand the developing lives of children and young people, as is evidenced in the 'Growing Up in Ireland Study' (McCoy, Smyth and Banks 2012). It is in this context we believe that Bronfenbrenner's theory is exceptionally beneficial to us.

Bronfenbrenner and his bio-ecological approach

Bronfenbrenner's bio-ecological theory and framework (e.g. Bronfenbrenner 1977, 1979) is useful in conceptualising and understanding the lives of children and young people from a wide-ranging and encompassing perspective (Mc Guckin and Minton 2014). It is a concept whereby we can consider a child or young person's environment (ecology) as a multi-layered set of nested and interconnected systems, where the central 'agents' influence development,

Table 3.1 A comparison of different psychological theories

Theory	Useful reading	Brief overview
Jean Piaget – Theory of Cognitive Development	Donaldson (1978)	How our thinking and cognition develops across various developmental stages – being capable of increasing complexity in cognition as we grow from babies through childhood and into early adolescence
Erik Erikson – Theory of Psychosocial Development	Erikson ([1951] 1995)	A theory of psychosocial development that attempts to explain how we develop 'psycho-socially' – how people around us help us to develop a sense of who we are
The Behaviourists (e.g. Watson, Skinner, Thorndike) – Behaviourism Learning Theory	Schneider and Morris (1987), Malone (2014)	Understand learning as a series of 'stimulus-response' events. For example, when we teach a new puppy to 'sit', we can see that the more often we pair a treat with the command to sit, the puppy gradually learns that there is a relationship between you asking it to sit and getting that treat! Can you think of instances where you use this technique – either in education or at home with children?
Bandura – Social Learning Theory	Bandura and Walters (1977)	How children learn by 'imitation' and 'modelling'. Children learn by example, from watching what others are doing – modelling what they see
Vygotsky – Sociocultural Theory of Cognitive Development	Vygotsky (2012)	Notions of 'scaffolding' and the 'zone of proximal development' help us to understand that children can 'reach' beyond what they might be capable of when we support them in their trials and errors
Bowlby – Attachment Theory	Bowlby and Ainsworth (2013)	The quality, strength and consistency of our early attachments and relationships with others are important for healthy psychological development. For example, are our attachments warm, stable and consistent? Or, are they cold, detached and not predictable?
Dweck (and subsequent work of Mary Ainsworth and Mary Main in educational settings)	Dweck (2017)	Dweck helpfully posits that we have 'the power of yet' – the idea that while I got the answer incorrect this time, it is just that I do not know the answer or mechanics of how to resolve the problem 'yet'! The difference between having a 'fixed mindset' and a 'growth mindset'

each with varying degrees of directness. To demonstrate this, the 'systems model' can be illustrated by way of a series of concentric rings surrounding the young person. These systems are illustrated as rings (representing the micro-, meso-, exo-, macro- and chronosystems) and arranged in accordance with their influence, from the most proximal to the most distal and indirect, but nonetheless important. (Imagine a dart board where the inner ring is the microsystem and each ring as you move out represents the different systems in order, with the widest ring being the macrosystem – the chronosystem is the depth of the dart board and impacts on all systems.)

The microsystem is the social ecology's 'centre of gravity' and refers to the complex relations between the developing person and their immediate environment, including physical features, activities, social roles and interpersonal relationships (Bronfenbrenner and Morris 1998: 1645). The microsystem is characterised by those relationships that are often intimate and face-to-face (e.g. with mum, dad, siblings, relatives).

The mesosystem incorporates linkages between two or more microsystems in a young person's life and refers to the interrelationships between settings, such as those between home, school and peer groups, as well as attributes, belief systems, resources and opportunities, lifestyles and patterns of social interaction (Bronfenbrenner 1992). As such, the mesosystem includes home–school communication, parent–teacher relationships and interactions between schools (as in transitions).

The exosystem is comprised of the young person's experiences of systems in a social setting in which they are not directly involved, yet experience the 'indirect' effect of these systems, such as their parents' work settings and governmental agencies (Bronfenbrenner 1994). For example, although a learner is not yet directly involved in a school to which they will be transitioning, it remains part of their exosystem.

The macrosystem represents the wider socio-cultural context that provides 'blueprints' for explicit (e.g. laws) and implicit (e.g. normative expectations) social structures. These manifest as patterns of formal and informal interaction within the exo- and microsystems (Bronfenbrenner 1977). Coyne, Dempsey and Comiskey (2012) illustrated ways in which learners can be impacted by forces outside the microsystem. For example, Irish learners have shown concerns about the economic recession (macrosystem) through vicarious experiences of parental worry (exosystem).

The chronosystem, which shifted the model from an ecological to a bioecological model, accounts for time and enables the study of continuity and change as part of a life course perspective. For example, this includes the patterning and lifelong outcomes from environmental events, critical periods during development (e.g. divorce, long-stay hospital care) and transitions over the lifespan. Chronosystem events may be of a personal and individual nature, or representative of a cohort effect – for example, subtle but important differences between cohort experiences of life events before the global recession and cohort experiences of life events during or after the recession. Bronfenbrenner (2005) offered the following mathematical equation:

Development is a function of P-E (Person-Environment) across Time
[D = f (P-E-T)]

Considering that the chronosystem is hugely relevant to the lived experience of a person with SEN, perhaps especially compared to many of their peers, an educator can really start to understand the profound effects of life's adversities and how these can continue to have a reverberating impact on experiential events within the person's micro- and mesosystems, and of the added challenges that might be brought about by developments in the more 'outer' rings (e.g. changes in government policy). That is, the individual's developmental growth and potential across the lifespan may be inextricably linked to a chronosystem event (e.g. acquired impairment, SEN, long-term illness in childhood).

The evolution of the original theory

Bronfenbrenner continued to update his model over his lifetime, with reference made to the role of biological maturation in individual development in all iterations (Bronfenbrenner 1995). He finalised his theory on developing an idea about 'proximal processes', suggesting a process-person-context-time (PPCT) model (Bronfenbrenner and Ceci 1994; Bronfenbrenner 1995; Bronfenbrenner and Evans 2000).

The development of the PPCT model is based on the idea that human development should not only be viewed objectively but must also include elements of experience or activity (Engeström 2016). In other words, the PPCT model shifted its thinking from viewing the developing person as 'passive' to having an 'active' role to play in their own development. An example of this would be the Individual Educational Planning (IEP) process, which endeavours to ensure the learner becomes the driver in their (learning) system (Bergin and Logan 2013); actively participating in the dynamic, responsive and reciprocal interaction with the surrounding environments through person-context interaction (Bronfenbrenner and Morris 2006).

PPCT further explored

In the PPCT model, proximal processes (or process) is defined as a reciprocal interaction between an active developing individual and their immediate external environment. According to Bronfenbrenner, these interactions are located within the microsystems of development and 'occur on a fairly regular basis over extended periods of time' (1995: 620). Scholars (Rosa and Tudge 2013; O'Toole, Hayes and Mhathúna 2014; Hayes, O'Toole and Halpenny 2022) researching in the area of education transition, early childhood studies and inclusive education often view the process as the core component of the PPCT model, as it emphasises the significance of a network of shared relationships that an individual develops. Such shared relationships are not only limited to biopsychological human organisms (the child or other persons), but also include surrounding objects and symbols (Bronfenbrenner 1995). In education contexts, these relationships could involve child–adult, child–child and child–object (e.g. books, technology) interactions in a variety of regularly occurring activities, such as playing, reading and school outings.

For Bronfenbrenner and Morris (2006), proximal processes operate either to facilitate or impede the development of the child, depending on the quality of the interactions, as well as the quality of the contexts where interactions occur. For educators working in busy classrooms with learners with SEN, or those who are able and talented, or both (dual exceptionality), the word 'quality' is often defined in terms of learner–teacher ratios, class size, availability of support staff, physical facilities and teaching resources. However, when 'quality' is viewed through the lens of processes within the PPCT model, school becomes a prominent feature of the environment of relationships in which all (both learners and educators) develop. Therefore, focusing on the power of quality relationships in the learning environment is the key for identifying the connections between and among the learners with SEN, their relationships and learning experiences. Conversely, the importance of ensuring that quality relationships in school are positive, strong, stimulating, anticipatory and reliable, leads to an emphasis on the skills and personal attributes of the educators (McLinden et al. 2017).

The power of movement

Although proximal processes are considered the primary mechanism for an individual's development, the power of these processes is mutually influenced by the person – that is, the learner. That is to say, there is movement and the approach becomes more dynamic.

The characteristics of the learner and both the direct and distant environmental characteristics over time can all influence proximal processes (Bronfenbrenner and Morris 1998, 2006). To be more specific, Bronfenbrenner and Morris (1998) summarised three characteristics that are direct influencers: (i) demand, (ii) resource and (iii) force. *Demand* characteristics include aspects such as a developing individual's appearance, age, gender and ethnicity. These characteristics are easy to observe and can act as immediate stimuli that influence initial interaction. *Resource* characteristics are not as immediately recognisable. These relate to the developing individual's own biopsychological assets (e.g. past experiences, knowledge, skills and intelligence), developmental liabilities (e.g. genetic inheritances, SEN, neurodivergence), as well as social and material resources, such as access to food, housing, educational opportunities and support services. Finally, *force* characteristics are those that relate to the developing individual's dynamic traits of personality, including temperament, self-efficacy, persistence and level of motivation (Smit, Preston and Hay 2020). Research has found that the personal psychological resources of professionals, characteristics of the learners, and contextual sources of stress and support, all have an important role to play in shaping learner–professional relationships (Bardach, Klassen and Perry 2022).

For those of us working towards a more inclusive society, allowing the 'learner' to play an active part in the relationship provides us with unique opportunities. It is a dynamic approach that enables reflection on our beliefs about inclusion, while challenging assumptions, together with the beliefs of those learners we work with. As Bronfenbrenner reminds us: 'Every child needs at least one adult who is irrationally crazy about him or her' (Brendtro 2006: 163).

Staying grounded

Staying grounded while navigating the relationships in the dynamic learning contexts is perhaps most challenging. Therefore, minding and understanding the critical influences of the various contexts that exist in the learning environment provides an insight into the reciprocal nature of the relationships in an educational context (Bronfenbrenner and Ceci 1994).

However, contexts are dynamic and situations change in our work – nothing ever stays the same. Bearing this in mind, understanding the environment we engage with, and how it evolves, helps us to better navigate working relationships. Regular reflections on our own beliefs and values have positive influence, with careful and critical consideration about new assumptions. Professional supervision plays a part in this process.

The winds of change

Bronfenbrenner and Morris (1998) further identified three ways in which time could impact on the proximal processes of a person's development: (i) microtime, (ii) mesotime and (iii) macrotime. While the concept and impact of timing is not new, it is especially relevant when major events have an impact on a learner's lifespan, such as the COVID-19 pandemic. We then recognise the power of proximal processes (P), the characteristics of the individual learner (P), the complex and dynamic contexts where learning occurs (C) and, most importantly, how our current practice shapes the landscape of inclusion for future generations (T).

Adopting a more dynamic inclusive approach

While the notion of inclusion is a wonderful concept, it has become largely restricted to a subset of learners – those with an additional need and/or difference and those that teach them. In this section of the chapter, we encourage you to consider reframing your professional approach to inclusion rather than consider it 'somebody else's business' (McCarthy, Quirke and Mc Guckin 2019).

An approach for inclusion that easily co-exists with Bronfenbrenner's bio-ecological model is that offered by Universal Design (UD) and Universal Design for Learning (UDL). While Bronfenbrenner offers us an opportunity to understand the learning environment in a broader and more dynamic way, UD and UDL offer opportunities to design, redevelop and implement positive inclusive approaches in environments that are continuously changing and evolving. Importantly, the core philosophy of UD and UDL is that we create inclusive thinking in all aspects of our work, so that it can be accessed by the greatest number of learners possible (Story, Mueller and Mace 1998) – from the 'get-go' (Quirke and McCarthy 2020).

The demands of twenty-first-century learners necessitate ongoing changes in the areas of curriculum, teaching and assessment. Indeed, with the increasing utility of technology in our work (Wang, Mc Guckin and Quirke 2022), inclusion is continually evolving – and we need to evolve with it! Combining your knowledge of Bronfenbrenner together with UD and UDL thinking across all aspects of your work – from inception, through development, to implementation and review – will contribute to a more dynamic and responsive approach to inclusion.

So what is Universal Design (UD)?

Universal Design is a concept that originated from architecture and the built environment and is based on design thinking. The social model of disability set the course for this new way of thinking. A UD approach seeks to create products and services, from the very outset, so that they can engage with the greatest number of users possible (Mace 2008). While UD seeks to include 'many' individuals, it is important to note that the word 'universal' does not mean the design can accommodate each and every individual. Rather, there is inbuilt recognition that no single approach can include everyone. Like Bronfenbrenner's bio-ecological approach, UD is a dynamic process and demands constant reflection. Remember, UD simply asks that we seek to include 'with intent' or from 'the get-go', while constantly re-evaluating the work that we are engaged with (Quirke, Mc Guckin and McCarthy 2020).

Universal Design was proposed by Ron Mace, an architect who had a physical disability. Mace appreciated an individual's need and desire to belong meaningfully, and his approach advocated for a move away from the traditional medical 'add-on' or 'reactionary' thinking about inclusion. While primarily focused on physical spaces, the seven UD principles that Mace devised with colleagues to frame the design process (Story, Mueller and Mace 1998), have been successfully applied in a variety of environments, including learning. The essence of the principles is that they encourage a mindful and perhaps more 'constructive approach' to inclusion. If UD is to be allowed to reframe our relationships and thinking with the learning environment, it is important to explore these seven guiding principles.

1 *Equitable use*: the design should be useful and have appeal.
2 *Flexibility in use*: the design should accommodate a wide range of individual preferences and abilities.
3 *Simple and intuitive*: the design should be easy to understand, making no assumptions about ability, communication skills or ability to focus.

4 *Perceptible information*: the design should share all necessary information with ease, regardless of the user's sensory abilities.
5 *Tolerance for error*: the design should minimise hazards and possible adverse consequences of accidental or unintended actions.
6 *Low physical effort*: the design should be efficient and comfortable to use, and not require unnecessary energy.
7 *Size and space for approach and use*: the design should be cognizant of the size and space (whether physical or virtual) and considerate of the user's body size, posture, mobility, or context they are engaged in.

While the seven principles were developed for architects and designers, we too are architects and designers – building and creating with Bronfenbrenner and a UD approach (Quirke and Mc Guckin 2019). With confidence, we can easily reinterpret these principles for our work.

What is Universal Design for Learning (UDL)?

The seven principles of UD have been interpreted for use in educational settings in a number of theories (Mcguire, Scott, and Shaw 2006), with the best known, and most widely applied approach, being Universal Design for Learning (UDL) (Rose and Meyer 2006; CAST 2018). The CAST model of UDL, underpinned by theories and research from the fields of learning (e.g. Vygotsky) and neuroscience, appreciates pedagogical approaches, learning and educational settings (Rose and Meyer 2002). The CAST model is framed by 'pillars':

1 *Multiple means of engagement* (the 'why' of learning): focuses on enabling learners to engage positively, enjoy and appreciate their learning.
2 *Multiple means of representation* (the 'what' of learning): focuses on how we offer choice in learning content.
3 *Multiple means of action/expression* (the 'how' of learning): focuses on offering very real choice in assessment (e.g. multiple options – not just an essay) while meeting curriculum goals and learning outcomes.

Box 3.1   Examples of 'UDL in action'

Example 1: An example of the UDL principle: 'Why' – 'Regular Feedback'

Jenny was struggling with maths, and it was starting to result in a lot of anxiety. She found concentrating challenging, so when she could not follow or keep up, she believed she was failing. She started to believe that maths was just not her subject and moreover was starting to avoid her maths class. She had engaged with her teacher, Mr Evans, who had set aside time to review some of the learning with her. However, this 'once-off approach' did not resolve the issue.

Mr Evans knew he was losing a good learner and decided to reassess his approach, using UDL. He redesigned his lessons, setting out clear goals at the beginning of each class, signposting challenges, recognising effort rather than result, and offering all his students feedback, on a weekly basis. This meant that he was not singling out Jenny while he was addressing the issue. It was a big change – not just in terms of his approach but also from within himself, as it took time to change and was not what he was used to doing. As he initiated his changes, he recognised that there was an unexpected benefit for himself – a new and more positive engagement with his learners. While his students now embraced challenges positively, they did so together with their teacher.

Example 2: An example of the UDL principle: 'What' – 'Flexible Learning'

Jo found the science lab too busy – he had hearing issues and was particularly challenged by background noise. Mr Jones, his teacher, recognised that Jo had a genuine interest and showed real potential for the subject. Mr Jones, having explored UDL, quickly identified that by simply reorganising his science lab, he could offer flexibility in so many ways. He redesigned the layout, designed signage using clear visuals for all students, using clear images and plain English so that all would engage in hands-on learning and lab work safely. He also allowed Jo to wear headphones when engaging in his work independently while encouraging him to share and engage in projects with small groups. Soon, other students also requested to wear headphones – they also appreciated listening to music and podcasts when learning! Mr Jones agreed to a trial period and together they designed the structure of the class – clear instruction leading to practical assignments and science theory towards the end. All learners engaged and when he needed their attention, Mr Jones simply flashed the lights three times.

Example 3: An example of the UDL principle: 'How' – 'Redesigning Assessment'

History was proving to be a challenge to teach. Ms Hughes's class comprised a wide variety of learners, and she often wondered if some might have some learning difficulties. Moreover, assessment (essay writing) was challenging, as the learners did not engage with the content in the first instance. Traditional assignments by way of composing essays and completing printed worksheets was becoming tedious. Ms Hughes recognised that while the year-end assessment would be an essay, learners first needed to develop their thinking, understanding and appreciation of the content. Ms Hughes, having researched UDL, decided to 'teach' using an alternative assessment approach – re-enacting scenes from times past or debating at great length different historical events. Classes changed – they became exciting and engaging. And at the end of every week, she asked for one short written piece. By year end, learners were not as challenged by the assessment.

For our purposes, inclusion within a UDL approach highlights that there is more than one optimal solution for every learner. UDL seeks to be relevant to the unique nature of each learner, creating experiences that maximise their potential (Rose and Meyer 2002). While UDL asks that inclusive learning environments be designed with intent (Quirke et al. 2018; Quirke and McCarthy 2020), it is important to stress that some adjustments may be required for some learners – either all or some of the time, depending upon learning requirements. UDL also shifts the focus of inclusion to be of concern to everyone – not the 'special education specialist' – recognising we are all specialists when it comes to being inclusive in our work. This is an important development, in that the new focus is upon the learning relationship we have with our learners (Quirke and McCarthy 2020; Mc Guckin and O'Síoráin 2021).

When Bronfenbrenner meets UD and UDL

Both UD and UDL emerged from the social and rights-based models of disability, approaches that believe society may in fact cause barriers and ask that inclusion be reframed. Bronfenbrenner also espoused the need to appreciate the person, process and context over time if we are to realise meaningful results in our work. The usefulness of bringing these theories together is that it enables our view of inclusion in education to continue to develop – it can continue to include new understandings about learning, respond to the growing diversity of learners, while also appreciating ever-changing learning environments. The result is 'inclusion in action'.

Inclusion in action

We can appreciate that starting a chapter which sets out to explain one theory, Bronfenbrenner, introduces another theory (Universal Design) and proposes a new way of looking at things, is a bit like asking you to watch a firework display! But this is what happens when you explore theory!

Bronfenbrenner's theory enables us to consider and reconsider the environment in which we work – and, moreover, to reflect on the relationships at play and the context within which they sit. UD and UDL offer us an opportunity to move away from models that built on a legacy of segregation, shifted to integration and struggled with inclusion, by allowing us to redesign and refresh our thinking while embracing values of inclusion.

Inclusion, as framed by UDL and Bronfenbrenner (Quirke and Mc Guckin 2019, 2020), demands a subtle but important shift. While recognising we are seeking to include and adapt using design approaches, it demands our professional practice for inclusion is personal, reflexive, emotive, dynamic, ethical and value-driven – it takes an 'inclusion as process' approach (Quirke, Mc Guckin and McCarthy 2022). While all the parts are moving, the one thing you can control is yourself. Perhaps it is time to place yourself in the centre of Bronfenbrenner's bio-ecological model, with a UDL hat on (!)

and reflect on the shift this has for inclusion, inclusive practice and your learning environment.

Such thinking places responsibility and a renewed focus on the practitioner's view of 'inclusion', and it must be remembered it does not mean starting over. There are decades of 'inclusive education' developments and resultant adjustments in our work. Taking the time to reflect on what you know to be authentic, workable and true as you plan for a future version of 'inclusion in action' is worthwhile.

Activities – further reading and development

Just as Bronfenbrenner recognised the importance of understanding the ecology within which we work and the influence of relationships, it is also important that we appreciate how we, as practitioners, today, relate to 'inclusion' and 'inclusive practice' in and of itself.

> *Activity 1*
> Reflect on what you know to be true
>
> Be honest and reflexive as you engage with inclusion. 'Inclusion as process' (Quirke, Mc Guckin and McCarthy 2022) is an example of a method that benefitted from the thinking enshrined in Bronfenbrenner's UD and UDL theory. It sets out how we need to value our approach to inclusion in research, while it can be adapted for other practice.
>
> **Q.** How do you think you need to reframe your thinking if you are to adopt a dynamic inclusive approach in your work?
>
> *Activity 2*
> Our work, our ecology and inclusion demand change
>
> The 'Theory of Change' approach (Ren and Mc Guckin 2022) promotes collaborative engagement with others. Collective participatory approaches not only ensure the voices of all are heard, but also allows those of us directly involved to make change happen and effectively influence policy.
>
> **Q.** Can you recall a time when you observed exclusion in learning? Knowing what you now know, how might you affect positive change?
>
> *Activity 3*
> Appreciate your place in the system as you reframe your approach to inclusion using Bronfenbrenner!
>
> Bronfenbrenner is about being truly human and appreciating relationships – it is personal, value-driven and, most importantly, dynamic. It demands we get emotional about inclusion – that we engage with others.
>
> **Q.** Who do you need to build relationships as you develop your inclusive practice and develop your community of practice?

Conclusion

Congratulations for getting to this final part of the chapter! You have taken the time to do something very few of us ever feel we have time to do in our busy work as educators – you have taken the time to 'stop and stand and stare'. But, in addition, we hope you were able to read and think about the content in a reflexive manner, remembering your own experiences of educational and social inclusion, and questioning your approach to what you do in education. We mentioned at the start of the chapter that we did not want to present a checklist or recipe for how to 'do inclusion'. Rather, we wanted to share our knowledge of two great approaches, that are easy to understand and apply, in a way that might encourage you to 'have a go'. Education and inclusion are far from straightforward endeavours. As you leave us, we do hope you will continue your work with the words of Beckett (1983) guiding you: have a go!

References

Bandura, A. and Walters, R.H. (1977) *Social Learning Theory*, vol. 1. Englewood-Cliffs, NJ: Prentice-Hall.

Bardach, L., Klassen, R.M. and Perry, N.E. (2022) Teachers' psychological characteristics: do they matter for teacher effectiveness, teachers' well-being, retention, and interpersonal relations? An integrative review, *Educational Psychology Review*, 34 (1): 259–300.

Beckett, S. (1983) *Worstward Ho*. London: John Calder.

Bergin, E. and Logan, A. (2013) An individual education plan for pupils with special educational needs: how inclusive is the process for the pupil?, *REACH: Journal of Inclusive Education in Ireland*, 26 (2): 79–91.

Bowlby, J. and Ainsworth, M. (2013) The origins of attachment theory, *Attachment Theory: Social, Developmental, and Clinical Perspectives*, 45 (28): 759–775.

Brendtro, L.K. (2006) The vision of Urie Bronfenbrenner: adults who are crazy about kids, *Reclaiming Children and Youth*, 15 (3): 162–166.

Bronfenbrenner, U. (1977) Toward an experimental ecology of human development, *American Psychologist*, 32 (7): 513–531.

Bronfenbrenner, U. (1979) *The Ecology of Human Development: Experiments by Nature and Design*. Cambridge. MA: Harvard University Press.

Bronfenbrenner, U. (1986) Ecology of the family as a context for human development: research perspectives, *Developmental Psychology*, 22 (6): 723–742.

Bronfenbrenner, U. (1992) *Ecological Systems Theory*. London: Jessica Kingsley.

Bronfenbrenner, U. (1994) Ecological models of human development, *International Encyclopedia of Education*, 3 (2): 37–43.

Bronfenbrenner, U. (1995) Developmental ecology through space and time: a future perspective, in P. Moen, G.H. Elder and K. Luscher (eds.), *Examining Lives in Context: Perspectives on the Ecology of Human Development*. Washington, DC: American Psychological Association.

Bronfenbrenner, U. (2005) The bioecological theory of human development, in U. Bronfenbrenner (ed.), *Making Human Beings Human: Bioecological Perspectives on Human Development*. Thousand Oaks, CA: Sage.

Bronfenbrenner, U. and Ceci, S.J. (1994) Nature-nurture reconceptualized in developmental perspective: a bioecological model, *Psychological Review*, 101 (4): 568–586.

Bronfenbrenner, U. and Evans, G.W. (2000) Developmental science in the 21st century: emerging questions, theoretical models, research designs and empirical findings, *Social Development*, 9 (1): 115–125.

Bronfenbrenner, U. and Morris, P.A. (1998) The ecology of developmental processes, in W. Damon and R.M. Lerner (eds.), *Handbook of Child Psychology, vol. 1: Theoretical Models of Human Development*, 5th edition. Hoboken, NJ: Wiley.

Bronfenbrenner, U. and Morris, P.A. (2006) The bioecological model of human development, in W. Damon and R.M. Lerner (eds.), *Handbook of Child Psychology, vol. 1: Theoretical Models of Human Development*, 6th edition. New York: Wiley.

CAST (2018) *Universal Design for Learning Guidelines*, Version 2.2. Available at: http://udlguidelines.cast.org/

Coyne, I., Dempsey, O. and Comiskey, C. (2012) *Life as a Child and Young Person in Ireland: Report of a National Consultation*. Dublin: Department of Children and Youth Affairs.

Donaldson, M. (1978) *Children's Minds*. London: Fontana.

Dweck, C.S. (2017) *Mindset: Changing the Way You Think to Fulfil Your Potential*, updated edition. London: Hachette UK.

Engeström, Y. (2016) *Studies in Expansive Learning: Learning What is Not Yet There*. New York: Cambridge University Press.

Erikson, E.H. ([1951] 1995) *Childhood and Society*. London: Vintage.

Hayes, N., O'Toole, H. and Halpenny, A.M. (2022) *Introducing Bronfenbrenner: A Guide for Practitioners and Students in Early Years Education*. London: Routledge.

Mace, R.L. (2008) *Ronald L. Mace*. Retrieved from: https://projects.ncsu.edu/ncsu/design/cud/about_us/usronmace.htm

Malone, J.C. (2014) Did John B. Watson really 'found' behaviorism?, *The Behavior Analyst*, 37 (1): 1–12.

McCarthy, P., Quirke, M. and Mc Guckin, C. (2019) *UDL – Can you see what I see … Is it an Exclusive Model or an Inclusive Model?* Abstract posted to the Third Pan-Canadian Conference on Universal Design for Learning: 'Connecting the Dots – Sharing Promising Practices across Country', 2–4 October, Royal Roads University, Victoria, Canada.

McCoy, S., Smyth, E. and Banks, J. (2012) *The Primary Classroom: Insights from the Growing Up in Ireland Study*. Dublin: ESRI.

Mc Guckin, C. and Minton, S. (2014) From theory to practice: two ecosystemic approaches and their applications to understanding school bullying, *Australian Journal of Guidance and Counselling*, 24 (1): 36–48.

Mc Guckin, C. and O'Síoráin, C.A. (2021) The professional self and diverse learning needs, in S. Soan (ed.), *Why Do Teachers Need to Know about Diverse Learning Needs? Strengthening Professional Identity and Well-Being*. London: Bloomsbury.

Mcguire, J.M., Scott, S.S. and Shaw, S.F. (2006) Universal design and its applications in educational environments, *Remedial and Special Education*, 27 (3): 166–175.

McLinden, M., Douglas, G., Hewett, R., Cobb, R. and Lynch, P. (2017) Facilitating participation in education: the distinctive role of the specialist teacher in supporting learners with vision impairment in combination with severe and profound and multiple learning difficulties, *Journal of Blindness Innovation and Research*, 7 (2). Available at: https://nfb.org/images/nfb/publications/jbir/jbir17/jbir070203.html

O'Toole L., Hayes N. and Mhathúna M.M. (2014) A bio-ecological perspective on educational transition, *Procedia – Social and Behavioral Sciences*, 140: 121–127.

Quirke, M. and McCarthy, P. (2020) *A Conceptual Framework of Universal Design for Learning (UDL) for the Irish Further Education and Training Sector: Where Inclusion Is Everybody's Business*. Dublin, IE: SOLAS and AHEAD Ireland. Available at: https://www.solas.ie/f/70398/x/b1aa8a51b6/a-conceptual-framework-of-universal-design-for-learning-udl-for-the-ir.pdf.

Quirke, M., McCarthy, P., Treanor, D. and Mc Guckin, C. (2018) Tomorrow's disability officer: a cornerstone on the Universal Design Campus, *Journal of Inclusive Practice in Further and Higher Education (JIPFHE)*, 11 (1): 29–42.

Quirke, M. and Mc Guckin, C. (2019) *Career guidance needs to learn from 'disability' if it is to embrace an uncertain future.* Abstract posted to the European Conference on Educational Research (ECER): 'Education in an Era of Risk – The Role of Educational Research for the Future', 3–6 September, Universität Hamburg, Hamburg.

Quirke, M. and Mc Guckin, C. (2020). Career guidance needs to learn from 'disability' if it is to embrace an uncertain future. *European Conference on Educational Research (ECER): "Educational Research (Re)connecting Communities"*, University of Glasgow, Glasgow, Scotland, 24th–28th August 2020.

Quirke, M., Mc Guckin, C. and McCarthy, P. (2022) How to adopt an 'inclusion as process' approach and navigate ethical challenges in research, *SAGE Research Methods Cases*. Available at: https://doi.org/10.4135/9781529605341

Ren, K. and Mc Guckin, C. (2022) Using theory of change as both theory and method in educational research, *SAGE Research Methods Cases*. Available at: https://doi.org/10.4135/9781529601596

Rosa, E.M. and Tudge, J. (2013) Urie Bronfenbrenner's theory of human development: its evolution from ecology to bioecology, *Journal of Family Theory and Review*, 5 (4): 243–258.

Rose, D.H. and Meyer, A. (2002) *Teaching Every Student in the Digital Age: Universal Design for Learning*. Alexandria, VA: Association for Supervision and Curriculum Development (Product #101042).

Rose, D.H. and Meyer, A., eds. (2006) *A Practical Reader in Universal Design for Learning*. Cambridge, MA: Harvard Education Press.

Sapon-Shevin, M. (2003) Equity, excellence and school reform: where does gifted education fit and why is finding common ground so hard?, in J. Borland and L. Wright (eds.), *Rethinking Gifted Education: Contemporary Approaches to Meeting the Needs of Gifted Students*. New York: Teachers College Press.

Schneider, S.M. and Morris, E.K. (1987) A history of the term radical behaviorism: from Watson to Skinner, *The Behavior Analyst*, 10 (1): 27–39.

Smit, S., Preston, L. and Hay, J. (2020) The development of education for learners with diverse learning needs in the South African context: a bio-ecological systems analysis, *African Journal of Disability*, 9: art. 670. Available at: https://doi.org/10.4102/ajod.v9i0.670

Story, M.F., Mueller, J.L. and Mace, R.L. (1998) *The Universal Design File: Designing for People of all Ages and Abilities*, revised edition. Available at: https://files.eric.ed.gov/fulltext/ED460554.pdf

Vygotsky, L.S. (2012) *The Collected Works of LS Vygotsky: Scientific Legacy*. Berlin: Springer.

Wang, X., Mc Guckin, C. and Quirke, M. (2022) The importance of social competence for twenty-first century citizens: the use of mixed reality for social competence learning in mainstream education, in A. Correia and V. Viegas (eds.), *Methodologies and Use Cases on Extended Reality for Training and Education*. New York: IGI Global.

4 Migrant children with special educational needs: dynamic and complex ecologies and their implications for educational practice

Clara Rübner Jørgensen and Graeme Dobson

By the end of this chapter, you will be able to:
- understand ecological systems theory as it applies to migrant children with SEN
- understand that migrant children with SEN pass through different ecologies
- understand what practitioners need to know about migrant children with SEN to best support them in educational settings
- understand the need for cultural sensitivity when working with migrant children with SEN and their families.

Introduction

Migrant children represent a substantial and growing group in schools across the world, bringing a diversity of languages and cultural practices to classrooms and educational settings. Migrant children come from a range of geographic, socio-economic, cultural and educational backgrounds, and their experiences vary significantly depending on the reasons for their migration, the nature of their journey and their reception in the settlement country (Bartlett 2015; European Commission/EACEA/Eurydice 2019). Migrant children who also have a special educational need and/or disability may experience particular challenges in education, making it important for practitioners to be aware of the many possible factors impacting on their education and how best to approach them (Jörgensen, Perry and Dobson 2021b). This chapter draws on Bronfenbrenner's ecological systems theory (described in Chapter 3), in particular its later iterations (Bronfenbrenner 1994) and educational adaptations (e.g. Anderson, Boyle and Deppler 2014), to present and organise the many intersecting variables impacting on assessments, interventions and support mechanisms for migrant children with SEN. It begins by describing some of the ways in which ecological systems theory has been applied in the context of migration and SEN, arguing for the importance of acknowledging the journeys of migrant children with SEN through different pre-migration, trans-migration and post-migration ecologies. Following this, we discuss the different factors that impact on the education of migrant children with SEN within these ecologies, the many relations between them and the multifaceted role of practitioners in responding to them. The chapter concludes with key implications for practice.

Ecological systems theory in the context of migration and SEN

Bronfenbrenner's ecological systems theory is a widely used model for describing the psychosocial influences shaping children's development. It locates the child in the centre of a series of nested subsystems, which include the different settings, people and contexts directly or indirectly interacting with the child (see Chapter 3 for a detailed description). In the field of migration, adaptations of Bronfenbrenner's framework have been applied to explore the education, mental health and adaptation of migrant children (e.g. Moinolnolki and Han 2017; Adbul-Majied and Kinkead-Clark 2022), albeit in different ways. For example, Paat (2013) has framed migration as a personal transition over time as part of the chronosystem, while Mackenzie, Zizzo and Redmond (2018) have focused on contexts, such as 'previous family homes', 'refugee camps' and 'current family home', within migrant children's microsystem. Anderson et al. (2004) provide a different way of adapting Bronfenbrenner's model, by emphasising the journeys of migrant children through separate pre-migration, trans-migration and post-migration ecologies (Figure 4.1).

In this chapter, we similarly argue that the many dynamic and complex contexts affecting the education of migrant children with SEN are difficult to contain within a single ecology, and thus better understood as part of three separate, but interlinked pre-, trans- and post-migration ecologies. Practitioners should be conscious of the journeys that migrant children undertake through these different ecologies and aware that their pre- and trans-migration ecologies may influence their situation and encounters with practitioners in the post-migration ecology. The following sections outline some of the many factors influencing the educational journeys of migrant children with SEN, examining first the broader and overarching factors in the macrosystem, followed by the influences closer to the child within the exosystem, and those that work directly with the child within the micro- and mesosystems. Finally, acknowledging that

Migrant children with special educational needs 49

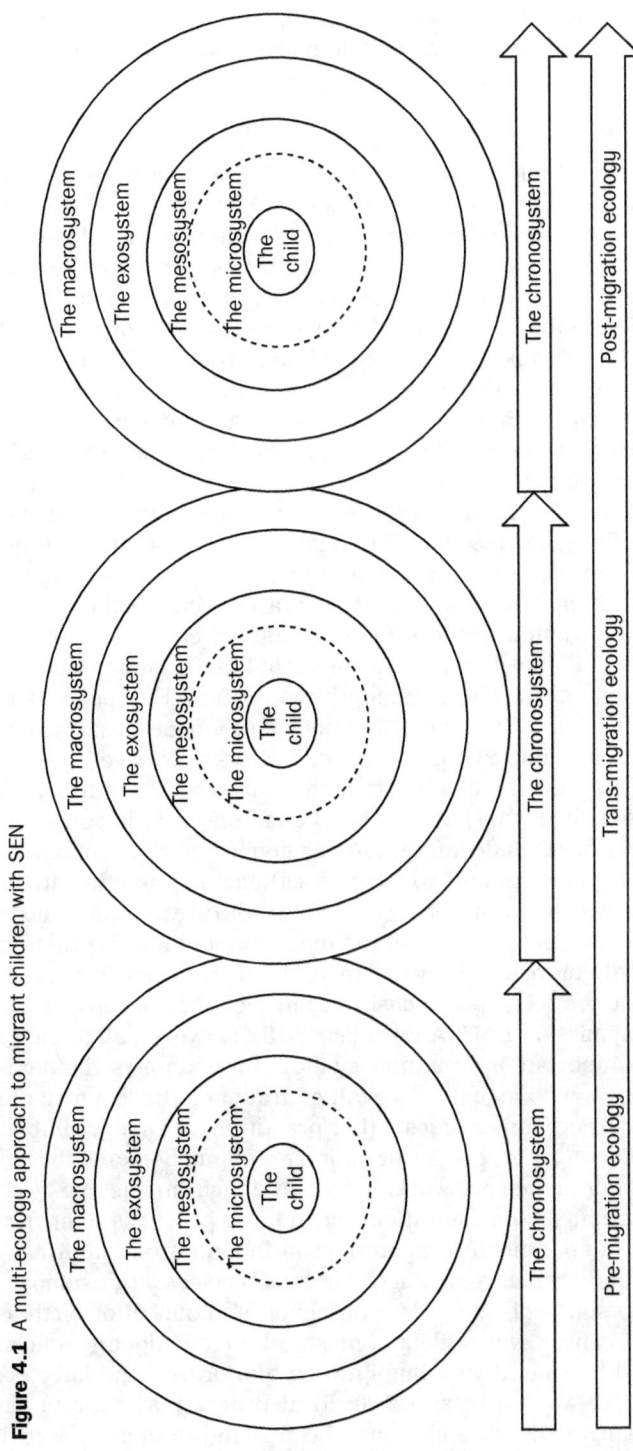

Figure 4.1 A multi-ecology approach to migrant children with SEN

Adapted from Anderson et al. (2004)

all factors discussed in the model may change over time, we briefly consider the chronosystem, before concluding with implications for practice.

The macrosystem

The macrosystem of migrant children with SEN encompasses different national approaches to the definition, identification and assessment of SEN, as well as approaches to inclusion and support of migrant children and children with SEN (Jörgensen, Dobson and Perry 2021a). Countries vary significantly in their approach to SEN and the extent to which they provide any national guidance in relation to identification, referral and assessments (Jörgensen, Perry and Dobson 2021b). In Europe, for example, children who are identified as having an official decision of SEN range from 1.1 per cent to 20.5 per cent across countries (European Agency for Special Needs and Inclusive Education 2018), showing wide variation in perceptions of SEN and systems of formal assessment. The way in which SEN is conceptualised and acted on at the macro-level in the post-migration ecology may thus differ significantly from the pre- and trans-migration ecology.

National policies and discourses in relation to migration is another important macrosystemic context in the trans- and post-migration ecology. Countries use different categories as a basis for data collection and this shapes the background information about different groups of children available to practitioners. Some national school datasets include information about children's country of birth or residence/immigration status (European Commission/EACEA/Eurydice 2019: 52); others, like the UK school census, classify children according to their ethnic background (e.g. DfE 2021). None of these categories in themselves is sufficient to understand the complex lives of migrant children, let alone those of them who have SEN. For example, focusing on a child's country of birth does not include information on countries they may have resided in between country of birth and country of settlement, and ethnicity categories do not allow for a distinction between children who are migrants and those who belong to more established minority ethnic communities. In practice, schools may operate with more specialised categories, such as 'newly arrived children' or use language proficiency as a basis for interventions or separate instruction (European Commission/EACEA/Eurydice 2019). However, all broad categories may still omit important information, such as, for example, whether a migrant child is a refugee, who may have sustained trauma in the country of origin or during their journey. This suggests that practitioners have an important role informally collecting their own information to fully understand the situation of the migrant children they are working with and their families.

National discourses on migration and related practices may furthermore influence the way parents feel regarding sharing important information about their children and/or their reluctance to access services. For example, the decision in 2016 to start collecting data on children's country of birth as part of the UK school census was widely contested by campaigners concerned that the data would be shared with immigration authorities, and later abandoned (Whittaker 2021). Walton et al. (2020: 5) also note that migrant families in both the Global North and South have been found to underreport disability, because they worry it might affect their immigration or school admissions status or because they do not want to be seen to be 'demanding or complaining'. While practitioners themselves may not be able to change national policies or discourses, it is important for them to be aware of their impact on migrant families, in order to understand the decisions and rationale of migrant parents and children and how best to support them.

Finally, national school systems have different approaches to cultural diversity and identification of need. Language proficiency and other factors associated with migration may, to varying degrees, be seen as part of SEN in national definitions guiding educational policy. For example, in some countries, like Italy and Spain, SEN definitions include characteristics which may potentially overlap with migration ('linguistic and cultural disadvantage' in Italy and 'late entrants into the system' in Spain). Contrary to this, the English SEND code of practice specifically states that 'difficulties related solely to learning English as an additional language are not SEN' (DfE/DoH 2015: 96). These differences constitute important policy distinctions, which may feed into teacher practices and school approaches towards migrant children with (or with suspected) SEN. Migrant children with SEN who have attended schools in different national settings may therefore have been subject to different systems and taught under different categories.

Reflection
Within your national context, explore how a child comes to be identified with a special educational need. Consider, for example:

- Is there a definition of SEN in law?
- Who is responsible for the identification?

Reflection
Consider, from your experience, the different categories and labels that can be used to identify:

- Migrant children – for example, migrant children who have English as a second language or refugee children.
- Special educational needs – for example, children with autism or physical disabilities.

The exosystem

The exosystem consists of contextual factors that do not directly engage with the child but are nevertheless important for their development or education. Parental employment may be one such factor (Bronfenbrenner 1994). Parents' employment situation may change from pre- to post-migration ecology, with migrants commonly taking on less secure jobs they may be overqualified for

(Fernández-Reino and Rienzo 2022). Besides having an impact on the family's economic situation, employment conditions may also be a barrier for parents attending appointments with school and thus directly influence school–home interactions. When assessing parents' ability to get involved in school, setting up appointments or developing interventions for the children, practitioners need to consider wider family contexts, including, for example, transnational caring arrangements and precarious employment situations (Oliver and Singal 2017), and avoid misinterpreting limited parental engagement as lack of interest (Paniagua 2015).

School funding is another important exosystemic factor. Insufficient funding for education may affect staff turnover and teacher training in schools, both of which have been identified as key to the inclusion of migrant children with SEN (Caldin and Cinotti 2018; McIntyre and Hall 2018). Schools may adopt a 'wait and see approach', if they think a suspected SEN may be a language issue and resolve over time, particularly if the alternative is considered too costly (Jörgensen, Perry and Dobson 2021b). Arbitrary processes for identifying SEN, for example based on subjective teacher assessments and lacking coordination with specialists, have been identified in the literature (Paniagua 2017; Migliarini 2018), where it has furthermore been noted that interventions often focus on the individual children (by, for example, drawing on support teachers) rather than inclusion more broadly (Migliarini, D'Alessio and Bocci 2018; see also Chapters 1 and 2).

Finally, attitudes and beliefs about SEN within migrant communities are an important exosystemic factor, as there may be tensions between these and accepted practices within the post-migration ecology. Stigma and shame attached to SEN have been documented in some communities (Fox et al. 2017; Steigmann 2020), but some migrant parents have also been found to explicitly reject community attitudes and beliefs, for example by openly talking about their children and refusing to hide them away (Fox et al. 2017; Hussein, Pellicano and Crane 2018). As this illustrates, migrant parents are not a homogeneous group, and understandings of SEN vary within communities (Steigmann 2020). Nevertheless, practitioners need to be knowledgeable of cultural beliefs around SEN and work sensitively with parents to best support their children (see also Chapter 14 for a discussion).

Reflection
Explore current approaches to supporting migrant children with SEN in schools within your context. Consider, for example:

- Are the children included within classrooms with their peers or do they attend separate provision, either based on language or SEN?
- Is there a particular member of staff responsible for delivering or coordinating provision for this group of children?
- Are parents involved in conversations about provision and, if they are, what form does this communication take?

The following two subsections consider the two systems closest to the child: the microsystem, which includes people whom the child directly interacts with, and the mesosystem, which acknowledges that many of these microsystems interact with one another, as in communication between families and professionals.

The microsystem

In the case of migrant children, interactions in the post-migration microsystem (for example, between the children and their parents and/or teachers) cannot be seen in isolation from the children's pre- and trans-migration experiences. When migrating, children often leave established and trusted support networks behind (Caldin 2014), and thus go through a phase of making new networks and settling into an unfamiliar community (Hamilton 2013). They may also have to work out ways to manage any pre- and trans-migration contacts transnationally. Digital communication provides an important context for such 'cross-ecological networks' and illustrates that in the contemporary world, interactions in the microsystems may not always be *physically* proximate.

When children migrate with their parents, child–parent interactions form a 'continuous' microsystem across pre-, trans- and post-migration ecologies. However, the nature of these interactions may change in the family's journey through the three ecologies, such as when parents need to work more hours to sustain the family, or if children take on the roles of translators or 'cultural interpreters' (Orellana 2009). Additionally, the common practice of serial migration (Suarez-Orosco, Bang and Kim 2011) may involve children being left with extended family over significant periods of time until their parents are ready to collect them. The close family microsystem may thus significantly change across ecologies. Furthermore, in cases where the pre-migration or trans-migration ecology has involved conflict and war, children may bring experiences of trauma and potential loss of close caregivers with them to the post-migration ecology. Trauma may impact children's cognitive functioning, and a lack of understanding of a child's history and related contextual factors when assessing for SEN may therefore risk misdiagnosis (Kaplan et al. 2016).

Internationally, children with disabilities are among the most marginalised in education (UNESCO 2015) and the microsystem of migrant children with SEN pre- and trans-migration may have involved various and shifting levels of engagement with educational settings and teachers. Migrant children are 'bearers of pre-migratory resources and previous knowledge' but their pre- and trans-migration experiences are often understood through a 'deficit-perspective' (Nilsson and Brunar 2016: 411) and in terms of special needs by practitioners in the post-migration ecology (Paniagua 2017; Migliarini, Stinson and D'Alessio 2019). Practitioners have been found to commonly draw on their own cultural references when interacting with or trying to assess migrant children, and this may result in deficit thinking in relation to the children and their prior education or family situation (Jörgensen, Perry and Dobson 2021b). Such bias may be exacerbated by the fact that assessment tools are commonly not adapted to multicultural groups of children (Hurley et al. 2014) or those who have travelled through multiple ecologies.

Language is another important context in the microsystem of migrant children with SEN, and one which is often emphasised by practitioners, who describe difficulties of assessing students for SEN when the children also lack proficiency in the language of instruction (Sinkkonen and Kyttälä 2014; Paniagua 2017; McIntyre and Hall 2018). Teachers may be reluctant to refer children for SEN assessment if they think there could be a language issue, and this may result in delays of assessment (Hurley et al. 2014; Jörgensen, Perry and Dobson 2021b). However, research has also found that teachers may use SEN labels as a way to get extra resources for migrant students, when the system provides insufficient support for language difficulties alone (Migliarini et al. 2019). This emphasises the close link between policy and funding decisions made in the macrosystem and educational practices responding to these in the microsystem. Language also plays an important role in the children's social and cultural competencies (Arakelyan and Ager 2021) and their degree of social inclusion among peers – another important part of the microsystem. However, the peer relations of migrant children with SEN are a very under-researched area, perhaps due to the fact that most studies have explored the views of parents or professionals, rather than the children themselves. This highlights the importance of practitioners directly eliciting the voices of migrant children with SEN in their practice, to understand their experiences of social in/exclusion in the classroom.

The mesosystem

In the case of migrant children with SEN, effective communication between the family and the professionals who work with them is essential to understand the family situation, assess whether a suspected SEN should be investigated, and/or whether an intervention should be put in place to support the child. However, communication between educational practitioners and migrant parents of children with SEN have been found to be an area susceptible to misunderstandings (Paniagua 2015; Oliver and Singal 2017; Migliarini 2018). Parental lack of proficiency in the school language is an issue frequently mentioned in the literature as complicating communication between migrant parents and schools. For example, Paniagua (2017) and Caldin (2014) document how migrant families may not always understand what teachers are saying to them, or the training and interventions they suggest for the children.

Where parents are not proficient in the language of the settlement country, translators may be employed to facilitate communication. However, in the case of potentially complex meetings about SEN, translators need knowledge of both SEN and the educational system (Jörgensen, Perry and Dobson 2021b), and must be able to act as 'cultural interpreters' (Bešić and Hochgatterer 2020) to ensure they provide sufficient explanation and context to parents. To improve communication between schools and families, Oliver and Singal (2017) recommend employing linguistically and ethnically diverse migrant support staff. Bešić and Hochgatterer (2020) also report positively on the use of 'parent guides' who know the language of the families they work with and help them by attending appointments, completing applications, translating documents, selecting childcare and school settings, and employment issues.

In the case of migrant children, the mesosystem also includes communication between pre-, trans and post-migration settings within and across countries. Practitioners working with migrant children with SEN post-migration have commented on the common lack of information accompanying the children from the pre-migration setting, for example, assessments done in the country of origin (Oliver and Singal 2017; Jòrgensen, Dobson and Perry 2021a). Depending on the extent of communication between schools within the post-migration ecology, teachers and practitioners may also lack information from previous settings the child has been part of, and this may delay assessments, particularly in the case of highly mobile migrant children. This highlights the importance of knowledge transfer across settings and ecologies. However, given the complexity of acquiring knowledge about a child across settings, let alone borders, practitioners often have to rely on information provided by the people in the child's microsystem, further emphasising the need for positive communication and trust.

The chronosystem

The chronosystem acknowledges the importance of historical and developmental time and how the two interact. Time is an important context for migrant children, including those who have SEN. Hayes (2021), for example, mentions the length of time children have been displaced, their age, and the time taken to put support or intervention in place for them, as all important for their education. In the specific context of refugees' mental health, Arakelyan and Ager (2021) have similarly discussed the importance of understanding how historical time (pre-flight, flight, temporary settlement and settlement) interacts with developmental age. Reflecting the importance of time, Jòrgensen, Perry and Dobson (2021b) have shown how the education of migrant children with SEN can usefully be considered as a set of 'journeys'. These journeys are not only the children's individual journeys, but also those of their families and the educational settings they attend. For migrant families, the journey is both literal – as they move from the pre- to the post-migration ecology, and metaphorical – as they may shift in their understanding and acceptance of SEN and their knowledge of educational inclusion (Papoudi et al. 2021). Similarly, practitioners may develop in their approach to diversity and SEN, for example, through training or by becoming more knowledgeable about the pre-, trans- and post-migration ecologies of the children in their classrooms. Such shifts may also be driven by macrosystemic shifts, such as around approaches to inclusion and migration within society.

Implications for practice

The education of migrant children with SEN is, as this chapter has shown, a process, by which the child journeys through a series of complex, dynamic ecologies. These include many contexts, settings and relationships which, directly or indirectly, influence the inclusion and educational experiences of the child over time. The intersection of migration and SEN is a relatively nascent area of research and therefore we are not aware of any evidence-based interventions for working with this particular group of children. However, as we have discussed in this chapter, the adapted ecological systems model provides a useful tool for educational settings to approach migrant children with SEN holistically and can help practitioners move away from singular questions, such as 'is it a language or special educational need?' As noted by Anderson et al. (2014: 9), school environments are 'messy', and they therefore specify that their ecology of inclusive education is 'not an attempt to neaten the messiness'. Similarly, we have not attempted to simplify the factors impacting on the education of migrant children with SEN. Rather, we have tried to organise them in a way in which the 'messiness' of language, culture, SEN, etc. can be understood holistically across and within pre-, trans- and post-migration ecologies, and be of use to practitioners in trying to understand and support this growing group of children.

Box 4.1   Case study

A child enters your setting. He speaks Italian as an additional language. You are aware that he comes from a country in the Middle East. The child appears withdrawn and despite intervention does not seem to be acquiring basic English language skills. Teachers have reported that he is disengaged in lessons.

Activity

- Make a list of the contextual factors that might affect the child (consider, for example: who does the child live with, what might he have experienced along his journey to the UK?).
- Categorise the contextual factors according to their place in the ecological system (micro-, meso-, exo- or macrosystem) and their location within the pre-, trans- or post-migration ecology.
- What information would you need to obtain to be able to support the child?
- What support might you or your setting put in place for the child?

Conclusion

The main implication of the chapter is the advice for practitioners to acquire knowledge of the complex and multifaceted backgrounds of migrant children with SEN and being aware of the different pre-, trans- and post-migration ecologies they have journeyed through. More specifically, the importance of practitioners seeking knowledge of the children's educational and migration history and other relevant contextual factors through trusting relationships and applying this knowledge when assessing for SEN. As we have argued, practitioners need to show sensitivity and understanding of the family's general situation when communicating with parents and developing interventions for children. Practitioners are also encouraged to make themselves aware of dominant national policies and discourses, as these may shape the experiences of migrant children with SEN and their families. Finally, we invite practitioners to consider and engage with the children's experiences of social inclusion in the educational settings, of which they are part.

> *Resources*
> Here are some additional resources in case you would like to learn more about migrant children with SEN and how to support them in the classroom.
>
> Migrant Children with Special Educational Needs – emerging findings from a recent review and their implications for educational practice: https://my.chartered.college/research-hub/migrant-children-with-special-educational-needs-ai-emerging-findings-from-a-recent-review-and-their-implications-for-educational-practice/
>
> NALDIC – EAL and Special Educational Needs: https://www.naldic.org.uk/eal-teaching-and-learning/eal-resources/eal-sen/
>
> Special Needs Jungle – The law on educational provision to support Ukrainian children with SEN and disabilities arriving in England: https://www.specialneedsjungle.com/law-educational-provision-ukrainian-children-sen-disabilities-england/

References

Adbul-Majied, S. and Kinkead-Clark, Z. (2022) Exploring the early years needs of Venezuelan migrant children in Trinidad and Tobago, *International Journal of Early Years Education*, 30 (2): 216–234.

Anderson, A., Hamilton, R., Moore, D., Loewen, S. and Frater-Mathieson, K. (2004) Education of refugee children: theoretical perspectives and best practice, in R.J. Hamilton and D. Moore (eds.), *Educational Interventions for Refugee Children: Theoretical Perspectives and Implementing Best Practice*. New York: Routledge.

Anderson, J., Boyle, C. and Deppler, J. (2014) The ecology of inclusive education: reconceptualising Bronfenbrenner, in H. Zhang, P. Wing Keung Chan & C. Deppler (eds.), *Equality in Education: Fairness and Inclusion*. Rotterdam: Sense Publishers.

Arakelyan, S. and Ager, A. (2021) Annual research review: a multilevel bioecological analysis of factors influencing the mental health and psychosocial well-being of refugee children, *Journal of Child Psychology and Psychiatry*, 62 (5): 484–509.

Bartlett, L. (2015) *Access and quality of education for international migrant children.* Paper commissioned for the EFA Global Monitoring Report 2015, 'Education for All 2000–2015: Achievements and Challenges. Available at: https://unesdoc.unesco.org/ark:/48223/pf0000232474

Bešić, E. and Hochgatterer, L. (2020) Refugee families with children with disabilities: exploring their social network and support needs, *Frontiers in Education*, 5. Available at: https://www.frontiersin.org/articles/10.3389/feduc.2020.00061/full.

Bronfenbrenner, U. (1994) Ecological models of human development, in M. Gauvain and& M. Cole (eds.), *Readings on the Development of Children*, 2nd edition. New York: Freeman.

Caldin, R. (2014) Inclusive social networks and inclusive schools for disabled children of migrant families, *Alter*, 8 (2): 105–117.

Caldin, R. and Cinotti, A. (2018) Migrant families with disabilities: social participation, school and inclusion, *Interdisciplinary Journal of Family Studies*, 23 (1): 6–25.

Department for Education (DfE) (2021) *Special Educational Needs in England: Academic Year 2021/2022.* Available at: https://explore-education-statistics.service.gov.uk/find-statistics/special-educational-needs-in-england (accessed 26 August 2022).

Department for Education and Department of Health (DfE/DoH) (2015) *Special Educational Needs and Disability Code of Practice: 0 to 25 Years.* London: DfE. Available at: https://www.gov.uk/government/uploads/system/uploads/attachment_data/file/398815/SEND_Code_of_Practice_January_2015.pdf (accessed 26 August 2022).

European Agency for Special Needs and Inclusive Education (2018) *European Agency Statistics on Inclusive Education: 2016 Dataset Cross-Country Report.* Odense: European Agency for Special Needs and Inclusive Education.

European Commission/EACEA/Eurydice (2019) *Integrating Students from Migrant Backgrounds into Schools in Europe: National Policies and Measures.* Eurydice Report. Luxembourg: Publications Office of the European Union. Available at: https://eurydice.eacea.ec.europa.eu/publications/integrating-students-migrant-backgrounds-schools-europe-national-policies-and-measures

Fernández-Reino, M. and Rienzo, C. (2022) *Migrants in the UK labour market: an overview.* Briefing, Migrant Observatory, Oxford University. Available at: https://migrationobservatory.ox.ac.uk/resources/briefings/migrants-in-the-uk-labour-market-an-overview/ (accessed 26 August 2022).

Fox, F., Aabe, N., Turner, K., Redwood, S. and Rai, D. (2017) 'It was like walking without knowing where I was going': a qualitative study of autism in a UK Somali migrant community, *Journal of Autism and Developmental Disorders*, 47 (2): 305–315.

Hamilton, P. (2013) Including migrant worker children in the learning and social context of the rural primary school, *Education 3–13*, 41 (2): 202–217.

Hayes, S.W. (2021) Deepening understanding of refugee children and adolescents using Bronfenbrenner's bioecological and PPCT models – a commentary on Arakelyan and Ager (2020), *Journal of Child Psychology and Psychiatry*, 62 (5): 510–513.

Hurley, J.J., Warren, R.A., Habalow, R.D., Weber, L.E. and Tousignant, S.R. (2014) Early childhood special education in a refugee resettlement community: challenges and innovative practices, *Early Child Development and Care*, 184 (1): 50–62.

Hussein, A.M., Pellicano, E. and Crane, L. (2018) Understanding and awareness of autism among Somali parents living in the United Kingdom, *Autism*, 23 (6): 1408–1418.

Jorgensen, C.R., Dobson, G. and Perry, T. (2021a) *Supporting migrant children with special educational needs: What information do schools need and how can it be collected?* Project Report, University of Birmingham. Available at: https://www.birmingham.ac.uk/documents/college-social-sciences/education/publications/migrant-children.pdf (accessed 26 August 2022).

Jørgensen, C.R., Perry, T. and Dobson, G. (2021b) Migrant children with special educational needs in European schools – a review of current issues and approaches, *European Journal of Special Needs Education*, 36 (3): 438–453.

Kaplan, I., Stolk, Y., Valibhoy, M., Tucker, A. and Baker, J. (2016) Cognitive assessment of refugee children: effects of trauma and new language acquisition, *Transcultural Psychiatry*, 53 (1): 81–109.

Mackenzie, C., Zizzo, G. and Redmond, G. (2018) *Using web-based interactive mapping to inform an ecological systems understanding of young migrants' support networks*. Paper presented to the Third World Conference on Qualitative Research, 17–19 October, Lisbon.

McIntyre, J. and Hall, C. (2018) Barriers to the inclusion of refugee and asylum-seeking children in schools in England, *Educational Review*, 72 (5): 583–600.

Migliarini, V. (2018) 'Colour-evasiveness' and racism without race: the disablement of asylum-seeking children at the edge of fortress Europe, *Race Ethnicity and Education*, 21 (4): 438–457.

Migliarini, V., D'Alessio, S. and Bocci, F. (2018) SEN policies and migrant children in Italian schools: micro-exclusions through discourses of equality, *Discourse: Studies in the Cultural Politics of Education*, 41 (6): 887–900.

Migliarini, V., Stinson, C. and D'Alessio, S. (2019) 'SENitizing' migrant children in inclusive settings: exploring the impact of the Salamanca Statement thinking in Italy and the United States, *International Journal of Inclusive Education*, 23 (7/8): 754–767.

Moinolnolki, N. and Han, M. (2017) No Child Left Behind: what about refugees?, *Childhood Education*, 93 (1): 3–9.

Nilsson, N. and Bunar, N. (2016) Educational responses to newly arrived students in Sweden: understanding the structure and influence of post-migration ecology, *Scandinavian Journal of Educational Research*, 60 (4): 399–416.

Oliver, C. and Singal, N. (2017) Migration, disability and education: reflections from a special school in the east of England, *British Journal of Sociology of Education*, 38 (8): 1217–1229.

Orellana, M.F. (2009) *Translating Childhoods: Immigrant Youth, Language, and Culture*. New Brunswick, NJ: Rutgers University Press.

Paat, Y. (2013) Working with immigrant children and their families: an application of Bronfenbrenner's ecological systems theory, *Journal of Human Behavior in the Social Environment*, 23 (8): 954–966.

Paniagua, A. (2015) The participation of immigrant families with children with SEN in schools: a qualitative study in the area of Barcelona, *European Journal of Special Needs Education*, 30 (1): 47–60.

Paniagua, A. (2017) The intersection of cultural diversity and special education in Catalonia, *Anthropology & Education Quarterly*, 48 (2): 141–158.

Papoudi, D., Jørgensen, C.R., Guldberg, K. and Meadan, H. (2021) Perceptions, experiences and needs of parents of culturally and linguistically diverse children with autism: a scoping review, *Review Journal of Autism and Developmental Disorders*, 8 (2): 195–212.

Sinkkonen, H.M. and Kyttälä, M. (2014) Experiences of Finnish teachers working with immigrant students, *European Journal of Special Needs Education*, 29 (2): 167–183.

Steigmann, F. (2020) Inclusive education for refugee children with disabilities in Berlin – the decisive role of parental support, *Frontiers in Education*, 5. Available at: https://doi.org/10.3389/feduc.2020.529615.

Suarez-Orosco, C., Bang, H.J. and Kim, H.Y. (2011) I felt like my heart was staying behind: psychological implications of family separations & reunifications for immigrant youth, *Journal of Adolescent Research*, 26 (2): 222–257.

UNESCO (2015) *Education for All 2000–2015: Achievements and Challenges*. Paris: UNESCO. Available at: https://www.unesco.org/gem-report/en/efa-achievements-challenges

Walton, E., McIntyre, J., Awidi, S.J., Wet-Billings, N. de, Dixon, K., Madziva, R. et al. (2020) Compounded exclusion: education for disabled refugees in Sub-Saharan Africa, *Frontiers in Education*, 5. Available at: https://doi.org/10.3389/feduc.2020.00047

Whittaker, F. (2021) DfE finally deletes pupil nationality and birth country data, *Schoolsweek*, 18 March. Available at: https://schoolsweek.co.uk/dfe-finally-deletes-pupil-nationality-and-country-of-birth-data/ (26 August 2022).

Part II

Specific Areas of Need

In Part 2, we examine some of the most common SEN within mainstream classrooms associated with differences in social and communication preferences, learning, and/or social, emotional and/or mental health. We begin with a chapter on the needs of children with autism (Chapter 5). Next, we move on to explore the broad area of need known as social, emotional and mental health (Chapter 6), and then look at two types of need within this area: the effect of social inequalities on child development and mental health (Chapter 7) and attention deficit hyperactivity disorder (Chapter 8). Finally, we explore specific learning differences, using the examples of developmental dyslexia (Chapter 9) and developmental maths difficulties/dyscalculia (Chapter 10). In addition to being among the more common SEN observed in educational settings, there is frequently reported co-occurrence between these needs. These chapters are structured so that we hope you develop an understanding of (a) identification, assessment and understanding of needs, and (b) responses, including research-inspired intervention, teaching, accommodations and adaptations. As you read, try to consider the following questions:

- What approach (special versus inclusive) is present within each chapter – does one dominate?
- Is the focus more on difficulties, as a result of differences, or are the difficulties attributed to external factors?
- Is the response more about changing the environment (or person-environment relationship) or changing the person?

5 Autism and inclusive practice

Rachael Davis, Margaret Laurie and Laura Crane

By the end of this chapter, you will be able to:
- introduce different lenses through which autism can be understood
- consider how traditional theories of autism can be reframed by taking a neurodiversity-affirmative approach
- reflect on how to best support autistic learners in a classroom environment.

Introducing autism – what teachers need to know

In this first part of the chapter, we discuss what autism is and how our understanding of autism has changed over time. We also consider how autism is increasingly being viewed through the lens of neurodiversity.

What is autism?

The answer to this question is not as simple as it may seem! Our understanding of autism is both constantly evolving and widely contested. Early clinical accounts of autism (e.g. Kanner 1943; Asperger 1944) defined autism in terms of 'extreme autistic aloneness', 'obsessive preservation of sameness' and 'restricted interest in activities'. It was in the 1980s and 1990s that the term autism spectrum disorders (ASDs) was first listed as a formal cluster of diagnoses (e.g. autistic disorder, Asperger's disorder), all connected by characteristic impairments in social interaction and communication, alongside the presence of restricted and repetitive behaviours, interests and activities (APA 1994). However, this classification of autism has since changed. For example, despite the subgrouping of ASDs being the norm for decades, there was growing recognition that this was problematic (see Box 5.1 for an example). Nowadays, anyone meeting core diagnostic criteria (detailed next) would receive a diagnosis of autism spectrum disorder (ASD).

> **Box 5.1 Autism and Asperger syndrome**
>
> Sam and Jaime are two autistic 15-year-olds. Their autistic characteristics are largely indistinguishable from one another; for example, both struggle to make friends with their non-autistic peers, find it challenging to communicate verbally at times, display very intense interests in particular areas, and struggle with some sensory environments (e.g. the school canteen). Both are doing very well academically, excelling in certain subjects. Yet while Sam was given a diagnosis of autism, Jaime received a diagnosis of Asperger's disorder (often referred to as Asperger syndrome). This difference in label is simply because Sam did not speak until she was five years old, and early language delay was the key criterion differentiating autism from Asperger syndrome. These different labels meant that Sam and Jaime were eligible for different support services at school and in their community, but also that they were treated differently by those around them (e.g. Jaime often had her challenges overlooked because everyone assumed her to be a very 'high-functioning'-like character with Asperger syndrome they had seen on television and in films). Today, both young people would receive a diagnostic label of ASD.

Today, the official diagnostic criteria for ASD are that children, young people and adults need to display 'persistent deficits' in three key areas of social communication and interaction:

- Socio-emotional reciprocity (e.g. difficulties with back-and-forth conversations, failing to initiate or respond to social interactions).
- Non-verbal communicative behaviours (e.g. unusual eye contact, body language or use of gesture).
- Developing, understanding and maintaining relationships (e.g. difficulties making friends, a lack of interest in peers).

They would also need to show at least two of the four 'restricted, repetitive' patterns of behaviour, interests and activities:

- Repetitive motor movements (e.g. hand flapping), use of objects (e.g. lining up toys) or speech (e.g. repeating specific words or phrases).
- Insistence on sameness (e.g. becoming extremely distressed at what appear to be small changes), inflexible adherence to routines (e.g. struggling with transitions) or engaging in rituals (e.g. eating the same food every day).
- A restricted range of very intense interests (e.g. topics, activities).
- Unusual sensory reactions (e.g. indifference to pain, intolerance of sensory aspects of the environment such as lights, sounds or smells).

The above characteristics need to be present in early life, even if they may be 'masked' or not fully apparent until later in life; need to have a significant impact on a person's day-to-day functioning; and are not better explained by other clinical labels (e.g. intellectual disability). Within this broad diagnostic label, we see children with a range of strengths and challenges (see Box 5.2 for examples). Additionally, the nature, extent and impact of these characteristics can change over the course of a day, a year, even a lifetime.

Activity
Reflect on the diversity of autistic profiles described in Box 5.2, focusing on the characteristics you have seen in the children and young people you have worked with. Which students would you feel most able to support given your skills, experience and expertise? And what types of support may be useful for each of these young people?

Box 5.2 Diversity of autism

Jude is 4 years old, in a nursery school

- Does not speak
- Shows very little interest in anyone around him, except when they are blowing bubbles, which he loves
- Often described as being in his own world

Jody is 16 years old, in a mainstream school

- Bullied and isolated from his peers
- Has a diagnosis of both anxiety and depression
- Is receiving ongoing interventions from his local mental health service

Lily is 10 years old, in specialist provision for autistic children

- Speaks a few two-word phrases
- Really enjoys being around other people
- Has meltdowns* when routines are changed

Sam is 19 years old, starting her second year at university

- Academically very intelligent and has a passion for history, which is the focus of her degree
- Incredible memory for dates and facts
- Has a really close peer group within her history society, who all share a common interest

* Meltdowns can be described as 'an intense response to an overwhelming situation. It happens when someone becomes completely overwhelmed by their current situation and temporarily loses control of their behaviour. A meltdown is not the same as a temper tantrum. It is not bad or naughty behaviour' (National Autistic Society). See also Phung et al. (2021) for more information.

An important consideration to be aware of is the impact of labels often used to categorise autistic people (see Box 5.3 for more information). Two common labels are 'high-' versus 'low-functioning'. While these are not clinical terms, 'high-functioning' is more often used to describe autistic people with average/above-average IQ and fluent language, who are assumed to have more positive, long-term outcomes (Alvares et al. 2020). However, by using these terms, we fail to consider how well people can cope in other aspects of their lives or how their skills and abilities vary over time (den Houting 2018; Alvares et al. 2020). Furthermore, it is important to understand the difference between functioning based on IQ versus the concept of adaptive functioning – the levels at which a person can cope with everyday life experiences (e.g. maintaining friendships, creating a routine, getting to work on time, self-care skills). Crucially, an autistic person's IQ may not correlate with their level of adaptive functioning.

> **Box 5.3 Language preferences and why they matter**
>
> There is debate around the most appropriate language to use when talking about autism. Traditionally, there has been a preference (particularly among professionals) to use person-first language (i.e. child with autism). Such language is thought to put the person before the disability; recognising their autism is a part of who a person is, and not necessarily a defining part. Though motivated by good intentions, autistic advocates have more recently called for the use of identity-first language (i.e. autistic child) instead. There are several reasons why identity-first language is thought to be preferable. For example, a person cannot be separated from autism, just as someone cannot separate themselves from other characteristics (e.g. sexual orientation). As autism defines the way that a person interprets and lives in the world, identity-first language makes sense for many autistic people (see Gernsbacher et al. 2017). Therefore, we have chosen to use identity-first language in this chapter. It is worth noting, however, that individual language preferences vary. Furthermore, there may be different preferences across countries and/or cultures. For instance, a recent study in the Netherlands showed that most adults with a diagnosis of autism preferred person-first language (Buijsman, Begeer and Scheeren 2022). Therefore, it is advisable to ask individuals what their personal preference is and model their use of language. See Chapter 1 for an in-depth discussion of language choices and how this preference may differ between groups.
>
> *Activity:* Reflective questions
>
> - Reflect on your own language choices with pupils. What was the reason for those choices – e.g. personal preference, asking individuals about their own preferences, good practice?
> - Consider whether those language choices would be different now – if so, what are the reasons they have changed?

Identifying autistic children

There is no definitive 'test' for autism (e.g. a blood test or brain scan). Rather, the decision to pursue an assessment for autism will depend on those people closest to the child, such as parents and teachers, noticing that the child's behaviour might be different to that of their typically developing peers. Parents are often (but not always) the first to notice such signs, which tend to relate to social development and behaviour (see Crane et al. 2016). While many autistic children are referred for an assessment at an early age, this is not always the case, especially those who do not have a co-occurring intellectual disability or early language delay (who were once referred to as having Asperger's disorder or Asperger's syndrome). Many people do not receive an autism diagnosis until late childhood or even well into adulthood (e.g. Russell et al. 2022). Delayed or missed diagnoses may relate to common myths and misconceptions about autism (see Table 5.1).

What role do teachers play in the identification and diagnosis of autism?

Around 1 in 60 people meet the criteria for an autism diagnosis in the UK (Roman-Urrestarazu et al. 2022), and the number of autistic pupils has risen considerably over the last two decades (McConkey 2020). As such, it is very likely that teachers will have an autistic child in their class at some point. Some of these children will have a formal diagnosis of autism; others may be on the autism diagnostic pathway; still for others, it may yet to be considered that they are autistic. Indeed, there are certain groups of autistic children and young people who often 'fly under the radar' (see Table 5.2 for examples).

Teachers may face dilemmas if they think a child might be autistic. First, they may worry whether they should mention their suspicions to the child or their parents and, if so, how they might react. Alternatively, they may worry in case they are wrong and cause unnecessary anxiety among the child and their parents. There is debate around the ideal solutions in these cases. While it has been suggested that teachers should have a better understanding of who to refer a child to, and to support parents with navigating a diagnostic process, others have questioned whether this could have unintended negative consequences such as leading to the over-referral of some children (e.g. a child putting their hands over their ears could occur for several reasons that are not necessarily related to autism).

What makes a good teacher of autistic children?

Research by Hummerstone and Parsons (2021) elicited staff and student views on what makes a good teacher of autistic children. Generally, staff tended to put the needs of the class before the needs of individual students, providing additional guidance and explanation to autistic students where needed. Yet autistic students felt they needed more tailored support from their teachers to meet their needs. Students also emphasised that they did not feel that their needs were always understood by their teachers, which perhaps underpinned

Table 5.1 Common myths and misconceptions about autism

Myth: Autism is more common in boys
Reality: Boys are more likely to be diagnosed as autistic than girls, but this does not necessarily mean that girls are less likely to be autistic. Rather, it may be that autistic girls tend to be overlooked as their autistic characteristics may be different to those of boys. For example, girls often show intense interests but in areas that align with those of their non-autistic peers (McLinden and Sedgewick 2023).

Importantly, autistic children are also more likely to identify outside the gender binary, with autistic children being between four (Hisle-Gorman et al. 2019) and eight (Strang et al. 2014) times more likely to be gender-diverse.

Myth: Autistic children don't want to make or have friends
Reality: Autistic children can and do make friends. The quantity and quality of these friendships may be different to that seen in non-autistic children (e.g. autistic children often value companionship over closeness) but, importantly, children are often 'content' with these friendships (Calder et al. 2013).

Autistic children also note that they sometimes value time alone (e.g. at break time or recess), which can help them regulate after time in the classroom (Calder, Hill and Pellicano 2013). However, it is important not to conflate this with the misconception that autistic children prefer to be alone all the time or lack motivation to make friends (Jaswal and Akhtar 2019). Indeed, some autistic children report feelings of loneliness and isolation (Libster et al. 2023).

Myth: Autistic children have extraordinary talents
Reality: There are high-profile accounts of autistic savants who have extraordinary talents in relation to art, memory or language learning, for example. So-called 'savantism' is more common in autistic people relative to the general population, but the number of autistic children with savant skills is relatively small: it is estimated that around 10 per cent of autistic people have some level of savantism (Treffert 2009).

Savantism can include splinter skills (i.e. a preoccupation with and memorisation of facts in a niche area), talents (i.e. those with an intellectual disability who have a honed skill in a specific area) and prodigious abilities (i.e. a talent so rare and extraordinary that it would be impressive when compared with the general population).

the lack of appropriate support they felt they were receiving. These findings suggest that while it is important to equip teachers with knowledge of autism, it is perhaps even more essential for teachers to take the time to really understand their pupils as individuals, learning about their needs and the type of support that is helpful for them. More broadly, teachers should be aware that not all their autistic pupils will have a diagnosis of autism or have even considered that they might be autistic. As such, this principle should apply to *all* children within their class.

Table 5.2 Examples of autistic children and young people who may 'fly under the radar'

Autistic girls
Autistic girls may show subtly different characteristics of autism to autistic boys. Research suggests the current diagnostic criteria are geared more towards male characteristics, and that this diagnostic bias means that we do not diagnose girls as often (e.g. Dworzynski et al. 2012).

Autistic children who have English as an additional language (EAL)
It can sometimes be difficult to tease apart whether the challenges that autistic children with EAL are experiencing at school are due to differences relating to their autism diagnosis, or due to language delays and/or barriers in being assimilated into a majority language classroom without being proficient in English (also potentially endangering the maintenance of a child's home language, and access to their cultural and linguistic identity). See Chapter 14 for more about bilingual children and SEN.

Autistic children from minority ethnic groups
Some early markers of autism in Western populations (e.g. lack of eye contact) do not always indicate autism in non-Western populations (Davis, Fletcher-Watson and Digard 2021). As a result, autistic children from minority ethnic groups are more likely to be diagnosed later (Shattuck et al. 2009) or even misdiagnosed (Harris, Barton and Albert 2014). Indeed, negative stereotypes have led to a significant level of misdiagnosis of Black children. For example, African American children were five times more likely to be misdiagnosed with a conduct disorder before being diagnosed as autistic (Mandell et al. 2007). See Chapter 4 for more information about migrant children and SEN.

Let's end this part of the chapter with a couple of suggested videos:

- First, from Fergus Murray, an autistic teacher and advocate, who talks about his own experiences of school, and what teachers can do for the next generation of students: https://www.youtube.com/watch?v=47x5d39aY70&t=851s
- Second, a talk from Beckett Cox, an autistic school student. They talk about their experiences within mainstream and specialist autism schools: https://www.youtube.com/watch?v=nFfWMzUoKbA

Psychological theory and evidence-based frameworks for classroom practices.

In this second part of the chapter, we discuss psychological theories and supports and how they could be better understood through the lens of neurodiversity.

Viewing autism through the lens of neurodiversity

Traditional definitions of autism position it as a *deficit* or *impairment* inherent to a child or young person, compared with peers who do not have a diagnosis of autism. In education, this positioning yields classroom approaches that focus on *fixing* the student and making them more like their non-autistic peers. Yet an alternative view has been attracting increased interest within education – neurodiversity (see Box 5.4).

Box 5.4   What is neurodiversity?

Walker (2014) explains that 'neurodiversity is a natural and valuable form of human diversity'. Walker adds: 'The idea that there is one "normal" or "healthy" type of brain or mind is culturally constructed fiction, no more valid … than the idea that there is one "normal" or "right" ethnicity, gender, or culture'.

In discussing neurodiversity within education, Aitken and Fletcher-Watson (2022) argue that education and societal systems tend to be built for and by neurotypical people. As a result, neurotypical children and young people are more likely to thrive in these systems. They argue that inclusive education needs to accommodate all pupils, and that means providing resources and support for different types of need as the norm in a school system (https://www.bps.org.uk/psychologist/neurodiversity-affirmative-education-why-and-how).

See also Chapter 1 for a discussion of neurodivergence and the affirmative model of disability.

Reframing social deficits

Next, we consider how we might reframe long-standing and pervasive views of autism through the lens of neurodiversity, using the example of Theory of Mind (ToM). Theory of Mind refers to the ability to understand that others may have thoughts, beliefs and emotions that may differ to one's own, but also from reality. A seminal study on this topic (Baron-Cohen, Leslie and Frith 1985) suggested that autistic people struggle with ToM understanding, leading them to struggle to empathise with, and read the behaviours of, non-autistic people (see Box 5.5, below, for an example of a ToM task).

Yet researchers have questioned the reasons why autistic people may fail standard ToM tasks, and whether this really is due to problems in empathising with, and reading the behaviours of, others. For instance, ToM tasks often require children to keep track of a story being told to them, answer a question about the story by taking the perspective of one of the characters, and provide a verbal response. These tasks involve lots of complex skills at once, which could overwhelm children and negatively impact on task performance (Glenwright et al. 2021).

Task complexity aside, researchers have questioned whether the whole premise of ToM deficits in autistic children is flawed. The Double Empathy Problem (Milton 2012) suggests that when people who have very different experiences of the world interact (e.g. autistic and non-autistic people), they may struggle to empathise with one another. As such, the difficulties commonly ascribed to autistic people (e.g. poor ToM) may be better framed as an issue in *two-way* communication. Indeed, research has consistently shown that non-autistic people often misunderstand autistic people. For example, non-autistic people have been found to be less accurate at inferring the mental states of autistic people (Edey et al. 2016); less willing to interact with autistic people; and overestimate how helpful they have been to autistic people (Heasman and Gillespie 2018). Research has also tested this mismatched communication directly by comparing how people of different neurotypes (e.g. autistic versus non-autistic) interact with one another. These studies suggest that in some situations, autistic people are more comfortable with other autistic people, and that there could be specific ways of communicating that allow for this effective communication (Heasman and Gillespie 2018; Crompton et al. 2020).

Overall, these studies suggest that we should question deficit-led theories such as the idea that autistic children lack a ToM. In the following subsection, we consider the implications of applying deficit-focused versus neurodiversity-affirmative theories within educational practice.

Activity

Here are some reflective questions

- Can you reflect on a time where there may have been such a miscommunication in class with a pupil?
- Looking from the perspective of the Double Empathy Problem, can you consider how you might reframe your understanding of that miscommunication; reflecting on their understanding of the situation and how this might be similar to and/or different from your own understanding of the situation?

Box 5.5 Theory of mind example task

A seminal ToM study is the Strange Stories task (Happé 1994). The task focuses on children's ability to understand subtle aspects of ToM such as white lies, deception and pretence. As one example (white lie), children are told the following story before being asked the questions below:

One day, Aunt Jane came to visit Peter. Now, Peter loves his Aunt very much, but today she is wearing a new hat; a new hat which Peter thinks is very ugly indeed. Peter thinks his aunt looks silly in it, and much nicer in her old hat. But when Aunt Jane asks Peter, 'How do you like my new hat?' Peter says, 'Oh, it's very nice.'

> Q: Was it true, what Peter said?
> Q: Why did he say it?
>
> If children have an understanding of ToM, they will confirm that Peter told a lie, and they will explain that he did this so as not to offend Aunt Jane.

Applying theories of autism to educational practice

It is beyond the scope of this chapter to comprehensively review all educational practices for autistic children and young people (for an accessible and brief review, see Davis et al. 2022). Yet several research studies have shown that autistic children and young people have negative educational experiences (Sproston et al. 2017; Macmillan, Goodall and Fletcher-Watson 2018). As such, our current approaches to supporting autistic young people in education may need to be rethought. Specifically, supports and practices that are rooted in a deficit-based model of autism could be seen to exacerbate negative educational experiences, as they attempt to change the child rather than dismantle the environmental barriers around them (Davis et al. 2022). In relation to this idea, we critically evaluate two examples of deficit-based supports next.

Interventions targeted at alleviating ToM deficits

Interventions targeting ToM skills do not achieve the significant and sustained outcomes that would be predicted by psychological theories. In a systematic review of ToM interventions, Fletcher-Watson et al. (2014) found that while ToM skills can be taught to autistic people, there is very little evidence that this teaching actually extends to real-life settings, or that they extend to other related cognitive skills. While a range of interventions were included in this review, one example of a ToM intervention is using 'thought bubbles' to demonstrate to autistic children how to understand others' thoughts or beliefs.

In addition to the lack of positive effects from such interventions, Davis et al. (2022) note that it is critical to question what a positive effect looks like. Interventions targeting ToM deficits often frame a positive outcome as a child appearing less autistic and more neurotypical in terms of their social and communication-based behaviours. We argue here that this should not be a desired outcome from an intervention, and instead, introduce two types of supports (Boxes 5.6 and 5.7; see below) that aim to create inclusive learning environments for *all* students, and to improve the educational experiences of neurodivergent children and young people.

Peer modelling

Peer modelling is an approach where, in this case a non-autistic person, is instructed or expected to demonstrate 'appropriate' behaviour or target skills to an autistic person. In other cases, the peer role can be undertaken by a parent or caregiver, a teacher, a video demonstration, a robotic demonstration or another young person (Chang and Locke 2016). There is some evidence that these types of interventions are effective, however, the literature is dominated by small-scale and non-rigorous studies (Dean and Chang 2021). There are several assumptions inherent within this approach that stem from historical views of autism. For instance, there is an assumption that the peer is modelling an appropriate behaviour that the autistic person 'should' be doing. There is the further assumption that, despite the difficulties that autistic people may have in interpreting social cues from others, autistic people will be able to recognise and imitate such behaviours from other people and internalise them in a way that will lead to a sustained behaviour across different contexts. Peer modelling may have some merits in terms of allowing different groups of people to spend time together, but – as with interventions targeting ToM deficits – our theoretical understanding of autism has changed and therefore new approaches are needed to create more inclusive spaces.

Neurodiversity-affirming supports in educational practice

Neurodiversity-affirming practices include (1) schools focusing on changing the environment to provide support for autistic pupils, and (2) schools avoiding the promotion of supports that attempt to 'normalise' differences in autistic children, instead focusing on all children becoming more aware, understanding and accepting of difference. Here we include some examples of neurodiversity-affirmative approaches to support autistic children and young people.

Autistic peer support

In educational settings, there is often a push towards inclusion, or encouraging autistic people to spend time with, and learn from, non-autistic people (akin to the peer modelling approaches previously described). However, it can be beneficial for autistic people to spend time with other autistic people. This sense of connection is what young people (Hummerstone and Parsons 2021) have suggested could help them to feel more understood and have a sense of belonging in school (Macmillan, Goodall and Fletcher-Watson 2018), and provides an opportunity to talk about their diagnosis (Crane et al. 2021).

So far, there is a limited amount of research in this area. However, one study asked autistic adults to reflect on their educational experiences and consider what would make good autistic peer support (Crompton et al. 2022). Supporting the ideas above, no participant stated that they would have preferred support from neurotypical pupils. Yet they said they would be interested in a neurodivergent (versus autism-specific) peer-support; recognising that similar issues could affect autistic pupils and neurodivergent pupils more broadly. Participants also highlighted that autistic peer support should be structured around a shared interest or common goal that was defined by pupils and not staff, and that these activities could take many forms (e.g. music, outdoor activities, yoga, etc.). Intervention programmes that bring autistic people together, such as in

Box 5.6, are found to be effective. Anecdotal evidence and feedback from such programmes have highlighted that having children share similar experiences with each other is an enriching experience for young people (Owens et al. 2008; Ringland 2019). Crucially, programmes that are led by children themselves, rather than modelled by one particular peer or an adult, are also powerful at supporting the development of self-confidence and leadership skills.

Taken together, these findings suggest that having opportunities for autistic children and young people to meet and interact with other autistic people could be beneficial for learning and social well-being. Furthermore, there is also a notion that shared experiences with neurodivergent people can support effective learning (Crompton et al. 2020). Such approaches contrast with long-standing, deficit-focused theories of autism (e.g. ToM), and highlight the need for neurodiversity to be embraced within the curriculum.

Box 5.6   Case example: Minecraft™ Club

Earlier in this chapter, we considered the reverse of peer modelling: bringing autistic children together to foster an inclusive and supportive space where they have things in common with one another. Consider this example: one school has noticed that a group of children have a shared interest in Minecraft™, a block-building video game where players can build their own landscapes. The children gather in the computer room at break time to discuss their Minecraft builds and share tips. One teacher, who also enjoys playing Minecraft, decided to set up a club where children would come together to play Minecraft together. As a group, they decided to build a re-imagined model of the school building.

Activity: Reflective questions

- In what ways might an initiative like this foster authentic autistic interactions?
- How could initiatives like this support positive autistic identities?
- What has the teacher done, or could they do, to create an inclusive environment for autistic children?

Embracing neurodiversity in the curriculum

Social skills programmes that bring autistic people together are certainly valuable, but they do little to break down the silos between children and young people of different neurotypes. So, how do we create an inclusive environment for all learners? Recent research has highlighted that neurodiverse environments, which include both autistic and non-autistic people, can better foster creativity than environments made up of people with the same neurotype (Axbey et al. 2023). Therefore, as well as fostering spaces where autistic students can connect, it is also important to create inclusive spaces where everyone is welcomed and accepted.

Particularly at school, autistic people report a general lack of awareness, understanding and acceptance of neurodivergence, which leads to stigmatising experiences (Pellicano and den Houting et al. 2022). One solution to this issue is to provide education about neurodiversity to *everyone*. Resources such as the Learning about Neurodiversity in Schools (LEANS) programme are available as a classroom-wide initiative to teach primary school students about neurodiversity as a concept, and how it impacts children at school. Underpinning the LEANS programme is the idea of teaching children about equity: that everyone has needs, and having those needs met is the right of every child. Across learning environments, giving children and young people the opportunities and capabilities to advocate for their own needs is key to reaching real inclusion.

> **Box 5.7 Learning about neurodiversity at school**
>
> The Learning about Neurodiversity at School (LEANS) package is the first interactive resource pack for primary teachers in the UK to teach children aged 8–11 years about neurodiversity. Delivered to the whole class, it encourages children to explore and learn about different components of the neurodiversity paradigm, such as equity and acceptance. LEANS was co-designed with a neurodiverse team of educators and researchers over a series of sessions. The aim is to upskill all students in the class (and, eventually, the whole school) rather than thinking about LEANS as an intervention for perceived 'difficulties' that are experienced by some children.
>
> At the time of writing, the LEANS resource pack includes seven units: introducing neurodiversity, classroom experiences, communication, needs and wants, fairness, friendship, and reflecting on our actions. LEANS is free and available online and is being evaluated in schools: https://salvesen-research.ed.ac.uk/leans

Conclusion

In this chapter, we have provided an overview of autism and how our understanding of autism has changed over time. We have shown how a focus on autistic *deficits* may have hindered the support provided to autistic children and young people, and explained how a neurodiversity-affirmative approach might provide a better lens through which to understand how to support autistic differences in the classroom. Underpinning all approaches to supporting autistic learners should be a focus on staff appreciating and accepting difference and diversity, along with an understanding that each young person is an individual, and that we need to reflect on how best to support them.

References

Aitken, D. and Fletcher-Watson, S. (2022) Neurodiversity-affirmative education: why and how?, *The Psychologist*, 15 December. Available at: https://www.bps.org.uk/psychologist/neurodiversity-affirmative-education-why-and-how

Alvares, G.A., Bebbington, K., Cleary, D., Evans, K., Glasson, E.J., Maybery, M.T. et al. (2020) The misnomer of 'high functioning autism': intelligence is an imprecise predictor of functional abilities at diagnosis, *Autism*, 24 (1): 221–232.

American Psychiatric Association (APA) (1994) *Diagnostic and Statistical Manual of Mental Disorders*, 4th edition (DSM-IV). Washington, DC: APA.

Asperger, H. (1944) Die 'Autistischen psychopathen' im kindesalter, *Archiv für psychiatrie und nervenkrankheiten*, 117 (1): 76–136.

Axbey, H., Beckmann, N., Fletcher-Watson, S., Tullo, A. and Crompton, C.J. (2023) Innovation through neurodiversity: diversity is beneficial, *Autism*. Available at: https://doi.org/10.1177/13623613231158685

Baron-Cohen, S., Leslie, A.M. and Frith, U. (1985) Does the autistic child have a 'theory of mind?', *Cognition*, 21 (1): 37–46.

Buijsman, R., Begeer, S. and Scheeren, A.M. (2022) 'Autistic person' or 'person with autism'? Person-first language preference in Dutch adults with autism and parents, *Autism*, 27 (3): 788–795.

Calder, L., Hill, V. and Pellicano, E. (2013) 'Sometimes I want to play by myself': Understanding what friendship means to children with autism in mainstream primary schools, *Autism*, 17 (3): 296–316.

Chang, Y.C. and Locke, J. (2016) A systematic review of peer-mediated interventions for children with autism spectrum disorder, *Research in Autism Spectrum Disorders*, 27: 1–10.

Crane, L., Chester, J.W., Goddard, L., Henry, L.A. and Hill, E. (2016) Experiences of autism diagnosis: a survey of over 1000 patients in the United Kingdom, *Autism*, 20 (2): 153–162

Crane, L., Lui, L.M., Davies, J. and Pellicano, E. (2021) Autistic parents' views and experiences of talking about autism with their autistic children, *Autism*, 25 (4): 1161–1167.

Crompton, C.J., Ropar, D., Evans-Williams, C.V., Flynn, E.G. and Fletcher-Watson, S. (2020) Autistic peer-to-peer information transfer is highly effective, *Autism*, 24 (7): 1704–1712.

Crompton, C.J., Hallett, S., McAuliffe, C., Stanfield, A.C. and Fletcher-Watson, S. (2022) 'A group of fellow travellers who understand': interviews with autistic people about post-diagnostic peer support in adulthood, *Frontiers in Psychology*, 13. Available at: https://doi.org/10.3389/fpsyg.2022.831628

Davis, R., Fletcher-Watson, S. and Digard, B.G. (2021) Autistic people's access to bilingualism and additional language learning: identifying the barriers and facilitators for equal opportunities, *Frontiers in Psychology*, 12. Available at: https://doi.org/10.3389/fpsyg.2021.741182

Davis, R., den Houting, J., Nordahl-Hansen, A. and Fletcher-Watson, S. (2022) Helping autistic children, in P.K. Smith and C.H. Hart (eds.), *The Wiley-Blackwell Handbook of Childhood Social Development*, 3rd edition. Hoboken, NJ: Wiley-Blackwell.

Dean, M. and Chang, Y.C. (2021), A systematic review of school-based social skills interventions and observed social outcomes for students with autism spectrum disorder in inclusive settings, *Autism*, 25 (7): 1828–1843.

den Houting, J. (2018) Neurodiversity: an insider's perspective, *Autism*, 23 (2): 271–273.

Dworzynski, K., Ronald, A., Bolton, P. and Happé, F. (2012) How different are girls and boys above and below the diagnostic threshold for autism spectrum disorders?, *Journal of the American Academy of Child & Adolescent Psychiatry*, 51 (8): 788–797.

Edey, R., Cook, J., Brewer, R., Johnson, M.H., Bird, G. and Press, C. (2016) Interaction takes two: typical adults exhibit mind-blindness towards those with autism spectrum disorder, *Journal of Abnormal Psychology*, 125 (7): 879–885.

Fletcher-Watson, S., McConnell, F., Manola, E. and McConachie, H. (2014) Interventions based on the Theory of Mind cognitive model for autism spectrum disorder (ASD), *Cochrane Database of Systematic Reviews*, 3: CD008785. Available at: https://doi.org/10.1002/14651858.CD008785.pub2.

Gernsbacher, M.A. (2017). Editorial perspective: The use of person-first language in scholarly writing may accentuate stigma. *Journal of Child Psychology and Psychiatry*, 58(7), 859–861. https://doi.org/10.1111/jcpp.12706

Glenwright, M., Scott, R.M., Bilevicius, E., Pronovost, M. and Hanlon-Dearman, A. (2021) Children with autism spectrum disorder can attribute false beliefs in a spontaneous-response preferential-looking task, *Frontiers in Communication*, 6. Available at: https://doi.org/10.3389/fcomm.2021.669985

Happé, F.G. (1994) An advanced test of theory of mind: understanding of story characters' thoughts and feelings by able autistic, mentally handicapped, and normal children and adults, *Journal of Autism and Developmental Disorders*, 24 (2): 129–154.

Harris, B., Barton, E.E. and Albert, C. (2014) Evaluating autism diagnostic and screening tools for cultural and linguistic responsiveness, *Journal of Autism and Developmental Disorders*, 44 (6): 1275–1287.

Heasman, B. and Gillespie, A. (2018) Perspective-taking is two-sided: misunderstandings between people with Asperger's syndrome and their family members, *Autism*, 22 (6): 740–750.

Hisle-Gorman, E., Landis, C.A., Susi, A., Schvey, N.A., Gorman, G.H., Nylund, C.M. et al. (2019) Gender dysphoria in children with autism spectrum disorder, *LGBT Health*, 6 (3): 95–100.

Hummerstone, H. and Parsons, S. (2021) What makes a good teacher? Comparing the perspectives of students on the autism spectrum and staff, *European Journal of Special Needs Education*, 36 (4): 610–624.

Jaswal, V.K. and Akhtar, N. (2019) Being versus appearing socially uninterested: challenging assumptions about social motivation in autism, *Behavioral and Brain Sciences*, 42: e82. Available at: https://doi.org/10.1017/S0140525X18001826.

Kanner, L. (1943) Autistic disturbances of affective contact, *Nervous Child*, 2 (3): 217–250.

Libster, N., Knox, A., Engin, S., Geschwind, D., Parish-Morris, J. and Kasari, C. (2023) Sex differences in friendships and loneliness in autistic and non-autistic children across development, *Molecular Autism*, 14 (1): 1–12.

Macmillan, K., Goodall, K. and Fletcher-Watson, S. (2018) Do autistic individuals experience understanding in school?, *OSF Preprints*, 12 November. Available at: https://doi.org/10.31219/osf.io/awzuk

Mandell, D.S., Ittenbach, R.F., Levy, S.E. and Pinto-Martin, J.A. (2007) Disparities in diagnoses received prior to a diagnosis of autism spectrum disorder, *Journal of Autism and Developmental Disorders*, 37 (9): 1795–1802.

McConkey, R. (2020) The rise in the numbers of pupils identified by schools with autism spectrum disorder (ASD): a comparison of the four countries in the United Kingdom, *Support for Learning*, 35 (2): 132–143.

McLinden, H. and Sedgewick, F. (2023) 'The girls are out there': professional perspectives on potential changes in the diagnostic process for, and recognition of, autistic females in the UK, *British Journal of Special Education*, 50 (1): 63–82.

Milton, D.E.M. (2012) On the ontological status of autism: the 'double empathy problem', *Disability & Society*, 27 (6), 883–887.

Owens, G., Granader, Y., Humphrey, A. and Baron-Cohen, S. (2008) LEGO® therapy and the Social Use of Language Programme: an evaluation of two social skills interventions for children with high functioning autism and Asperger syndrome, *Journal of Autism and Developmental Disorders*, 38 (10): 1944–1957.

Pellicano, E. and den Houting, J. (2022) Annual research review: ShiftPsychology & ing from 'normal science' to neurodiversity in autism science, *Journal of Child Psychiatry*, 63 (4): 381–396.

Phung, J., Penner, M., Pirlot, C. and Welch, C. (2021) What I wish I knew: insights on burnout, inertia, meltdown, and shutdown from autistic youth, *Frontiers in Psychology*, 12. Available at: https://doi.org/10.3389/fpsyg.2021.741421

Ringland, K.E. (2019) A place to play: the (dis)abled embodied experience for autistic children in online spaces, in *Proceedings of the 2019 CHI Conference on Human Factors in Computing Systems*, 1–14, Glasgow, 4–9 May.

Roman-Urrestarazu, A., Yang, J.C., van Kessel, R., Warrier, V., Dumas, G., Jongsma, H. et al. (2022) Autism incidence and spatial analysis in more than 7 million pupils in English schools: a retrospective, longitudinal, school registry study, *The Lancet Child & Adolescent Health*, 6 (12): 857–868.

Russell, G., Stapley, S., Newlove-Delgado, T., Salmon, A., White, R., Warren, F. et al. (2022) Time trends in autism diagnosis over 20 years: a UK population-based cohort study, *Journal of Child Psychology and Psychiatry*, 63 (6): 674–682.

Shattuck, P.T., Durkin, M., Maenner, M., Newschaffer, C., Mandell, D.S., Wiggins, L. et al. (2009) Timing of identification among children with an autism spectrum disorder: findings from a population-based surveillance study, *Journal of the American Academy of Child & Adolescent Psychiatry*, 48 (5): 474–483.

Sproston, K., Sedgewick, F. and Crane, L. (2017) Autistic girls and school exclusion: perspectives of students and their parents, *Autism & Developmental Language Impairments*, 2. Available at: https://doi.org/10.1177/2396941517706172

Strang, J.F., Kenworthy, L., Dominska, A., Sokoloff, J., Kenealy, L.E., Berl, M. et al. (2014) Increased gender variance in autism spectrum disorders and attention deficit hyperactivity disorder, *Archives of Sexual Behavior*, 43 (8): 1525–1533.

Treffert, D.A. (2009) The savant syndrome: an extraordinary condition. A synopsis: past, present, future, *Philosophical Transactions of the Royal Society B: Biological Sciences*, 364 (1522): 1351–1357.

Walker, N. (2014) Neurodiversity: some basic terms an& definitions, *Neuroqueer*. Available at: https://neuroqueer.com/neurodiversity-terms-and-definitions/

6 Understanding and responding to social, emotional and mental health needs

Kate Carr-Fanning

By the end of this chapter, you will be able to:

- identify and describe social, emotional and mental health difficulties
- critically consider the concept and personal assumptions about challenging behaviours
- critically consider labelling, stigma and mental health practices
- develop an understanding of promoting mental health and well-being and positive education
- develop a psychologically informed understanding of what may underlie challenging behaviours, how this informs interventions, and things to think about when designing or selecting an intervention.

This chapter explores the extremely broad area of needs that fall under the category social, emotional and mental health (SEMH) – how we understand the term, what may underlie challenging behaviour and mental health difficulties, some challenges in the area, and things to consider when it comes to responding to SEMH needs.

Before we begin, reflect on your assumptions and beliefs about 'challenging behaviours'.

Activity
What do you think about when we say 'challenging behaviours'? List the kinds of challenging behaviours learners exhibit in your experience.

- Prioritise the most common.
- Prioritise those that are the most disruptive in school (e.g. classrooms, groupwork, etc.), the most difficult to manage, and the most challenging or stressful to the adult.
- Prioritise those that are the most disruptive to the learner's development and the most stressful for them.
- Are there any differences between the above?

What are social, emotional and mental health needs?

This section will consider SEMH needs in terms of all learners' mental health needs, but first we will focus on the group showing difficulties in this area.

In search of a definition for difficulties

In 2019, 14.9 per cent of learners were recognised as having some form of SEN, and 17.1 per cent of them were identified as having SEMH difficulties as their primary need (DfE 2019). These learners are particularly disadvantaged when it comes to inclusion as they experience disproportionate rates of school exclusion (Bowman-Perrott et al. 2013), placing them at risk for a range of other negative outcomes.

According to the SEN Code of Practice (DfE/DoH 2015: 98), SEMH difficulties are defined broadly as 'social and emotional difficulties' that manifest in varied ways, including:

- *Challenging behaviours* (e.g. 'withdrawn', 'isolated', 'disruptive' or 'disturbing'). Such behaviours 'may reflect underlying mental health difficulties such as anxiety or depression, self-harming, substance misuse, eating disorders or physical symptoms that are medically unexplained'.
- *Disorders* (e.g. ADHD, attachment disorder, conduct disorder, oppositional-defiant disorder, generalised anxiety disorder).

Clearly, a range of needs, difficulties and disorders are included under SEMH – the definition is so broad that it is infinitely interpretable, potentially unhelpful, and at worst harmful. A significant problem with this (and previous categories) is that the needs included are so varied, while others are more specific (e.g. ADHD). Although these needs are extremely varied, approaches to understanding and responding (e.g. interventions) to them is often done indiscriminately (e.g. Carroll and Hurry 2018).

SEMH difficulties can manifest as 'acting-out' or externalising (e.g. aggression) and 'acting-in' or internalising (e.g. anxiety and depression) behaviours. However, teachers appear to be more concerned with externalising behaviours, especially those that challenge authority (Armstrong 2017). Learners who internalise, the so-called 'quiet children', can sometimes fly under the radar and be missed (Pedersen et al. 2019).

A significant contribution of the new definition in the 2015 Code was the shift from a focus on 'behaviour' to a focus on SEMH difficulties that are assumed to underlie these behaviours. The previous heading – social, emotional and behavioural difficulties or disorders (S/EBD) – focused on 'behaviour', which prevented a meaningful understanding of what was going on for the learner.

The thing about mental health is that everyone has it

The concept of mental health is sometimes used to imply difficulty, or a problem. However, everyone has mental health, and so all learners have SEMH needs. We can understand SEMH on a continuum: at one end, there is mental health that is associated with well-being and flourishing, which should be promoted in all learners; at the other, there are mental health difficulties, where a minority of learners will need support and intervention. Positive psychology contributes to our understanding of learners' mental health and well-being.

According to Seligman and Csikszentmihalyi (2000: 5), psychology needed to move away from 'repairing the worst things in life' towards the study of positive experiences, personal strengths and positive institutions. Focusing on strengths does not negate weaknesses, it merely suggests that identifying and promoting strengths and resources is more practical and effective than responding reactively to problems (Wright, Lopez and Magyar 2021).

The application of positive psychology to schools is known as positive education, which Gable and Haidt define as, 'the study of the conditions and processes that contribute to the flourishing or optimal functioning of people, groups, and institutions' (2005: 104). Positive psychology promotes concepts and evidence-based practices applicable to most facets of school life, contributing to preventative interventions, mental health promotion programmes, collaborative practices, and developing the competencies and resiliency of all learners (Wright, Lopez, and Magyar 2021).

Positive education is focused on developing the whole learner, encompassing social, emotional, moral and academic learning (Waters 2011). Using the PERMA model, Seligman (2011) provides a framework to understand needs in this area, consisting of five characteristics which can be enhanced and are intrinsically motivating: positive emotions, engagement, relationships, meaning and achievement (see Figure 6.1).

Figure 6.1 PERMA model

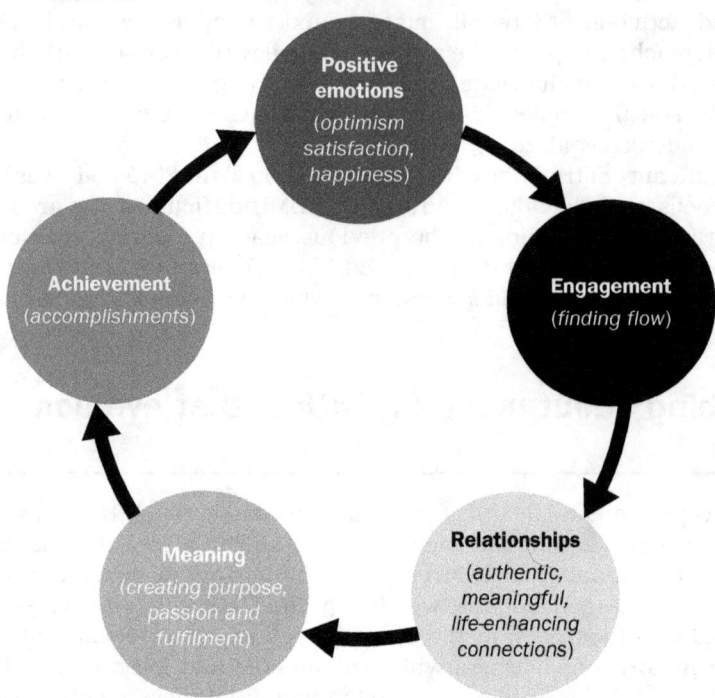

Seligman worked with the Geelong Grammar School in Australia to apply this model to education, embedding these principles within the curriculum and the practices of the whole school. For example, pupils discussed the character strengths of King Lear in English Literature (character strengths are linked to engagement) and volunteered within their community (linked to meaning).

A critical look at mental health: stigma, labelling and diagnosis

Mental health practices have a number of significant problems and limitations, and these are considered here.

Reflection
Before we begin, consider your current beliefs. What are mental health disorders? How would you identify them? What, if any, are the problems with diagnosing and labelling children?

Stigma and labelling

As discussed in Chapter 1, the use of labels and the impact of stigma are ever present within special and inclusive education. Learners with SEMH difficulties are among the most stigmatised group because their behaviours (especially externalising ones) are considered 'difficult difference' (Flynn 2013). More importantly, however, these learners have consistently been found to hold negative self-beliefs, and consistently report negative self-perceptions: 'sad, bad, or mad' (Armstrong 2017). In their systematic review of the literature on the views and experiences of learners with SEMH, Hickinbotham and Soni (2021) found positive and negative effects associated with the label. While there may be benefits associated with diagnosis (e.g. access to knowledge and services), learners reportedly do not understand the SEMH label and view it negatively, as meaning they are 'mentally ill'. They also consistently report feeling stigmatised, blamed for their difficulties, and viewed as undesirable, unwanted and disempowered in school. The label also reportedly has significant consequences for their identity.

Lauchlan and Boyle (2007) outline a number of advantages to the use of labels to different stakeholders. Educators can use them to understand difficulties, they can reduce ambiguity and help with planning. For parents and children, they can 'explain' their difficulties and build positive identities and belonging. The Lancet Psychiatry convention (i.e. person-first terminology) is often discussed in terms of a more respectful approach. However, in line with the affirmative model of disability (see Chapter 1; Swain and French 2000), insiders and disability advocates wishing to 'reclaim' their identity and/or construct a positive disability identity are choosing disorder-first language. For example, they are self-identifying as an 'ADDer' or 'Autistic'.

A question we also need to ask, with regards to labelling and stigma, is whether the stigma arises from the label, the behaviours or a combination of the two. For example, in a survey of 3,998 Australian adults, Jorm and Griffiths (2008) reported that medical labels are not the cause of stigma, but rather the behaviours themselves and perceptions of control or responsibility, for example, the belief that difficulties people with SEMH experience are the result of personal weakness.

Critical psychopathology

Mental health practice is often focused on understanding and managing behaviours (or symptoms). There are significant problems with assumptions about what underlies these behaviours and how these behaviours are used to diagnose disorders.

Any critique of mental health practice draws on ideas from the social model and the problems with the individual/medical model, which focuses on the person and ignores the environment (see Chapter 1). How we make decisions about how 'abnormal' a behaviour is, is subjective. So, we need to be careful we are not pathologising behaviours based on societal expectations about what is normal or optimal functioning.

As discussed in Chapter 1, Foucault (1994) argued that the use of diagnosis and treatment as a method to control behaviour emerged as traditional forms of control in schools (e.g. corporal punishment and exclusion) were removed. So, we can understand diagnosis and treatment as a new way of punishing undesirable behaviour. Others (e.g. Maddux 2021) have argued that society has become increasingly more perfectionist in what it expects from people, and less tolerant of what used to be considered normal distress or individual difference. Human emotions are adaptive and we would struggle to navigate the world without them – emotions are involved in functioning and learning. However, negative emotions can be pathologised, viewed as things that are bad and undesirable, rather than normal, healthy and adaptive. For example, during the COVID-19 pandemic, reports of a mental health 'crisis' were rampant. However, we can view these increases in feelings of anxiety or depression as healthy responses to fear for oneself or one's loved ones, or as the natural consequence of social isolation. These medicalising tendencies are observable through the language we use. For example, a learner might say an upcoming exam is causing them 'anxiety', rather than making them 'worried'.

> *Reflection*
> Think of a time when you or someone you know medicalised emotions in their choice of language.

More issues with mental health practice exist within how disorders are diagnosed. We often think of mental health difficulties as 'facts' about a person. However, we need to question how we know someone is 'disordered' and how accurate that diagnosis is.

Diagnostic systems for mental health difficulties focus on discrete categories of disorders, similar to the way medical diseases are diagnosed. Diagnostic texts (e.g. DSM-5) provide lists of disorders and a checklist of associated behavioural symptoms, meaning complex difficulties are understood as clusters of behaviours/symptoms. Due to considerable debate about what 'causes' disorders, diagnostic systems like the DSM-5 have adopted an atheoretical perspective, and so ignore cause.

Diagnostic systems use a categorical approach – they use interviews and psychometrics to identify the presence or absence of 'abnormal' behaviours to diagnose a disorder. So, when someone receives a diagnosis, they have 'depression'. However, these disorders (and the associated behaviours) may be better understood as dimensional – that is, as more or less severe (e.g. how sad someone experiencing depression feels may vary from person to person) or as more or less frequent (e.g. how anxious a person feels may vary from day-to-day) (Maddux 2021). Diagnostic manuals have been further criticised for the number of disorders, and with each revision more disorders are added. The situation is further complicated by the fact that co-existing (or co-morbid) diagnoses are common. For example, the co-occurrence of autism and mental health difficulties may be as high as 70 per cent (Lai, Lombardo and Baron-Cohen 2014). Additional problems arise around differential diagnosis, since difficulties can overlap (e.g. depression and anxiety both have similar symptoms linked to feeling anxious).

Diagnostic systems use Wakefield's (1992) notion of 'harmful dysfunction' to classify a disorder, which requires both a 'functional' and a 'factual' criterion. So, for a disorder to be a disorder, the person has to have a psychobiological deficit (factual) that causes dysfunction in more than one area of functioning (e.g. social, academic, family). Therefore, the personal-deficit 'causes' the dysfunction, which (again) ignores the environment. Furthermore, if SEMH difficulties are caused solely by an impairment, then diagnosis would be reliable and valid across contexts and treatment would be unwaveringly effective. If a difficulty is caused by the same deficit, then it should be recognisable and respond similarly to treatment. Unfortunately, how difficulties manifest and impair varies from person to person, diagnosis is influenced by the clinician's skills and beliefs/biases, and some treatments work better for some than for others (Desforges and Lindsay 2010).

> *Reflection*
> Return to your reflections from the beginning of this section: would you change any of your responses?

What underlies challenging behaviours?

A significant shift in the definition of SEMH difficulties was the focus on what underlined challenging behaviours and functional difficulties. A child's behaviour is shaped through a dynamic interactive process with other people (e.g. parents, teachers, peers) in different contexts (e.g. school and home) across their lifetime. Any variances in this process (within the child) are the focus of developmental psychology (Armstrong 2018). Thus, a significant contribution of psychology to educational inclusion is an understanding of what might underlie and/or contribute to SEMH difficulties.

Differences in psychobiology, thoughts, feelings and behaviours

Educators cannot ignore or underestimate the social, family and environmental contexts. However, to understand what underlies SEMH difficulties, it is helpful to consider variances at the level of the child. In educational contexts, the psychobiological, behavioural and social-cognitive are the main psychological approaches.

Psychobiology

Psychobiological approaches would seek to understand SEMH difficulties in terms of neurochemicals and structures, family genetics or stress hormones. In relation to the relationship between neurology and behaviour, for example, we can study the effects of the neurotransmitter serotonin on depressive behaviours. Cognitive neuroscience focuses on the correlations between behaviour, cognition, and the physical and chemical make-up of the brain. Brain imaging studies, for instance, demonstrate the long-term effects of prolonged exposure to stress hormones (associated with traumatic experiences) on early brain development, which impacts cognitive processes such as memory (van der Kolk 2014).

Behaviourism

Based on the work of Pavlov, Watson and Skinner, behavioural approaches focus on objective behaviours that can be observed. They are not concerned with internal processes, such as thoughts and feelings.

The assumption is that behaviour is 'learnt' through experiences in the child's environment, and so if one changes the environment, the child can change their behaviours or develop entirely new ones. In understanding challenging behaviour, the emphasis should be on identifying what features within the environment develop or maintain it and then to adjust these. Skinner's (2019) work on operant conditioning or 'contingency management' has been particularly influential in schools. This approach suggests that behaviour is motivated by consequences, both positive (e.g. praise) and negative ones (e.g. exclusion) that are commonly encountered in schools.

The legacy of behaviourism in education cannot be underestimated. Behaviourism dominates school behaviour policies (Maguire, Ball and Braun 2010) and practices (Armstrong 2018), such as Positive Behaviour Support. The reason for this is partly due to the efficacy of the approach, as the majority of learners respond well. However, behaviourism may ignore other factors to the detriment of the child. Behavioural management focuses on overt behaviour and its control; it can ignore or minimise many of the processes involved in behavioural development and change. It often fails to ask important questions, like:

- What is going on with you?
- How are things at home, in your community, with your peers?
- How do you think and feel today?
- What are your self-perceptions? Do you think you can achieve at school?
- Do you feel secure, safe and a sense of belonging?
- Are you experiencing significant stress and adversity?
- What can you learn and how can you grow from this mistake/situation?

Armstrong (2021) argued that learners with SEN that affects their behaviour and/or have SEMH difficulties experience 'disadvantage, suspension or exclusion' as a direct result of the application of this model in practice. He further argued for a need to reject 'wholeheartedly' ineffective approaches based on behavioural management and discipline, support teachers who are (or at risk of) burnout, incentivise schools to keep (i.e. not exclude) these learners, and to base educational responses on research (especially developmental psychology).

Social and cognitive approaches

While less influential, many programmes of intervention and responses within schools draw upon social and cognitive approaches, including the principles of cognitive behaviour therapy (CBT), such as the Why Try! programme.

Cognitive approaches are focused on cognitive processes – how a learner perceives events, thinks about them, plans and problem-solves. According to this view, a child's interpretation of events will determine their behaviour. So, to change behaviour, one needs to change how the child 'perceives' events. These perceptions are based on a number of psychological processes (e.g. self-esteem, attributions, attitudes and cognitive skills).

Bandura's (1986) social learning theory straddles cognitive approaches and behaviourism with its emphasis on learnt behaviour, as well as its recognition of internal mental processes, such as observational learning and beliefs (in particular self-efficacy).

The concept and educational practice of developing social and emotional learning (SEL) refers to the process whereby learners develop and use their knowledge and skills to support healthy development and relationships. A broad range of skills have been included under the terms SEL. According to the CASEL (2015) model (see the 'Resources' box below), SEL encompasses self-awareness, self-management, responsible decision-making, relationship skills and social awareness.

SEL is applicable to all children, and so a promotional approach. Promotional approaches target positive development that contribute to well-being and flourishing. This is distinct from responding to difficulties, which is the case with treatment or intervention (see further explanation on different approaches below). For example, social and emotional skills have been found to be better determinants of academic attainment than IQ (e.g. Duckworth and Seligman 2005). Social and emotional skills can be developed through interventions, or used to prevent the development of SEMH difficulties. For example, in a meta-analysis of 270,034 learners, Durlak et al. (2011) found that universal SEL programmes enhanced behavioural adjustment, increased prosocial behaviours, and reduced conduct and internalising problems. Drawing on data from the 1946 British birth cohort study, Richards and Huppert (2011) found that children rated as having 'positive' attributes (e.g. make friends easily) had better mental health in adulthood. Due to the associated outcomes, it has been argued that a lack of social and emotional skills places children at a severe disadvantage, and schools play a critical role in SEL (Elias, Ferrito and Moceri 2015; Domitrovich et al. 2017; Elias 2019).

Humanistic psychology

Humanistic psychology draws on the work of Carl Rogers and Abraham Maslow, and encompasses educational approaches such as Montessori and Steiner. Humanism is premised on the belief that people are innately good and born with a drive to develop. Humanistic psychology emphasises child-centred or student-centred practices, whereby educators trust and 'follow' the child's innate tendencies (Rogers 1969; Sinnott 2008).

In this approach, the educator acts as a facilitator, trusting the child's innate drive to develop and grow, and providing enriching environments where the child is free to explore. Key traits of the educator include empathy, genuineness and caring about students. The focus is on the development of the 'whole child' – their academic, social, emotional, artistic and practical competencies, with an emphasis on the development of self-esteem, setting and achieving goals, and becoming independent and autonomous.

Children who present with any adverse psychosocial behaviours or experiences are viewed as deviating from their natural tendencies. As a result, child-centred approaches that emphasise empathy, unconditional positive regard for the child, supporting the child to explore emotional experiences, and develop emotional and other personal competencies would fall within humanistic education.

'What's going on for you?'

Approaches informed by psychoanalytic and attachment theory, and an understanding of the effects of adversity and trauma in childhood have shifted the focus from 'what's wrong with you' to 'what's going on for you' – these approaches inform educational responses, such as the nurture approaches and trauma-informed education (Thomas, Crosby and Vanderhaar 2019).

Psychoanalytic theory

Psychodynamic perspectives, originating in the work of Freud, place significance on early childhood experiences and relationships with primary caregivers. These early experiences reside within the unconscious mind and inform relationships with others (e.g. teachers) and behaviours. While it has not been particularly influential in most educational contexts, it has influenced a range of ideas and practice which are.

Attachment theory

Drawing on the work of Freud, Bowlby (1977) introduced notions of attachment or 'psychological connectedness' between a child and their primary carer.

These early attachment relationships have significant outcomes, forming the basis for future attachments with other people and institutions (e.g. schools), and fostering resiliency and learner engagement (Bomber 2007; Centre on the Developing Child at Harvard University 2015). Attachment to school can be defined as:

> the degree of commitment towards and engagement with schooling ... Students who have a strong attachment to school believe that success in school will lead to significant rewards in later life. Weak attachment to school is characterized by indifference or hostility towards teachers and scepticism about the value of schooling.
> (Cooper and Jacobs 2011: 38)

In contrast, learners with SEMH difficulties are consistently found to be disengaged from school, and often do not feel accepted or respected (Cooper and Jacobs 2011). Such disengagement and attachment difficulties may arise due to adversity, stress or trauma.

Stress and adversity

All children's development includes – even necessitates – some degree of risk and stress. The goal is for the risk/stress to be balanced out by factors that promote positive development and/or protect (buffer) against stress (Masten and Cicchetti 2016). Here, we will consider risks/stress in the absence of such buffers.

Trauma is 'an emotional response to a terrible event' (APA 2015). Trauma can cause problems with emotional regulation (e.g. outbursts, anxiety), social relationships (e.g. making friends, new teachers), cognitive processes (e.g. memory, attention, executive functioning, reward processing), as well as lead to the development of physical symptoms (e.g. stomach aches, insomnia, chest pains). It can negatively affect the development of the stress response/regulation system and make children less resilient to adversity or challenge. In a birth-cohort study of 2,232 children born in England and Wales in 1994–95, it was found found that by age 18 years, 31.1 per cent had been exposed to trauma (Lewis et al. 2019).

Trauma can take many forms: it can involve families, communities, even whole populations (e.g. war), and it can refer to a single event ('simple trauma') or more chronic exposure known as 'developmental trauma' (van der Kolk 2014). Simple trauma can have some of the most powerful and immediate effects on learners' behaviours. Developmental trauma is the exposure to trauma multiple times, for longer periods of time, often within the context of important interpersonal relationships that are threatening or violent (e.g. abuse, neglect, bulling). Over time, developmental trauma, if it remains unrecognised or unaddressed, has the potential to be more devastating to learners than simple trauma. Developmental trauma can have a lasting physical, emotional and cognitive impact.

Many children experience trauma – including developmental trauma – through adverse childhood experiences (ACEs), which are highly stressful or traumatic events that occur within childhood/adolescence. In their landmark study, Felitti et al. (1998) collected data over two years from 17,000 adults in the USA exploring their exposure to ten categories of abuse, neglect and household dysfunction. They found correlations between childhood trauma and a range of poor personal and social outcomes, including negative effects on physical and mental health, educational and occupational outcomes. Drawing on findings from the WHO survey of mental health, Kessler et al. (2010) established the link between ACE and mental health difficulties. Follow-up studies have reported additional adversities; these expanded (community-level) ACEs include racism, witnessing violence, unsafe neighbourhoods, bullying/victimisation and being in foster care (Cronholm et al. 2015). With cumulative exposure, the more adversity you experience, the more likely you are to experience worse outcomes. In England, Bellis et al. (2014) found that almost half (46 per cent) of the adult population had experienced at least one ACE, while 8 per cent had been affected by four or more.

While trauma-informed education, based on an understanding of the impact of stress and adversity, is not a unified or clearly defined approach, it has made a significant contribution to understanding the needs and the behaviours (particularly avoidance, aggression and disengagement) of learners with SEMH difficulties. It emphasises the importance of the school environment, with a particular focus on building and sustaining meaningful relationships (between members of staff, between staff and learners, and between the learners themselves) and promoting a sense of consistency, safety and security (Thomas, Crosby and Vanderhaar 2019). Similarly, in their systematic review of the literature, Hobfoll et al. (2007) identified several essential elements for trauma-informed practice: providing a sense of 'safety' and 'calming' to ameliorate the fear/stress response and 'connectedness'. Connectedness has been found to be the most significant protective factor in the development of post-traumatic stress disorder (McDermott, Berry and Cobham 2012). Hobfoll et al. also suggest that educators can provide opportunities to develop a sense of 'efficacy' and foster a sense of 'hope' about the future.

> Reflection
> Many of the origins of ACEs, stress and trauma are located outside educational settings. What can educators do to help learners if they experience any of these?

The whole child: a holistic approach

A holistic and systemic approach is essential for understanding and responding to SEMH difficulties and/or challenging behaviours. To address these difficulties and behaviours, we must understand the reciprocal *interactions* between child-level factors (e.g. temperament, traits, differences, strengths) and their environment (e.g. social, family, school, community) over time. Bronfenbrenner's (2005) bio-ecological model (see Chapters 3 and 4) and Engel's (1977) biopsychosocial model (see Chapter 1) provide good frameworks for educational practice with learners with SEMH difficulties. In this way, behaviour can be understood to emerge from complex interactions between biology, psychology, and the social, environmental and cultural contexts.

Responding to SEMH difficulties – what you need to consider

Most interventions or programmes aimed at addressing SEMH difficulties focus on the child, their parents and family environment. However, children and young people spend a lot of their time at school where they interact with peers and teachers, and encounter academic, emotional, behavioural and social challenges. Taken together with the increase in demand for mental health services and support, this makes school an exciting environment to deliver services to a larger number of children and young people. This section will outline some of the key features of broadly defined intervention programmes and what you should consider when evaluating, recommending or choosing one.

Different approaches: intervention, prevention and promotion

You may have come across a number of terms referring to mental health programmes such as interventions, prevention programmes, well-being promotion or tiers of treatment. All these relate to different approaches to SEMH needs and have a number of key aims, which we briefly outline below.

1 *Promotion*: includes strategies that focus on developing strengths and skills such as improving self-esteem and confidence, emotional self-regulation and resilience. Such approaches are usually delivered to all learners (e.g. entire school or class). *Note: this could also be considered an early prevention step.*
2 *Prevention*: includes strategies or programmes that attempt to prevent difficulties arising or from becoming worse. Such approaches are usually delivered to individuals without present difficulties and focus either on all learners or selected groups who are considered 'at risk'.
3 *Intervention*: includes targeted intervention programmes that focus on supporting learners with identified difficulties.

When choosing an approach, there are a number of key considerations, which we will now consider.

Children's profiles

A key factor in developing the appropriate response is to develop an understanding of the learner or the group. SEMH difficulties are heterogeneous in nature. Furthermore, two learners who seem to experience the same difficulty 'on the surface' may have a different set of needs. Co-morbid difficulties further complicate this picture. Co-morbidity refers to the co-occurrence of more than one difficulty (or disorder, in clinical terms) in the same individual. This suggests that learners may have very different profiles in terms of strengths and difficulties, which is important to consider because selecting the most effective programme largely depends on the type of difficulty that is being addressed (Paulus, Ohmann and Popow 2016). Because of that, a large number of programmes remain quite focused and are designed to address specific difficulties. For example, Fabiano and Pyle (2019) introduced best-practice recommendations that are specific to learners with ADHD. These might include classroom contingency management strategies or training in organisational skills. Another example comes from Liber and colleagues (2013), who highlighted the positive effect of school-based CBT on disruptive behaviour. Ideally, learners' profiles of strengths and difficulties should be considered here, however, we acknowledge the pitfalls of such specificity when delivering programmes to larger groups of children.

In considering the needs of the learner or learners, we need to understand them holistically (see p. 11). A child's behaviour and SEMH difficulties can only be understood as the cumulative effects of their interactions and lived experiences across their lifetime. So, it is important to consider their family and cultural background, ethnicity/race, gender and so forth, as these will have implications for responding appropriately. Do not forget to consider their preferences and wishes too! Learners with SEMH difficulties are often left out of decision-making (Flynn 2013).

Choosing 'the one'

Once you have considered the complexity of the learner or group of learners, you need to figure out which is the most appropriate programme for them.

There have been a number of reviews of school-based interventions for child mental health, looking at the strength of evidence to support their effectiveness (see Paulus, Ohmann and Popow 2016; Dray at al. 2017; O'Reilly et al. 2018). Children's profiles and the highest standard of evidence should be key considerations here. Randomised controlled trials (RCTs) are considered the 'gold standard' in the intervention literature. They include random allocation to various conditions (e.g. condition A versus condition B), which reduces the risk of there being systematic differences between treatment groups (i.e. different intervention groups). When conducted robustly with factors such as 'concealment of allocation' (concealing whether a participant is allocated to condition A or B), 'blinding' (the researcher is unaware of allocation), 'intention-to-treat analysis' (all participants, regardless of randomisation, intervention or whether they complete the study are included in the analysis), and having a sufficiently large sample size, RCTs can provide a reliable assessment of effectiveness. With the hope of facilitating the interpretation of trial findings and their critical evaluation, there is a set of recommendations on reporting trials called CONSORT (Consolidated Standards of Reporting Trials). Familiarisation with these guidelines will help researchers and practitioners to choose the most effective interventions (see the 'Resources' box below).

Delivery

An important consideration in any programme is the knowledge, skills and values of the educators and practitioners, as it is they who will implement the programme and address SEMH difficulties in schools. Another consideration is deciding to whom the programme should be delivered. Programmes can be delivered at a whole-school level, which involves all parts of the school working together and being committed, or to smaller groups. The latter approach focuses on whole-class delivery or smaller groups of learners with similar needs (as discussed earlier, children's profiles in terms of difficulties and needs should be considered). Finally, a programme could be delivered on a one-to-one basis. For mental health promotion, whole-school or group approaches are typical, as they focus on teaching lifelong socio-emotional skills. However, when it comes to prevention or intervention, small-group/classroom-based or individual approaches are more common. A meta-analysis of 249 studies investigating school-based interventions for disruptive behaviours showed that the most effective approaches were universal programmes (i.e. delivered to entire classrooms) and those targeted at selected groups of children (Wilson and Lipsey 2007). The type of programme and difficulty should drive delivery decisions, as well as availability of resources and feasibility of programme implementation in the educational setting.

Children's voice

Finally, remember from Chapter 2 that children's voice is central to inclusion. Nowhere is this as important, and perhaps as neglected, than in provision for children with SEMH difficulties. These children often feel chronically disempowered, rejected and excluded; as Cooper says, these children are the 'least empowered and least liked group of all' (2006: 69). Involving them in meaningful discussion is key to understanding their behaviour and its resolution (Carr-Fanning 2015; Cosma and Soni 2019). Therefore, when weighing up an approach and deciding on whether and how it should be delivered, the child should be involved in the decision-making process. However, their experiences to date may make them less likely to trust adults or their behaviour/difficulties may mean educators need also to think about 'how' they communicate with these learners, because conventional or non-authentic methods may not be effective (Carr-Fanning and Mc Guckin 2017; Cosma and Soni 2019).

Conclusion

This chapter has critically explored the social, emotional and mental health needs of learners. We began with an overview of the breadth and complexity of SEMH needs; on one hand, SEMH needs include difficulties, disorders and challenging behaviours; on the other, all learners have mental health which needs to be protected and promoted. We also explored the problems with mental health practice. There are significant issues with labelling, whether that be of the child or the behaviour, due to its links with stigma and its potential to affect self-identity. We also took a critical look at problems inherent in diagnostic and treatment practices (see the critique of the social model in Chapter 1), and cautioned against the pathologising of all negative emotions and behaviour. We reviewed different psychological approaches to understanding SEMH difficulties, and how developing the appropriate educational response requires an understanding of the unique needs, difficulties and strengths of the child. A child's behaviour is shaped through a dynamic interactive process with other people (e.g. parents, teachers, peers) in different contexts (e.g. school and home) across their lifespan. Therefore, choosing 'the one' that suits the child's profile as informed by the evidence base, considering how it is to be delivered, and involving the voice of the child throughout the process, should help educators develop more effective responses to SEMH difficulties.

Resources

The resources below will support you in developing a better understanding of SEMH needs and designing appropriate educational responses.

CASEL model of SEL – Fundamentals of SEL: https://casel.org/fundamentals-of-sel/

Consolidated Standards of Reporting Trials (CONSORT): http://www.consort-statement.org/

Geelong Grammar School's Positive Education Model: What is positive education?: https://www.ggs.vic.edu.au/learning/wellbeing/what-is-positive-education/#:~:text=Good%20health%2C%20frequent%20positive%20emotions,has%20flourishing%20at%20the%20heart

Professor Martin Seligman on PERMA – YouTube videos, e.g. https://www.youtube.com/watch?v=jqqHUxzpfBI

The Association for Child and Adolescent Mental Health (ACAMH): https://www.acamh.org/

Education Scotland (2022) *Nurture, Adverse Childhood Experiences and Trauma Informed Practice: making the links between these approaches*: https://education.gov.scot/improvement/Documents/inc83-making-the-links-nurture-ACES-and-trauma.pdf

References

American Psychological Association (APA) (2015) *Trauma*. Available at: www.apa.org/topics/trauma (accessed 20 August 2022).

Armstrong, D. (2017) Wicked problems in special and inclusive education, *Journal of Research in Special Educational Needs*, 17 (4): 229–236.

Armstrong, D. (2018) Addressing the wicked problem of behaviour in schools, *International Journal of Inclusive Education*, 22 (9): 997–1013.

Armstrong, D. (2021) Can school psychologists be inclusive when delivering evidence-based behavioural interventions in special schools, behaviour units or clinics? A systematic mapping literature review, *Review of Education*, 9 (3): e3271. Available at: https://doi.org/10.1002/rev3.3271

Bandura, A. (1986) *Social Foundations of Thought and Action: A Social Cognitive Theory*. Englewood Cliffs, NJ: Prentice-Hall.

Bellis, M.A., Lowey, H., Leckenby, N., Hughes, K. and Harrison, D. (2014) Adverse childhood experiences: retrospective study to determine their impact on adult health behaviours and health outcomes in a UK population, *Journal of Public Health*, 36 (1): 81–91.

Bomber, L. (2007) *Inside I'm Hurting: Practical Strategies for Supporting Children with Attachment Difficulties in Schools*. London: Worth Publishing.

Bowlby, J. (1977) The making and breaking of affectional bonds: I. Aetiology and psychopathology in the light of attachment theory, *British Journal of Psychiatry*, 130 (3): 201–210.

Bowman-Perrott, L., Benz, M.R., Hsu, H.-Y., Kwok, O.-M., Eisterhold, L.A. and Zhang, D. (2013) Patterns and predictors of disciplinary exclusion over time: an analysis of the SEELS national data set, *Journal of Emotional and Behavioral Disorders*, 21 (2): 83–96.

Bronfenbrenner, U. (2005) *Making Human Beings Human: Bio-ecological Perspectives on Human Development*. Thousand Oaks, CA: Sage.

Carr-Fanning, K. (2015) *There's nothing so wrong with you that what's right with you couldn't fix: a study of stress, emotion, and coping in students with ADHD*. PhD thesis, Trinity College Dublin.

Carr-Fanning, K. and Mc Guckin, C. (2017) Developing creative methods for children's voice research: potential and pitfalls when constructing verbal and visual methods for research with children with attention deficit hyperactivity disorder, *Sage Research Methods Cases*, Part 2: 2–20.

Carroll, C. and Hurry, J. (2018) Supporting pupils in school with social, emotional and mental health needs: a scoping review of the literature, *Emotional and Behavioural Difficulties*, 23 (3): 310–325.

Centre on the Developing Child at Harvard University (2015) *Supportive relationships and active skill building strengthen the foundations of resilience*, Working Paper 13. Available at: https://developingchild.harvard.edu/wp-content/uploads/2015/05/The-Science-of-Resilience.pdf (accessed 10 September 2022).

Cooper, P. (2006) *Promoting Positive Pupil Engagement: Educating Pupils with Social, Emotional and Behavioural Difficulties*. Malta: Miller Publications.

Cooper, P. and Jacobs, B. (2011) *Evidence of best practice models and outcomes in the education of children with emotional disturbance/behavioural difficulties: An international review*. NCSE Research Report #7. Dublin: National Council for Special Education. Available at: http://ncse.ie/wp-content/uploads/2016/08/Research_Report_7_EBD.pdf

Cosma, P. and Soni, A. (2019) A systematic literature review exploring the factors identified by children and young people with behavioural, emotional and social difficulties as influential on their experiences of education, *Emotional and Behavioural Difficulties*, 24 (4): 421–435.

Cronholm, P.F., Forke, C.M., Wade, R., Bair-Merritt, M.H., Davis, M., Harkins-Schwarz, M. et al. (2015) Adverse childhood experiences: expanding the concept of adversity, *American Journal of Preventive Medicine*, 49 (3): 354–361.

Department for Education (DfE) (2019) *National Statistics: SEN in England*. London: DfE.

Department for Education and Department of Health (DfE/DoH) (2015) *Special Educational Needs and Disability Code of Practice: 0 to 25 years*. London: DfE. Available at: https://www.gov.uk/government/uploads/system/uploads/attachment_data/file/398815/SEND_Code_of_Practice_January_2015.pdf

Desforges, M. and Lindsay, G. (2010) *Procedures Used to Diagnose a Disability and to Assess Special Educational Needs: An International Review*. Trim, Ireland: NCSE.

Domitrovich, C.E., Durlak, J.A., Staley, K.C. and Weissberg, R.P. (2017) Social-emotional competence: an essential factor for promoting positive adjustment and reducing risk in school children, *Child Development*, 88 (2): 408–416.

Dray, J., Bowman, J., Campbell, E., Freund, M., Wolfenden, L., Hodder, R.K. et al. (2017) Systematic review of universal resilience-focused interventions targeting child and adolescent mental health in the school setting, *Journal of the American Academy of Child and Adolescent Psychiatry*, 56 (10): 813–824.

Duckworth, A.L. and Seligman, M.E.P. (2005) Self-discipline outdoes IQ in predicting academic performance of adolescents, *Psychological Science*, 16 (12): 939–944.

Durlak, J.A., Weissberg, R.P., Dymnicki, A.B., Taylor, R.D. and Schellinger, K.B. (2011) The impact of enhancing students' social and emotional learning: a meta-analysis of school-based universal interventions, *Child Development*, 82 (1): 405–432.

Elias, M.J. (2019) What if the doors of every schoolhouse opened to social-emotional learning tomorrow: reflections on how to feasibly scale up high-quality SEL, *Educational Psychologist*, 54 (3): 233–245.

Elias, M.J., Ferrito, J.J. and Moceri, D.C. (2015) *The Other Side of the Report Card: Assessing Students' Social, Emotional, and Character Development*. Newbury Park, CA: Corwin Press.

Engel, G.L. (1977) The need for a new medical model: a challenge for biomedicine, *Science*, 196 (4286): 129–136.

Fabiano, G.A. and Pyle, K. (2019) Best practices in school mental health for attention-deficit/hyperactivity disorder: a framework for intervention, *School Mental Health*, 11 (1): 72–91.

Felitti, V.J., Anda, R.F., Nordenberg, D., Williamson, D.F., Spitz, A.M., Edwards, V. et al. (1998) Relationship of childhood abuse and household dysfunction to many of the leading causes of death in adults: the Adverse Childhood Experiences (ACE) study, *American Journal of Preventive Medicine*, 14 (4): 245–258.

Flynn, P. (2013) *Authentic listening to student voice and the transformative potential to empower students with social, emotional and behavioural difficulties in mainstream schools*. PhD thesis, Trinity College Dublin.

Foucault, M. (1994) Two lectures, in N. Dirks and S.B. Ortner (eds.), *Culture, Power, History*. Princeton, NJ: Princeton University Press.

Gable, S.L. and Haidt, J. (2005) What (and why) is positive psychology, *Review of General Psychology*, 9 (2): 103–110.

Hickinbotham, L. and Soni, A. (2021) A systematic literature review exploring the views and experiences of children and young people of the label Social, Emotional and Mental Health (SEMH), *Emotional and Behavioural Difficulties*, 26 (2): 135–150.

Hobfoll, S.E., Watson, P., Bell, C.C., Bryant, R.A., Brymer, M.J., Friedman, M.J. et al. (2007) Five essential elements of immediate and mid-term mass trauma intervention: empirical evidence, *Psychiatry*, 70 (4): 283–315.

Jorm, A.F. and Griffiths, K.M. (2008) The public's stigmatizing attitudes towards people with mental disorders: how important are biomedical conceptualizations?, *Acta Psychiatrica Scandinavica*, 118 (4): 315–321.

Kessler, R.C., McLaughlin, K.A., Green, J.G., Gruber, M.J., Sampson, N.A., Zaslavsky, A.M. et al. (2010) Childhood adversities and adult psychopathology in the WHO Surveys, *British Journal of Psychiatry*, 197 (5): 378–385.

Lai, M.C., Lombardo, M.V. and Baron-Cohen, S. (2014) Autism, *The Lancet*, 383 (9920): 896–910.

Lauchlan, F. and Boyle, C. (2007) Is the use of labels in special education helpful?, *Support for Learning*, 22 (1): 36–42.

Lewis, S.J., Arseneault, L., Caspi, A., Fisher, H.L., Matthews, T., Moffitt, T.E. et al. (2019) The epidemiology of trauma and post-traumatic stress disorder in a representative cohort of young people in England and Wales, *The Lancet Psychiatry*, 6 (3): 247–256.

Liber, J.M., De Boo, G.M., Huizenga, H. and Prins, P.J.M. (2013) School-based intervention for childhood disruptive behaviour in disadvantaged settings: a randomized controlled trial with and without active teacher support, *Journal of Consulting and Clinical Psychology*, 81 (6): 975–987.

Maddux, J.E. (2021) Stopping the 'madness': positive psychology and deconstructing the illness ideology and the DSM, in C.R. Snyder, S.J. Lopez, L.M. Edwards and S.C. Marques (eds.), *The Oxford Handbook of Positive Psychology*, 3rd edition. Oxford: Oxford University Press.

Maguire, M., Ball, S. and Braun, A. (2010) Behaviour, classroom management and student 'control': enacting policy in the English secondary school, *International Studies in Sociology of Education*, 20 (2): 153–170.

Masten, A.S. and Cicchetti, D. (2016) Resilience in development: progress and transformation, in D. Cicchetti (ed.), *Developmental Psychopathology: Risk, Resilience, and Intervention*. Chichester: Wiley.

McDermott, B., Berry, H. and Cobham, V. (2012) Social connectedness: a potential aetiological factor in the development of child post-traumatic stress disorder, *Australian & New Zealand Journal of Psychiatry*, 46 (2): 109–117.

O'Reilly, M., Svirydzenka, N., Adams, S. and Dogra, N. (2018) Review of mental health promotion interventions in schools, *Social Psychiatry and Psychiatric Epidemiology*, 53 (7): 647–662.

Paulus, F.W., Ohmann, S. and Popow, C. (2016) Practitioner review: school-based interventions in child mental health, *Journal of Child Psychology and Psychiatry*, 57 (12): 1337–1359.

Pedersen, M.L., Holen, S., Lydersen, S., Martinsen, K., Neumer, S.-P., Adolfsen, F. et al. (2019) School functioning and internalizing problems in young schoolchildren, *BMC Psychology*, 7: 88. Available at: https://doi.org/10.1186/s40359-019-0365-1

Richards, M. and Huppert, F.A. (2011) Do positive children become positive adults? Evidence from a longitudinal birth cohort study, *Journal of Positive Psychology*, 6 (1): 75–87.

Rogers, C.R. (1969) *Freedom to Learn*. Columbus, OH: Charles E. Merrill.

Seligman, M. (2011) *Flourish*. New York: Free Press.

Seligman, M.E.P. and Csikszentmihalyi, M. (2000) Positive psychology: an introduction, *American Psychologist*, 55 (1): 5–14.

Sinnott, J.D. (2008) Humanistic psychology, learning and teaching the 'whole person', *Journal on Educational Psychology*, 1 (4): 56–64.

Skinner, B.F. (2019) *The Behavior of Organisms: An Experimental Analysis*. Cambridge, MA: B.F. Skinner Foundation Reprint Series.

Swain, J. and French, S. (2000) Towards an affirmation model of disability, *Disability & Society*, 15 (4): 569–582.

Thomas, M.S., Crosby, S. and Vanderhaar, J. (2019) Trauma-informed practices in schools across two decades: an interdisciplinary review of research, *Review of Research in Education*, 43 (1): 422–452.

Van der Kolk, B. (2014) *The Body Keeps the Score: Mind, Brain and Body in the Transformation of Trauma*. London: Penguin.

Wakefield, J.C. (1992) Disorder as harmful dysfunction: a conceptual critique of DSM-III-R's definition of mental disorder, *Psychology Review*, 99 (2): 232–247.

Waters, L. (2011) A review of school-based positive psychology interventions, *Australian Educational and Developmental Psychologist*, 28 (2): 75–90.

Wilson, S.J. and Lipsey, M.W. (2007) School-based interventions for aggressive and disruptive behaviour: update of a meta-analysis, *American Journal of Preventive Medicine*, 33 (2): S130–S143.

Wright, B.A., Lopez, S.J. and Magyar, J.L. (2021) Widening the diagnostic focus: a case for including human strengths and environmental resources, in C.R. Snyder, S.J. Lopez, L.M. Edwards and S.C. Marques (eds.), *The Oxford Handbook of Positive Psychology*, 3rd edition. Oxford: Oxford University Press.

7 Social inequality in the classroom: exploring the effects of social inequality on child development and mental health

Patrycja J. Piotrowska and Richard Rowe

By the end of this chapter, you will be able to:

- define social inequality and discuss its measurement and the idea of social gradients
- discuss the impact of social inequality on child outcomes
- critically consider the issues of causality in social inequality research
- develop a psychologically informed understanding of potential mechanisms that link social inequality to child outcomes
- evaluate the impact of social inequality on the classroom and potential intervention steps.

Education has long been hailed as a societal priority and the key to social mobility. The importance of identifying the key educational experiences to achieve this goal is increasingly being recognised. We have finally accepted that children are not 'empty vessels' ready to be filled with knowledge; we acknowledge their personal and family experiences, their individual differences, their different strengths and difficulties, and what they bring with them to the classroom. Or at least we should actively acknowledge that. But not just that. We also need to consider the effect of children's experiences on their well-being, educational progress and the effect it may have on the classroom as a dynamic system. That dynamic system includes a group of children, each with their own personal journeys. One of those contextual life circumstances is children's experience of social inequality. Understanding that potential impact of social inequality on children and the classroom is the key to educational inclusion.

> **Activity**
> Try to reflect on inequality and socio-economic status. What is social inequality? What do you think it affects? What kind of impact does it have on children and young people's lives? List some examples.

Inequality refers to an unequal distribution of resources. Socio-economic inequality in particular has been linked to a number of negative child outcomes, such as poorer mental health and well-being, lower educational achievement and higher rates of school dropout (e.g. Reiss 2013; Winding and Andersen 2015). Socio-economic (or social) inequality can affect children on multiple levels, from poor nutrition and limited availability of educational resources (e.g. to attend after-school clubs or go on school trips), to their social position or standing in their peer group. In this chapter, we will focus on the importance of considering the effects of social inequality on children's social, emotional, behavioural, cognitive and educational outcomes. We introduce the field of social inequality as it applies to students, educators, clinicians and policymakers. We hope it will prompt readers to keep asking questions about the level of inequality that they observe in their daily lives, its impact and what we can all do about it.

Social inequality and child outcomes

Social inequality is often described as an unequal distribution of resources in a society. It refers to an individual's social position and their socio-economic resources – that is, where they stand in relation to others. This is our socio-economic status (SES). Social inequality at the individual or family level is most often measured using income, education, occupation, housing or car ownership. When discussing the importance of SES or inequality for child development, we look to their family's SES as it is associated with children's day-to-day experiences. The last few decades have made clear that the general increase in living standards as well as the costs of economic crises have not been shared equally across society.

> **Activity**
> In this section, we have introduced the concept of inequality and how it is often measured. Stop and reflect for a few minutes and consider which of the measures you would consider most relevant in the context of child development. For example, would household income or parental education have a greater impact on the child?

Over the years, a number of studies have found a consistent link between family SES and children's cognitive, educational, emotional and behavioural outcomes. In their review, Bradley and Corwyn (2002) indicated that SES affects children from before they are born; children from lower socio-economic backgrounds were more likely to be born prematurely, experience more accidents and injuries, have more health problems (e.g. respiratory illnesses) and experience higher levels of depression and emotional difficulties. They also linked SES to cognitive development, usually measured by children's academic achievement. A more recent systematic review found that out of 55 included studies, 52 indicated an inverse (negative) relationship between SES and mental health difficulties in children and adolescents (Reiss 2013). This review showed that children from lower SES backgrounds were two to three times more likely to experience mental health difficulties. In addition, our meta-analysis that synthesised the results from 133 studies showed that lower family SES was associated with higher levels of disruptive behaviour (e.g. aggression) in children and adolescents (Piotrowska et al. 2015a). Similarly, in a sample of 34,000 children and their families, Torvik and colleagues (2020) showed that low parental education was associated with higher levels of attention deficit hyperactivity disorder (ADHD), depression and academic difficulties experienced by their children. These results indicate that SES can be considered an important factor in academic or cognitive skills as well as emotional and behavioural difficulties. On average, children from lower SES backgrounds do less well than their more advantaged peers on a number of outcomes, and that the mental health and achievement gap keeps widening.

Social gradients

You might have heard about 'social gradients' before. Social gradients show that differences that we see in academic or mental health outcomes are present across the entire socio-economic continuum. That means that everyone is affected by it, and that being somewhere in the middle is better than being at the bottom, but worse than being on the top. In fact, for many outcomes, being just below the top is still far worse than being at the top. When considering that these middle or top socio-economic groups are far above the poverty line, it becomes clear that the effects of social inequality do not simply reflect a lack of resources faced by those in poverty. Said inequality affects everything: where children go to school, what they do in their free time, who they spend time with. The following activity provides an opportunity to consider what the shape of gradient might look like.

> *Activity*
> Using the empty graph shown in Figure 7.1, think about the effect of SES on child mental health difficulties across the spectrum from low to high SES. You can indicate the expected level of difficulties by drawing several dots representing the level of difficulty at different SES levels and then connecting them to form a single line. What do you think the gradient might look like?

Figure 7.1 Level of mental health difficulties graph exercise

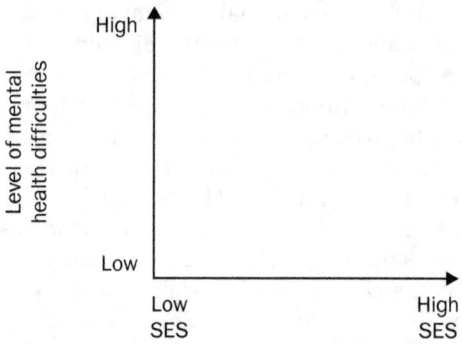

Figure 7.2 Prevalence rates of conduct disorder by income quintile

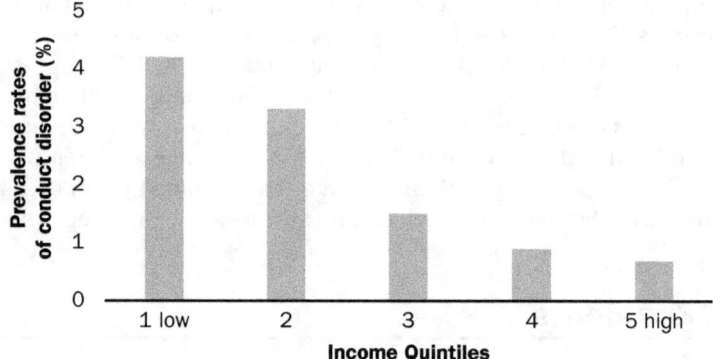

Based on data published in Piotrowska et al. (2015b)

You just drew a potential social gradient of child mental health difficulties. We will now have a look at some research that tried to measure social gradients. Conduct disorder (CD) is characterised by a persistent pattern of disruptive behaviour and violation of social norms with the main diagnostic criteria including aggression, destruction of property and stealing (APA 2013). Figure 7.2 presents a gradient of the prevalence of CD in the general population of children and adolescents (ages 5–16). These prevalence rates indicate the proportion (expressed as a percentage) of children having CD by level of income. Household income was divided here into five groups, called quintiles, ranging from low income (quintile 1) to high income (quintile 5). The graph shows that children and young people in the lower income quintiles had a higher prevalence of CD (above 3 per cent) than those in the high-income categories (prevalence rates below 1 per cent).

A similar gradient is presented in Figure 7.3. This time we look at the odds ratios representing the association between income quintiles and speech or language problems in a sample of boys aged 5–10 years. These odds ratios were

Figure 7.3 Odds ratios for prevalence rates of speech or language problems by income quintile

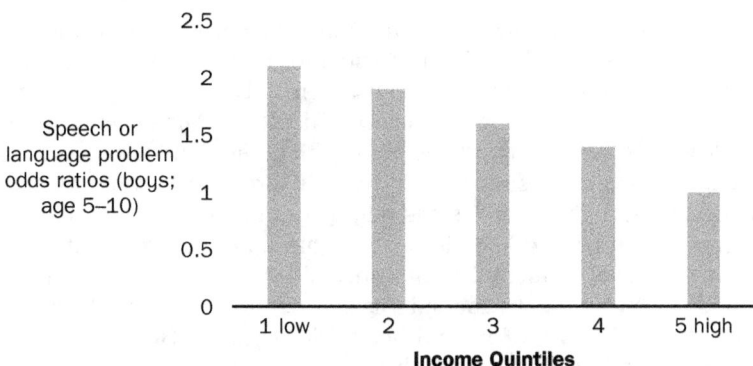

Based on data published in Emerson, Graham and Hatton (2006)

calculated through logistic regression modelling and represent the increased odds of speech or language difficulties in each of the lower income groups (quintiles) relative to the highest income quintile.

Figures 7.2 and 7.3 show examples of social gradients with children in the lower income groups having higher risk of difficulties than children in the higher income categories. The research into the shape of these gradients is still developing, but in a previous study that focused on behavioural difficulties such as CD, we found that the gradient was non-linear (Piotrowska et al. 2015b). We found that the steepest slope was in the middle-income groups, while it was flatter at both the low- and high-income ends of the scale. This suggests that income (or SES) can have a different effect on families in different income groups. For example, a small increase in income could make a substantial difference to people in the middle of the distribution, while those in the most disadvantaged contexts would require a larger increase in income to show the same improvement in outcomes. More research is needed to help us further understand social gradients and their shape across other mental health and cognitive outcomes.

Activity
Which of the below statements is correct?
 a Identifying causes of ill-health can help us design more targeted interventions
 b Experimental designs provide the strongest tests of causality
 c Mental health difficulties are known to have multiple causes
 d All of the above

Correct answer: d

Causality

So far, this chapter has shown that lower family SES is associated with a higher level of mental health and academic difficulties in children and we, in places, have implicitly assumed that this is a causal effect. But you could be wondering whether SES really causes mental health difficulties. This question is not that easy to answer as inequality and mental health do not lend themselves to fully experimental research designs that provide the strongest tests of causality. This is because experimental designs rely on randomly allocating participants to experimental and control conditions and this cannot be done with variables such as SES or level of mental health difficulties due to ethical and practical constraints (i.e. we cannot randomly assign people to different SES groups, or manipulate their level of mental health difficulties). However, reviews of studies that provide the best available evidence for studying these relationships do support the causal effect of family SES on children's outcomes (Jaffee, Strait and Odgers 2012; Maughan, Rowe and Murray 2017). For example, the systematic review of 34 studies designed to provide higher levels of causal evidence (such as randomised controlled trials, natural experiments, or advanced statistical modelling of longitudinal data) confirmed that children from poorer backgrounds have worse cognitive, socio-behavioural and health outcomes (Cooper and Stewart 2013). The strongest evidence presented in this review was in relation to school performance and cognitive development. The authors concluded that there is strong evidence of the negative relationship between SES and child outcomes and that it is causal. However, it is worth noting that the strength of the effect of that relationship often depends on the methods used, or socio-economic indicators chosen for a particular study.

More recently, Levesque and colleagues (2021) conducted a systematic review of 80 longitudinal studies that considered relationships between changes in family SES and subsequent changes in child and adolescent physical and mental health outcomes. By modelling changes in SES (i.e. social mobility) and child functioning over time, these studies provide a further test of the direction of the effect – that is, whether SES truly leads to changes in mental health and cognitive development. The review concluded that upward mobility (i.e. increase in household or parental income) was associated with better overall cognition, while negative changes in income predicted worse child cognition. A similar pattern was found for dental and overall parent-reported child health. The findings for child mental health were less consistent and dependent on the geographical location from which study participants were sampled. For example, studies conducted in the US indicated that increases in income were associated with fewer mental health difficulties, while decreases in income led to higher levels of difficulties. In the UK, however, it was persistent childhood poverty that most consistently predicted mental health difficulties. The majority of these studies (13 out of 24) also showed that negative changes in income were associated with worse socio-emotional behaviour.

Finally, when discussing causality, it is important to acknowledge the possibility of SES and mental health and education outcomes being influenced by a

Figure 7.4 Mechanisms linking social inequality to child outcomes

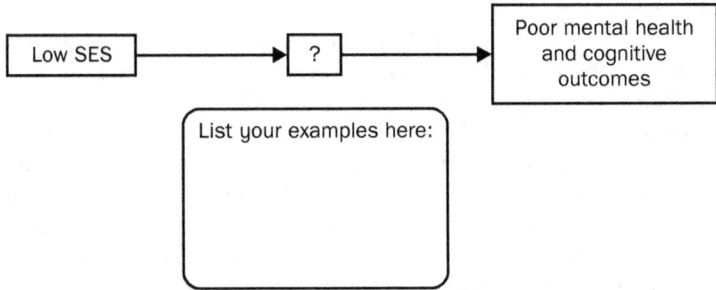

number of other factors, including genetics. It is possible that such unmeasured and unaccounted for variables contribute to family SES and affect children's academic and mental health outcomes. However, Torvik and colleagues (2020) found that the association between parental education and children's ADHD and academic difficulties remained after taking into account shared genetic factors in the families as well as family environmental factors. The story, however, was different for depressive symptoms, which were largely explained by shared genetic and family risk factors. This indicates that the strength of relationships and causality may differ between the outcomes studied, and highlights the importance of using research designs that can disentangle the genetic and environmental factors and their influence across generations.

> *Activity*
> We have discussed relationships between inequality and child outcomes, and the idea of social gradients. But why do we see these relationships? Can you think of any mechanisms that could explain social inequality in child mental health? In other words, how does inequality affect child mental health or cognitive development? Can you think of any intermediate factors that are influenced by low SES and in turn affect children? Take a look at Figure 7.4 and list two or three mechanisms linking social inequality to child outcomes.

Mechanisms

The 'how' has been the focus of a lot of recent social inequality research. In the absence of national-level policies that could reduce the level of inequality, identifying and addressing the potential mechanisms that link inequality to poor outcomes is a priority. What we mean by mechanisms are potential pathways that link the experience of socio-economic pressure and later changes in child and adolescent mental health or academic outcomes. What is it about SES that affects families?

The Family Stress Model (FSM; Masarik and Conger 2017) is one of the most influential theoretical models used to explain how inequality affects parents and children and may consequently lead to poorer academic or mental health outcomes. The model proposes that low income increases the risk of economic pressures that lower parental well-being and increase distress (e.g. depression, anxiety), which in turn leads to poorer parenting practices such as lower supervision, less attentive or supportive parenting, less quality time and harsher discipline, which likely lead to increased levels of child and adolescent mental health difficulties. This includes behavioural difficulties such as antisocial behaviour, substance use in older adolescents, emotional and depressive difficulties, as well as poor cognitive development outcomes such as lower literacy and maths performance. The recent versions of the model also involve interparental conflict or relationship difficulties which are considered to have a bidirectional association with suboptimal parenting; this means that parental distress can lead to more relationship difficulties and that these difficulties can lead to poorer parenting, but it is also possible that it is the suboptimal parenting that contributes to more relationship difficulties.

Despite the extensive research consistent with the pathways in the FSM, we need to remember that these risk factors or pathways do not act in isolation. The family is a dynamic system and a wider range of potential mechanisms and factors affecting these mechanisms need to be considered. For example, Straatmann and colleagues (2019) showed that children from low SES backgrounds, indexed by low maternal education, were four times more likely to experience mental health difficulties (socio-emotional and behavioural), and that this inequality was largely mediated by early life (preschool) factors across pre-birth, child, family, peer and neighbourhood levels. Some of these factors included maternal smoking or alcohol use in pregnancy, birth weight, school readiness and cognitive skills, maternal mental health and parenting style, bullying and neighbourhood safety. Similarly, early (preschool) verbal and non-verbal cognitive ability have been shown to partially explain the relationship between SES and children's school performance (von Stumm et al. 2020). This highlights the importance of considering mechanisms other than parenting that incorporate children's environments. For example, it is possible that impoverished environments affect language development very early on, which then translates to poorer school performance.

The idea of impoverished environments links to the investment perspective, which argues that inequality affects children's outcomes through limited physical resources such as not having books at home, poor nutrition and not being able to afford extracurricular activities. For example, social gradient in diet quality is largely explained by the cost of healthy food (Aggarwal et al. 2011). More recently, researchers have been working to combine the FSM and investment perspectives in order to present a more comprehensive framework for understanding how inequality affects families. Using data from the Growing

Up in Scotland survey, Sosu and Schmidt (2017) showed that the relationship between deprivation and conduct problems acted through increased parental stress and punitive discipline (family stress perspective) but also through educational investment and cognitive ability (investment perspective). More money can certainly help through alleviating parental stress and day-to-day life management, which is especially crucial in times when the cost of living is high. It is also important to consider supporting families, parenting or mental health programmes, and highlighting educational investment which can take place at home and at schools.

> *Activity*
> What policy changes would you recommend to improve educational investment in children from lower socio-economic backgrounds? How could such changes be enacted at the local level?

Finally, we should note that the relationship between inequality or socio-economic circumstances and family and child outcomes can also be understood at the biological level. For example, maternal responsiveness and chronic physiological stress might be the mechanisms underlying the relationship between early life poverty and adult executive functioning, which is a set of cognitive processes that help us pay attention, organise and plan (Evans, Farah and Hackman 2021). It has been shown that low SES can affect children's stress hormone response through cortisol secretion, which may lead to changes in the amygdala-prefrontal circuitry responsible for emotional regulation (Tian et al. 2021). This suggests a potential neurobiological mechanism that underlies social inequality in emotional difficulties, and highlights childhood as an important developmental stage where environmental life stressors such as low SES can affect brain development. Similarly, Yu and colleagues (2017) found that lower SES during early life was associated with hippocampal volume in children. Variations in this neural system relate to memory and may suggest further biological mechanisms by which low socio-economic background affects children, their cognitive abilities and school performance. The extent to which these biological pathways relate to the psychosocial pathways described in models such as the FSM is unknown.

> *Activity*
> You are the teacher. How are social inequalities affecting the classroom? Think about perceptions of SES, inequality and classroom interactions.

Social inequality in the classroom

In this section, we will consider inequalities in the classroom and associated biases. Structural inequalities are a well-known source of bias in society. The same applies to socio-economic inequalities, and to the classroom and educational environments. Individual characteristics are associated with differing perceptions of educators, counsellors, psychologists and other professionals involved in supporting children and young people. For example, a previous study showed that students from low SES backgrounds were perceived to have lower maths abilities by school counsellors (Auwarter and Aruguete 2008). Similarly, Ready and Wright (2011) showed that teachers in lower SES and lower-achieving contexts were more likely to underestimate students' language and literacy abilities. However, this is not always the case. For example, Abidin and Robinson (2002) showed that it was teachers' perceptions of behavioural and academic competence that predicted whether students would be referred for psycho-educational assessment, and that the referral decisions were not influenced by socio-economic or demographic factors. Similarly, a more recent study did not find a significant association between student socio-demographic characteristics (i.e. gender, SES, race) and likelihood of recommending alternative learning programmes by school counsellors (Dameron, Foxx and Flowers 2019). This is certainly encouraging, although it should be noted that the majority of studies in this field have involved educational settings in the US. Nonetheless, this literature emphasises the importance of recognising the effects that inequality may have on children, potential mechanisms and whether this can be addressed in a school setting. It is also crucial to emphasise the importance of unconscious bias awareness and training to ensure that children from lower SES backgrounds are not additionally disadvantaged by the perceptions of their educators or counsellors.

What can we do?

This final section focuses on identifying inclusive and evidence-based practice with regard to social inequality and child mental health and academic outcomes. Despite some researchers indicating potential counsellor and teacher bias when it comes to children's educational achievements, or emotional and behavioural difficulties, it is clear that the gap between children from low and high SES backgrounds exists, and that it likely starts before a child's first day at school. The question remains what we can do to support all children, though especially those from disadvantaged backgrounds, to help them thrive academically and emotionally.

Early interventions to improve child mental health and accessible evidence-based mental health services are primary actions that are often suggested to address mental health inequalities (Roberts et al. 2016). Promoting both physical and psychological health as well as developing young people's mental health literacy and resilience are key priorities (Hostinar and Miller 2019). However, academic interventions have been shown to improve child outcomes and at least partially address the existing mental health and achievement gap; as such, these should be considered as a potential intervention strategy. A systematic review and meta-analysis of 101 studies investigating the effectiveness of academic interventions showed that tutoring (additional pedagogical support, individual or group), feedback and progress monitoring (e.g. individualised feedback or detailed information on child's progress), and cooperative learning (learning through peer support) improved academic achievement of children from lower SES backgrounds (Dietrichson et al. 2017). Despite these promising results, additional activities such as tutoring are often associated with higher costs for the school, and that progress monitoring and cooperative learning have better potential to be more easily accessible and incorporated into existing curricula.

There has been an increase in research exploring the relationship between green spaces and mental health, with a recent review emphasising the importance of better access to nature and public open spaces for child mental health (Alderton et al. 2019). These are often considered neighbourhood-level factors. However, schools are embedded in these neighbourhoods and further investments in good quality public spaces or school playgrounds is crucial. Finally, Roberts, Donkin and Marmot (2016) identified the potential of social media and other online sources in supporting young people's mental health. This is often the first contact point for young people wishing to access support. This raises issues of ensuring that children and young people are signposted to the most effective resources, and that they have fair access to these. This further highlights the importance of investment in resources and supporting children and young people through mental health literacy trainings and academic interventions that can help close the inequality gap. It is our hope that the future holds the implementation of multi-layered and systematic ways to support children and their families in addressing the investment and stress mechanisms discussed above, but also reducing the level of social inequality.

Conclusion

This chapter has provided a brief introduction to the field of social inequality and the wide-ranging effects that SES can have on children and families. The research clearly identifies that mental health and cognitive difficulties are more common in children from low SES backgrounds, and that the social gradient exists across numerous outcomes. We highlighted that it is important to consider potential mechanisms through which social inequality affects children so that these mechanisms can become intervention targets and help reduce the mental health and achievement gap. The key frameworks that contribute to our understanding of these mechanisms include family and parental factors such as poor parental mental health and suboptimal parenting, but also educational investment and resources available to children. It is crucial that these effects and mechanisms are considered in educational settings and inform further efforts to address social inequality in the classroom.

> *Resources*
> If you would like to learn more about social inequality and the wide-ranging effects that SES can have on children and families, access the resources below.
>
> TED Talk – How economic inequality harms societies (Professor Richard Wilkinson): https://www.youtube.com/watch?v=cZ7LzE3u7Bw
>
> Inequality – the big picture (Professor Danny Dorling) https://www.youtube.com/watch?v=3bbWyG9-CIE
>
> Equality Trust: https://equalitytrust.org.uk/
> Joseph Rowntree Foundation: https://www.jrf.org.uk/
>
> *Further reading*
> Wilkinson, R. and Pickett, K. (2010) *The Spirit Level: Why Equality is Better for Everyone*. London: Penguin.

References

Abidin, R.R. and Robinson, L.L. (2002) Stress, biases, or professionalism: what drives teachers' referral judgments of students with challenging behaviors?, *Journal of Emotional and Behavioral Disorders*, 10 (4): 204–212.

Aggarwal, A., Monsivais, P., Cook, A. J. and Drewnowski, A. (2011) Does diet cost mediate the relation between socioeconomic position and diet quality and quest, *European Journal of Clinical Nutrition*, 65 (9): 1059–1066.

Alderton, A., Villanueva, K., O'Connor, M., Boulangé, C. and Badland, H. (2019) Reducing inequities in early childhood mental health: how might the neighborhood built environment help close the gap? A systematic search and critical review, *International Journal of Environmental Research and Public Health*, 16 (9): 1516. Available at: https://doi.org/10.3390/ijerph16091516

American Psychiatric Association (APA) (2013) *Diagnostic and Statistical Manual of Mental Disorders, DSM-5*. American Psychiatric Association.

Auwarter, A.E. and Aruguete, M.S. (2008) Counselor perceptions of students who vary in gender and socioeconomic status, *Social Psychology of Education*, 11 (4): 389–395.

Bradley, R.H. and Corwyn, R.F. (2002) Socioeconomic status and child development, *Annual Review of Psychology*, 53: 371–399.

Cooper, K. and Stewart, K. (2013) *Does money affect children's outcomes? A systematic review*. York: Joseph Rowntree Foundation. Available at: https://sticerd.lse.ac.uk/dps/case/cr/casereport80.pdf

Dameron, M.L., Foxx, S.P. and Flowers, C. (2019) The impact of race, gender, and socioeconomic status on school counselors' alternative learning program placement decisions: an experimental study, *The Urban Review*, 51 (5): 699–723.

Dietrichson, J., Bòg, M., Filges, T. and Jörgensen, A.-M.K. (2017) Academic interventions for elementary and middle school students with low socioeconomic status: a systematic review and meta-analysis, *Review of Educational Research*, 87 (2): 243–282.

Emerson, E., Graham, H., and Hatton, C. (2006) Household income and health status in children and adolescents in Britain, *European Journal of Public Health*, 16 (4): 354–360.

Evans, G.W., Farah, M.J. and Hackman, D.A. (2021) Early childhood poverty and adult executive functioning: distinct, mediating pathways for different domains of executive functioning, *Developmental Science*, 24 (5): e13084. Available at: https://doi.org/10.1111/desc.13084

Hostinar, C.E. and Miller, G. E. (2019) Protective factors for youth confronting economic hardship: current challenges and future avenues in resilience research, *American Psychologist*, 74 (6): 641–652.

Jaffee, S.R., Strait, L.B. and Odgers, C.L. (2012) From correlates to causes: can quasi-experimental studies and statistical innovations bring us closer to identifying the causes of antisocial behavior?, *Psychological Bulletin*, 138 (2): 272–295.

Levesque, A.R., MacDonald, S., Berg, S.A. and Reka, R. (2021) Assessing the impact of changes in household socioeconomic status on the health of children and adolescents: a systematic review, *Adolescent Research Review*, 6 (2): 91–123.

Masarik, A.S. and Conger, R.D. (2017) Stress and child development: a review of the Family Stress Model, *Current Opinion in Psychology*, 13: 85–90.

Maughan, B., Rowe, R. and Murray, J. (2017) Family poverty and structure, in J.E. Lochman and W. Matthys (eds.), *The Wiley Handbook of Disruptive and Impulse-Control Disorders*. Hoboken, NJ: Wiley.

Piotrowska, P.J., Stride, C.B., Croft, S.E. and Rowe, R. (2015a) Socioeconomic status and antisocial behaviour among children and adolescents: a systematic review and meta-analysis, *Clinical Psychology Review*, 35: 47–55.

Piotrowska, P.J., Stride, C.B., Maughan, B., Goodman, R., McCaw, L. and Rowe, R. (2015b) Income gradients within child and adolescent antisocial behaviours, *British Journal of Psychiatry*, 207 (5): 385–391.

Ready, D.D. and Wright, D.L. (2011) Accuracy and inaccuracy in teachers' perceptions of young children's cognitive abilities: the role of child background and classroom context, *American Educational Research Journal*, 48 (2): 335–360.

Reiss, F. (2013) Socioeconomic inequalities and mental health problems in children and adolescents: a systematic review, *Social Science and Medicine*, 90: 24–31.

Roberts, J., Donkin, A. and Marmot, M. (2016) Opportunities for reducing socioeconomic inequalities in the mental health of children and young people – reducing adversity and increasing resilience, *Journal of Public Mental Health*, 15 (1): 4–18.

Sosu, E.M. and Schmidt, P. (2017) Economic deprivation and its effects on childhood conduct problems: the mediating role of family stress and investment factors, *Frontiers in Psychology*, 8: 1580. Available at: https://doi.org/10.3389/fpsyg.2017.01580

Straatmann, V.S., Lai, E., Lange, T., Campbell, M.C., Wickham, S., Andersen, A.-M.N. et al. (2019) How do early-life factors explain social inequalities in adolescent mental health? Findings from the UK Millennium Cohort Study, *Journal of Epidemiology and Community Health*, 73 (11): 1049–1060.

Tian, T., Young, C.B., Zhu, Y., Xu, J., He, Y., Chen, M. et al. (2021) Socioeconomic disparities affect children's amygdala-prefrontal circuitry via stress hormone response, *Biological Psychiatry*, 90 (3): 173–181.

Torvik, F.A., Eilertsen, E.M., McAdams, T.A., Gustavson, K., Zachrisson, H.D., Brandlistuen, R. et al. (2020) Mechanisms linking parental educational attainment with child ADHD, depression, and academic problems: a study of extended families in the

Norwegian Mother, Father and Child Cohort Study, *Journal of Child Psychology and Psychiatry*, 61 (9): 1009–1018.

von Stumm, S., Rimfeld, K., Dale, P. S. and Plomin, R. (2020) Preschool verbal and non-verbal ability mediate the association between socioeconomic status and school performance, *Child Development*, 91 (3): 705–714.

Winding, T.N. and Andersen, J.H. (2015) Socioeconomic differences in school dropout among young adults: the role of social relations, *BMC Public Health*, 15: 1054. Available at: https://doi.org/10.1186/s12889-015-2391-0

Yu, Q., Daugherty, A.M., Anderson, D.M., Nishimura, M., Brush, D., Hardwick, A. et al. (2017) Socioeconomic status and hippocampal volume in children and young adults, *Developmental Science*, 21 (3): e12561. Available at: https://doi.org/10.1111/desc.12561

8 The psychology of including learners with attention deficit hyperactivity disorder

Kate Carr-Fanning

By the end of this chapter, you will be able to:
- identify and describe the primary characteristic (strengths and differences) of ADHD
- identify a range of ADHD-related difficulties
- critically consider the role of culture, stigma and the social meaning of ADHD
- identify and apply evidence-based interventions and accommodations to support learners with ADHD.

This chapter will explore the needs associated with attention deficit hyperactivity disorder (ADHD). ADHD falls within the framework of social, emotional and mental health needs discussed in Chapter 6. The needs of learners with ADHD (differences, strengths, difficulties and stigma) will be considered, and a synopsis of evidence-based responses (interventions, accommodations and collaboration) will be provided. The aim is to understand the whole learner (their strengths and difficulties) and work 'with' them to create inclusive solutions, so that these children do not just survive education, but thrive!

Before we begin, take a moment to reflect on your own definition of ADHD. It has a long history and has changed shape over time. From Crichton's 1798 account of 'mental restlessness' (cited in Sharkey and Fitzgerald 2007), through Still's (1902) 'affliction' in moral deficits, to ongoing debates about presentations and the role of 'hyperactivity' (e.g. *Diagnostic and Statistical Manual*, 4th and 5th editions – DSM-4, DSM-5).

Activity
Reflect on your own definition of ADHD.

a) Which is it?
   1. *Under-activity*
   2. *Inattention*
   3. *Impulsivity*
   4. *Inattention + impulsivity with or without hyperactivity*
   5. *Hyperactivity + inattention + impulsivity*
   6. *Hyperactivity + inattention + impulsivity+ behaviour problems*
   7. *Hyperactivity + impulsivity and/or inattention.*
b) Is ADHD a mental health problem or a learning difficulty?

Whatever your response to the above two questions, you are correct. ADHD is classified differently across different diagnostic texts (e.g. DSM-5 versus International Classification of Diseases (ICD)-10). It is categorised in some countries with learning difficulties and in others with mental health (e.g. USA versus UK). Different models or theories of ADHD emphasise different characteristics.

What is ADHD?

This section considers how you would identify and understand ADHD-related characteristics, or differences, including both strengths and difficulties.

Characteristics, prevalence and persistence of ADHD

According to the DSM-5, ADHD is a neurodevelopmental disorder characterised by 'inattention' and/or 'hyperactive-impulsivity' (APA 2013). Within a neurodivergence framework, ADHD is associated with *differences* in sustained attention, effort and motivation, and inhibiting behaviour, where ADHD is a neurodevelopmental difference. The *neuro*developmental label is applied because of what Barkley (2016) refers to as 'overwhelming' and 'irrefutable' evidence for the role of neurological and genetics in causing these differences. It is not that the learner does not know what to do, it is about performance, doing what one knows.

ADHD affects approximately 5–6 per cent of learners (Polanczyk et al. 2007), which means there is likely one learner with ADHD in every classroom. While both the severity of ADHD and co-occurrence have an impact, for those diagnosed with ADHD in childhood, most will continue to either meet the diagnostic criteria or struggle due to their ADHD-related difficulties into adulthood (Uchida et al. 2018).

According to the DSM-5 (APA 2013), ADHD presents itself in one of three ways:

1. Combined (hyperactive-impulsive-inattentive) presentation
2. Hyperactive-impulsive presentation
3. Inattentive presentation.

Diagnostic rates vary based on presentation. One epidemiological survey found that in childhood, the combined presentation was the most common, followed by hyperactivity-impulsivity, with the inattentive presentation being the least diagnosed (Larsson et al. 2011). Perhaps it occurs less often, or inattention may go unrecognised. Possibly because they don't 'fit in' with the stereotypical view of the hyperactive child, and/or inattentive behaviours are not as disruptive and challenging for teachers.

The differences experienced by children with ADHD are best understood as dimensional (Barkley 2016) – as more or less different, or as more or less severe. For example, we could think of a child as being more or less active. Dimensional rather than categorical, so they are not 'hyperactive' in the way someone is or is not pregnant.

Executive functions

Learners need lots of skills to be successful academically and socially. Skills like following instructions, planning, prioritising, following multi-step directions, staying focused or switching focus when necessary, and using self-control are

Table 8.1 ADHD-type behaviours

Hyperactive-impulsive	Inattentive
• Fidgets with hands or feet, squirms in seat • Leaves seat when expected to remain seated • Runs about or climbs when others would not do so • Unable to play or play quietly • Seems often 'on the go', as if 'driven by a motor' • Talks a lot more than other children • Blurts out an answer prematurely • Cannot wait • Interrupts or intrudes on others' activities	• Fails to pay close attention to details • Makes careless mistakes • Differences in sustaining attention to activities or work • Doesn't seem to listen when spoken to • Difficulty following through on instructions • Fails to finish work • Difficulty organising tasks and activities • Avoids, dislikes or seems reluctant to engage in anything that require sustained effort • Loses things needed to do work or other activities • Is easily distracted • Forgets things

Figure 8.1 Brown's model of executive function differences

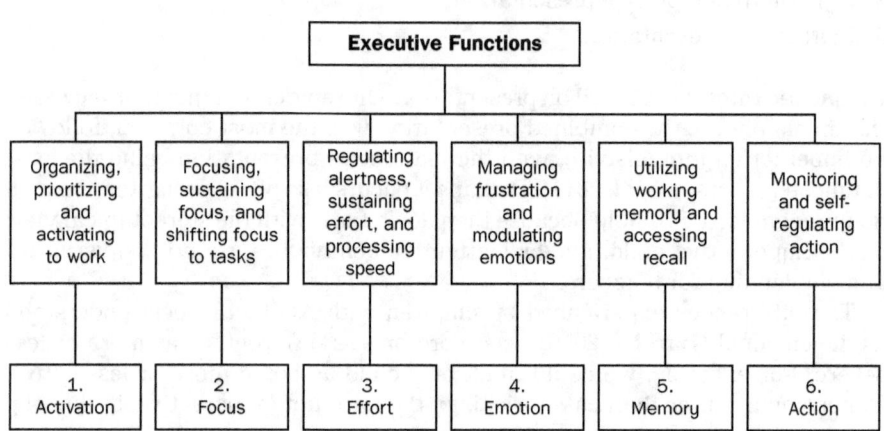

Source: Brown Attention-Deficit Disorder Scales. © 2001 NCS Pearson. Reproduced with permission.

known as executive function skills. Think of these as advanced thinking skills. Many academics and practitioners understand the differences associated with ADHD as being due to differences in these thinking skills (e.g. Barkley 2016; Brown 2001). Brown (2001) has provided a model to explain the executive function (EF) differences in children with ADHD (see Figure 8.1).

The majority of children with ADHD fall into the bottom 7 per cent in measures of EF (Barkley 2016). However, there is a lack of universality – that is, not all children with ADHD present with EF differences and EF profiles differ across children with ADHD (Willcutt et al. 2005).

> *Activity*
> Can you identify one barrier-to-participation (see Chapter 1 for explanation) that learners with ADHD might experience in your school for each EF difference? Would there be any differences in the barriers between primary and secondary school?

ADHD in girls

There are significant gender differences associated with ADHD, as it is more commonly diagnosed in boys in childhood, about 5:1 boys to girls; in most studies, however, diagnostic rates even out between the genders in adulthood to roughly 1:1 (Barkley, Murphy and Fischer, 2010; Kooij, S.J. et al. 2010). One way to understand these differences is presentation: girls tend to present with inattention and internalising difficulties (e.g. anxiety and depression) and with fewer externalising difficulties (e.g. hyperactivity) (de Schipper et al. 2015). These 'quiet' children are often not disruptive at home and in school, and so they may fly under the radar. However, evidence from the Zurich cohort study suggests that ADHD-related behaviours vary (across the genders) in early adolescence, and the typical characteristics listed above might not become apparent in girls until this age (Murray et al. 2019). This creates challenges for diagnostic guidelines, which require presentation before the age of 12 years (DSM-5).

It is not only about identification, gender-based attitudes may also be involved in responses. For example, Pisecco, Huzinec and Curtis (2001) found that teachers viewed medical management much more positively for boys than girls.

ADHD and strengths

By adopting a strengths-based and neuro-affirmative approach to ADHD, we can understand differences in terms of their positive contributions.

The ADHD community boasts many famous and talented people among its ranks, from entrepreneurs and inventors to musicians and actors. By embracing a neuro-affirmative approach to ADHD, we can use Hartmann's (2005) hunter-farmer theory: people with ADHD are hunters living in a 'farmer's world'. ADHD-type behaviours had adaptational value in hunter-gatherer society. For example, increased activity (i.e. hyperactivity) would support gathering and moving with the climate. Today, educational settings can adapt to the needs and preference of these types of learners.

Identifying and developing the strengths of a learner may support them with their development and cope with their condition. In a study of 174 experts across 11 disciplines and 45 counties, the following positive qualities of ADHD were noted (de Schipper et al. 2015):

- creative
- energetic
- fun to be around
- flexible
- multitasking
- resiliency
- risk-taking.

While 'risk-taking' might at times be considered a difficulty, it can be a real asset in many circumstances. For example, learning depends on one's ability to leave one's comfort zone (Vygotsky), and it's generally true that you need to be willing to take risks to set up your own business or audition for and preform on stage. One study found that university learners with greater ADHD-like behaviours were more likely to have entrepreneurial intentions (Verheul et al. 2015).

Another way to adopt a strengths-based approach is to focus on promoting factors that are known to protect (buffer) against risks or promote resiliency. In their review, Dvorsky and Langberg (2016) identified a range of social, individual and familial factors linked to resiliency in young people with ADHD. In particular, they found that research consistently identifies social acceptance and positive self-perceptions as protective factors, and the promotive effects of positive parenting. Chan et al. (2022) compared resiliency and demographic data in children with and without ADHD to identify ADHD-specific resiliency factors. They found that higher IQ and anxiety levels, and lower levels of oppositional defiant disorder (ODD) and fewer learning difficulties were associated with higher resilience in children with ADHD. They found that higher socio-economic status (see also Chapter 7) was a protective factor for children without ADHD, suggesting children with ADHD do not experience its buffering effects in the same way.

ADHD-related difficulties

ADHD is linked to a range of difficulties in many, if not all, areas of functioning. A synopsis of some of these key areas is given here.

Relationships: peers, teachers and family

Children with ADHD tend to have poorer social skills, be less liked by their peers, have fewer friends, and experience rejection from an early age (Wehmeier, Schacht and Barkley 2010; Carr-Fanning 2015). Together with risk-taking behaviours, these traits may be linked with a tendency to associate with more deviant peer groups in adolescence (Barkley 2016). Children with ADHD have been found to be more likely to be both the victims and perpetrators of bullying (Žic Ralić, Cvitković and Šifner 2016). Learners with ADHD who also present with aggression may be even more likely to be victimised. These types of behaviours seem to be viewed by their peers as particularly unacceptable, and so the child with ADHD is targeted as a result. Although there is a relationship between ADHD and the perpetration of bullying, we need to exercise caution, because children with ADHD might respond to victimisation by being aggressive, and as a result may be viewed by teachers as bullies (Wiener and Mak 2009). Conversely, positive relationships characterised by acceptance and understanding may provide much needed buffers for people with ADHD (de Schipper et al. 2015).

Unfortunately, other relationships also seem to be characterised by conflict, such as those with teachers and family members (Carr-Fanning 2015). Indeed, ADHD is associated with greater family dysfunction (see Carr-Fanning and Mc Guckin 2022), in that having a child with ADHD can cause a lot of stress for parents and siblings and can contribute to conflict and financial difficulties (e.g. sometimes one parent needs to stay at home, treatments often cost money, lost or damaged items need to be replaced). Parents might struggle with their own sense of parent efficacy, such as viewing themselves as a 'bad mother' for example, and they might feel stigmatised and judged by others, and so isolate themselves. Due to high heritability there may be multiple family members with ADHD, which can lead to even greater stress and dysfunction in the home. Adults with ADHD may struggle to stick to routines, provide structure and remain calm, which are essential skills when raising a child with ADHD.

Academic difficulties

As Barkley (2016) observed, the majority of learners with ADHD will experience some degree of academic difficulties, regardless of their intelligence or academic ability. Leaners with ADHD are more likely than learners without ADHD to experience failure, be held back a year, or drop out of secondary school (Breslau et al. 2011). ADHD's association with academic difficulties is reportedly not accounted for by other personal or contextual factors (Martin 2014). A longitudinal study in the USA found that students with ADHD were less likely to attend university (Kuriyan et al. 2013). However, findings consistently point to two predictors: 'academic problems' and 'disciplinary problems'. Learners with ADHD who also have higher levels of one or both of these risk factors, are less likely to progress to tertiary education. Knowing what makes the difference means we know where to target interventions, which is important in preventing some of the outcomes linked with ADHD, such as unemployment, lower earning potential and struggling to hold down a job (Kuriyan et al. 2013).

Co-occurring difficulties

ADHD tends to co-occur with other difficulties; indeed, this tendency is the rule rather than the exception. People with ADHD may experience more stress and feel overwhelmed, possibly as a result of trying to fit in and live up to social expectations. ADHD is associated with a range of internalising and externalising difficulties. People with ADHD report poorer self-concepts and lower self-esteem, as well as higher levels of anxiety, depression, self-harm and suicide (Harpin 2005; Spencer 2006; Wehmeier at al. 2010; de Schipper et al. 2015). ADHD is also linked with a range of behavioural and learning difficulties (Reale et al. 2017), and autism spectrum disorder (ASD; Antshel, Zhang-James and Faraone 2013). Co-occurrence is associated with more severe difficulties and may require particular types of intervention (Reale et al. 2017).

> Reflection
> Why do you think learners with ADHD experience these difficulties? Is it due to ADHD characteristics, or social structures in education and society (e.g. having to sit still in class)?

Activity
Try to identify the differences, strengths and difficulties experienced by Sarah (see Box 8.1).

Box 8.1   Case study: Sarah

Sarah is 10 years old and lives with her parents and younger sister. Her parents met while doing their master's degrees and her mother believes she has undiagnosed ADHD.

Sarah is very intelligent and has a brilliant memory for historical facts and quickly grasps scientific concepts. However, she is not doing well in most subjects, except those she loves and can 'hyper-focus' on. Sarah is highly sensitive and emotionally reactive; she can fly into a temper quickly, get easily excited or upset with classmates, especially if she thinks someone doesn't like her. Sarah loves watching TV and physical activities like swimming and playing hockey. But, she never remembers her kit and doesn't know the name of her club.

Sarah makes friends easily, but struggles to keep them, which is a source of distress for her. She can be easily influenced by others and her teachers describe her as 'immature', which is why she was kept back a year. Recently, she has begun avoiding social situations (e.g. sitting alone at lunchtime). Sarah finds it hard to pay attention in class, and she needs constant reminders to do her work. She used to be very active, but she has become less so recently. She still does things without thinking (e.g. shouting out answers in class). She recognises this, calling it 'weird', but doesn't know why she does it or how to stop. She often dominates conversations. Her teachers describe her as 'bossy' and 'domineering'. Sarah doesn't seem to recognise this.

At home, her parents say she struggles to sleep at night and mornings are stressful and disorganised. At night, it's difficult to get her to do her work or get her material ready for the following day. She is often late and does not have what she needs for school. Her parents and teachers are worried about her transitioning to secondary school and managing socially and academically.

Culture, meaning and stigma

A considerable evidence base attests to the presence, persistence and consequences of stigmatisation of ADHD. The term 'stigma' refers to negative attitudes and often inaccurate beliefs that are attached to labels like ADHD

(Kranke et al. 2011). Stigma is influenced by policy and legislation (Singh 2008), as well as the media (Gilmore 2010). Soppitt (2016) described the 'media myths' of ADHD, such as newspapers running headlines such as 'ADHD is an excuse for bad parenting', stoking the controversy that surrounds ADHD.

Stigma has significant consequences (see Chapter 1 and 6). Singh's (2012) trans-cultural research concluded that children with ADHD may be 're-victimised' by the 'public face' or the social meaning of ADHD. Singh found that ADHD was viewed as a disorder of associated with anger and aggression in the UK and learning in the USA. This socially negotiated meaning of ADHD impacted parent/teacher beliefs about responses and how the children viewed themselves. Overwhelmingly, evidence suggests learners with ADHD hold negative self-perceptions (e.g. Carr-Fanning 2015).

The meaning of ADHD is negotiated within the cultures of family, school and peer group, as well as the country at large. Evidence suggests that efforts to change this culture from one of rejection and stigma to acceptance of ADHD has positive effects in terms of the social inclusion of children with ADHD (Mikami, Smit and Khalis 2017).

Reflection
Reflect on your beliefs about ADHD. Are any of them negative/stigmatising, where do these come from?

What works in practice?

This section focuses on what we can do in educational practice, including interventions, accommodations and collaboration with parents/carers and learners. This review is evidenced-based, drawing on some studies, but is mainly focused on meta-analyses and systematic literature reviews.

This discussion draws on practices from both special and inclusive educational approaches – try to identify the approach as you read. The educational responses to ADHD with the strongest evidence base have some limitations. There is an over-abundance of studies exploring contingency management to the neglect of other areas, such as skills development and more inclusive approaches around accommodations. As a result, the literature is dominated by special educational approaches. So, when developing educational responses, although it is essential to draw on the evidence base, it is necessary to apply it critically, reflexively and involve the learner in any decision-making. Much of the evidence relates to primary school children, and so early years and post-primary educational responses are less well understood.

Interventions

Here, we consider school-based interventions for learners with ADHD. In a meta-analysis of 60 studies conducted between 1996 and 2010, academic, contingency management and self-regulation interventions showed moderate to large improvements in both academic and behavioural functioning (DuPaul, Eckert and Vilardo 2012).

Functional assessments: the ABC model

Functionally based interventions (FIs) support more individualised interventions. According to one meta-analysis of 82 studies and 168 participants (Miller and Lee 2013), FIs were associated with significantly larger effects, maybe because FIs are more tailored to the specific needs of the learner, rather than having a one-size-fits-all approach.

FIs are based on the idea that a behaviour serves a 'function' for the learner (e.g. behaviour may attract attention or materials, enable escape/avoidance, or provide self-stimulation). The goal is to understand the function of the behaviour. One can assess the function of the behaviour using the Antecedent-Behaviour-Consequence (ABC) model. The ABC model depends on multiple good quality observations of a child's behaviour in context. It involves identifying a target Behaviour and then considering what led to that behaviour (Antecedents) and what comes after the behaviour (Consequences). Once we understand the function of the behaviour, we can then work towards changing it. It is useful to have a framework that enables us to view and consider behaviours more objectively, adopting the role of 'teacher as behaviour detective', if you like. But remember, to do this inclusively, your focus should be on the social and environmental context that the student is struggling with and placing the child's voice at the centre of this process. Table 8.2 and Box 8.2 provide a step-by-step approach to conducting your own functional assessment.

Figure 8.2 The ABC model: understanding the function of a behaviour

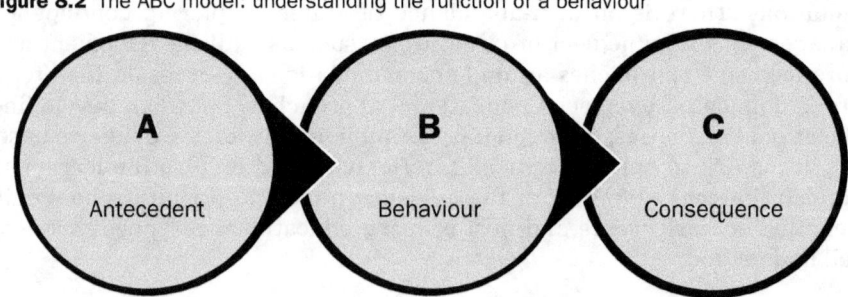

Source: Brown (2001)

Table 8.2 Functional intervention: step by step

1. *Define*	Define target behaviour so you can measure it
2. *Observe*	Identify and explore Antecedent and Consequences through observation and collaboration (see p. 122). For observations, decide 'how' you will measure (record) the target behaviour and 'when' you will measure it (schedule). For example, you may record each time the behaviour presents or you may choose specific times in the day across a number of days or weeks. Aim for quality and objective data.
3. *Analyse*	Analyse the behaviour and generate an hypothesis about possible Antecedents and Consequences.
4. *Positive behaviours*	Define the positive behaviour you want to develop. Focus on teaching specific skill(s) to replace problems and on academic performance (e.g. work completed accurately, not on-task behaviour). Remember to consider the child's neurodivergence and their wishes within this – it's not about getting them to 'fit in' with their non-ADHD peers, but rather to develop skills and achieve goals valued by them.
5. *Strategise*	Design 'proactive strategies' which manipulate Antecedents to prevent challenging behaviour (e.g. use a teaching assistant, adapt the environment, adapt teaching methods, promote acceptance and belonging), and 'reactive strategies' which introduce positive and/or negative Consequence to increase or decrease behaviour. It's best when these are co-constructed with parents and learners (see p. 122).
6. *Implement*	Implement strategies to test your hypothesis and change behaviour.
7. *Evaluate*	Evaluate the strategies' effectiveness with parents and learners.

Box 8.2 ABC model example

Connor is eight years old, was diagnosed with ADHD, and struggles academically and with his behaviour. Connor has regular emotional outbursts in class. Over two weeks, every time Connor disrupts the class by verbally shouting out or getting out of his seat (target behaviour) his teacher records what happened before (Antecedent) and after (Consequence). She notices a theme. This behaviour most frequently occurs after learners are asked to get their English books; when she asks Connor he admits he is worried he will be called on to read aloud (Antecedent). The teacher's response (Consequence) is to send him to speak with his Year Head (as a negative consequence). To Connor, this is a positive consequence because he escapes his fears (Consequence). His teacher agrees with Connor that she will not call on him to read and provides teaching assistant support (proactive strategies). And Connor receives tokens when he positively engages in English that he can exchange for a reward (reactive strategy).

Contingency management

A preponderance of evidence supports the efficacy of behavioural change programmes for learners with ADHD (e.g. Pfiffner and DuPaul 2016). However, they are also the most studied school-based intervention for ADHD.

Contingency management programmes can be delivered by teachers, parents or be peer-mediated, and they can be group or individual based. They usually involved both:

- *Positive consequences*: praise, tangible rewards and token economies (where the child receives token that can be exchanged for a reward).
- *Negative consequences*: reprimands, response costs (loss of a reinforce/reward) or time out.

Praise or positive consequences alone may not be enough to motivate learners with ADHD (Pfiffner and DuPaul 2016). A combination of token reinforcement and response costs works best, showing improvements in on-task behaviour, seatwork, productivity and accuracy, with similar effect sizes to medication (DuPaul and Stoner 2014). While behavioural management systems are common, what is distinct with learners with ADHD is 'how' and 'when' consequences are used. Possibly linked to differences in how children with ADHD process emotions and are motivated.

Positive consequences are most effective when they are immediate, brief, consistent, salient and frequently delivered (Pfiffner and DuPaul 2016). Due to their decreased sensitivity to reward and differences in sustained attention, when a reinforcer is used inconsistently or is weak, it will not be as effective. A reinforcement needs to be used frequently and be powerful, and may need to be changed regularly. In this way, in a token economy, a learner receives a token each time they achieve a certain behaviour, which they can exchange for a tangible reward later that day or at the end of the week. Identifying 'powerful' rewards is an important part of this process, so that learners are motivated to sustain effort. It is also challenging, as there is a need to continue to change the reward to sustain motivation and attention.

Negative consequences when used need to be immediate, unemotional, brief and consistent (Pfiffner and DuPaul 2016). Consequences that are consistently strong, rather than increasing in severity across a term or semester, are more beneficial. Proximity is another important characteristic identified in Pfiffner and DuPaul's (2016) review; rather than called from across a room, a consequence delivered in close proximity may have more of an effect. Suspension has not been found to be effective for leaners with ADHD (Atkins et al. 2002), possibly due to the need for the sanction to be immediate.

A frequently studied approach known as the Daily Report Card (DRC) method is a home-based contingency programme (Iznardo et al. 2020). With this method, the parent and teacher identify around four or five target behaviours (positive behaviours everyone wants to develop) that will be reported on each day. It is useful to include one or two behaviours that a child already presents with. Every day the teacher reports on these and the parents implement the contingencies at home. Owens et al. (2012) reported that over 70 per cent of learners will show improvements within one month and further gains across several months. These can be adapted for use in secondary school as a 'note home' (Volpe and Fabiano 2013). A challenge is the delay in consequences and parent skills (DuPaul and Stoner 2014).

Once contingency-based methods are established, the aim is to make the behaviour generalisable, so it is preferable to fade out the programme over time, rather than for it to come to an abrupt end (Pfiffner and DuPaul 2016). In general, research supports the use of contingency management in primary schools and somewhat for early childhood, but less so for secondary school or beyond (Fabiano and Pyle 2019). However, in their systematic review, Sibley et al. (2014) did find support for its use with this age group. In secondary school, there may be greater need and efficacy for skills training.

Skills development

Another target for development is the specific academic, social and behavioural skills of the learner. This can be considered an area for intervention and proactive (antecedent-based) strategies.

Cognitive-behavioural interventions for ADHD focus on self-regulation, including self-monitoring, self-reinforcement and cognitive training (self-instruction and problem-solving), which target academic and social skills. The focus of these interventions is 'self-control', a core difference in learners with ADHD. Meta-analyses and literature reviews consistently find low effects for cognition (Pfiffner and DuPaul 2016), which might be preferable, because the aim is to fix neurocognitive deficits, and raises questions about respect for the rights of neuro-minorities (i.e. those considered neurodivergent).

According to Mikami, Jia and Na (2014), social skills training may not be effective because social difficulties are not caused by a lack of knowledge, but an inability to perform (e.g. respond appropriately); training programmes also tend to ignore context, such as peer stigma and contextual rules for behaviour. Social skills training also raises questions about a neuro-affirmative stance and trying to get the child to 'fit in' and behave like other children. Indeed, when Mikami, Smit and Khalis (2017) developed a social skills intervention programme that also targeted peer groups, promoting greater social acceptance of ADHD-type behaviour, they reported much better results. This has clear implications for the neuro-affirmative paradigm in education – making changes to the environment and promoting acceptance and belonging.

Self-regulation strategies, which tend to focus on self-monitoring and self-reinforcement, have been found to be more effective. The child learns to self-monitor by learning to observe, record and evaluate their own behaviour, and then to self-reward (e.g. points or tokens). Student can do this independently or be prompted by a teacher or timer. One meta-analysis of 16 studies between 1974 and 2003 found large effects related to on-task behaviour, challenging behaviour, accuracy and productivity (Reid, Trout and Schartz 2005). Similarly, in a meta-analysis of school-based interventions including 8/60 outcome studies (mostly single-subject design), DuPaul, Eckert and Vilardo (2012) found large effects on behaviour and academic outcomes. Significantly, the behavioural effects were larger than for contingency management alone or academic interventions.

Teaching learners self-regulatory behaviour has become increasingly common; however, Harrison et al. (2019) observed that the once broad approach to self-regulation has become more focused on self-management in academic settings. Educators tend to focus more on the skills required for independent functioning in classrooms, although it is also important to consider other self-regulation skills that learners need in all areas of functioning, both now and in the future.

A review of evidence-based interventions by Evans, Owens and Bunford (2014) determined that organisational skills training is 'well-established'. There are a range of skills and programmes that involve teaching skills to learners and teachers, and often parents; those that involve organisational skills and contingency management usually provide rewards for the effective use of skill at home and/or school. These programmes have been found to improve organisational skills, family functioning, and academic performance and achievement.

> *Activity*
> Consider Sarah's situation (see case study, Box 8.1). What interventions would you recommend for her now (in primary school) and what might she need (now or in the future) to do well in secondary school?

Accommodation

At the heart of inclusion is accommodation, it is about adapting or redesigning the learning experience based on the needs and preferences of the learner (see Chapter 1 and 3). They can be understood within the ABC model as proactive (antecedent-based) strategies. Learners with ADHD need more structure (external support, guidance and 'scaffolding') and accommodations to classroom assignments and tasks (Barkley 2016).

Teaching methods, in particular instructional strategies, have a significant evidence base with regards to learners with challenging behaviour (e.g. Nelson, Benner and Mooney 2008), and so is often recommended for learners with ADHD (DuPaul and Stoner 2014). In particular, explicit instruction, with the following steps: (1) clearly identify 'what' will be learnt; (2) teach (knowledge, skills, etc.) is small steps with multiple concrete examples; (3) continuously assess understanding; and (4) use active participation. The pace should be predictable, perhaps follow a similar format each day, and use a variety of activities to maintain interest/attention. Any transitions should be clearly directed (Pfiffner and DuPaul 2016).

Teachers can change the classroom environment and actively teach to expectations (Pfiffner and DuPaul 2016). A range of classroom and task modifications have been suggested. Teachers can design learning experiences that are ability-matched, using multisensory teaching methods due to learners with ADHD having a preference for 'active' methods (Pfiffner and DuPaul 2016). They can 'chunk' or break down assignments or teaching into smaller tasks, and use timers to provide feedback, make time 'real' and enable self-monitoring (Barkley 2016). Movement breaks can be used, especially later in the day (Pfiffner and DuPaul 2016), which can involve the type of learning experience, sensory breaks or be integrated into the classroom (e.g. fidget toys or sitting on balls or swivel seats). As Dunlap et al. (1994) found, an important point when it comes to instruction is giving learners with ADHD choices to improve behaviour and academic performance (e.g. give the learner the choice of which maths problem to do).

Externalising information reduces demands on executive function. Such demands may be reasonable for many students, but they may not suit individuals with ADHD (for a review, see Barkley 2016). Children with ADHD might experience 'time blindness' and so educators can make time 'real' by representing time and time periods physically (e.g. visual timetables or using egg timers to guide students on how long to continue with a task). To reduce the demands on executive functions like working memory, expectations and instructions can be provided clearly, briefly and visually/externally. For example, providing positive behaviour support cards or handouts with directions (e.g. homework).

Accommodation research is limited by the fact that very few single-case designs have been conducted, and further research in this area is needed to support its use (Harrison et al. 2019).

> *Activity*
> Consider Sarah's situation (see case study, Box 8.1). What accommodations would you recommend for her now (in primary school) and what might she need to do well in secondary school?

Collaboration

The use of collaboration is an important element for developing and evaluating educational responses (e.g. Pfiffner and DuPaul 2016). Collaborative working is important in a number of ways when including learners with ADHD: multi-agency working (e.g. school, CAMHS, social care), home-school collaboration and learner voice, with notions of children's voice and participation being central to both inclusion and neuro-affirmative paradigms.

Home-school collaboration

An important consideration in terms of effective intervention for ADHD is home-school collaboration; indeed, challenging behaviours are likely to create difficulties across these contexts and 'consistency' is key when it comes to ADHD. Many of the intervention programmes reviewed above involved parents/carers. DuPaul and Stoner (2014) suggest the evidence-based model for home-school collaboration, owing to its effects on positive academic and behavioural outcomes for learners with ADHD, and that it is based on collecting data about the behaviour before and after the intervention. This model focuses on problem-solving across four stages: problem identification, problem analysis, intervention and evaluation.

Educators should also be aware that a parent/carer may also have ADHD-related differences and experience difficulties, which may need external support, accommodation during collaboration, and/or create challenges for implementing interventions at home. For example, contingency management requires skills such as consistency, structure and routine, which a parent/carer with ADHD may struggle with (Carr-Fanning and Mc Guckin 2022).

Working with learners with ADHD

Positive student-teacher relationships are essential when it comes to learners with ADHD (de Schipper et al. 2015). However, learners with ADHD often feel misunderstood and rejected by teachers (Carr-Fanning 2015). A part of understanding 'the problem' and it's 'solution', as in the case of functional assessment, requires learner involvement.

Learners with ADHD may be the most neglected when it comes to voice (Carr-Fanning 2015). When trying to collaborate with learners, you need to take into account their specific communication differences. For example, think about emotions and executive function, as they may have difficulties with memory, planning and sequencing (e.g. sequencing events or relaying stories). Try to be as clear as you can when asking questions, and repeat back what you have heard to make sure you have understood. Learners with ADHD may have experienced a lot of rejection, and so may be less inclined to trust adults (Carr-Fanning and Mc Guckin 2017).

Collaboration is about recognising that it is important to work 'with' learners and parents, to co-construct knowledge about difficulties and strengths. It is also about recognising that responses will be more effective, and the learner will be more engaged and empowered, when they are involved (Carr-Fanning 2015).

Greene (2010) designed an evidence-based, step-by-step approach to this co-construction process, known as collaborative and proactive solutions (CPS: see Table 8.3). CPS is a cognitive-behavioural intervention, which shifts the focus to 'solving problems', not modifying behaviours. It asks educators to reconsider their mindset. It suggests that if a learner had the skills to cope with the demands (e.g. schoolwork or social interaction), they would not exhibit challenging behaviours. So, when challenging behaviour does occur, there is (a) an unsolved problem and (b) a 'lagging skill' or cognitive difference (e.g. self-regulation or problem-solving). This approach differs from other cognitive-behavioural interventions, because the emphasis is on adult–child problem-solving, rather than trying to change a learner to fit-in.

Table 8.3 Collaborative problem-solving: step by step

1. *Empathy*	The learner describes the problem from their perspective and the educator listens with empathy and curiosity.
2. *Define*	The educator shares their concerns and the learner listens (they don't have to agree).
3. *Invitation*	This begins with a restatement of problems identified in steps 1 and 2. Here the educator and learner collaborate, the educator inviting the learner to help develop options and then solve the problem. They agree a solution.

Reflection
What approach do you usually take when it comes to collaborating? Does it differ when collaborating with colleagues, parents or children? What might you need to consider when talking to a child with ADHD?

Summary and conclusion

ADHD relates to the cognitive, behavioural and affective domains of attentional processing, executive functioning, response inhibition and/or increased levels of activity. An understanding of strengths and difficulties will enable you to design learning experiences that create a better fit between the learner with ADHD and their educational system.

Learners with ADHD can be supported using contingency management (especially functional interventions) and the teaching of specific skills (e.g. organisation and self-regulation). Working inclusively, systemic changes can be made, adapting the classroom environment and educational experience, and importantly creating a culture of acceptance of neurodivergence among ADHD learners' teachers and their peers, and so promote a sense of belonging. An important part of this process is collaboration with parents and learners with ADHD, to better understand their differences and to co-construct inclusive and empowering responses.

Resources
Below are some additional resources to help in your understanding of ADHD: Brown's model of executive functioning and Barkley's excellent synthesis of evidence-based accommodations in practice.

Thomas Brown's website: https://www.brownadhdclinic.com/the-brown-model-of-add-adhd.

Barkley, R.A. (2016) *Managing ADHD in School: The Best Evidence-Based Methods for Teachers.* Eau Claire, WI: PESI.

References

American Psychiatric Association (APA) (2013) *Diagnostic and Statistical Manual of Mental Disorders: DSM-5*. Washington, DC: APA.

Antshel, K.M., Zhang-James, Y. and Faraone, S.V. (2013) The comorbidity of ADHD and autism spectrum disorder, *Expert Review of Neurotherapeutics*, 13 (10): 1117–1128.

Atkins, M.S., McKay, M.M., Frazier, S.L., Jakobsons, L.J., Arvanitis, P., Cunningham, T. et al. (2002) Suspensions and detentions in an urban, low-income school: punishment or reward?, *Journal of Abnormal Child Psychology*, 30 (4): 361–371.

Barkley, R.A. (2016) *Managing ADHD in School: The Best Evidence-Based Methods for Teachers*. Eau Claire, WI: PESI.

Barkley, RA, Murphy, KR, and Fischer, M (2010). *MADHD in adults: what the science says*. Guildford Press: New York.

Breslau, J., Miller, E., Chung, W.-J.J. and Schweitzer, J.B. (2011) Childhood and adolescent onset psychiatric disorders, substance use, and failure to graduate high school on time, *Journal of Psychiatric Research*, 45 (3): 295–301.

Brown, T. (2001) *Manual for Attention Deficit Disorder Scales for Children and Adolescents*. San Antonio, TX: Psychological Corporation.

Carr-Fanning, K. (2015) *'There's nothing so wrong with you that what's right with you couldn't fix': a study of stress, emotion, and coping in children with ADHD*. PhD thesis, Trinity College Dublin.

Carr-Fanning, K. and Mc Guckin, C. (2017) Developing creative methods for children's voice, in B. Flett (ed.), *Sage Cases in Methodology: A Unique Collection of over 500 Case Studies for Use in the Teaching of Research Methods*. London: Sage.

Carr-Fanning, K. and Mc Guckin, C. (2022) 'I find it really difficult to control myself too': a qualitative study of the effects on the family dynamic when parent and child have ADHD, *Educational Sciences*, 12 (11): 758. Available at: https://doi.org/10.3390/educsci12110758

Chan, E.S., Groves, N.B., Marsh, C.L., Miller, C.E., Richmond, K.P. and Kofler, M.J. (2022) Are there resilient children with ADHD?, *Journal of Attention Disorders*, 26 (5): 643–655.

de Schipper, E., Lundequist, A., Wilteus, A.L., Coghill, D., de Vries, P.J., Granlund, M. et al. (2015) A comprehensive scoping review of ability and disability in ADHD using the International Classification of Functioning, Disability and Health-Children and Youth Version (ICF-CY), *European Child & Adolescent Psychiatry*, 24 (8): 859–872.

Dunlap, G., dePerczei, M., Clarke, S., Wilson, D., Wright, S., White, R. et al. (1994) Choice making to promote positive adaptive behaviour for students with emotional and behavioural challenges, *Journal of Applied Behaviour Analysis*, 27 (3): 505–518.

DuPaul, G.J. and Stoner, G. (2014) *ADHD in the School*, 3rd edition. New York: Guilford Press.

DuPaul, G.J., Eckert, T.L. and Vilardo, B. (2012) The effects of school-based interventions for attention deficit hyperactivity disorder: a meta-analysis 1996–2010, *School Psychology Review*, 41 (4): 387–412.

Dvorsky, M.R. and Langberg, J.M. (2016) A review of factors that promote resilience in youth with ADHD and ADHD symptoms, *Clinical Child and Family Psychology Review*, 19 (4): 368–391.

Evans, S.W., Owens, J.S. and Bunford, N. (2014) Evidence-based psychosocial treatments for children and adolescents with attention-deficit/hyperactivity disorder, *Journal of Clinical Child & Adolescent Psychology*, 43 (4): 527–551.

Fabiano, G.A. and Pyle, K. (2019) Best practices in school mental health for attention-deficit/hyperactivity disorder: a framework for intervention, *School Mental Health*, 11 (1): 72–91.

Fabiano, G.A., Vujnovic, R.K., Pelham, W.E., Waschbusch, D.A., Massetti, G.M., Pariseau, M.E. et al. (2010) Enhancing the effectiveness of special education programming for children with ADHD using a daily report card, *School Psychology Review*, 39 (2): 219–239.

Gilmore, L. (2010) Community knowledge and beliefs about ADHD, *Australian Educational and Developmental Psychologist*, 27 (1): 20–30.

Greene, R.W. (2010) *The Explosive Child: A New Approach for Understanding and Parenting Easily Frustrated, 'Chronically Inflexible' Children*, 4th edition. New York: HarperCollins.

Harpin, V.A. (2005) The effect of ADHD on the life of an individual, their family, and community from preschool to adult life, *Archives of Diseases in Childhood*, 90 (1): i2–i7.

Harrison, J.R., Soares, D.A., Rudzinski, S. and Johnson, R. (2019) Attention deficit hyperactivity disorders and classroom-based interventions: evidence-based status, effectiveness, and moderators of effects in single-case design research, *Review of Educational Research*, 89 (4): 569–611.

Hartmann, T. (2005) *The Edison Gene: ADHD and the Gift of the Hunter Child*. Randolph, VT: Inner Traditions/Bear & Co.

Iznardo, M., Rogers, M.A., Volpe, R.J., Labelle, P.R. and Robaey, P. (2020) The effectiveness of daily behavior report cards for children with ADHD: a meta-analysis, *Journal of Attention Disorders*, 24 (12): 1623–1636.

Kooij, S.J. et al. (2010) European consensus statement on diagnosis and treatment of adult ADHD: The European network adult ADHD, *BMC Psychiatry*, 10: 67.

Kranke, D.A., Floersch, J., Kranke, B.O. and Munson, M.R. (2011) A qualitative investigation of self-stigma among adolescents taking psychiatric medication, *Psychiatric Services*, 62 (8): 893–899.

Kuriyan, A.B., Pelham, Jr., W.E., Molina, B.S.G., Waschbusch, D.A., Gnagy, E.M., Sibley, M.H. et al. (2013) Young adult educational and vocational outcomes of children diagnosed with ADHD, *Journal of Abnormal Child Psychology*, 41 (1): 27–41.

Larsson, H., Dilshad, R., Lichtenstein, P. and Barker, E.D. (2011) Developmental trajectories of DSM-IV symptoms of ADHD: genetic effects, family risk and associated psychopathology, *Journal of Child Psychology & Psychiatry*, 52 (9): 954–963.

Martin, A.J. (2014) The role of ADHD in academic adversity: disentangling ADHD effects from other personal and contextual factors, *School Psychology Quarterly*, 29 (4): 395–408.

Mikami, A.Y., Jia, M. and Na, J.J. (2014) Social skills training, *Child and Adolescent Psychiatric Clinics*, 23 (4): 775–788.

Mikami, A.Y., Smit, S. and Khalis, A. (2017) Social skills training and ADHD – what works?, *Current Psychiatry Reports*, 19: 93. Available at: https://doi.org/10.1007/s11920-017-0850-2

Miller, F.G. and Lee, D.L. (2013) Do functional behavioral assessments improve intervention effectiveness for students diagnosed with ADHD? A single-subject meta-analysis, *Journal of Behavioral Education*, 22 (3): 253–282.

Murray, A.L., Booth, T., Eisner, M., Auyeung, B., Murray, G. and Ribeaud, D. (2019) Sex differences in ADHD trajectories across childhood and adolescence, *Developmental Science*, 22 (1): e12721. Available at: https://doi.org/10.1111/desc.12721

Nelson, J.R., Benner, G.J. and Mooney, P. (2008) *Instructional Practices for Students with Emotional and Behavioural Disorders: Applications in Schools*. New York: Guilford Press.

Owens, J.S., Holdaway, A.S., Zoromski, A.K., Evans, S.W., Himawan, L.K., Girio-Herrera, E. et al. (2012) Incremental benefits of the daily report card intervention over time for youth with disruptive behaviour, *Behaviour Therapy*, 43 (4): 848–861.

Pfiffner, L.J. and DuPaul, G. (2016) Treatment of ADHD in school settings, in R.A. Barkley (ed.), *Attention Deficit Hyperactivity Disorder: A Handbook for Diagnosis and Treatment*. New York: Guilford Press.

Pisecco, S., Huzinec, C. and Curtis, D. (2001) The effect of child characteristics on teachers' acceptability of classroom-based behavioral strategies and psychostimulant medication for the treatment of ADHD, *Journal of Clinical Child Psychology*, 30 (3): 413–421.

Polanczyk, G., Silva de Lima, M., Horta, B.L., Biederman, J. and Rohde, L.A. (2007) The worldwide prevalence of ADHD: a systematic review and metaregression analysis, *American Journal of Psychiatry*, 164 (6): 942–948.

Reale L., Bartoli, B., Cartabia, M., Zanetti, M., Costantino, M.A., Canevini, M.P. et al. (2017) Comorbidity prevalence and treatment outcome in children and adolescents with ADHD, *European Child & Adolescent Psychiatry*, 26 (12): 1443–1457.

Reid, R., Trout, A.L. and Schartz, M. (2005) Self-regulation interventions for children with attention deficit/ hyperactivity disorder, *Exceptional Children*, 71 (4): 361–377.

Sharkey, L. and Fitzgerald, M. (2007) Diagnosis and classification of ADHD in childhood, in M. Fitzgerald, M. Bellgrove and M. Gill (eds.), *Handbook of Attention Deficit Hyperactivity Disorder*. Chichester: Wiley.

Sibley, M.H., Kuriyan, A.B., Evans, S.W., Waxmonsky, J.G. and Smith, B.H. (2014) Pharmacological and psychosocial treatments for adolescents with ADHD: an updated systematic review of the literature, *Clinical Psychology Review*, 34 (3): 218–232.

Singh, I. (2008). *ADHD, culture and education. Early Child Development and Care*, 178 (4): 347–361.

Singh, I. (2012) *VOICES Study: Final Report*. London: ADHD Voices. Available at: http://www.adhdvoices.com/adhdreport/.

Soppitt, R. (2016) Attention deficit hyperactivity disorder (or hyperkinetic disorder), in L. Peer and G. Reid (eds.), *Special Educational Needs: A Guide for Inclusive Practice*. London: Sage.

Spencer, T.J. (2006) ADHD and comorbidity in childhood, *Journal of Clinical Psychiatry*, 67 (suppl. 8): 27–31.

Still, G.F. (1902) Some abnormal psychical conditions in children, *Lancet*, 1: 1008–1012, 1077–1082, 1163–1168.

Uchida, M., Spencer, T.J., Faraone, S.V. and Biederman, J. (2018) Adult outcome of ADHD: an overview of results from the MGH longitudinal family studies of pediatrically and psychiatrically referred youth with and without ADHD of both sexes, *Journal of Attention Disorders*, 22 (6): 523–534.

Verheul, I., Block, J., Burmeister-Lamp, K., Thurik, R., Tiemeier, H. and Turturea, R. (2015) ADHD-like behavior and entrepreneurial intentions, *Small Business Economics*, 45 (1): 85–101.

Volpe, R.J. and Fabiano, G.A. (2013). *Daily Behavior Report Cards: An Evidence-based System of Assessment and Intervention*. New York: Guilford Press.

Wehmeier, P.M., Schacht, A. and Barkley, R.A. (2010) Social and emotional impairment in children and adolescents with ADHD and the impact on quality of life, *Journal of Adolescent Health*, 46 (3): 209–217.

Wiener, J. and Mak, M. (2009) Peer victimization in children with attention-deficit/hyperactivity disorder, *Psychology in Schools*, 46 (2): 116–131.

Willcutt, E.G., Doyle, A.E., Nigg, J.T., Faraone, S.V. and Pennington, B.F. (2005) Validity of the executive function theory of attention-deficit/hyperactivity disorder: a meta-analytic review, *Biological Psychiatry*, 57 (11): 1336–1346.

Žic Ralić, A., Cvitković, D. and Šifner, E. (2016) The relation between school bullying and victimization in children with ADHD, *Journal of Special Education and Rehabilitation*, 17(3/4): 105–121.

9 Dyslexia: recognition of needs and overcoming literacy barriers through evidence-based practices

Georgia Niolaki, Aris Terzopoulos, Jennifer Donovan and Jackie Masterson

---

By the end of this chapter, you will be able to:

- discuss if it is possible to have a widely accepted definition of dyslexia
- understand the range of different risk factors linked to dyslexia
- gain an awareness of the strengths and challenges an individual encounters within the different domains (literacy, cognition and ability), as well as the frequently neglected social and emotional elements
- identify important theoretical frameworks and discuss their application to teaching practice.

Box 9.1 The case of Rosie

Rosie's parents requested a diagnostic assessment for her when she was 10 years old (UK Year 5). According to her parents, she was having 'troubles with schoolwork', and they thought that she was 'a little bit lazy'. They also had concerns because she complained of having a stomach ache every Friday morning. Furthermore, her parents were worried that she frequently missed class or was late on Fridays due to her complaints. Rosie abhorred spelling tests, and Fridays were spelling test days! She found long words tricky, she spelled <stretchy> as <striche> and <coming> as <comeing>. But shorter words were not much better: <which> as <wich>, <two> as <tow> and <other> as <over>.

> *Activity*
> Why did Rosie fear the prospect of a spelling test? What else would you like to know about Rosie?

Rosie has a learning difficulty called developmental dyslexia. There is still no widely accepted definition of dyslexia and even some local educational authorities in the UK do not accept the dyslexia diagnosis. This hinders the process of early recognition of needs and support, which is crucial for improving educational attainment and academic performance (Elliott and Grigorenko 2014). As such, in the current chapter, we will focus on describing the strengths and challenges individuals with dyslexia face. In line with the evidence-informed and best practice in this area, this chapter will adopt principles and practices from both special and inclusive educational approaches. We argue that both are needed to support the needs and development of learners with developmental dyslexia. As you read this chapter, take time to reflect and try to identify which approach is being adopted – is it special or inclusive education? But first, let us begin with the critical question: *Does dyslexia exist?*

> **Box 9.2 Definitions of dyslexia**
>
> We list here the two most widely adopted definitions.
>
> *British Dyslexia Association*
> The British Dyslexia Association (BDA) definition is tailored upon the Rose (2009) review:
>
> > Dyslexia affects word reading and spelling accuracy and fluency. Individuals with dyslexia have difficulties in phonological awareness, verbal memory and processing speed. Dyslexia occurs across the spectrum of intellectual abilities. Response to intervention can be considered as a criterion of the severity and remediation of the dyslexic difficulties (https://www.bdadyslexia.org.uk/dyslexia/about-dyslexia/what-is-dyslexia).
>
> *Specific Learning Disorder (APA 2013)*
> Dyslexia is a neurodevelopmental and biological difficulty with word reading accuracy or fluency, poor decoding and spelling being significantly below age expectations. These difficulties cannot be due to intellectual ability or any other developmental, motor or neurological disorders. The difficulties should be present for more than six months. The definition is mainly used by psychologists and clinicians in the UK and abroad.

> *Activity*
> Compare the definitions in Box 9.2 side-by-side and consider whether their purposes and applications can enhance or hinder understanding.

We live in the era of information, and those who cannot easily access information are set to be excluded from jobs that require skilful reading and writing (Pan, Rickard and Bjork 2021). This was not a problem for previous generations as vocational education programmes were linked to employment opportunities. Literacy difficulties can emerge from sensory disabilities (hearing and vision difficulties, neurological difficulties, etc.). They can also arise without any sensory or intellectual challenges (i.e. dyslexia). Researchers have used different terms to describe and define it, such as 'reading disability', 'specific reading difficulties', 'dyslexia', and so on. The most prevalent term is considered to be 'developmental dyslexia' (see Box 9.2). Much of the confusion around what dyslexia is stems from the lack of a single, universally accepted definition or description (Snowling, Hulme and Nation 2020).

The debate: dyslexia or no dyslexia

Dyslexia constitutes a long-standing difficulty described initially by the pioneers in the reading difficulties field: Morgan (1896), Hinshelwood (1900) and Orton (1966). Since then, although our understanding has improved significantly, a vigorous debate still exists around the definition. Consequently, many even question who should be identified as having dyslexia and who not. But even individuals who have dyslexia do not always feel that they fit the usual profile, or that their needs are a lot more neurodivergent and complex, not only nested within literacy.

The main difficulty with defining dyslexia is the lack of a clear set of criteria. Many researchers in the past asserted that intellectual ability should be a criterion; however, this view has been strongly criticised (cf. Stanovich 1994). Others argue that dyslexia has a genetic origin. Dehaene wrote: 'Genetic research is now rapidly moving ahead, and I am confident that a full causal chain linking genes to dyslexic behaviour will be available shortly' (2009: 244). Similarly, Olson et al. (2014), in a review of genetic and behavioural studies with twins from English-speaking countries, provide research evidence that genetic factors contribute to children's reading ability by the end of Grade 1. Friend, DeFries and Olson (2008) stated that the performance of children with learning difficulties whose parents had received higher education was more influenced by genetic than environmental factors, compared with children from less well-educated families. In addition, Friend and colleagues reported that children from low educated families and with environmental obstacles to their educational attainment may be good readers, and this could be due to their genetic heritage. On the other hand, according to Bishop (2014), there is not enough evidence to support genetic correlations.

Recap
A family history of dyslexia/reading difficulties can be an early indicator of literacy difficulties, and a reason early intervention and support needs to be put in place by the class teacher.

Twenty-five per cent of pupils in the UK currently fail to reach the expected standard in reading and writing (DfE 2019), and these children are frequently at risk for dyslexia. Dyslexia is highly prevalent, affecting up to 20 per cent of the population, according to estimates, and affects both genders equally (Shaywitz, Shaywitz and Shaywitz 2021). These facts are worrisome when seen alongside data published by the National Literacy Trust (Clark and Teravainen-Goff 2020), which indicate that just 26 per cent of under-18s spent time each day reading.

Elliot and Grigorenko (2014) raised an important question: Do children assigned as dyslexic and those falling in the broader category of poor readers receive appropriate intervention? Castles and colleagues (2014) provide a potential answer to this question. Assigning the label of dyslexia is not as important as the possibility to increase our knowledge of how improvement occurs because of intervention for literacy difficulties, since this is not well understood (Kohnen et al. 2008).

Researchers and practitioners generally agree that dyslexia is a significant reading and spelling difficulty that is not easy to address, even when interventions are tailored to each child's specific needs (Niolaki et al. 2014). Until recently, interventions for dyslexia have focused on phonology. However, current research suggests other non-phonological causes of literacy difficulties (Peyrin et al. 2012; Niolaki and Masterson 2013).

> *Activity*
> Could the latter point mean that different types of intervention are effective depending on various underlying challenges? If this is the case, reflect how easy it is to administer individualised interventions in a busy classroom. What steps should be taken in order to tailor an effective intervention for a child with phonological difficulties only, or sight-word recognition difficulties only?

The weight is therefore not on the label but on the recognition of needs, which will guide a suitable tailored intervention that will eventually help the child develop strategies to overcome or compensate for the difficulty.

> *Activity*
> Considering how difficult it is for a classroom teacher to implement specialist tailored one-to-one sessions, consider solutions that could benefit not only the child with dyslexia but the whole class. Make a list of simple solutions, for example:
> - we could use multisensory strategies and chunking techniques in the teaching of spelling for the whole classroom
> - we could use audio books as well as hard copies for all the children
> - we could provide oral and written feedback to all the students in the classroom.

Learning to read is an effortful procedure for a child with literacy difficulties. It may cause negative emotions, and it is crucial to 'find the principles that will allow children to learn to read without tears' (Dehaene 2009: 308). To achieve this, findings from educational neuroscience, psychology and education should jointly inform the optimal design of interventions for all children that are falling behind. We agree with Castles and colleagues' (2014) concluding remarks, that 'deciding what label to use to identify children who struggle with learning to read is not nearly so important as ensuring they receive the support they need'. The spectrum approach is much more suitable for the *No Child Left Behind* and *Every Child Matters* policies put in place in the USA and UK, respectively. In that way, we emphasise the recognition of needs and how to support them rather than the cognitive/distal underlying aspects of development, which are more challenging to target via intervention (Coltheart 2015). For example, it is more effective to target directly the teaching of letter recognition and letter-sound mapping than distal cognitive and environmental obstacles (genetic predispositions and/or policy decisions in the way children are taught to read).

What are the profiles of children who have dyslexia?

Returning to Rosie, she finds it hard to pronounce the words on the page, which affects her ability to understand the text. If she can read successfully, she is slow, and she struggles to remember the sounds of the letters correctly. However, her listening comprehension and vocabulary are appropriate for her age. Successful reading requires identifying letters, making letter-sound associations, creating phonic chunks, knowing the word meanings, making connections between the concepts, using effective strategies, asking questions, understanding the different genres, as well as many other skills.

The complexity involved in reading can be understood using the Simple View of Reading (SVoR) formula (Hoover and Tunmer 2020), which suggests that reading equals the product of decoding and comprehension ($R = D*C$):

- *Decoding*: using spelling-sound correspondences to map letter strings to sounds, for example 'c' 'a' 't' = 'cat' and whole-word recognition of familiar words (sight vocabulary).
- *Comprehension*: understanding reading and listening – for example, understanding that 'cat' is a small furry animal.

The updated version replaced C with LC, linguistic comprehension, to identify the wider skills involved in the processing and understanding of oral language at the word, sentence and discourse level (see Kilpatrick 2015). Rosie and many other children with dyslexia we have assessed do not present difficulties in linguistic comprehension as her scores on a standardised test of listening comprehension were within the average range. Learners who also present with difficulties in oral language skills are considered to have dyslexic difficulties and speech, language and communication needs (SLCN).

> *Activity*
> According to the SVoR formula, reading comprehension is the product of decoding and linguistic comprehension (RC = WR*LC) and not just a sum. This means if someone reads WR = 45 per cent of words in a text and understands (LC) 95 per cent, the overall reading comprehension (RC) is 42.7 per cent.
>
> Calculate the reading comprehension skill of a child who is 85 per cent accurate (WR) and understands (LC) 98 per cent of the text!

In another case, the first author (G.N.) assessed Tammy, whose listening comprehension score was within the below-average range (79 standard score (SS)). In addition, assessment of general ability revealed higher visual than verbal ability. To further check for SLCN, Tammy was assessed on a standardised test of grammar reception (Bishop 2003). Her score in this test was in the below-average range (78 SS). All these scores indicate that apart from dyslexia, Tammy might have an additional need in the language domain (SLCN). See Table 9.1 for a guide to interpreting the SS.

> *Activity*
> Difficulties in both literacy and language can co-occur. How easy do you think it is for a classroom teacher to spot these overlapping difficulties? Make a list of differences and similarities between children with literacy difficulties and language difficulties? Is it easy to say who has dyslexia and who has SLCNs?

Table 9.1 Guide to interpretation of standard scores

SS (range)	Descriptive label
131 or more	Well above average
116–130	Above average
111–115	High average
90–110	Mid Average
85–89	Low average
70–84	Below average
69 or less	Well below average

Note: The labels above are used to describe performance, although some manuals use different terms. The descriptive labels are often more easily understood by laypersons, and thus they facilitate the communication of test results.

Returning our attention to the SVoR, the initial decoding skill proposed by Hoover and Tunmer (2020) has been replaced by the broader term 'word recognition' (WR). This could be seen as an umbrella term that includes both sublexical (= phonological) and lexical (= orthographic) processes. Phonology refers to the organisation of sounds in language – that is, the different sounds and the way they combine to form speech. Orthography relates to the rules governing the written form of the language, for example, no words begin with <cc> in English. Both sublexical and lexical processes are needed to successfully read words (Niolaki et al. 2020b), especially for the English orthography, which has less straightforward letter-sound and sound-letter associations compared with more transparent orthographies such as Greek, Italian and Turkish (Seymour, Aro and Erskine 2003).

> *Activity*
> Think about how a decoding technique would help you to read words such as <have> and <save>. Similarly, try <yacht> and <part>!

Unsurprisingly, research has demonstrated that children with dyslexia might find it easier to read regular words like <leg> rather than irregular words like <yacht>. Children with difficulties in irregular word reading and no weaknesses in phonology are considered to have surface dyslexia. Such a case was presented by Castles (1996). Children with surface dyslexia tend to make more phonologically appropriate errors in reading and spelling (e.g. <night> can be spelled <nite>), as the sublexical route is not compromised and they might not have any difficulties in phonological ability. The latter is considered to be the skill whereby children are able to identify and manipulate speech sounds in words.

On the other hand, there are children with significant phonological difficulties who might use the lexical route to compensate for their sublexical difficulties (Hanley and Gard 1995). These learners can successfully read irregular words such as <yacht>, but they are unable to use their phonological decoding skills. They make errors in reading and spelling that are not phonologically appropriate (<night> could be spelled <knirte>). The mistakes they might make include omission, transposition, substitution or addition of letters (Spruhan et al. 2022).

> *Reflection*
> Have you met learners in your classroom with difficulties in phonological decoding (letter-sound associations) but who are good at irregular word reading? Have you ever worked with learners with the opposite profile – good at phonological decoding but with challenges in irregular word reading? How frequent are these profiles in our classrooms?

Figure 9.1 How do we read words? A depiction of the dual-route model of reading

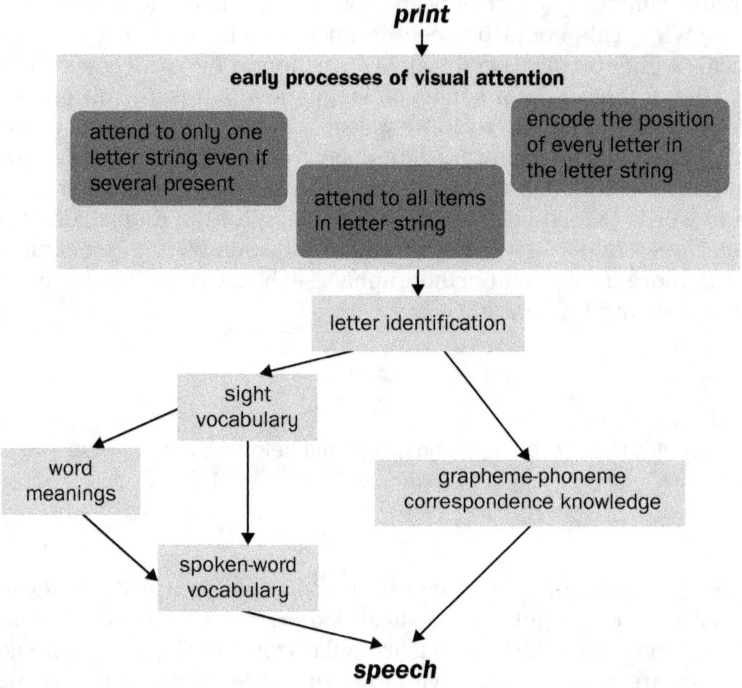

print

→ early processes of visual attention
- attend to only one letter string even if several present
- attend to all items in letter string
- encode the position of every letter in the letter string

↓ letter identification

→ sight vocabulary
→ grapheme-phoneme correspondence knowledge
→ word meanings
→ spoken-word vocabulary

speech

Adapted from Coltheart (2015: 108)

However, a large proportion of learners (Sprenger-Charolles et al. 2011) like Rosie will have difficulties with both processes, lexical (irregular word and familiar word reading) and sublexical (phonological decoding). Figure 9.1 presents a depiction of the dual-route model (Coltheart 2015), a model of how we read familiar as well as unfamiliar words. There are two routes after a child has identified the letters in a word. The sublexical route involves using phonological decoding skills to read. The lexical route, on the other hand, involves identifying stored words (sight vocabulary), and is supported by knowing what the words mean. Since this second route requires fewer phonological skills, it is faster. Rosie reads high-frequency regular and irregular words and pseudowords less accurately than her peers. See examples of items read in Table 9.2.

Aetiologies of unexpected reading difficulties

Many theories have been developed to explain reading difficulties. We agree with Pennington (2006) that a single deficit theory (which requires phonological and reading accuracy difficulties) cannot explain the spectrum of difficulties that learners with dyslexia display. Dyslexia should be considered

Table 9.2 Examples of words tapping the lexical and sublexical routes

Irregular words (primarily the lexical route)	Regular (both routes)	Made-up items (pseudowords) or real words never encountered before (primarily the sublexical route)
these	cup	sratnim
have	make	trouse

Note: The items in the table are similar to those in the single-word reading test, the Diagnostic Test of Word Reading Processes (FRiLL 2012), which was developed to identify strengths and weaknesses in lexical and sublexical processes.

as a spectrum of literacy difficulties that may need support (Snowling 2019). Several children might be missed or excluded only because they struggle with reading speed and spelling and not with reading accuracy and prose. Many individuals have difficulties beyond phonology, for example with memory (verbal, visual and working memory), visual attention span, and so on. Children with dyslexia may have problems remembering verbal instructions, times tables and visual information. The idea of a spectrum of difficulties can help educational psychologists, teachers and specialist dyslexia assessors to identify and support children who might not have a 'pure' dyslexic profile.

As we saw in Chapters 1 and 3, inclusion requires a systemic approach. A hybrid model proposed by Niolaki et al. (2020a) includes all aspects of development (biological, cognitive, behavioural, environmental and social/emotional) without adhering to a single stumbling block in any domain. There was no history of dyslexia or other specific learning difficulties in Rosie's family and her hearing and vision were typical. She did not present any visual processing difficulties, according to the optometrist. However, other children do. The profiles of individuals with dyslexia are diverse. Not everyone with dyslexia has visual problems or reports that the letters tend to move on the page. Frequently, when someone talks about dyslexia, they envision a child who confuses /b/ and /d/, but this is not always the case.

According to the hybrid model, it is not enough to explore difficulties and strengths in the cognitive, biological, environmental and behavioural domains. We also need to look at the often neglected emotional factors. A recent meta-analysis by Francis et al. (2019) demonstrated moderate links to anxiety and depression. A potential association could be low self-esteem in the academic domain due to reading difficulties. There is ample research evidence demonstrating strong links between low self-esteem and anxiety (Sowislo and Orth 2013). In a recent study, Negoita et al. (2022) found that individuals with dyslexia had high levels of anxiety and low feelings of self-compassion. This demonstrates that difficulties build up and in adulthood, these low feelings of self-worth do not mitigate, but can potentially affect not only emotional aspects such as self-compassion but even somatic aspects (i.e. high blood pressure and autoimmune diseases; Song et al. 2018). These links have not yet been thoroughly explored in relation to dyslexia.

We tend to focus our attention on challenges and ignore the incredible strengths individuals with dyslexia have. Rosie, like Stephanie, has significant strengths in visual ability. On the Diamonds subtask in the Wide Range Intelligence Test (Glutting, Adams and Heslow 2000), Rosie scored SS = 140, which places her performance in the high superior range, while her reading score in a single-word reading test (Wechsler 2017) was SS = 63 (i.e. in the well below average range). This highlights the importance of moving away from the deficit model and to start building a model that highlights strengths – a neuro-affirmative approach (see Chapter 1).

> *Activity*
> Based on the strengths one has, is it possible to develop an intervention programme? Think of classroom examples where you use the learner's strengths to teach concepts?

In 2013, we published a paper on an emergent bilingual girl, Eda, whose first language was English. Instead of building again on an already unsuccessful support programme that had targeted phonics, we used visual imagery and whole-word recognition (multisensory spelling strategies) and Eda improved significantly (Niolaki et al. 2014; see also Chapter 14).

So, what can be done?

Although identification has been considered by some to be discriminatory in the past, as traditional assessment and diagnosis locates difficulties within the child rather than broader society, we agree with Jordan, who argued 'that there could be no true inclusion that does not include the needs of all from the start' (1999: 29). Recognition of needs can provide the foundation for building a 'prosthetic environment' (Jordan 1999). 'Prosthetic environment' means that we offer the appropriate reasonable adjustments to help the child with dyslexia enjoy school on a par with their peers.

Several interventions have been designed for individuals with dyslexia; our own review includes evidence from randomised controlled trials and single-subject designs. As with any intervention aiming to support individuals with SEN, the main principle is not to fit the intervention to the individual. Frequently, a single intervention or approach is not enough. The educator needs to reflect by following a four-part cycle (assess, plan, do, review) (DfE/DoH 2015; see also Chapter 2).

One of the main approaches suggested based on the Rose review (2009), and implemented by many schools in the UK and the USA, is the response to intervention (RTI) model. This is a multi-layered approach dependent on the needs of each individual. Learners with more severe reading needs will be placed into intensive interventions in small groups (Tier or Wave 2) or one-to-one support (Tier or Wave 3). However, evidence from the UK and USA indicates that RTI may not be the best course of action, as evidence for effectiveness is limited (Miciak and Fletcher 2020). Miciak and Fletcher suggest the possible reason for this could be a mismatch between the learners' needs and the reading intervention provided. The school that learners attended and the school's policy for identification and support can also impact on the success of the intervention. The intervention lasted a short time, specifically the one administered in the UK (with a small effect size in return), and the point in time of the delivery of the intervention (end of Year 6) was deemed to be an additional negative factor (Gorard, Siddiqui and See 2014). Although the evidence is inconclusive, one should not ignore the strengths of RTI, such as identifying learners' needs, and evaluation and continuous reflection, to determine adjustment. Also, the studies reported in Miciak and Fletcher were school based, so the findings are ecologically valid.

Some recent metanalytic reviews have highlighted the effect of how valid small-group interventions are in closing the attainment gap in reading, spelling and writing. All reviews highlight the importance of using approaches that simultaneously target phonics, orthography and morphological instruction. These can have a moderate to high effect on spelling when coupled with explicit teaching (Galuschka et al. 2020). Similar findings were reported in a single case study targeting all three concepts of literacy using direct and explicit instruction combined with guided discovery (Niolaki et al. 2021).

There has been much discussion as to whether it is preferable for children with dyslexia to use discovery learning or avoid it as a teaching strategy. Weakland stresses that 'discovery learning should be avoided and instead provide the learners with the shortest paths possible to learning' (2021: 262). This is accomplished via explicit and direct instruction coupled with the teacher modelling the taught/learned concept. This is included in best teaching practices for those with dyslexia, such as breaking the new learning into simple and discrete parts; specifically, telling and showing the students what to do and what they need to know, re-teaching and re-modelling combined with multisensory techniques, and providing opportunities for overlearning and giving immediate corrective feedback. Such questions as 'let's discover what patterns exist in specific words' should be avoided (Weakland 2021). Weakland also highlights the importance of repetition (actively practising the same skill in multiple ways) and distributed practice skills, essential for automaticity and generalisation. Distributed practice is the opportunity to practise the skill in different environments or tasks. Practising a specific letter-sound correspondence in reading, spelling and writing is a good example.

For interventions to be ecologically valid and useful, they should be tailored around the learner's specific interests. Interventions must treat literacy as an integral whole, simultaneously targeting reading (guided and independent), spelling, grammar, syntax and writing (Niolaki et al. 2021).

In another metanalytic review targeting writing in students with learning disabilities in Grades 1–12, Gillespie and Graham (2014) found that explicit and direct modelling of strategies for planning, revising and editing, use of a dictaphone to aid memory, the setting of goals linked to what the learners expect to achieve, and being explicitly aware of the writing processes and expectations (metawriting skills) had a positive impact on overall writing quality. The researchers also concluded that several limitations should be addressed in future studies, which is also valid for most intervention studies involving students with dyslexia. For example, the design of 'true experiments that control for instructor effects, report reliability of outcome measures, and provide treatment fidelity data' (Gillespie and Graham 2014: 467) should be the norm and not the exception.

We are aware that we started our presentation of metanalytic reviews by looking at spelling, then writing and finally reading. This was purposefully done because there is a tendency to emphasise reading and forget the importance of spelling and writing. There is now strong evidence that spelling is much more difficult to support due to its firm reliance on memory of the sequence of letters in a word. Therefore, spelling is harder to conquer due to its multi-layered arbitrary representation. Perfetti (2007) characterises spelling as 'idealised' due to the many cognitive processes involved in this skill (sequencing, memory and pattern perception). If any of these processes fails, the representation of the word in our mental dictionary will be of low quality, and as a result, this will produce an error.

This is not the case with reading. Owing to context and recognition of some of the letters (the ones positioned at the most salient parts of the word; Pitchford, Ledgeway and Masterson 2008), one can effectively decode and pronounce the word with almost 99 per cent accuracy. In a large-scale study looking at spelling and reading of regular and irregular words and pseudowords in UK primary school children, Niolaki et al. (2019) found that for reading, the lexicality effect (reading real words better than pseudowords) is achieved in Year 2, whereas for spelling this occurs in Year 5. This confirms that spelling as a written-production task is more complicated than reading. Our findings (Figure 9.2) accentuate the need to focus on this neglected aspect of literacy (spelling). As Pan et al. say, 'in the early 21st century ... scepticism about the importance of spelling has grown, some schools have de-emphasised or abandoned spelling instruction altogether' (2021: 1). Also, there is strong evidence that spelling interventions can also facilitate reading (Graham and Santangelo 2014).

Al Otaiba et al. (2022) reviewed 14 metanalyses and systematic reviews that explored the effects of reading and writing interventions for primary age children with dyslexia and other reading difficulties. Their findings confirm that interventions that combine reading and spelling instruction are the most promising. The length of the intervention also seems to have a powerful impact. Other factors identified as important are small-group or one-to-one interventions combined with explicit and systematic teaching, addressing code-focused reading skills (phonemic awareness, letter-sound knowledge and whole-word recognition). Interventions that target only meaning (reading

Figure 9.2 Mean spelling (a) and reading (b) accuracy for irregular and regular words and pseudowords by year group (max. correct spelling 36 items and reading 30 items)

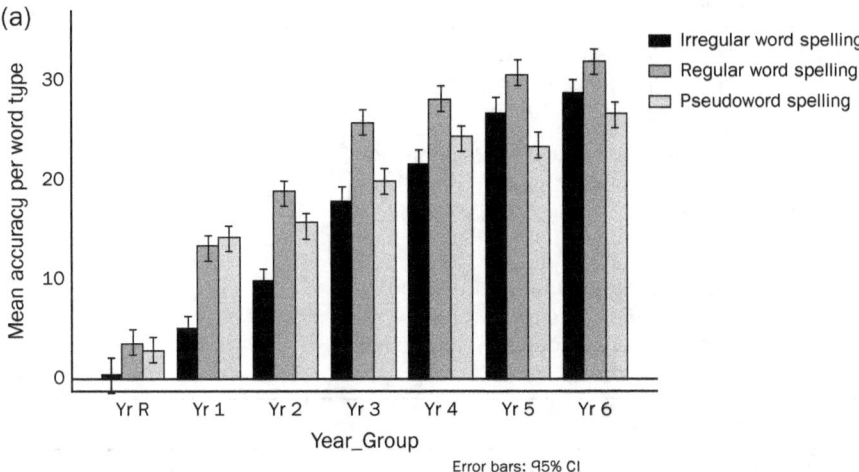

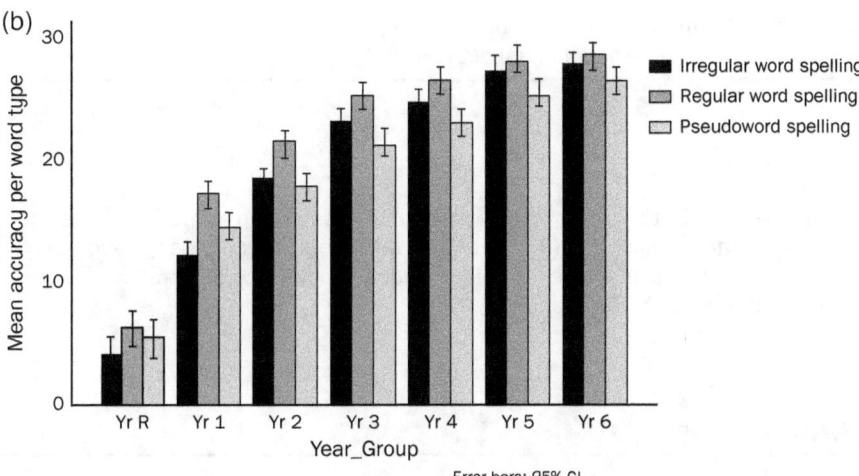

and listening comprehension, vocabulary and oral expression) were less successful for reading.

Having the specialist and evidence-informed knowledge, as mentioned earlier, the specialist dyslexia teacher (SDT) is able to design the learner's profile using a similar table of strengths and challenges as in Table 9.3. This summary profile will help the SDT tailor a bespoke intervention that will target the specific needs that the child with dyslexia has in literacy but also the social and emotional areas of need.

Table 9.3 Table of strengths and challenges

Summary profile		
a. Behavioural: reading, spelling, phonics, orthography, morphology, syntax, handwriting … (you can always add to the list)	Strengths	Challenges
b. Cognitive: memory, attention, perception, concentration, phonological ability, processing, speed/automaticity … (you can always add to the list)		
c. Social/emotional: temperament, attachment, self-esteem, self-efficacy, copy strategies, self-compassion, group dynamics, mindfulness … (you can always add to the list)		
Proposed intervention		
SMART long-term aims linked to behavioural, cognitive and social/emotional aspects		
SMART short-term aims linked to behavioural, cognitive and social/emotional aspects		

Activity
Use Table 9.3 to design an appropriate intervention based on Rosie's strengths and challenges (Box 9.1) that will target not only behavioural and cognitive aspects but also social/emotional ones according to the hybrid model proposed in this chapter.

Conclusions

The aim of this chapter was to provide an applied and theoretical understanding of dyslexia, bringing together evidence from psychology and education in an inclusive context. Challenges defining dyslexia and an understanding of needs were unpicked. Our review included randomised control trials and single-subject designs; we presented their potencies and shortcomings as we believe their findings can contribute equally to everyday classroom practice. We hope that the synthesis provided here can support and empower the teacher, the specialist dyslexia assessor and the educational psychologist during the challenging journey of recognition of needs and support. Although we focused our attention on the individual with dyslexia, the proposed teaching strategies can be used for the benefit of all the children in the classroom. Modelling, explicit teaching, giving time to the learners to think and respond, scaffolding the learning and breaking it down into smaller chunks, all are helpful for any learner, not only the child with dyslexia. Therefore, by adopting a dyslexia-friendly teaching style, everyone in the classroom can benefit.

Resources
The following further reading and web resources will help you to find out more about dyslexia.

American Psychiatric Association (APA) (2013) *Diagnostic and Statistical manual of Mental Disorders: DSM-5*. Washington, DC: APA.

Bishop, D. (2014) *My thoughts on the dyslexia debate*. Available at: http://deevybee.blogspot.co.uk/2014/03/my-thoughts-on-dyslexia-debate.html (accessed 8 September 2022).

British Dyslexia Association (2010) *What is dyslexia?* Available at: https://www.bdadyslexia.org.uk/dyslexia/about-dyslexia/what-is-dyslexia (accessed 14 March 2022).

Castles, A., Wheldall K. and Nayton, M. (2014) Should we do away with 'dyslexia'?, *The Conversation*, 19 March. Available at: https://theconversation.com/should-we-do-away-with-dyslexia-24027 (accessed 15 May 2022).

Department for Education (DfE) (2019) *National statistics: National Curriculum assessments at Key Stage 2 in England* (interim). Available at: https://www.gov.uk/government/publications/national-curriculum-assessments-key-stage-2-2019-interim/national-curriculum-assessments-at-key-stage-2-in-england-2019-interim (accessed 15 May 2022).

Department for Education and Department of Health (DfE/DoH) (2015) *Special Educational Needs and Disability Code of Practice: 0 to 25 years*. London: DfE. Available at: https://www.gov.uk/government/uploads/system/uploads/attachment_data/file/398815/SEND_Code_of_Practice_January_2015.pdf (accessed 15 May 2022).

Rose, J. (2009) *Independent Review of the Primary Curriculum: Final Report*. London: DCSF Publications. Available at: http://www.educationengland.org.uk/documents/pdfs/2009-IRPC-final-report.pdf (accessed 15 May 2022).

Weakland, M. (2021) *How to Prevent Reading Difficulties, Grades PreK–3: Proactive Practices for Teaching Young Children to Read*. Thousand Oaks, CA: Corwin Press (many links to YouTube resources are included in this book).

https://www.bdadyslexia.org.uk/

https://dyslexiaida.org/

https://dyslexiaaction.org.uk/

https://dyslexiaguild.org.uk/

https://www.patoss-dyslexia.org/

References

Al Otaiba, S., McMaster, K., Wanzek, J. and Zaru, M.W. (2022) What we know and need to know about literacy interventions for elementary students with reading difficulties and disabilities, including dyslexia, *Reading Research Quarterly*, 58 (2): 313–332.

American Psychiatric Association (APA) (2013) *Diagnostic and Statistical manual of Mental Disorders: DSM-5*. Washington, DC: APA.

Bishop, D. (2003) *Test for Reception of Grammar*, 2nd edition (TROG-2). London: Pearson Assessment.

Bishop, D. (2014) *My thoughts on the dyslexia debate*. Available at: http://deevybee.blogspot.co.uk/2014/03/my-thoughts-on-dyslexia-debate.html (accessed 8 September 2022).

Castles, A. (1996) Cognitive correlates of developmental surface dyslexia: a single case study, *Cognitive Neuropsychology*, 13 (1): 25–50.

Castles, A., Wheldall K. and Nayton, M. (2014) Should we do away with 'dyslexia'?, *The Conversation*, 19 March. Available at: https://theconversation.com/should-we-do-away-with-dyslexia-24027 (accessed 15 May 2022).

Clark, C. and Teravainen-Goff, A. (2020) *Children and young people's reading in 2019: findings from our Annual Literacy Survey*. Research Report. London: National Literacy Trust. Available at: https://cdn.literacytrust.org.uk/media/documents/Reading_trends_in_2019_-_Final.pdf

Coltheart, M. (2015) What kinds of things cause children's reading difficulties?, *Australian Journal of Learning Difficulties*, 20 (2): 103–112.

Dehaene, S. (2009) *Reading in the Brain: The New Science of How We Read*. London: Penguin Viking.

Department for Education (DfE) (2019) *National statistics: National Curriculum assessments at Key Stage 2 in England* (interim). Available at: https://www.gov.uk/government/publications/national-curriculum-assessments-key-stage-2-2019-interim/national-curriculum-assessments-at-key-stage-2-in-england-2019-interim (accessed 15 May 2022).

Department for Education and Department of Health (DfE/DoH) (2015) *Special Educational Needs and Disability Code of Practice: 0 to 25 years*. London: DfE. Available at: https://www.gov.uk/government/uploads/system/uploads/attachment_data/file/398815/SEND_Code_of_Practice_January_2015.pdf (accessed 15 May 2022).

Elliott, J.G. and Grigorenko, E.L. (2014) *The Dyslexia Debate*, Cambridge Studies in Cognitive and Perceptual Development #14. Cambridge: Cambridge University Press.

Forum for Research into Language and Literacy (FRiLL) (2012) *Diagnostic Test of Word Reading Processes (DTWRP)*. London: GL Assessment.

Francis, D.A., Caruana, N., Hudson, J.L. and McArthur, G. (2019) The association between poor reading and internalising problems: a systematic review and meta-analysis, *Clinical Psychology Review*, 67: 45–60.

Friend, A., DeFries, J.C. and Olson, R.K. (2008) Parental education moderates genetic influences on reading disability, *Psychological Science*, 19 (11): 1124–1130.

Galuschka, K., Görgen, R., Kalmar, J., Haberstroh, S., Schalmz, X. and Schulte-Körne, G. (2020) Effectiveness of spelling interventions for learners with dyslexia: a meta-analysis and systematic review, *Educational Psychologist*, 55 (1): 1–20.

Gillespie, A. and Graham, S. (2014) A meta-analysis of writing interventions for students with learning disabilities, *Exceptional Children*, 80 (4): 454–473.

Glutting, J., Adams, W. and Heslow, D. (2000) *Wide Range Intelligence Test (WRIT)*. Lutz, FL: Psychological Assessment Resources.

Gorard, S., Siddiqui, N. and See, B.H. (2014) *Response to intervention: Evaluation report and executive summary.* London: Education Endowment Foundation. Available at: https://educationendowmentfoundation.org.uk/public/files/Projects/Evaluation_Reports/EEF_Project_Report_ResponseToIntervention.pdf

Graham, S. and Santangelo, T. (2014) Does spelling instruction make students better spellers, readers, and writers? A meta-analytic review, *Reading and Writing*, 27 (9): 1703–1743.

Hanley, J.R. and Gard, F. (1995) A dissociation between developmental surface and phonological dyslexia in two undergraduate students, *Neuropsychologia*, 33 (7): 909–914.

Hinshelwood, J. (1900) Congenital word-blindness, *The Lancet*, 155 (4004): 1506–1508.

Hoover, W.A. and Tunmer, W.E. (2020) The cognitive foundations of reading acquisition, in *The Cognitive Foundations of Reading and its Acquisition*. Springer: Cham.

Jordan, R. (1999) *Autistic Spectrum Disorders: An Introductory Handbook for Practitioners.* London: David Fulton.

Kilpatrick, D.A. (2015) *Essentials of Assessing, Preventing, and Overcoming Reading Difficulties.* London: Wiley.

Kohnen, S., Nickels, L., Brunsdon, R. and Coltheart, M. (2008) Patterns of generalisation after treating sub-lexical spelling deficits in a child with mixed dysgraphia, *Journal of Research in Reading*, 31 (1): 157–177.

Miciak, J. and Fletcher, J.M. (2020) The critical role of instructional response for identifying dyslexia and other learning disabilities, *Journal of Learning Disabilities*, 53 (5): 343–353.

Morgan, W.P. (1896) A case of congenital word blindness, *British Medical Journal*, 2 (1871): 1378. Available at: https://www.ncbi.nlm.nih.gov/pmc/articles/PMC2510936/?page=1.

Negoita A., Niolaki, G., Terzopoulos, A., Vousden, J. and Masterson, J. (2022) *The dyslexic jigsaw: beyond dyslexia, the role of self-compassion in adults with dyslexia.* Paper presented to the Experimental Psychology Society Meeting, Keele University, 30–31 March.

Niolaki, G.Z. and Masterson, J. (2013) Intervention for a multi-character processing deficit in a Greek-speaking child with surface dyslexia, *Cognitive Neuropsychology*, 30 (4): 208–232.

Niolaki, G.Z., Masterson, J. and Terzopoulos, A.R. (2014) Spelling improvement through letter-sound and whole-word training in two multilingual Greek- and English- speaking children, *Multilingual Education*, 4: 20. Available at: https://doi.org/10.1186/s13616-014-0020-3

Niolaki, G., Vousden, J., Terzopoulos, A.R. and Taylor, L. (2019) *Spelling predictors in a large cross-sectional study investigating the role of phonological ability and rapid naming.* Paper presented to the 19th European Conference on Developmental Psychology, Athens, 29 August–1 September.

Niolaki, G., Taylor, L.M., Terzopoulos, A.R. and Davies, R. (2020a) Literacy difficulties in higher education: identifying students' needs with a hybrid model, *Educational & Child Psychology*, 37 (2): 80–92.

Niolaki, G.Z., Vousden, J., Terzopoulos, A.R., Taylor, L.M., Sephton, S. and Masterson, J. (2020b) Predictors of single word spelling in English speaking children: a cross sectional study, *Journal of Research in Reading*, 43 (4): 577–596.

Niolaki, G., Vousden, J., Terzopoulos, A.R., Taylor, L. and Masterson, J. (2021) A linguistic awareness intervention targeting spelling and written expression in a 10-year-old dyslexic child, *Preschool & Primary Education*, 9 (1): 1–27.

Olson, R.K., Keenan, J.M., Byrne, B. and Samuelsson, S. (2014) Why do children differ in their development of reading and related skills?, *Scientific Studies of Reading*, 18 (1): 38–54.

Orton, J.L. (1966) The Orton-Gillingham approach, in J. Money (ed.), *The Disabled Reader: Education of the Dyslexic Child*. Baltimore, MD: Johns Hopkins University Press.

Pan, S.C., Rickard, T.C. and Bjork, R.A. (2021) Does spelling still matter – and if so, how should it be taught? Perspectives from contemporary and historical research, *Educational Psychology Review*, 33 (4): 1523–1552.

Pennington, B.F. (2006) From single to multiple deficit models of developmental disorders, *Cognition*, 101 (2): 385–413.

Perfetti, C. (2007) Reading ability: lexical quality to comprehension, *Scientific Studies of Reading*, 11 (4): 357–383.

Peyrin, C., Lallier, M., Démonet, J., Pernet, C., Baciu, M., Le Bas, J.F. et al. (2012) Neural dissociation of phonological and visual attention span disorders in developmental dyslexia: FMRI evidence from two case reports, *Brain & Language*, 120 (3): 381–394.

Pitchford, N.J., Ledgeway, T. and Masterson, J. (2008) Effect of orthographic processes on letter position encoding, *Journal of Research in Reading*, 31 (1): 97–116.

Rose, J. (2009) *Independent Review of the Primary Curriculum: Final Report*. London: DCSF Publications. Available at: http://www.educationengland.org.uk/documents/pdfs/2009-IRPC-final-report.pdf (accessed 15 May 2022).

Seymour, P.H., Aro, M. and Erskine, J.M. (2003) Foundation literacy acquisition in European orthographies, *British Journal of Psychology*, 94 (2): 143–174.

Shaywitz, S.E., Shaywitz, J.E. and Shaywitz, B.A. (2021) Dyslexia in the 21st century, *Current Opinion in Psychiatry*, 34 (2): 80–86.

Snowling, M.J. (2019) *Dyslexia: A Very Short Introduction*. Oxford: Oxford University Press.

Snowling, M.J., Hulme, C. and Nation, K. (2020) Defining and understanding dyslexia: past, present and future, *Oxford Review of Education*, 46 (4): 501–513.

Song, H., Fang, F., Tomasson, G., Arnberg, F.K., Mataix-Cols, D., Fernández de la Cruz, L. et al. (2018) Association of stress-related disorders with subsequent autoimmune disease, *Journal of the American Medical Association*, 319 (23): 2388–2400.

Sowislo, J.F. and Orth, U. (2013) Does low self-esteem predict depression and anxiety? A meta-analysis of longitudinal studies, *Psychological Bulletin*, 139 (1): 213–240.

Sprenger-Charolles, L., Siegel, L.S., Jiménez, J.E. and Ziegler, C. (2011) Prevalence and reliability of phonological, surface, and mixed profiles in dyslexia: a review of studies conducted in languages varying in orthographic depth, *Scientific Studies of Reading*, 15 (6): 498–521.

Spruhan, H., Niolaki, G., Vousden, J., Terzopoulos, L. and Masterson, J. (2022) Spelling performance of 6- and 8-year-old Irish children: is it < analice > or <analyze>?, *Journal of Educational Research*, 115 (1): 87–97.

Stanovich, K. (1994) Annotation: does dyslexia exist?, *Journal of Child Psychology and Psychiatry*, 35 (4): 579–595.

Weakland, M. (2021) *How to Prevent Reading Difficulties, Grades PreK–3: Proactive Practices for Teaching Young Children to Read*. Thousand Oaks, CA: Corwin Press

Wechsler, D. (2017) *Wechsler Individual Achievement Test, Third UK Edition* (WIAT-III UK). London: Pearson.

10 Why are circles so smart? Because they have 360 degrees!

Donna-Lynn Shepherd

By the end of this chapter, you will be able to:

- understand how mathematical skills and understanding develop
- identify learners experiencing maths difficulties
- understand, apply and critically evaluate psychological models of numerical cognition, developmental dyscalculia and maths anxiety
- create and implement inclusive, evidence-based approaches to support all maths learners.

Numeracy is arguably more important than literacy (Parsons and Bynner 2005; Geary 2015; OECD 2018). Numeracy refers to our ability to understand and confidently use basic maths in daily life (National Numeracy 2022), and is just one aspect of the extensive field of mathematics which includes topics such as algebra, geometry, statistics and calculus. Successful financial, physical and mental health outcomes – even avoiding prison! – are all positively correlated with numeracy (Parsons and Bynner 2005; Ritchie and Bates 2013). Being numerate is important for having a good life (Box 10.1).

Box 10.1 'We are all numbers people' (Fuller 2019)

Today, have you:

- bought something?
- checked the weather/time/date?
- been to the gym or played a sport?
- followed a recipe?
- checked your driving speed?

- used time or direction words (left, right, in, over, under, later, now, soon)?
- watched the news?
- counted the weeks or days until your holiday (always too many!)?

These all involve maths. Doing even one (including reading this sentence) makes you a numbers person. Welcome to the club!

Despite the undeniable importance of numeracy, many people have less understanding and confidence – and fewer strategies – to tackle mathematical difficulties (Swars, Daane and Giesen 2006; Costa, Outhwaite and Van Herwegen 2021; Ferrie 2022). This chapter aims to address this gap. It begins with a brief discussion of mathematical development, explains how to identify pupils who may be experiencing mathematical learning difficulties, presents psychological models to explain these difficulties, and offers suggestions for support. The chapter is written from the perspective of inclusion and emphasises the importance of identifying and removing barriers to learning and making maths accessible for everyone.

Mathematical development

Why were the Romans the best civilisation at algebra? Because x was always ten!

[Those of you who are not 'mathsphiles' may be surprised to know there are many freely available websites with lists of (very funny) maths jokes. Jokes in this chapter have been adapted from: https://happynumbers.com/blog/30-funniest-jokes-for-math-teachers/ and http://www.mrbartonmaths.com/jokes/.]

Mathematical Development consists of children's progressive development of concepts, skills, knowledge and understanding in:

- solving mathematical problems
- communicating mathematically
- reasoning mathematically. (DCELLS 2008: 5)

Maths learning is cumulative; each concept/skill must be secure before moving on (De Smedt, Verschaffel and Ghesquière 2009; Fuchs et al. 2010).

Mathematical development begins with number sense – an understanding of basic number concepts (e.g. an intuitive grasp of the 'two-ness' of two). Although debated (Wilkey and Ansari 2020), number sense is assumed to be innate because it is evident in newborns and not limited to humans

(Dehaene 2001; Xu, Spelke and Goddard 2005; Caicoya et al. 2021) – even fish count! (Butterworth 2022)

Early skills include subitising (recognising small numbers without counting, e.g. that • • • is 3), counting, digit recognition, magnitude comparison (estimating, without counting, which amount is larger), mapping quantities to number symbols and vice versa. Between the ages of 1 and 7, children learn the count sequence (stable order principle) and other counting principles: for example, one-to-one principle (count each item only once); cardinal word principle (the final count number gives the set size); order irrelevance principle (the order in which items are counted is irrelevant) (Gelman and Gallistel 1978; Dowker 2008). Recent research (Lyons and Ansari 2015; Cahoon, Gilmore and Simms 2021) has shown that order processing – the ability to order numbers according to their relative size – is another important feature (also see Box 10.2).

Box 10.2   Deepen your understanding

Camilla Gilmore explains the complexities of learning maths here:
https://www.youtube.com/watch?v=RMPM1yADsyY

As children progress through primary school, they develop fluency in retrieving and applying number facts (number bonds, times tables), learn the four arithmetic operations, and develop calculation and problem-solving strategies. In secondary school, students learn to solve complex problems such as applying the Pythagorean theorem in three dimensions. This shift from simple counting to deeper, conceptual understanding and sophisticated mathematical reasoning depends on cognitive, biological and environmental factors (see Table 10.1).

Influence and interaction

The influence – and interaction – of cognitive, biological and environmental factors implies that challenges in any one area can lead to maths difficulties. For example, if a child grows up in a society where maths is not considered important, even if the child is developmentally ready and has good access to high-quality teaching, attainment may be lower than if the child grew up in a culture where maths is respected and valued. This is a particular problem in the UK because being 'bad at maths' is culturally acceptable and even considered a badge of honour (Brewer 2018). This dismissive mindset and negative relationship to maths has resulted in less focus on mathematical development and learning difficulties, which, in turn, has contributed to a significant lag in our understanding (Morsanyi et al. 2018; Ferrie 2022; see Box 10.3). As an excellent example, consider the position of this chapter within the book – it is definitely not in pole position!

Table 10.1 Factors affecting mathematical development

Domain	Description
Cognitive	Includes executive function (working memory, attention, processing speed and inhibition) (Bull and Scerif 2001; Gilmore et al. 2013; Caviola et al. 2020; Gordon et al. 2022) and developmental readiness (Piaget [1936] 1977). For example, although four-year-olds could be taught to chant the Pythagorean theorem as 'A squared plus B squared equals C squared' (much as they learn nursery rhymes), until they have reached an appropriate stage of cognitive development, they will not be able to understand or apply it. Cognitive difficulties, such as sustaining attention or understanding mathematical relationships (e.g. knowing that division is the inverse of multiplication), are highly likely to affect mathematical development.
Biological	Includes genetics, brain structure and neurological functioning. Although the link between specific genes and mathematical learning difficulties is not well understood (Carvalho et al. 2014; Davis et al. 2014; Peters and Ansari 2019), difficulties seem to run in families (Shalev et al. 2001).
	There is strong evidence that the intraparietal sulcus (IPS) plays a role in maths (Dehaene et al. 2003; Schel and Klingberg 2017). Some studies have found structural and/or functional differences in the IPS of individuals with mathematical learning difficulties when compared with their typical peers (Molko et al. 2003; Kaufmann et al. 2009; Roell et al. 2021).
Environmental	Includes educational experiences, the home learning environment (HLE) and cultural attitudes to maths. These have all been found to influence mathematical outcomes. For example: 1 Interactions with more confident and knowledgeable people who can scaffold children's learning (Vygotsky [1934] 1986). This shows the importance of high-quality teaching (Winheller, Hattie and Brown 2013) and places maths learning in a social context. 2 A favourable HLE, especially in the early years (Benavides-Varela et al. 2016). The interest, guidance and support of a child's family, irrespective of the family's socio-economic circumstances, are positively correlated with maths attainment (Sammons et al. 2015; Purpura et al. 2020). 3 A culture that values and supports mathematics (Hu, Leung and Teng 2018). Pupils' learning is influenced by interactions with their peers, extended family and the wider community.

> **Box 10.3 'Bad' at maths**
>
> My parent/carer and student consultation evenings are full of comments like, 'They take after me – I was always rubbish at maths!' accompanied by an apologetic laugh and shrug of the shoulders. Many colleagues, including teachers, teaching assistants and school leaders express their dislike of, and 'badness' at, maths (if I was paid every time someone told me they are 'no good' at maths, I would be very rich!).
>
> Consider the impact this may have on students. How could we encourage parents/carers and school staff to develop and demonstrate more positive behaviours, emotions and attitudes to maths? What difference might this make?

Identifying learners with mathematical learning difficulties, developmental dyscalculia and maths anxiety

Never argue with 90-degree angles – *they're always right*!

Mathematical learning difficulties

Mathematical learning difficulties (MLD) are exactly that – difficulties with learning maths. They may occur across all areas of maths, in response to a specific maths topic (e.g. fractions), or result from another difficulty or difference (e.g. Down syndrome, foetal alcohol spectrum disorder). For example, pupils with attention deficit hyperactivity disorder (ADHD) may have lower maths attainment than their peers because they struggle to focus in lessons rather than because of a specific maths difficulty. The Special Educational Needs and Disability Code of practice (DfE/DoH 2015) stresses the importance of using the graduated approach to determine a child's specific barrier(s) to learning before attributing cause(s) or implementing support.

Developmental dyscalculia

Developmental dyscalculia (DD) is a learning difficulty specific to maths. For learners with DD, difficulties persist despite appropriate educational opportunities, high-quality teaching and support. Some researchers suggest DD represents more (and more extreme) difficulties on a spectrum (Mammarella et al. 2021). Others view DD as a qualitative difference: a different way of processing numbers (Butterworth, Varma and Laurillard 2011). Educators and parents will recognise learners with DD as those with little understanding of number and whose progress lags significantly behind their peers (see Table 10.2).

A key challenge is that different cut-off points (e.g. WHO 2021; APA 2022; also see Box 10.4) are used, which makes diagnosis and interpreting research difficult. Diagnostic criteria usually include:

- performing significantly below age-matched peers on standardised maths assessments (often below the 10th percentile)
- behavioural differences (using early strategies, such as finger-counting, for much longer than expected)
- difficulties cannot be explained by other factors, such as cognitive delay/difficulties or environmental factors (e.g. extended absence from school)
- difficulties persist over time (at least 6 months).

> **Box 10.4   What is dyscalculia?**
>
> Watch Daniel Ansari's four-minute description here:
> https://www.youtube.com/watch?v=GRJS-jeZ7Is

Table 10.2 Difficulties experienced by individuals with developmental dyscalculia

Difficulties with …	Looks like …
… subitising	… counting an array of 3 dots rather than just 'knowing' there are 3
… using advanced counting procedures to solve simple arithmetic problems (e.g. starting with the larger number and counting on)	… when solving 5 + 2, counting from 1 up to 5 first, then counting on another 2 … may continue to count on fingers for much longer than their peers
… decade numbers: omitting/crossing boundaries, especially when counting backwards	… may count: 88, 89, 91 or 43, 42, 41, 42
… discriminating between numbers that sound similar	… may confuse 'teen' and 'ty' (e.g. 18 and 80)
… retrieving arithmetic facts from memory	… may not know times tables or other age-appropriate number facts

(continued)

Table 10.2 (Continued)

Difficulties with ...	Looks like ...
... estimating quantity	... unsure whether a pencil weighs 10 g or 10 kg
... understanding the place-value system	... in primary school, difficulty identifying tens, hundreds and thousands and correctly lining digits up for column addition or subtraction ... beyond primary school, being unable to say which is more: 0.1 vs. 0.015 (may say 0.015 is bigger because 15 is bigger than 1)
... understanding mathematical procedures and concepts	... struggle to apply prior knowledge of triangles and rectangles to understand why the area of a triangle is half the area of the associated rectangle (may calculate the area of a triangle as base times height without halving it)
... decomposing problems into smaller steps	... 'If a year group has 35 girls and 75 boys, what percentage of the students are girls?' Students with DD might not break the problem down into first finding the total number of students and then calculating the percentage of girls
... decomposing and rearranging numbers	... to solve 26 + 15, may not know how to decompose the numbers into tens (20 + 10 = 30), ones (6 + 5 = 11), and then combine them (30 + 11 = 41)
... time, especially reading analogue clocks	... may confuse the hour and minute hands, e.g. read 1:15 as 3:05 (and write the time as 3:5 or 3:50) ... may often be late; if there is no access to a digital clock, older children and young people may find an excuse not to give the time or may repeatedly ask the time (or 'how long is left?') during lessons
... judging whether answers are 'sensible'	... a Year 5 pupil (age 9–10) might guess that 20 × 30 = 60 instead of 600 (difficulty understanding place value) ... a Year 10 student (age 14–15) might not know whether the distance from London to Brighton is 60 or 600 miles – even if they live in one of those cities (difficulty estimating)

Prevalence and co-occurrence

Estimates of the prevalence of MLD are as high as 22 per cent (around 6–7 children in every class of 30; Kaufmann et al. 2013) and around 6 per cent for DD (about 1–2 pupils in every class of 30; Morsanyi et al. 2018; also see Box 10.5). Co-occurrence with other learning difficulties (especially dyslexia, ADHD and dyspraxia) is reported to be common (Moll et al. 2014) and more frequent than would be expected by chance (Peters and Ansari 2019).

> **Box 10.5 What is it like to have dyscalculia?**
>
> Watch BBC financial expert Fiona Bains talking about having DD:
> https://twitter.com/BBCMorningLive/status/1526949642142990336

Maths anxiety

Maths anxiety results from individuals' feelings about maths rather than challenges with the subject itself. A simple definition is 'a state of discomfort caused by performing mathematical tasks' (Devine et al. 2012: 2), although the fear (some say terror) associated with maths anxiety can be debilitating. Maths anxiety can develop at a very young age (Cargnelutti, Tomasetto and Passolunghi 2017), influences maths performance (Ashcraft and Moore 2009), and has important implications for mathematical development, education and adult functioning (Dowker, Sarkar and Looi 2016). Although prevalence estimates vary considerably, the latest Programme for International Student Assessment (PISA) results found 60 per cent of students expressed anxiety about maths (OECD 2018; also see Box 10.6).

> **Box 10.6 Case study: Will**
>
> Seventeen-year-old Will was enjoying his psychology A-level and achieving well until the research methods topic. During one lesson, students practised calculating basic statistics. Will panicked when he realised he had no idea how to start the set task. He became so anxious, he made up an excuse to leave the lesson early. Consider how maths anxiety might affect a learner's education, career choices and personal life.

Psychological models of numerical cognition, developmental dyscalculia and mathematics anxiety

Why was the maths book so sad? *Because it had so many problems*!

Numerical cognition

Models of numerical cognition help researchers and practitioners predict and explain mathematical behaviours. The best-known is Dehaene's (1992) triple code model (TCM). Dehaene and Cohen (1991) observed that in individuals with brain injuries, not all mathematical capabilities were equally affected — suggesting number is processed using different codes and routes.

Dehaene (1992) proposed three number codes that can each be transcoded (mapped) to any of the others:

- two symbolic, non-semantic codes that include verbal number words and visual Arabic digits
- one non-symbolic, semantic analogue magnitude (size/quantity) code,

and two processing routes, selected depending on the task and output requirements:

- an exact number system using memory and symbols (knowing that 3 + 2 = 5 exactly)
- an approximate number system using representations of magnitude (estimating that 360 + 430 will be around 800 but not 80 or 8000).

Difficulties with transcoding and/or either of the processing routes predict maths difficulties. For example, the TCM explains why an individual might be able to know which of two quantities is larger, match counting names to written digits, but not be able to work out 3 + 2. There is both support for and debate around the model (Siemann and Petermann 2018; Skagenholt et al. 2018; Malone et al. 2019).

Developmental dyscalculia

There is no agreed model of DD. The key distinction between the three main hypotheses concerns the origins of the difficulties.

The domain-specific hypothesis

The domain-specific hypothesis refers to a fundamental difficulty specific to understanding, representing and/or processing number (Landerl, Bevan and Butterworth 2004; Butterworth et al. 2011). Some researchers (Piazza et al. 2010; Mazzocco, Feigenson and Halberda 2011) have suggested that number sense difficulties underpin DD. Others (Mussolin, Mejias and Noël 2010; De Smedt et al. 2013) propose that difficulties with symbolic magnitude discrimination (the ability to compare Arabic digits) underlie DD. Schwenk and colleagues' (2017) meta-analysis concluded that independent of age, children with DD do, in fact, have slower response times on symbolic, but not non-symbolic, magnitude comparison tasks compared with typical peers.

The 'access deficit' hypothesis

This model suggests that challenges in DD result from difficulties mapping non-symbolic number representations to their symbolic (Arabic digit) representations (knowing that • • = 2). Although some researchers have found that children with MLD have slower response times when comparing symbolic (versus non-symbolic) magnitudes (Rousselle and Noël 2007; De Smedt and Gilmore 2011), the hypothesis is not presently fully supported (Benavides-Varela and Reoyo-Serrano 2021).

The domain-general hypothesis

This approach proposes that DD is the result of more general cognitive difficulties (Peng, Wang and Namkung 2018). Mathematical development relies on executive functions such as working memory and inhibition and many researchers have found strong evidence for their role in maths (Cowan et al. 2011; Menon 2016; Gordon et al. 2022; Li, Zhang and Zhang 2022). Cowan and Powell (2014) found both domain-specific and domain-general difficulties co-occur in many children with MLD.

Maths anxiety

It is unclear whether maths anxiety results in lower attainment because it interferes with working memory and/or because it prevents engagement with maths, or whether lower attainment leads to maths anxiety (Ma and Xu 2004). Recent research suggests that attainment and maths anxiety are not always linked. Devine et al. (2018) found that high maths anxiety was not necessarily associated with poorer maths attainment and vice versa. In the classroom, there are certainly high-attaining maths students who show considerable anxiety as well as low-attaining students who appear to have none.

> *Activity: Discrimination?*
> In 2022, the UK government proposed restricting student loan eligibility to those with at least a grade 4/C (pass) in GCSE English and maths. They want to raise academic standards as the UK performs poorly amongst OECD countries (Kuczera, Field and Windisch 2016; Drayton and van der Erve 2022).
>
> Is it fair to deny loans to students who may find it harder to achieve those grades (especially as many students with DD will not have a formal diagnosis), or are minimum academic qualifications an important prerequisite for higher education?

Supporting learners with mathematical learning difficulties

Did you hear about the mathematicians who were afraid of negative numbers? *They'd stop at nothing to avoid them*!

Providing effective support for pupils with MLD is challenging because individual needs vary and inconsistencies in the research make generalisation difficult (Fastame 2021). Additionally, there is little evidence to show that improvements from interventions that target specific skills are sustained and generalise to other numeracy skills (Monei and Pedro 2017; Szücs and Myers 2017). To understand individual maths-related needs, complete the activity in Box 10.7.

> **Box 10.7 Case study: Samira**
>
> Samira's teacher is worried about her progress. He notices that although Samira understands other maths topics, she struggles with fractions. He plans some targeted support. If Samira's maths does not improve, what does this suggest about her difficulties (e.g. MLD, DD and/or maths anxiety)? Throughout this section, consider how she could be supported.

In the literature (Kroesbergen and Van Luit 2003; Dennis et al. 2016; Marita and Hord 2017; Powell et al. 2021), common themes around best practice include:

- a developmental pedagogy based on conceptual understanding (mastery) and developing mathematical reasoning
- using concrete, manipulable resources
- personalised teaching and support
- allowing enough time
- supporting cognition (executive function, metacognition)
- explicitly teaching mathematical language
- addressing affective factors (anxiety, resilience and attitudes).

Pedagogy

Pedagogy refers to the interaction between teachers and pupils that facilitates learning. It includes teachers' beliefs, strategies and resources (Siraj-Blatchford et al. 2019). Practitioners should use a developmental approach to build conceptual understanding (mastery) and develop mathematical reasoning (Dienes 1963; Skemp 1976; Emerson and Babtie 2014; Chinn and Ashcroft 2017; Bird 2022) by breaking learning down into tiny components and not moving on until previous learning is secure (Table 10.3). In support of this approach, the Education Endowment Foundation (EEF) found that Year 1 children taught using a mastery approach made better progress than their matched peers (Vignoles, Jerrim and Cowan 2015).

Resources

Bruner (1977) proposed that children are active participants in their own learning (Ozdem-Yilmaz and Bilican 2020), so learning relies on discovering facts and relationships by interacting with the environment. Teaching should

Table 10.3 Strategies to build mastery

Strategies	
• Focus on mathematical reasoning and strategies rather than getting the 'right answer'. • Explicitly model your own thinking. • Break learning down into tiny components. • Do not move on until the learner is fluent, accurate and confident.	• Show pupils how to make links between what they already know and what they are trying to find. • Encourage pupils to explain out loud what they are doing – and why – to each other and to the teacher/teaching assistant.

In the classroom

- Emphasise understanding and strategy over getting the right answer. Ask pupils, 'How did you work that out?' rather than 'What did you get?'
- Treat mistakes (including your own!) as opportunities for learning. Ask, 'Why did you think that? What will you do differently next time?'
- Only change one aspect of a problem at a time.

therefore begin with concrete resources to build models, support visualisation and develop conceptual understanding (Emerson and Babtie 2014; Chinn and Ashcroft 2017; Bird 2022). Using practical activities and games also shows maths is a 'doing' subject that can be lots of fun! (Bird 2022)

Sharma (2005) adapted Bruner's (1977) ideas when creating the concrete-pictorial-abstract (CPA) approach. Using CPA, pupils explore new ideas using concrete materials and models (e.g. small toys, counters, fraction discs). They then use sketches and drawings to model problems and develop/support their solutions (e.g. bar models to visualise and compare halves and quarters). Finally, at the abstract level, learners use mathematical symbols and formulae (e.g. 1/4 + 1/2 = 3/4). At each stage, resources from the previous stage(s) remain available, so the links between the different representations are clear (also see Table 10.4).

Personalisation

Learning should be personalised by carefully matching teaching to identified areas of difficulty and including the learner's interests (Emerson and Babtie 2014; Chinn and Ashcroft 2017; Siraj-Blatchford et al. 2019; Bird 2022). Chinn suggests that recognising an individual's cognitive (learning) style (sequential 'inchworm' versus relational 'grasshopper'), and understanding that individuals may adopt these flexibly, could help teachers to tailor support more effectively (Chinn and Ashcroft 2017; Chinn 2020) (see Table 10.5).

Time

Allow plenty of time for learners to fully develop their understanding of concepts and solutions to problems and to practise strategies until they have mastered

Table 10.4 Strategies to develop conceptual understanding

Strategies

- Use concrete models to explain and demonstrate concepts.
- Provide manipulable resources for pupils to explore concepts by building their own models and solutions.
- Explicitly teach how to use the resources to create concrete, pictorial and abstract models.
- Only move to the next stage of CPA when pupils have thoroughly understood the previous one.

In the classroom

- Use maths-specific resources such as Numicon, Cuisenaire rods, Dienes blocks, counters, manipulable 2- and 3-dimensional shapes, algebra tiles, etc.
- Use real-world resources: buttons, toys, money, playing cards, dice, scales, measuring cups, etc.
- When moving to pictorial and abstract methods, keep the concrete resources available too.
- There is now a wide range of resources available to help students move from concrete to pictorial to abstract methods (e.g. White Rose Maths workbooks, workbooks and worksheets based on Singapore Maths).

Table 10.5 Strategies to identify areas of strength and difficulty

Strategies

- Identify learners' specific strengths and areas of difficulty.
- Progress at the learner's pace.
- Include pupils' interests and preferred ways of working.

In the classroom

- Discuss with students what they find hard (even very young children can do this).
- Link pupils' interests to the material being taught (e.g. use children's names in questions and problems, make problems about the things they like).
- Incorporate pupils' preferred ways of working into the learning activities (do they like to build, to move, to listen to stories or to game?).

them (Emerson and Babtie 2014; Vignoles et al. 2015; Chinn and Ashcroft 2017; Bird 2022). Time can be one of the most problematic issues, as many countries (including England) have overloaded curricula (OECD 2020). The OECD (2020) reports shallower learning, lower attainment and less student satisfaction as potential limitations of this approach (though a broader curriculum can offer more relevant and engaging topics). Providing enough time to develop conceptual understanding, fluency and confidence is essential (Emerson and Babtie 2014; Chinn and Ashcroft 2017; Bird 2022; also see Table 10.6).

Table 10.6 Strategies to combat time imposed difficulties

Strategies

- Break teaching down into minute components and move at the pupil's pace.
- Allocate time for pupils to experiment and build models with concrete materials.
- Include regular and frequent revision.
- Take time to regularly check understanding and address misconceptions on the spot – don't wait!
- Adjust the timing in the scheme of work or syllabus to fit the pupil (not the other way around).

In the classroom

- Adjust the pace to the learners, even when this means slowing down and/or not achieving all of the learning outcomes.
- Ask frequent questions to check understanding and revisit prior learning as often as necessary.

Cognitive factors

Supporting executive function (e.g. working memory, attention, inhibition, flexibility)

The role of executive function, especially working memory, in maths attainment has been well-documented (Alloway and Passolunghi 2011; Menon 2016; Avgerinou and Tolmie 2020; Gordon et al. 2022). Consider the cognitive load (the amount of information to be remembered and manipulated) and other cognitive requirements (e.g. attention, inhibition control, mental flexibility) of learning activities and provide appropriate support (Emerson and Babtie 2014; Chinn and Ashcroft 2017; Bird 2022).

Metacognition

The EEF has concluded there is considerable and robust support for the impact of metacognition on learning (EEF 2022). This also applies to learning maths (Desoete and De Craene 2019). Learners should be encouraged to ask questions, explain their thinking and be taught a range of strategies for when they are 'stuck' (Emerson and Babtie 2014; Chinn and Ashcroft 2017; Lee and Johnston-Wilder 2017; Desoete and De Craene 2019; Bird 2022; also see Table 10.7).

Mathematical language

Explicitly teaching mathematical vocabulary and the accurate use of mathematical terminology is important for developing conceptual understanding and mathematical reasoning and facilitating communication (Lee and Johnston-Wilder 2013; Emerson and Babtie 2014; Chinn and Ashcroft

Table 10.7 Strategies to support cognition and metacognition

Strategies

- Teach students that their thinking affects their performance.
- Model 'think aloud' (explaining the thought process out loud while solving a problem on the board) and encourage students to do this too.
- Explicitly teach strategies for planning how to solve a problem.
- Encourage pupils to ask lots of questions.
- Remind students to check their answers using a different method.
- Use mistakes as opportunities for additional exploration of concepts and misconceptions.

In the classroom

- Remind students what they did the previous lesson (without criticising them), as they may not be able to retain information from one lesson to the next.
- Use lots of repetition – little and often.
- Continue to revisit topics throughout the term/school year and into the next (and the next, and the next …).
- To support working memory, in addition to verbal explanations and instructions, include these on the board and on the activities/exercises themselves.

Table 10.8 Strategies to support mathematical language development

Strategies

- Explicitly teach mathematical vocabulary.
- Model the correct use of mathematical language.
- Explain language that has multiple meanings (e.g. 'mean'), is ambiguous or misleading.
- Clearly enunciate words that are often confused (e.g. eigh**ty** versus eigh**teen**).
- In general, avoid mathematically meaningless acronyms and mnemonics such as 'bus stop method' (division) or KFC (dividing fractions).

In the classroom

- Use the correct mathematical language and teach it explicitly (e.g. subtract, zero, multiple, factor, numerator, denominator, exchange).
- Write key vocabulary on the board and, where possible, provide copies for pupils to have on their desks or in their books.
- Use memory aids such as maths mats that include key vocabulary, definitions and examples.
- Relentlessly ask, 'What does that word mean? Can you give me an example?'

2017; Bird 2022; also see Table 10.8). Mathematical vocabulary also plays an important role in fostering a resilient approach to learning maths (Lee and Johnston-Wilder 2017).

Affective factors

Affective support is included last not because it is less important (for some, it is the most important) but because it is a different kind of support. How pupils feel about maths directly influences their performance and how they engage with it (Dowker, Sarkar and Looi 2016).

Anxiety

Anxiety exerts a greater influence on tasks like maths that rely on working memory (Ashcraft and Kirk 2001) and is found in all levels of maths attainers (Devine et al. 2018). Some researchers (Ramirez and Beilock 2011; Park, Ramirez and Beilock 2014) have found that allowing students to write about their worries for 10 minutes improves maths performance. Creating a safe environment is important for reducing anxiety (Whyte and Anthony 2012) and promoting inclusion (Monsen, Ewing and Kwoka 2014). Additionally, creating a positive classroom ethos, with an emphasis on good relationships, fairness, kindness and acceptance, is an important characteristic of effective pedagogy leading to good outcomes (Siraj-Blatchford et al. 2019).

Mathematical resilience

There is evidence to show that developing mathematical resilience – a positive mindset, valuing mathematics and adopting a range of behaviours and strategies for managing challenge – may mitigate the effects of maths anxiety and, consequently, increase engagement and improve outcomes (Lee and Johnston-Wilder 2017; Yeager and Dweck 2020; Lee and Ward-Penny 2022; also see Table 10.9).

Maths apps

Many maths apps are now available, although few have been effectively evaluated. Outhwaite and colleagues' (2022) systematic review identified app characteristics that are more likely to lead to success:

- Areas of difficulty are clearly identified
- Skills and learning are broken down into tiny steps
- Lots of built-in practice
- Clear links to the curriculum and maths in the real world
- Opportunities for questions, feedback and further explanations
- Appropriate pace — the learner does not move on until the previous step is secure
- The strengths of the learner are utilised (a learner who enjoys gaming is likely to engage better with a game).

Table 10.9 Strategies to combat anxiety and build resilience

General and maths-specific anxiety

Strategies

- Use an inclusive pedagogy focused on conceptual understanding rather than getting answers right.
- Create a safe, inclusive environment where everyone is welcome and valued.
- Use clear, unambiguous communication.
- Ensure students know how to communicate that they are struggling.
- Allow students to express their anxiety.
- Establish predictable routines.

In the classroom

- Establish good relationships so students know you are there to support them.
- Be positive about mistakes and ensure pupils understand these are opportunities for learning.
- Encourage students to write down their 'maths worries'.
- Do not allow children to laugh at each other. Promote empathy ('How would that make you feel?') and ensure there are clear consequences for those who do.
- Check in regularly with pupils who struggle so they know they will not have to wait long or draw attention to themselves.
- Stay calm. Remember that many behaviours that appear defiant or disruptive are not deliberate (e.g. children don't choose to have difficulties with attention or organisation) and are indications further support is needed.
- Have an open escape route. Some students are anxious when they cannot see a way out of the classroom, so keep the doorway (and the path to it) clear.

Self-regulation and self-efficacy

Strategies

- Actively support students to regulate their own emotions and behaviour.
- Encourage open discussions about self-regulation.
- Explicitly teach metacognitive strategies to help students deal with the emotional elements of challenge (fear, frustration).
- Emphasise the importance of brain stimulation at the right level of challenge for optimal development.

In the classroom

- Explain the purpose of what students are learning.
- Offer choices (e.g. Red or blue exercise book? Five or ten question starter today?).
- Provide sensory supports (therapy putty, sensory timers, Unifix cubes).
- Share your own self-regulation strategies.

(continued)

Table 10.9 *(Continued)*

Promote positive feelings towards maths

Strategies

- Show your own enthusiasm for maths.
- Highlight links between maths in the classroom and real-world maths.
- Present challenge as a positive experience.
- Promote resilience.

In the classroom

- Share your favourite maths topics with students – in an overtly enthusiastic way.
- Also share what you find difficult and how you navigate these challenges.
- Regularly remind students to take pride in the progress they have already made.
- Incorporate students' individuality into lessons and share some of yours.
- Include some variety and fun activities (computer lessons, games).
- Promote the profile of maths by investigating mathematicians who have made a difference (link to themes such as Black History Month, International Women's Day).
- Highlight famous people who struggle with maths (e.g. Robbie Williams, Cher, journalist Iona Bain) and link to developing coping strategies and resilience.
- Celebrate National Numeracy Day and Dyscalculia Day

Additional app features to consider are the amount of adult support required and whether the app provides feedback that explains errors *and* encourages the learner (Outhwaite et al. 2022).

Although many apps designed to support general mathematical development could easily be adapted to help learners with difficulties, some are designed specifically to support learners with DD (inclusion is not an endorsement):

- The Number Race (ages 4–8)
- The Number Catcher (ages 5–10 but suitable for older children and adults too)
- Calcularis (age 7+)
- Dynamo (ages 6–11).

Most apps are aimed at primary school pupils and there is a real lack of support for older learners.

Home support

The home numeracy environment is a significant factor in mathematical development (Purpura et al. 2020), so encouraging parents/carers to actively support their children with maths is important. Good strategies include promoting positive parental attitudes (maths is important and accessible to all) and suggesting practical activities that can be completed at home (discussing maths in real-world contexts, such as shopping and reading bus/train timetables, playing board games; also see Box 10.8).

> **Box 10.8 Mathematical difficulties, symptoms and strategies**
>
> For a more in-depth discussion, watch Jo Van Herwegen discuss mathematical difficulties, symptoms and strategies here:
> https://mediacentral.ucl.ac.uk/Play/86359

Conclusion

Mathematical learning difficulties encompass a heterogeneous group of behaviours, emotions and difficulties that can significantly influence an individual's life outcomes. Although controversy around the causes and most effective support continues, more (and more rigorous) research is now taking place to improve our understanding. In the meantime, current best practice advocates promoting mathematical inclusion by adopting a mastery approach, personalising learning and support, and addressing anxiety and attitudes through safe and accepting learning environments. Identifying learners' unique strengths, areas of difficulty and preferences, as well as supporting them to become resilient learners of mathematics, offers a promising and positive way forward.

> *Resources*
> If you want to know more about maths and how to support learners, check out the additional resources below.
>
> Chinn, S. (2015) *The Routledge International Handbook of Dyscalculia and Mathematical Learning Difficulties*. London: Routledge.
>
> Gilmore, C., Göbel, S.M. and Inglis, M. (2018) *An Introduction to Mathematical Cognition*. London: Routledge.
>
> Mammarella, I.C., Caviola, S. and Dowker, A., eds. (2019) *Mathematics Anxiety: What is Known, and What is Still Missing*. London: Routledge.
>
> For some fantastic (and many free!) dyscalculia resources: http://www.ronitbird.com/

References

Alloway, T.P. and Passolunghi, M.C. (2011) The relationship between working memory, IQ and mathematical skills in children, *Learning and Individual Differences*, 21 (1): 133–137.

American Psychiatric Association (APA) (2022) *Diagnostic and Statistical Manual of Mental Disorders*, 5th edition (DSM-5). Washington, DC: APA.

Ashcraft, M.H. and Kirk, E.P. (2001) The relationships among working memory, math anxiety, and performance, *Journal of Experimental Psychology*, 130 (2): 224–237.

Ashcraft, M.H. and Moore, A.M. (2009) Mathematics anxiety and the affective drop in performance, *Journal of Psychoeducational Assessment*, 27 (3): 197–205.

Avgerinou, V.A. and Tolmie, A. (2020) Inhibition and cognitive load in fractions and decimals, *British Journal of Educational Psychology*, 90 (suppl. 1): 240–256.

Benavides-Varela, S. and Reoyo-Serrano, N. (2021) Small-range numerical representations of linguistic sounds in 9- to 10-month-old infants, *Cognition*, 213: 104637. Available at: https://doi.org/10.1016/j.cognition.2021.104637

Benavides-Varela, S., Butterworth, B., Burgio, F., Arcara, G., Lucangeli, D. and Semenza, C. (2016) Numerical activities and information learned at home link to the exact numeracy skills in 5–6 years-old children, *Frontiers in Psychology*, 7: 94. Available at: https://doi.org/10.3389/fpsyg.2016.00094

Bird, R. (2022) *Overcoming Dyscalculia & Difficulties with Number*, 2nd edition. London: Corwin Press.

Brewer, K. (2018) British people often boast about being 'bad at maths'. Here's why that causes genuine harm, *The Guardian*, 12 September. Available at: https://www.theguardian.com/education/shortcuts/2018/sep/12/british-people-often-boast-about-being-bad-at-maths-heres-why-that-causes-genuine-harm?msclkid=97f24c48ced111eca3781fa0931992b5 (accessed 21 July 2022).

Bruner, J.S. (1977) *The Process of Education*. Cambridge, MA: Harvard University Press.

Bull, R. and Scerif, G. (2001) Executive functioning as a predictor of children's mathematics ability: inhibition, switching and working memory, *Developmental Neuropsychology*, 19 (3): 273–293.

Butterworth, B. (2022) *Can Fish Count? What Animals Reveal About Our Uniquely Mathematical Mind*. London: Quercus.

Butterworth, B., Varma, S. and Laurillard, D. (2011) Dyscalculia: from brain to education, *Science*, 332 (6033): 1049–1053.

Cahoon, A., Gilmore, C. and Simms, V. (2021) Developmental pathways of early numerical skills during the preschool to school transition, *Learning and Instruction*, 75: 101484. Available at: https://doi.org/10.1016/j.learninstruc.2021.101484.

Caicoya, A.L., Colell, M., Holland, R, Ensenyat, E. and Amici, F. (2021) Giraffes go for more: a quantity discrimination study in giraffes (*Giraffa camelopardalis*), *Animal Cognition*, 24 (3): 483–495.

Cargnelutti, E., Tomasetto, C. and Passolunghi, M.C. (2017) How is anxiety related to math performance in young students? A longitudinal study of Grade 2 to Grade 3 children, *Cognition and Emotion*, 31 (4): 755–764.

Carvalho, M.R.S., Vianna, G., Oliveira, L.F.S., Costa, A.J., Pinheiro-Chagas, P., Sturzenecker, R. et al. (2014) Are 22q11.2 distal deletions associated with math difficulties?, *American Journal of Medical Genetics*, 164A (9): 2256–2262.

Caviola, S., Colling, L.J., Mammarella, I.C. and Szücs, D. (2020) Predictors of mathematics in primary school: magnitude comparison, verbal and spatial working memory measures, *Developmental Science*, 23: e12957. Available at: https://doi.org/10.1111/desc.12957

Chinn, S. (2020) *More Trouble with Maths: A Complete Manual to Identifying and Diagnosing Mathematical Difficulties*, 3rd edition. London: Routledge.

Chinn, S. and Ashcroft, R. (2017) *Mathematics for Dyslexics and Dyscalculics: A Teaching Handbook*, 4th edition. Chichester: Wiley.

Costa, H.M., Outhwaite, L.A. and Van Herwegen, J. (2021) Preschool teachers' training, beliefs and practices concerning mathematics in pre-schools in the UK: Implication for education and practice, *PsyArXiv*, 23 February. Available at: https://doi.org/10.31234/osf.io/rdx6c (accessed 23 August 2022).

Cowan, R. and Powell, D. (2014) The contributions of domain-general and numerical factors to third-grade arithmetic skills and mathematical learning disability, *Journal of Educational Psychology*, 106 (1): 214–229.

Cowan, R., Donlan, C., Shepherd, D.-L., Cole-Fletcher, R., Saxton, M. and Hurry, J. (2011) Basic calculation proficiency and mathematics achievement in elementary school children, *Journal of Educational Psychology*, 103 (4): 786–803.

Davis, O.S.P., Band, G., Pirinen, M., Haworth, C.M.A., Meaburn, E.L., Kovas, Y. et al. (2014) The correlation between reading and mathematics ability at age twelve has a substantial genetic component, *Nature Communications*, 5: 4204. Available at: https://doi.org/10.1038/ncomms5204

Dehaene, S. (1992) Varieties of numerical abilities, *Cognition*, 44 (1/2): 1–42.

Dehaene, S. (2001) Précis of the number sense, *Mind & Language*, 16 (1): 16–36.

Dehaene, S. and Cohen, L. (1991) Two mental calculation systems: a case study of severe acalculia with preserved approximation, *Neuropsychologia*, 29 (11): 1045–1074.

Dehaene, S., Piazza, M., Pinel, P. and Cohen, L. (2003) Three parietal circuits for number processing, *Cognitive Neuropsychology*, 20 (3): 487–506.

Dennis, M.S., Sharp, E., Chovanes, J., Thomas, A., Burns, R.M., Custer, B. et al. (2016) A meta-analysis of empirical research on teaching students with mathematics learning difficulties, *Learning Disabilities Research & Practice*, 31 (3): 156–168.

Department for Children, Education, Lifelong Learning and Skills (DCELLS) (2008) *Mathematical Development*. Cardiff: Welsh Assembly Government. Available at: https://dera.ioe.ac.uk/15795/1/mathdevelopmentepdf_lang%3Den#:~:text=Mathematical%20Development%20consists%20of%20children's,communicating%20mathematically%20s%20reasoning%20mathematically (accessed 21 July 2022).

Department for Education and Department of Health (DfE/DoH) (2015) *Special Educational Needs and Disability Code of Practice: 0 to 25 years*. London: DfE. Available at: https://www.gov.uk/government/uploads/system/uploads/attachment_data/file/398815/SEND_Code_of_Practice_January_2015.pdf (accessed 21 July 2022).

De Smedt, B. and Gilmore, C.K. (2011) Defective number module or impaired access? Numerical magnitude processing in first graders with mathematical difficulties, *Journal of Experimental Child Psychology*, 108 (2): 278–292.

De Smedt, B., Verschaffel, L. and Ghesquière, P. (2009) The predictive value of numerical magnitude comparison for individual differences in mathematics achievement, *Journal of Experimental Child Psychology*, 103 (4): 469–479.

De Smedt, B., Noël, M.-P., Gilmore, C. and Ansari, D. (2013) How do symbolic and non-symbolic numerical processing skills relate to individual differences in children's mathematical skills? A review of evidence from brain and behavior, *Trends in Neuroscience and Education*, 2 (2): 48–55.

Desoete, A. and De Craene, B. (2019) Metacognition and mathematics education: an overview, *ZDM Mathematics Education*, 51: 565–575.

Devine, A., Fawcett, K., Szücs, D. and Dowker, A. (2012) Gender differences in mathematics anxiety and the relation to mathematics performance while controlling for test anxiety, *Behavioral and Brain Functions*, 8: 33. Available at: https://doi.org/10.1186/1744-9081-8-33

Devine, A., Hill, F., Carey, E. and Szücs, D. (2018) Cognitive and emotional math problems largely dissociate: prevalence of developmental dyscalculia and mathematics anxiety, *Journal of Educational Psychology*, 110 (3): 431–444.

Dienes, Z.P. (1963) On the learning of mathematics, *The Arithmetic Teacher*, 10 (3): 115–126.

Dowker, A. (2008) Individual differences in numerical abilities in preschoolers, *Developmental Science*, 11 (5): 650–654.

Dowker, A., Sarkar, A. and Looi, C.Y. (2016) Mathematics anxiety: what have we learned in 60 years?, *Frontiers in Psychology*, 7: 508. Available at: https://doi.org/10.3389/fpsyg.2016.00508

Drayton, E. and van der Erve, L. (2022) *The impact of student loan minimum eligibility requirements*. IFS Briefing Note #BN343. Institute for Fiscal Studies. London: Available at: https://ifs.org.uk/publications/impact-student-loan-minimum-eligibility-requirements

Education Endowment Foundation (EEF) (2022) *Teaching and Learning Toolkit*. London: EEF. Available at: https://educationendowmentfoundation.org.uk/education-evidence/teaching-learning-toolkit (accessed 21 July 2022).

Emerson, J. and Babtie, P. (2014) *The Dyscalculia Solution: Teaching Number Sense*. London: Bloomsbury.

Fastame, M.C. (2021) Visuo-spatial mental imagery and geometry skills in school-aged children, *School Psychology International*, 42 (3): 324–337.

Ferrie, B. (2022) *What is dyscalculia and how can it be spotted and supported in children and adults?* Brighton: National Numeracy. Available at: https://www.nationalnumeracy.org.uk/news/what-dyscalculia-and-how-can-it-be-spotted-and-supported-children-and-adults (accessed 21 July 2022).

Fuchs, L.S., Geary, D.C., Compton, D.L., Fuchs, D., Hamlett, C.L., Seethaler, P.M. et al. (2010) Do different types of school mathematics development depend on different constellations of numerical versus general cognitive abilities?, *Developmental Psychology*, 46 (6): 1731–1746.

Fuller, K. (2019) *International Women's Day: National Numeracy on why we are all numbers people*. Brighton: National Numeracy. Available at: https://www.nationalnumeracy.org.uk/news/international-womens-day-national-numeracy-why-we-are-all-numbers-people (accessed 23 August 2022).

Geary, D.C. (2015) The classification and cognitive characteristics of mathematical difficulties in children, in R. Cohen-Kadosh and A. Dowker (eds.), *The Oxford Handbook of Numerical Cognition*. Oxford: Oxford University Press.

Gelman, R. and Gallistel, R. (1978) *The Child's Understanding of Number*. Cambridge, MA: Harvard University Press.

Gilmore, C., Attridge, N., Clayton, S., Cragg, L., Johnson, S., Marlow, N. et al. (2013) Individual differences in inhibitory control, not non-verbal number acuity, correlate with mathematics achievement, *PLoS ONE*, 8 (6): e67374. Available at: https://doi.org/10.1371/journal.pone.0067374

Gordon, R., De Morais, D.S., Whitelock, E. and Mukarram, A. (2022) Mapping components of verbal and visuospatial working memory to mathematical topics in seven- to fifteen-year-olds, *British Journal of Educational Psychology*, 92 (1): 1–18.

Hu, X., Leung, F.K.S. and Teng, Y. (2018) The influence of culture on students' mathematics achievement across 51 countries, *International Journal of Science and Mathematics Education*, 16 (suppl. 1): S7–S24.

Kaufmann, L., Vogel, S.E., Starke, M., Kremser, C., Schocke, M. and Wood, G. (2009) Developmental dyscalculia: compensatory mechanisms in left intraparietal regions in response to nonsymbolic magnitudes, *Behavioral and Brain Functions*, 5: 35. Available at: https://doi.org/10.1186/1744-9081-5-35

Kaufmann, L., Mazzocco, M.M., Dowker, A., von Aster, M., Göbel, S.M., Grabner, R.H. et al. (2013) Dyscalculia from a developmental and differential perspective, *Frontiers in Psychology*, 4: 516. Available at: https://doi.org/10.3389/fpsyg.2013.00516

Kroesbergen, E.H. and Van Luit, J.E.H. (2003) Mathematics interventions for children with special educational needs: a meta-analysis, *Remedial and Special Education*, 24 (2): 97–114.

Kuczera, M., Field, S. and Windisch, H.C. (2016) *Building skills for all: A review of England*. Paris: OECD. Available at: https://www.oecd.org/unitedkingdom/building-skills-for-all-review-of-england.pdf

Landerl, K., Bevan, A. and Butterworth, B. (2004) Developmental dyscalculia and basic numerical capacities: a study of 8–9 year-old-students, *Cognition*, 93 (2): 99–125.

Lee, C. and Johnston-Wilder, S. (2013) Learning mathematics: letting the pupils have their say, *Educational Studies in Mathematics*, 83 (2): 163–180.

Lee, C. and Johnston-Wilder, S. (2017) The construct of mathematical resilience, in U.X. Eligio (ed.), *Understanding Emotions in Mathematical Thinking and Learning*. London: Academic Press.

Lee, C. and Ward-Penny, R. (2022) Agency and fidelity in primary teachers' efforts to develop mathematical resilience, *Teacher Development*, 16 (1): 75–93.

Li, D., Zhang, X. and Zhang, L. (2022) What skills could distinguish developmental dyscalculia and typically developing children: evidence from a 2-year longitudinal screening, *Journal of Learning Disabilities*. Available at: https://doi.org/10.1177/00222194221099674

Lyons, I.M. and Ansari, D. (2015) Numerical order processing in children: from reversing the distance-effect to predicting arithmetic, *Mind, Brain, and Education*, 9 (4): 207–221.

Ma, X. and Xu, J. (2004) The causal ordering of mathematics anxiety and mathematics achievement: a longitudinal panel analysis, *Journal of Adolescence*, 27 (2): 165–179.

Malone, S.A., Heron-Delaney, M., Burgoyne, K. and Hulme, C. (2019) Learning correspondences between magnitudes, symbols and words: evidence for a triple code model of arithmetic development, *Cognition*, 187: 1–9.

Mammarella, I.C., Toffalini, E., Caviola, S., Colling, L. and Szücs, D. (2021) No evidence for a core deficit in developmental dyscalculia or mathematical learning disabilities, *Journal of Child Psychology and Psychiatry*, 62 (6): 704–714.

Marita, S. and Hord, C. (2017) Review of mathematics interventions for secondary students with learning disabilities, *Learning Disability Quarterly*, 40 (1): 29–40.

Mazzocco, M.M.M., Feigenson, L. and Halberda, J. (2011) Preschoolers' precision of the approximate number system predicts later school mathematics performance, *PLoS ONE*, 6 (9): e23749. Available at: https://doi.org/10.1371/journal.pone.0023749.

Menon, V. (2016) Working memory in children's math learning and its disruption in dyscalculia, *Current Opinion in Behavioral Sciences*, 10: 125–132.

Molko, N., Cachia, A., Rivière, D., Mangin, J.F., Bruandet, M., LeBihan, D. et al. (2003) Functional and structural alternations of the intraparietal sulcus in a developmental dyscalculia of genetic origin, *Neuron*, 40 (4): 847–858.

Moll, K., Kunze, S., Neuhoff, N., Bruder, J. and Schulte-Körne, G. (2014) Specific learning disorder: prevalence and gender differences, *PLoS ONE*, 9 (7): e103537. Available at: https://doi.org/10.1371/journal.pone.0103537

Monei, T. and Pedro, A. (2017) A systematic review of interventions for children presenting with dyscalculia in primary schools, *Educational Psychology in Practice*, 33 (3): 277–293.

Monsen, J.J., Ewing, D.L. and Kwoka, M. (2014) Teachers' attitudes towards inclusion, perceived adequacy of support and classroom learning environment, *Learning Environments Research*, 17 (1): 113–126.

Morsanyi, K., van Bers, B.M.C.W, McCormack, T. and McGourty, J. (2018) The prevalence of specific learning disorder in mathematics and comorbidity with other developmental disorders in primary school-age children, *British Journal of Psychology*, 109 (4): 917–940.

Mussolin, C., Mejias, S. and Noël, M.-P. (2010) Symbolic and nonsymbolic number comparison in children with and without dyscalculia, *Cognition*, 115 (1): 10–25.

National Numeracy (2022) *What is numeracy?* Brighton: National Numeracy. Available at: https://www.nationalnumeracy.org.uk/what-numeracy (accessed 21 July 2022).

OECD (2018) *PISA 2018 results, vol. 1: What students know and can do.* Paris: OECD. Available at: https://www.oecd.org/pisa/publications/pisa-2018-results-volume-i-5f07c754-en.htm (accessed 23 August 2022)

OECD (2020) *Curriculum overload: A way forward.* Paris: OECD. Available at: https://www.oecd.org/education/curriculum-overload-3081ceca-en.htm.

Outhwaite, L., Early, E., Herodotou, C. and Van Herwegen, J. (2022) *Can maths apps add value to young children's learning? A systematic review and content analysis.* London: Institute of Education. Available at: https://discovery.ucl.ac.uk/id/eprint/10149354/

Ozdem-Yilmaz, Y. and Bilican, K. (2020) Discovery learning – Jerome Bruner, in B. Akpan and T.J. Kennedy (eds.), *Science Education in Theory and Practice.* Cham: Springer.

Park, D., Ramirez, G. and Beilock, S.L. (2014) The role of expressive writing in math anxiety, *Journal of Experimental Psychology: Applied*, 20 (2): 103–111.

Parsons, S. and Bynner, J. (2005) *Does numeracy matter more?* London: National Research and Development Centre for Adult Literacy and Numeracy. Available at http://nrdc.org.uk/wp-content/uploads/2005/01/Does-numeracy-matter-more.pdf (accessed 21 July 2022).

Peng, P., Wang, C. and Namkung, J. (2018) Understanding the cognition related to mathematics difficulties: a meta-analysis on the cognitive deficit profiles and the bottleneck theory, *Review of Educational Research*, 88 (3): 434–476.

Peters, L. and Ansari, D. (2019) Are specific learning disorders truly specific, and are they disorders?, *Trends in Neuroscience and Education*, 17: 100115. Available at: https://doi.org/10.1016/j.tine.2019.100115

Piaget, J. and Cook, M. ([1936] 1977) *The Origin of Intelligence in the Child*, trans. Margaret Cook. Harmondsworth: Penguin Books.

Piazza, M., Facoetti, A., Trussardi, A.N., Berteletti, I., Conte, S., Lucangeli, D. et al. (2010) Developmental trajectory of number acuity reveals a severe impairment in developmental dyscalculia, *Cognition*, 116 (1): 33–41.

Powell, S.R., Mason, E.N., Bos, S.E., Hirt, S., Ketterlin-Geller, L.R. and Lembke, S. (2021) A systematic review of mathematics interventions for middle-school students experiencing mathematics difficulty, *Learning Disabilities Research & Practice*, 36 (4): 295–329.

Purpura, D.J., King, Y.A., Rolan, E., Hornburg, C.B., Schmitt, S.A., Hart, S.A. et al. (2020) Examining the factor structure of the home mathematics environment to delineate its role in predicting preschool numeracy, mathematical language, and spatial skills, *Frontiers in Psychology*, 11: 1925. Available at: https://doi.org/10.3389/fpsyg.2020.01925

Ramirez, G. and Beilock, S.L. (2011) Writing about testing worries boosts exam performance in the classroom, *Science*, 331 (6014): 211–213.

Ritchie, S.J. and Bates, T.C. (2013) Enduring links from childhood mathematics and reading achievement to adult socioeconomic status, *Psychological Science*, 24 (7): 1301–1308.

Roell, M., Cachia, A., Matejko, A.A., Houdé, O., Ansari, D. and Borst, G. (2021) Sulcation of the intraparietal sulcus is related to symbolic but not non-symbolic number skills, *Developmental Cognitive Neuroscience*, 51: 100998. Available at: https://doi.org/10.1016/j.dcn.2021.100998

Rousselle, L. and Noël, M.-P. (2007) Basic numerical skills in children with mathematics learning disabilities: a comparison of symbolic vs non-symbolic number magnitude processing, *Cognition*, 102 (3): 361–395.

Sammons, P., Toth, K., Sylva, K., Melhuish, E., Siraj, I. and Taggart, B. (2015) The long-term role of the home learning environment in shaping students' academic attainment in secondary school, *Journal of Children's Services*, 10 (3): 189–201.

Schel, M.A. and Klingberg, T. (2017) Specialization of the right intraparietal sulcus for processing mathematics during development, *Cerebral Cortex*, 27 (9): 4436–4446.

Schwenk, C., Sasanguie, D., Kuhn, J.-T., Kempe, S., Doebler, P. and Holling, H. (2017) (Non-)symbolic magnitude processing in children with mathematical difficulties: a meta-analysis, *Research in Developmental Disabilities*, 64: 152–167.

Shalev, R.S., Manor, O., Kerem, B., Ayali, M., Badichi, N., Friedlander, Y. et al. (2001) Developmental dyscalculia is a familial learning disability, *Journal of Learning Disabilities*, 34 (1): 59–65.

Sharma, M.C. (2005). *Levels of learning mathematics.* Available at: https://www.westberkseducation.co.uk/Pages/Download/02153800-57ac-4aeb-a058-9de73bb1b7dc/PageSectionDocuments (accessed 28 October 2022).

Siemann, J. and Petermann, F. (2018) Evaluation of the Triple Code Model of numerical processing – reviewing past neuroimaging and clinical findings, *Research in Developmental Disabilities*, 72: 106–117.

Siraj, I., Taggart, B., Sammons, P., Melhuish, E., Sylva, K. and Shepherd, D.-L. (2019) *Teaching in Effective Primary Schools: Research into Pedagogy and Children's Learning.* London: UCL IOE Press.

Skagenholt, M., Träff, U., Västfjäll, D. and Skagerlund, K. (2018) Examining the Triple Code Model in numerical cognition: an fMRI study, *PLoS ONE*, 13 (6): e0199247. Available at: https://doi.org/10.1371/journal.pone.0199247.

Skemp, R. (1976) Relational understanding and instrumental understanding: Faux amis, *Mathematics Teaching*, 77 (1): 20–26.

Swars, S.L., Daane, C.J. and Giesen, J. (2006) Mathematics anxiety and mathematics teacher efficacy: what is the relationship in elementary preservice teachers?, *School Science and Mathematics*, 106 (7): 306–315.

Szűcs, D. and Myers, T. (2017) A critical analysis of design, facts, bias and inference in the approximate number system training literature: a systematic review, *Trends in Neuroscience and Education*, 6: 187–203.

Vignoles, A., Jerrim, J. and Cowan, R. (2015) *Mathematics mastery: primary evaluation report.* London: Education Endowment Foundation. Available at: https://d2tic4wvo1iusb.cloudfront.net/documents/projects/EEF_Project_Report_MathematicsMasteryPrimary.pdf?v=1666704852 (accessed 7 October 2022).

Vygotsky, L.S. ([1934] 1986) *Thought and Language*, ed. A. Kozulin. Cambridge, MA: MIT Press.

Whyte, J. and Anthony, G. (2012) Maths anxiety: the fear factor in the mathematics classroom, *New Zealand Journal of Teachers' Work*, 9 (1): 6–15.

Wilkey, E.D. and Ansari, D. (2020) Challenging the neurobiological link between number sense and symbolic numerical abilities, *Annals of the New York Academy of Sciences*, 1464 (1): 76–98.

Winheller, S., Hattie, J.A. and Brown, G.T.L. (2013) Factors influencing early adolescents' mathematics achievement: high-quality teacher rather than relationships, *Learning Environments Research*, 16 (1): 49–69.

World Health Organisation (WHO) (2021) *International Statistical Classification of Diseases and Related Health Problems*, 11th edition (ICD-11). Geneva: WHO.

Xu, F., Spelke, E.S. and Goddard, S. (2005) Number sense in human infants, *Developmental Science*, 8 (1): 88–101.

Yeager, D.S. and Dweck, C.S. (2020) What can be learned from growth mindset controversies?, *American Psychologist*, 75 (9): 1269–1284.

Part III

Physical and Sensory Needs

In Part III, we explore more physical- and sensory-based needs. We begin with developmental coordination disorder (DCD) in Chapter 11, which is related to physical needs associated with motor and coordination. We then move on to consider visual and auditory differences and difficulties. The chapter on visual impairments (Chapter 12) highlights the population's heterogeneity and the importance of acknowledging the significance of compensatory mechanisms and brain plasticity. Auditory processing difficulties (APD) and classroom implications are presented in Chapter 13. Carmel Capewell stresses the need for making an appropriate physical learning environment that will cater for the needs not only of children and young people with APD but for everyone in the classroom. We all learn better in a less noisy and disruptive environment.

As in Part II, the chapters are structured so that you develop an understanding of (a) identification, assessment and understanding of needs, and (b) responses, including research-inspired intervention, teaching, accommodations and adaptations. As you read, consider the following questions:

- What approach (special versus inclusive) is present within each chapter – does one dominate?
- Is the focus more on difficulties, as a result of differences, or are the difficulties attributed to external factors?
- Is the response more about changing the environment (or person-environment relationship) or changing the person?

11 Developmental coordination disorder: 'I'm falling ... through the cracks'

Tanya Rihtman and Susan Allen

After reading this chapter and completing the activities, you will:

- have an understanding of developmental coordination disorder (DCD) and its relationship to dyspraxia
- be able to identify types of school-based activities with which learners with DCD might struggle
- understand challenges faced by learners with DCD in accessing educational support in relation to the Special Educational Needs and Disability (SEND) Code of Practice: 0 to 25 years
- recognise the imperative for effective collaboration between allied health professionals, psychologists and education staff in achieving optimal outcomes for learners with DCD
- be able to implement school-based activities that lead to empowerment and enhanced outcomes of learners with DCD.

Introduction

Developmental coordination disorder (DCD) is a lifelong condition characterised by marked difficulties in learning and performing motor- and coordination-based tasks (Blank et al. 2019). Historically described using various labels, from 'clumsy child syndrome' to 'dyspraxia', DCD significantly impacts on children's functional day-to-day activities across all aspects of life. The motor coordination difficulties of DCD may initially appear mild, but they directly limit the child's ability to successfully engage in daily living and school activities, which, in turn, leads to longer-term social, physical and mental health effects (Blank et al. 2019). From the perspective of psychological and educational inclusion, participatory difficulties frequently become more marked when children with DCD enter structured educational settings, which introduce increased physical and organisational demands.

As the chapter is written from an allied health professional perspective of occupational therapy, it will follow principles and practices from both special and inclusive educational approaches, as both are needed to support the needs and development of learners with DCD. As you read this chapter, take time to reflect and try to identify which approach is being adopted – is it special or inclusive education? 'Occupation' is viewed by occupational therapists as 'everyday personalised activities that ... bring meaning and purpose to life' (American Occupational Therapy Association 2020: 79). Occupational therapists' professional remit lies in supporting people of any age to meaningfully 'occupy' their time.

Within educational settings, occupational therapists bring expertise to the identification of the *person-based, environmental* and *task* factors that may limit or facilitate optimal childhood development, participation and achievement of daily occupations (Royal College of Occupational Therapists 2021), potentially targeting interventions across any combination of these. This unique professional perspective, which supports children's broad occupational performance, closely complements the professional remit of other multidisciplinary educational team members who may work in educational settings, such as psychologists, speech and language therapists, and so on. This chapter explores practical application of evidence-based frameworks to support learners with DCD within inclusive, multidisciplinary educational settings.

Although different professionals may adopt different terminology and approaches, this chapter seeks to support collaborative educational working practices by emphasising professional similarities rather than differences. As you read, reflect on the language of educational inclusion (Chapter 1), and seek examples of professional similarities, such as evidence-based practice, structured approaches to support, and shared professional goals of maximising learner potential.

Background

Since DCD affects 5–6 per cent of the population (Lingam et al. 2009), it is statistically likely that every classroom has at least one learner with DCD. Motor-based performance difficulties are common within educational contexts, particularly in mainstream settings, where learners with DCD are most likely to be placed. Think about the motor demands for optimal school participation – the list is endless. From early years settings where children are learning to coordinate their muscles for nose-blowing or removing trousers for independent toileting, to young adults taking notes in class – hitting the correct keyboard letters through accurate finger location, or forming identifiable letters within constraints of lines and margins – the demands for moving our bodies accurately, with minimal energy expenditure, are never-ending.

Activity

If you are *right-handed*, find a pair of scissors you're used to using. On a piece of paper, draw a squiggly line (but not so squiggly that you wouldn't normally be able to cut around it). Holding the scissors in your *left hand* (assuming that you usually cut with your right hand), cut as accurately as you can along the squiggly line. Don't give up until the very end, ensuring that you cut exactly in the middle of the line.

If you are *left-handed*, take a right-handed can opener and open the can halfway with your right hand, and the other half with your left hand.

Now, take a moment to reflect on how the activity made you feel. Were you frustrated by the effort needed to perform these 'simple' tasks? How would you feel if every daily motor activity required that much effort? How do you think a learner with DCD might feel when facing similar challenges throughout the day?

There is much academic debate as to the neurological underpinnings of DCD, but it is evident that automaticity of motor learning is implicated. To understand this concept, think about driving. If you know how to drive, you may recall the amount of attention you initially needed to effectively perform all the motor movements. With time and experience, you now likely drive without actively thinking about each of the movements required (e.g. where to place your foot to find the brake). This is because movement sequences become automatic through integration of previous motor learning, coupled with practice. An early childhood example is that of learning to write. Initially, a child watches their hand as they try to control the pencil direction, and they build their writing repertoire through learning graphically simpler letters first. Over time, letter and word production becomes more automatic, with less reliance on visual feedback. For learners with DCD, there is a view that each time a new motor task is learned, they are 'starting from scratch'.

The UK Special Educational Needs and Disability (SEND) Code of Practice (DfE/DoH 2015) provides a national framework for inclusion of children with special or additional needs. However, difficulties experienced by learners with DCD are not usually considered to be life-threatening, and when educational/health services are stretched, their needs may not be prioritised. Dunford and Richards note that, 'children with DCD are doubly disadvantaged by having to compete for ... services against other children with apparently more severe disabilities' (2003: 18). In the UK, this type of prioritisation is reflected in notable inequity in geographical and socio-economic access to services. When coupled with a general lack of awareness of the characteristics and longer-term impacts of DCD, learners with DCD are at risk of falling through the cracks in relation to early intervention and/or ongoing support.

Identification, classification and definitions

There is a long history of attempts to classify early childhood difficulties. Understanding this history may help clarify why the terms 'DCD' and 'dyspraxia' are used interchangeably by some professionals but not by others, and may support more effective multidisciplinary professional communication.

The symptoms of DCD were first described in the early 1900s, when Collier coined the phrase, 'congenital maladroitness' (Dewey and Wilson 2001). Orton introduced 'impaired praxis' in 1937 as a central characteristic of 'maladroitness', while children displaying DCD symptoms were labelled with 'minimal brain dysfunction' in the 1960s (Clements 1966) and 'clumsy child syndrome' in the 1970s (Gubbay 1978). In this context, praxis refers to 'the ability to plan and execute skilled or non-habitual motor tasks' (Dewey and Wilson 2001: 6).

In the 1970s, Ayres proposed a theory of sensory integration to explain commonly observed early childhood functional difficulties (Ayres 1972). In simple evolutionary terms, the human body gains sensory information (e.g. noise, light, odour) from the world around it. The brain interprets sensory information to establish the need for a survival response (fight, flight or freeze). The response is then expressed through motor action (or inaction). In this manner, *sensory input* and *motor output* can be viewed as two sides of the same coin.

Ayres' theory of sensory integration suggests that motor coordination impairment results from inaccurate central nervous system interpretation and organisation of sensory information, and termed the resultant inaccurate or maladaptive motor responses 'dyspraxia'. Compared with other definitions of praxis, which tend to emphasise the *motor performance* component, Ayres' view of praxis encompasses motor planning as well as:

- planning and organisation required to have an idea/goal
- understanding motor choices available for goal attainment
- selection of the most appropriate motor action sequence
- initiation and completion of novel and complex movement tasks.

For those working with learners with motor coordination difficulties in educational settings, the complex and nuanced terminology is not always helpful in identifying potential causes for observed behaviours, referral pathways and access to evidence-based information. To simplify this in the most practical of terms (and for the purposes of this chapter):

- Dyspraxia is often used when sensory processing difficulties are suspected and is also frequently used in the context of UK-based research.
- DCD is viewed as the accepted term (Sugden 2007) to describe motor coordination difficulties in a way that facilitates common research and clinical language.

- DCD is a formal diagnosis within the Diagnostic and Statistical Manual of Mental Disorders (DSM-5) (APA 2013), while dyspraxia is not.
- Both terms feature synonymously in the International Statistical Classification of Diseases and Related Health Problems (ICD-10) (WHO 2016).

According to the DSM-5 (APA 2013), DCD is a 'neurodevelopmental disorder' with four diagnostic criteria:

- 'The acquisition and execution of coordinated motor skills is substantially below that expected given the individual's chronological age and opportunity for skill learning and use'.
- The difficulties with motor skills 'significantly and persistently [interfere] with activities of daily living [and impact] academic/school productivity, prevocational and vocational activities, leisure, and play'.
- Motor skills difficulties are evident from an early age.
- The motor difficulties are not explained by another diagnosis, e.g. intellectual delay, visual impairment or other movement-related neurological conditions.

According to the ICD-10 (WHO 2016: Section F82), DCD and dyspraxia are 'specific developmental disorders of motor function', characterised by:

- a 'serious impairment in the development of motor skills' that is not explained by 'intellectual retardation' or a 'neurological disorder'
- 'evidence of marked neurological immaturities'. For example, this may include choreiform movements that are involuntary and random movements, mirror movements where voluntary movement on one side is reflected with involuntary movement on the other side of the body, fine or gross motor difficulties.

The diagnosis is excluded if there are 'abnormalities of gait or mobility', if there is an 'isolated lack of coordination', or coordination difficulties are secondary to 'intellectual disability or other medical or psychosocial disorders'.

A DCD diagnosis requires clinical assessment to ascertain all four DSM-5 criteria. Motor coordination difficulties are present in many other developmental disorders, including autism, attention deficit hyperactivity disorder and dyslexia (Lino and Chieffo 2022) – which must be medically excluded. Standardised and observational assessment of motor skills is required by an appropriately trained allied health professional, to verify if motor skills are 'far below' expected age levels (see Table 11.1). In this process, the occupational therapist observes or seeks information on the functional motor impacts on activities of daily living (ADLs), academic/school productivity, leisure and play across both school and home environments.

Table 11.1 A selection of frequently used DCD screening and assessment tools

SCREENING TOOLS*	Authors	Age range	Description
The Little Developmental Coordination Disorder Questionnaire (LDCDQ) www.littledcdq.com	Rihtman, Wilson and Parush (2011)	3–4 years	A 15-item *parent* questionnaire designed to screen for coordination disorders in children aged 3–4 years. Comprises items related to control during movement, fine motor skills, and general coordination. This questionnaire is available for preschool teachers to use as a screening tool
The Developmental Coordination Disorder Questionnaire (DCDQ) www.dcdq.ca	Wilson et al. (2009)	5–15 years	A 15-item *parent* questionnaire designed to screen for coordination difficulties in children aged 5–15 years. Comprises items related to control during movement, fine motor/handwriting, and general coordination. This questionnaire can be used by teachers
Early Years Movement Skills Checklist	Chambers and Sugden (2006)	3–6 years	A 28-item *educator* checklist, comprising items across four categories: self-help skills, desk skills, general classroom skills, and recreational/playground skills. This questionnaire can be used by teachers
Movement Assessment Battery for Children, 2nd edition, Checklist (MABC-2 Checklist)	Henderson, Sugden and Barnett (2007)	5–12 years	A 43-item *parent or educator* checklist exploring the child's management of movement in everyday situations at home and in school. Items are organised according to movement in a predictable environment, movement in an unpredictable environment, and non-motor factors that might affect movement. This questionnaire can be used by teachers

(continued)

Table 11.1 (Continued)

ASSESSMENT TOOLS	Authors	Age range	Description
Movement Assessment Battery for Children, 2nd edition (MABC-2)	Henderson, Sugden and Barnett (2007)	3–16 years	Administered by a *professional* with appropriate training (https://www.pearsonclinical.co.uk/ordering/how-to-order/qualifications/qualifications-policy.html), the MABC-2 is a standardised assessment that identifies and describes motor impairment. Comprises tasks for three different age ranges (eight tasks each), covering: manual dexterity, ball skills, and static and dynamic balance
The Bruininks-Oseretsky Test of Motor Proficiency, 2nd edition (BOTMP-2)	Bruininks and Bruininks (2005)	4 years to 21 years and 11 months	Administered by a *professional* with appropriate training, the BOTMP-2 is a standardised assessment of motor skill. Comprises game-like tasks which generate six component scores: Fine manual control, manual coordination, body coordination, strength & agility, gross motor, and fine motor
Peabody Developmental Motor Scale, 2nd edition (PDMS-2)	Fewell and Folio (2000)	Birth to 5 years	Administered by a *professional* with appropriate training, the PDMS-2 provides an in-depth assessment of gross and fine motor skills across six subtests: reflexes, equilibrium, locomotion, object manipulation, grasping, and visual-motor integration
Beery-Buktenica Developmental Test of Visual-Motor Integration, 6th edition (VMI)	Beery, Beery and Buktenica (2010)	2 years to 99 years and 11 months	Administered by a *professional* with appropriate training, the VMI assesses the child's integration between their visual and motor abilities. The primary test of visual-motor integration is supported by two supplemental tests: visual perception and motor coordination

(continued)

Table 11.1 (Continued)

ASSESSMENT TOOLS	Authors	Age range	Description
The Sensory Profile 2 (SP-2)	Dunn (2014)	2–15 years	Completed by *parents or teachers* and interpreted by a *professional* with appropriate training, the SP-2 is a family of standardised questionnaire-based assessments that evaluate a child's sensory processing patterns. Age-appropriate versions are available for: infants, toddlers, and children and adolescents. A *School Companion* form is also available
Adolescent/Adult Sensory Profile	Dunn and Brown (2002)	11 years+	Completed by the *individual* and interpreted by a *professional* with appropriate training, this is a 60-item standardised questionnaire-based assessment that measures sensory processing patterns and their effects on functional performance
Sensory Processing Measure, 2nd edition (SPM-2)	Parham et al. (2021)	4 months to 87 years	Completed by *parents or teachers* and interpreted by a *professional* with appropriate training, the SPM-2 is a standardised questionnaire-based assessment that measures the individual's sensory processing difficulties across different settings
Detailed Assessment of Speed of Handwriting (DASH)	Barnett et al. (2007)	9 years to 16 years and 11 months	Administered by an individual working with a learner and interpreted by a *professional* with appropriate training, the DASH assesses handwriting speed. Comprises five subtests: fine motor, precision skills, speed, altering of performance, and free writing

*Unless otherwise stated, all assessments require registration as a healthcare professional or specialist training.

Historically, it was assumed that children with DCD outgrow their difficulties, but this is not the case (Tal-Saban and Kirby 2018). DCD is associated with significant long-term, social-emotional difficulties well into adulthood, including reduced participation across settings, lower social satisfaction, self-esteem and quality of life (Tal-Saban and Kirby 2018). At the other end of the age scale, even though DCD is rarely diagnosed prior to age 5 (Blank et al. 2019), symptoms are apparent before that age and we can reliably identify young children at risk of DCD to prevent the development of secondary difficulties (Lee and Zwicker 2021), which is vital to ensure appropriate early intervention support.

Supporting the identification of learners with DCD

Parental role

Parents of learners with DCD are intimately familiar with the impacts of their child's motor difficulties. They will have observed, experienced and shared their child's frustrations over time, and are often relieved to have these difficulties explained. The concerns of parents of children with DCD change over time; in the early years, parents are most concerned about motor skills and play, in middle childhood concerns relate to self-care, academic education and peer problems, and in later childhood self-esteem and emotional health are of greatest concern (Missiuna et al. 2007). Parents are frequently the strongest advocate for their child's individualised needs, and their involvement in the clinical DCD assessment process is vital.

Educationalist role

Educationalists have an important role in the identification of functional motor-based school performance concerns. Formal diagnosis of DCD requires clinical assessment, which frequently takes time, thus introducing undesirable delay to offers of support. However, valid and reliable screening tools for DCD may help direct educators and special educational needs (SEN) teams to consider the possible presence of DCD, and to encourage referral for more extensive clinical assessment (see Table 11.1).

> Activity
> Review the items in the DCDQ and LDCDQ screening tools (see Table 11.1). Have you ever witnessed a child or young person struggle with these tasks in your classroom? What might you previously have attributed their difficulties to? How did the child or young person respond in the face of their difficulty? How did you respond?

The tools in Table 11.1 are just some examples, and they have been developed around the world (such that some activities may not be culturally relevant); however, they may aid educationalists to provide support, as described in the following section. Moreover, through developing awareness of key DCD characteristics, and understanding their potential contribution to classroom-based difficulties (including compensatory or avoidant behaviours), educationalists are better placed to support these learners. Shifting our mindset about reasons for behaviour can – in and of itself – shift how we respond to a child or young person's response to their own experiences of difficulty.

Intervention, support and inclusive practices

If inclusion is the 'reinvention of the learning environment for each learner based on their unique strengths and differences' (chapter 1), learners with DCD are prime candidates to benefit from an inclusive education worldview. The school environment is a primary environment of childhood. The ubiquitous impacts of DCD on the developing child make it essential for educationalists to understand expressions of DCD and be familiar with best-practice approaches for support. In terms of embracing neurodiversity, inclusive practices for supporting learners with DCD should play to the child's strengths, particularly if social-emotional impacts are to be reduced. Clinical guidelines for learners with DCD emphasise that if diagnostic criteria are met, treatment and support should be provided (Blank et al. 2019).

> *Activity*
> Find a friend (or a friend's child!) and teach them a new motor task. The task will depend on their age – for example, you may teach them to tie their shoes, crochet or do the floss (https://www.yout-ube.com/watch?v=OKj3wWK-jMSQ). The important thing is that *you* should be confident performing the task.
>
> While teaching them, what teaching strategies did you use? Were they verbal, visual, hand-over-hand guidance? Did they struggle with any of the steps? If so, did you provide additional support? How?

Multidisciplinary working within mainstream educational settings to support learners with DCD

Many professionals working in educational settings have professional remits stemming from a predominantly educational perspective. The addition of a holistic occupational therapy perspective, which incorporates functional information from beyond educational contexts, can enable learners with DCD to develop effective strategies that prevent a school/non-school functional divide. Multidisciplinary, collaborative practice in school-based settings for learners with DCD is most effective when different professionals emphasise professional similarities over differences. Educationalists are all motivated to work with learners in evidence-based ways that support optimal outcomes. In this section, various interventions for supporting learners with DCD are described. While some are more specific to the occupational therapy remit, all members of the multidisciplinary team who work with learners with DCD can contribute to enhanced outcomes by:

- using cognitive strategies in the provision of educational support (e.g. statement of motor strategy before commencing motor tasks)
- reducing motor components of educational tasks (e.g. permitting learners with DCD to type on a computer if the educational intention is to demonstrate language or creativity)
- providing a rationale for gaining SEN support for further assessment, either via the Local Offer or via an Education Health Care Plan (EHCP) (DfE/DoH 2015).

> *Activity*
> Several ways in which educationalists may provide support to learners with DCD have been suggested. Name two potential benefits from increased educator ability to recognise potential signs of DCD for: (1) the child/young person, (2) the child/young person's family, and (3) the educator.

Intervention approaches for learners with DCD

Interventions for learners with DCD can be categorised according to those that address activities that the young person needs to perform (task-oriented approaches), and those that address underlying skills and abilities that are needed for successful completion of an activity (process-oriented approaches). The current DCD evidence base suggests that task-oriented approaches yield better functional performance outcomes, in less time, over process-oriented ones (Blank et al. 2019).

Task-oriented approaches

(a) *The Cognitive Orientation to daily Occupational Performance Approach*

> **Activity**
> To remind yourself of what it's like to learn a new motor task from scratch, watch this video (https://www.yout-ube.com/watch?v=9sxifROLtqk) and learn the steps. What were your initial thoughts about learning this task? Were you keen to try? Or do you usually avoid these kinds of activities?
>
> What strategies did you use to help you learn *individual steps* and *combined sequences*? Did you notice parts of your body move when you hadn't intended for them to move?

The Cognitive Orientation to daily Occupational Performance Approach (CO-OP™) (ICANCOOP n.d.) is a structured, task-oriented, 'performance-based … specifically tailored, active client-centred approach that engages the individual at the meta-cognitive level to solve performance problems'. Children are guided to articulate motor goals using collaborative goal-setting techniques and are supported in identifying and sequencing the steps required for task initiation and completion (using dynamic performance analysis). If needed, gentle prompting is used to help the child understand the motor task demands. On task completion, supportive, strengths-based reflection is used as a foundation for the transfer of CO-OP skills to other arenas of the child's life. This pragmatic problem-solving approach supports empowerment for physical and mental well-being throughout the life course.

Strong empirical evidence supports the effectiveness of the CO-OP approach (Blank et al. 2019). The approach is most commonly delivered by CO-OP-certified occupational therapists following formal training, but the foundational principles of empowering the young person through the development of transferable cognitive strategies to be drawn upon when faced with learning new motor tasks are highly applicable within educational settings.

(b) *Neuromotor Task Training*. Another example of an evidence-based, task-oriented approach commonly used with learners with DCD is Neuromotor Task Training (NTT) (Blank et al. 2019). This approach differs from CO-OP in that, although it also includes cognitive neuroscience principles, motor training is incorporated into the intervention, with motor tasks practised in gradually more challenging ways (Niemeijer, Smits-Engelsman and Schoemaker 2007). Motor learning is supported by repetition, making activities fun, and focusing on goals that are meaningful to the child.

(c) *Handwriting*. Handwriting is a complex motor task, so it is unsurprising that this is frequently highlighted as a functional concern of learners with DCD. Although some have claimed that modern technology has reduced the need for handwriting, evidence suggests that this is not the case (Santangelo and Graham 2016) and that handwriting difficulties remain a particular participatory challenge for learners with DCD. Some evidence demonstrates that direct motor instruction is not the optimal intervention approach for learners with handwriting difficulties, and that individualised handwriting instruction, combined with handwriting teaching via technology, leads to better handwriting improvement (Santangelo and Graham 2016). Clinical guidelines for learners with DCD state that if handwriting difficulties are present, activity-oriented intervention (including ways to self-evaluate performance) are advised. These interventions should be combined with early keyboarding instruction, to support legible recording of work (Blank et al. 2019).

Process-oriented approaches

(a) *Sensory processing*. Sensory processing is a broad term referring to the ability to detect, modulate, interpret and organise sensory information that enters the body through our sensory systems. An individual's ability to detect sensory input depends foremost on the physiological integrity of the sensory systems. In other words, visual input will not be modulated, interpreted or organised if blindness prevents the detection of visual stimuli in the first instance. But intact sensory systems are only the start to effective sensory processing.

Sensory *modulation* refers to the neurological ability to organise the way in which we respond to sensory input (Ayres and Robbins 2005). For typically developing children, this organisation usually occurs in a graded and adaptive manner, but some individuals will demonstrate difficulties with this. Children with neurological *hypersensitivity* will attribute too much importance to potentially unimportant sensory information and respond in ways that seem out of proportion to the stimulus, showing exaggerated physical or emotional responses that are based on principles of fight, flight or freeze. Children with *hyposensitivity* will not attribute enough neurological attention to important sensory information and may miss opportunities for engagement. After the brain decides how much of a response is required for a sensory stimulus, sensory *discrimination* enables the individual to understand sensory characteristics and qualities. For example, when we hold a pencil in our hand, sensory discrimination enables us to understand its size, shape and texture.

Evidence suggests that learners with DCD show notable difficulties with processing sensory information (e.g. Delgado-Lobete et al. 2020). This is highly significant for motor development. Think about a young child with hypersensitivity, whose sensory experiences are driven by survival-based responses (fight, flight or freeze) such that they miss vital early exploratory play that develops motor skills. Alternatively, think about the child with hyposensitivity, whose reduced engagement may limit opportunities for building the mental maps required for developing complex movement patterns. Then think about the child with sensory discrimination difficulties who struggles to integrate their understanding of the relationship between their physical self and their environments, such that the process of executing refined and adaptive movement becomes more laboured.

Although clinical DCD guidelines note that evidence remains inconclusive for the effectiveness of one-to-one sensory integration therapy interventions (Blank et al. 2019), the prevalence of sensory challenges in this population necessitates educator understanding of sensory impacts on participation, with a view to offering environmental or task-related adaptations. When sensory processing difficulties are suspected, referral for assessment by an occupational therapist (see Table 11.1) is recommended.

Activity

Now that you're familiar with DCD, write a sentence capturing your *unique* professional contribution to supporting learners with DCD in educational settings.

Next, name three other professionals who it would be beneficial to consult with to support learners with DCD in the educational setting in which you work (whether they currently work within the setting or not). For each of the professionals chosen, write a sentence defining their *unique* professional contribution to supporting learners with DCD in educational settings.

Review similarities and differences. Were there overlaps or complementary professional skills?

Box 11.1 Case-study: Queenie

Queenie is an 11½-year-old girl, born after a normal pregnancy and birth, who lives with her parents and two older siblings in a small village. There were 17 children in her single-form primary school class, and Queenie was always top of her class academically. Her teachers frequently commented on the presentation of Queenie's work, particularly as she moved into Key Stage 2, but since her parents are both doctors, they laughed it off saying that Queenie just had 'doctor's handwriting'. She transitioned into the local secondary school one term ago and is the youngest child in her class.

Her parents previously noticed some 'clumsiness' but they attributed this to lack of attention and carelessness. It took Queenie longer than her siblings to learn tasks such as toileting, dressing herself and feeding herself, and her parents often wonder why she always seems 'slovenly' compared with her sisters.

Queenie is strong-willed and her parents assumed that her lack of enthusiasm for group sports or swimming was simply due to personal preference for reading and problem-solving games. In fact, Queenie only recently learned to ride a bike after many failed attempts. She now rides with relative competence, and her parents are reassured that she was just waiting to learn this skill 'in her own time'.

Queenie is struggling to acclimatise to the large secondary school. Since the start of the school year, her parents have noticed that Queenie is frequently anxious about attending school (something that never happened in the past) and insists on taking all her books with her every day. Only after much prompting did she share that she finds it difficult to know what equipment she needs for her changing daily schedule. She has a school locker but has got lost a few times trying to find it, making her late for class, so she always carries everything with her 'just in case'. She's had some poor marks for schoolwork due to her handwriting, and her parents are worried about how withdrawn their previously happy-go-lucky Queenie is becoming. She always had close friendships with the village children, but they have started to form new friendships and Queenie is now avoiding social opportunities.

Queenie's form tutor has some awareness of DCD and suggested that her parents complete the DCDQ screening questionnaire (Table 11.1). Based on these results, Queenie was assessed by the family GP who confirmed the fourth DCD diagnostic criterion (*motor skill difficulties not better explained by intellectual delay, visual impairment, or other neurological conditions*) and recommended a referral for occupational therapy and educational psychology assessment. The results of the Wechsler Intelligence Scale for Children (WISC-V) administered by the educational psychologist suggest a full-scale IQ of 123 (which falls within the 'very high' category).

Queenie's standardised professional assessment results suggest that Queenie meets DSM-5 criteria for a DCD diagnosis (see Table 11.2). To date, Queenie's parents have paid privately for her assessments but are now looking to investigate her entitlement to educational support. They have heard about EHCPs and Local Offers and explore the information available online (see Table 11.3).

Activity
Explore the Local Offer of each location in Table 11.3. Consider the educational setting in which you work/are familiar with (you may wish to also explore the Local Offer that applies to the educational setting in which you work). Do the services available to Queenie differ across locations? How do they compare to the setting in which you work/are familiar with?

In each location, how might parents work with the school special educational needs coordinator (SENCo) to gain the educational support that Queenie needs? Is the information that the family needs easily available via the different council resources?

Activity
What day-to-day, practical adjustments could you make to support Queenie (Box 11.1), within the school setting? How would these change if she were still in KS2? How would these change if she were due to transition out of secondary school?

Which other professionals might you work with to support Queenie to achieve her full potential while limiting the secondary social-emotional difficulties commonly associated with DCD?

Table 11.2 Summary of Queenie's DCD assessment and relation to DSM-5 DCD diagnostic criteria (see Box 11.1).

DSM-5 CRITERION	Source of information	Assessment scores				What this means
			Component score	Standard score	Percentile	
1. Acquiring and execution of coordinated motor skills is far below expected level for age, given opportunity for skill learning	Standardised occupational therapy assessment: Movement Assessment Battery for Children, 2nd edition (MABC-2)	Manual Dexterity	12	3	1	This test component looks at how Queenie uses her hands and fingers in a coordinated way to grasp and manipulate objects and make precise movements. A percentile score of 1 means that, out of a large group of children, *Queenie's performance is worse than 99% of children*. This score alone is sufficient for DCD diagnostic purposes. In other words, Queenie seems to experience notable struggles with manual dexterity
		Ball Skills/ Aiming & Catching	14	7	16	This test component looks at how Queenie moves her body in a coordinated way during motor tasks that required rapid motor responses. A percentile score of 16 means that, out of a large group of children, *Queenie's performance is worse than 84% of children*. Although this is a comparative area of strength for Queenie, this score is suggestive of difficulties in this area

(continued)

Table 11.2 (Continued)

DSM-5 CRITERION	Source of information	Assessment scores		What this means
		Static & Dynamic Balance	15 5 5	This test component looks at how Queenie copes with motor activities that require maintaining balance while moving and while remaining in place. A percentile score of 5 means that, out of a large group of children, *Queenie's performance is worse than 95% of children*. This score suggestive that Queenie faces difficulties in this area
		Total Test Score	41 3 1	The MABC-2 may be used for diagnosis of DCD if the total percentile score is below 16 or one of the domain scores is below 5 (Blank et al. 2019). It is clear that this applies to Queenie

(*continued*)

Table 11.2 (Continued)

DSM-5 CRITERION	Source of information	Assessment scores				What this means
			Raw score	Standard score	Percentile	
	Standardised occupational therapy assessment: *Beery-Buktenica Developmental Test of Visual-Motor Integration, 6th edition (VMI)*	Visual-Motor Integration	17	65	1	This test component looks at how Queenie integrates her visual perception and motor abilities in a pencil-and-paper-based task. A percentile score of 1 means that, out of a large group of children, *Queenie's performance is worse than 99% of children*. In other words, visual-motor integration seems to be something that Queenie struggles significantly with
		Visual Perception	28	109	73	This test component looks at how Queenie perceives visual stimuli. A percentile score of 73 means that, out of a large group of children, *Queenie's performance is better than 73% of children*. In other words, her visual perceptual skills are in the upper average, and are a relative strength for Queenie

(continued)

Developmental coordination disorder and dyspraxia **197**

Table 11.2 (Continued)

DSM-5 CRITERION	Source of information	Assessment scores				What this means
			Raw score	Standard score	Percentile	
		Motor Control	18	65	1	This test component looks at Queenie's motor control abilities when using a pencil. A percentile score of 1 means that, out of a large group of children, *Queenie's performance is worse than 99% of children*. In other words, Queenie's visual perceptual strengths are not enough to overcome her difficulties in motor control when she has to perform visual-motor integration tasks
2. *Motor skill difficulties significantly interfere with activities of daily living (ADLs) and impact academic/school productivity, prevocational and vocational activities, leisure and play*	*Parent completion of the DCDQ* Parent report Teacher report Further verified by the visual perception component of the VMI and the WISC-V, which indicate above-average cognitive and perceptual skills	DCDQ: Total score = 52 (indicative of likely DCD)				Based on the 2016 Wechsler Intelligence Scale for Children (WISC-V), Queenie's full-scale IQ score is 123, which falls within the 'very high' category The available information suggests that Queenie is not achieving her full intellectual and participatory potential across home and school settings

(continued)

Table 11.2 (Continued)

DSM-5 CRITERION	Source of information	Assessment scores	What this means
3. Onset is in the early developmental period	Parent report GP – medical history		
4. Motor skill difficulties are not better explained by intellectual delay, visual impairment, or other neurological conditions that affect movement	GP – medical history GP – recent medical examination		

Developmental coordination disorder and dyspraxia **199**

Table 11.3 Information for parents regarding educational support via three local authorities

Queenie's family lives near Leeds	Queenie's family lives near Coventry	Queenie's family lives near Hillingdon
The parents explore the Local Offer here: https://leedslocaloffer.org.uk/#!/directory	The parents explore the Local Offer here: https://www.coventry.gov.uk/localoffer	The parents explore the Local Offer here: https://hillingdon.gov.uk/send
They find a 'one-minute guide' to the Local Offer (https://leedslocaloffer.org.uk/#!/model/page/service/3679) and learn that the majority of learners with SEN are eligible to have their needs met within their existing educational provision. They continue to explore the website which has clearly organised information for young people, parents and educators.	The homepage has an introductory video (https://youtu.be/fgddMVDuXrE) that provides a brief overview of the Local Offer as well as the resources that are available on the site. They are particularly grateful for the 'jargon buster' page (https://www.coventry.gov.uk/directory-record/42588/jargon-buster-frequently-used-send-terms), which they find very helpful in understanding many terms that they have recently heard only for the first time. Although the 'jargon buster' is useful, it does not include information about DCD, even though other diagnoses are listed and explained	The homepage is laid out with information in various categories. Queenie's parents are still unsure about what would apply to her, so they begin by exploring the heading 'I think my child has special needs' (https://hillingdon.gov.uk/article/4401/What-are-special-educational-needs). Despite trying many different avenues on the website, they are unable to find any information specifically related to 'DCD' or 'developmental coordination disorder'. When searching for 'dyspraxia', they find an encouraging example of a young person's experiences, but no specific guidance on how to gain support for Queenie's current educational challenges. They also find information about the Dyspraxia Foundation
They explore the links on the site and do a general search of 'DCD' and 'developmental coordination disorder'. At first, they are encouraged to see a large number of results, but then realise that many are general resources. When running a more specific search, they find a link to a private occupational therapy practice and to the Dyspraxia Foundation	They explore the links on the site and type in 'DCD' and 'developmental coordination disorder' but their search terms do not generate any results. They know that the term 'dyspraxia' is sometimes used and find a link to the Dyspraxia Foundation	

(*continued*)

Table 11.3 (Continued)

Queenie's family lives near Leeds	Queenie's family lives near Coventry	Queenie's family lives near Hillingdon
Queenie's parents find clear information that SEN support in the Leeds area is organised around different types of educational settings. Despite her diagnosis, Queenie does not seem to meet the criteria for schooling within any of the specialist school settings. Her provision needs to be offered via mainstream educational provision The Local Offer website refers Queenie's parents to the Leeds City Council site to explain the Local Offer of support in mainstream schools (https://www.leeds.gov.uk/schools-and-education/support-for-pupils-with-send/support-with-learning). From exploring the site, they come across information about a 'Graduated Approach' (https://leedslocaloffer.org.uk/#!/model/page/service/34148) Queenie's parents realise that they will need to gain the support and guidance from the school special educational needs coordinator (SENCo) in order to establish next steps for gaining optimal educational support	Queenie's parents learn that teachers are required to regularly assess the progress of all pupils. If a child is not making the expected educational progress, support should initially be provided by the teacher. If the child is still not making good progress, the school SENCo should be consulted to advise on extra help and support From scrolling through the website, they find info about Education, Health and Care Plans (EHCPs) (https://www.coventry.gov.uk/directory/86/send-local-offer-for-coventry/category/1158) and explore the information about Queenie's potential eligibility with the 'Graduated Pathway' (https://www.coventry.gov.uk/directory-record/42410/education-health-and-care-plan-ehcp-eligibility) From the available information, it is clear that Queenie's parents need to liaise closely with the school SENCo. Much emphasis is placed on the fact that an EHCP would only be available if Queenie is not making educational progress (as opposed to whether or not she is reaching her potential). Through this investigation, they learn that they need first and foremost to gain support via the routes that are 'ordinarily available' (http://www.coventry.gov.uk/downloads/file/23561/provision_ordinarily_available_for_students_without_an_ehc_plan)	They are guided to speak with their health provider as a first step if they feel that their child might have SEN. As they have already done this, they continue to search for information as to the next steps to gain educational support based on Queenie's clinical assessment. Some initial information is provided about the SEND Local Offer (https://hillingdon.gov.uk/article/4404/What-is-the-SEND-local-offer) with an embedded link to 'access the SEND Local Offer' but they find themselves back at the page they started at They explore the types of schools available (https://hillingdon.gov.uk/article/4408/Types-of-school-places-for-children-with-SEND) and find within the mainstream school page some brief information about EHCPs, but no links or further info. They also find the ordinarily available provision document (https://hillingdon.gov.uk/media/1961/Hillingdon-Ordinarily-Available-Provision/pdf/Hillingdon_Ordinarily_Available_Provision.pdf?m=15888847952827) but do not see any specific information in there about DCD or dyspraxia It becomes apparent that they will need to gain the support and direction from the school SENCo to understand what Queenie's rights and entitlements are, now that her diagnosis of DCD has been confirmed

Conclusion

Developmental coordination disorder (DCD) refers to a lifelong condition characterised by marked difficulties in learning and performing motor- and coordination-based tasks. Although often not diagnosed until secondary difficulties have already developed, DCD is evident from an early age, is not explained by any other condition, and has significant social and emotional impacts. From the perspective of psychological and educational inclusion, participatory difficulties tend to become more marked when children with DCD enter structured educational settings, and educationalists have a unique opportunity to support the long-term functional outcomes of children with DCD. This can be achieved through contribution to collaborative identification processes and adoption of evidence-based intervention strategies, such as breaking age-appropriate, classroom-based motor tasks into stages, and helping children to verbalise motor-based problem-solving strategies prior to performing a task.

Resources
If you would like to know more about DCD, check out the resources below.

Websites/online articles:
Dyspraxia Foundation: https://dyspraxiafoundation.org.uk/
CanChild: https://www.canchild.ca/en/diagnoses/developmental-coordination-disorder
Movement Difficulties in Children, The British Psychological Society (2011): https://www.bps.org.uk/psychologist/movement-difficulties-children
Telethon Kids Institute (Australia) video: https://youtu.be/KupoCLN6Yls
Telethon Kids Institute (Australia) report: https://www.telethonkids.org.au/globalassets/media/documents/projects/impact-for-dcd-report.pdf
Sensory Minis: https://www.youtube.com/channel/UCWKKMgblffBKOmdxJYrFTRA?app=desktop
Pathways: https://pathways.org

Recommended twitter accounts:
@DYSPRAXIAFDTN
@profamandakirby
@canchild_ca
@DyspraxiaKids
@DyspraxiaUK
@LittleDCDQ
@academy_coop

See also:
Cermak, S.A. and Larkin, D. (2002) *Developmental Coordination Disorder.* Albany, NY: Delmar Thomson Learning.
Kranowitz, C.S. (2006) *The Out-of-Sync Child: Recognizing and Coping with Sensory Processing Disorder.* New York: Penguin.

References

American Occupational Therapy Association (2020) Occupational Therapy Practice Framework: Domain and Process – fourth edition, *American Journal of Occupational Therapy*, 74 (suppl. 2): 7412410010. Available at: https://doi.org/10.5014/ajot.2020.74S2001

American Psychiatric Association (APA) (2013) *Diagnostic and Statistical Manual of Mental Disorders*, 5th edition (DSM-5). Arlington, VA: APA.

Ayres, A.J. (1972) *Sensory Integration and Learning Disorders*. Los Angeles, CA: Western Psychological Services.

Ayres, A.J. and Robbins, J. (2005) *Sensory Integration and the Child: Understanding Hidden Sensory Challenges*. Los Angeles, CA: Western Psychological Services.

Barnett, A., Henderson, S.E., Scheib, B. and Schulz, J. (2007) *Detailed Assessment of Speed of Handwriting*. London: Pearson.

Beery, K.E., Beery, N.A. and Buktenica, N.A. (2010) *Beery-Buktenica Developmental Test of Visual-Motor Integration*, 6th edition. London: Pearson.

Blank, R., Barnett, A.L., Cairney, J., Green, D., Kirby, A., Polatajko, H. (2019) International clinical practice recommendations on the definition, diagnosis, assessment, intervention, and psychosocial aspects of developmental coordination disorder, *Developmental Medicine and Child Neurology*, 61 (3): 242–285.

Bruininks, B.D. and Bruininks R.H. (2005) *Bruininks-Oseretsky Test of Motor Proficiency*, 2nd edition. London: Pearson.

Chambers, M. and Sugden, D. (2006) *Early Years Movement Skills: Description, Diagnosis and Intervention*. Chichester: Whurr Publishers.

Clements, S. (1966) *Minimal brain dysfunction in children*. Public Health Service Publication, #1414. US Department of Health, Education and Welfare.

Delgado-Lobete, L., Pértega-Díaz, S., Santos-del-Riego, S. and Montes-Montes, R. (2020) Sensory processing patterns in developmental coordination disorder, attention deficit hyperactivity disorder and typical development, *Research in Developmental Disabilities*, 100: 103608. Available at: https://doi.org/10.1016/j.ridd.2020.103608

Dewey. D. and Wilson, B.N. (2001) Developmental coordination disorder: what is it?, *Physical and Occupational Therapy in Paediatrics*, 20 (2/3): 5–27.

Department for Education and Department of Health (DfE/DoH) (2015) *Special Educational Needs and Disability Code of Practice: 0 to 25 years*. London: DfE. Available at: https://www.gov.uk/government/uploads/system/uploads/attachment_data/file/398815/SEND_Code_of_Practice_January_2015.pdf (accessed 16 October 2022).

Dunford, C. and Richards, S. (2003) *'Doubly disadvantaged': Report of a Survey on Waiting Lists and Waiting Times for Occupational Therapy Services for Children with Developmental Coordination Disorder*. London: College of Occupational Therapists.

Dunn, W. (2014) *The Sensory Profile*, 2nd edition. London: Pearson.

Dunn, W. and Brown, C.E. (2002) *Adolescent/Adult Sensory Profile: User's Manual*. London: Pearson.

Fewell, R.R. and Folio, M.R. (2000) *Peabody Developmental Motor Scales*, 2nd edition. London: Pearson.

Gubbay, S.S. (1978) The management of developmental apraxia, *Developmental Medicine and Child Neurology*, 20 (5): 643–646.

Henderson, S., Sugden, D. and Barnett, A. (2007) *Movement Assessment Battery for Children*, 2nd edition. London: Pearson.

ICANCOOP (n.d.) *The CO-OP Approach*. Available at: https://icancoop.org/pages/the-co-op-approach (accessed 16 October 2022).

Lee, E.J. and Zwicker, J.G. (2021) Early identification of children with/at risk of developmental coordination disorder: a scoping review, *Developmental Medicine and Child Neurology*, 63 (6): 649–658.

Lingam, R., Hunt, L., Golding, J., Jongmans, M. and Emond, A. (2009) Prevalence of developmental coordination disorder using the DSM-IV at 7 years of age: a UK population-based study, *Pediatrics*, 123 (4): e693–e700.

Lino, F. and Chieffo, D.P.R. (2022) Developmental coordination disorder and most prevalent comorbidities: a narrative review, *Children*, 9: 1095. Available at: https://doi.org/10.3390/children9071095

Missiuna, C., Moll, S., King, S., King, G. and Law, M. (2007) A trajectory of troubles: parents' impressions of the impact of developmental coordination disorder, *Physical and Occupational Therapy in Pediatrics*, 27 (1): 81–101.

Niemeijer, A.S., Smits-Engelsman, B.C. and Schoemaker, M.M. (2007) Neuromotor task training for children with developmental coordination disorder: a controlled trial, *Developmental Medicine and Child Neurology*, 49 (6): 406–411.

Parham, L.D., Ecker, C., Kuhaneck, H.M., Henry, D.A. and Glennon, T.J. (2021) *Sensory Processing Measure*, 2nd edition. Los Angeles, CA: Western Psychological Services.

Rihtman, T., Wilson, B.N. and Parush, S. (2011) Development of the Little Developmental Coordination Disorder Questionnaire for preschoolers and preliminary evidence of its psychometric properties in Israel, *Research in Developmental Disabilities*, 32 (4): 1378–1387.

Royal College of Occupational Therapists (2021) *Occupational therapy: Unlocking the potential of children and young people*. Available at: www.rcot.co.uk/files/occupational-therapy-unlocking-potential-children-and-young-people (accessed 16 October 2022).

Santangelo, T. and Graham, S. (2016) A comprehensive meta-analysis of handwriting instruction, *Educational Psychology Review*, 28 (2): 225–265.

Sugden, D. (2007) Current approaches to intervention in children with developmental coordination disorder, *Developmental Medicine and Child Neurology*, 49 (6): 467–471.

Tal-Saban, M. and Kirby, A. (2018) Adulthood in developmental coordination disorder (DCD): a review of current literature based on ICF perspective, *Current Developmental Disorders Reports*, 5 (1): 9–17.

Wechsler, D. (2016) *Wechsler Intelligence Scale for Children*, 5th UK edition (WISC-V UK). London: Pearson.

Wilson, B.N., Crawford, S.G., Green, D., Roberts, G., Aylott, A. and Kaplan, B.J. (2009) Psychometric properties of the revised Developmental Coordination Disorder Questionnaire, *Physical and Occupational Therapy in Pediatrics*, 29 (2): 182–202.

World Health Organisation (WHO) (2016) *International Statistical Classification of Diseases and Related Health Problems*, 10th revision (ICD-10). Geneva: WHO.

12 Psycho-educational assessment and instruction for students who have visual impairments

Vassilios Papadimitriou and Ayse Dolunay Sarica

By the end of this chapter, you will be able to:

- identify the development and education of individuals with visual impairments as a unique field of study
- highlight the top priority points related to the assessment of students with visual impairments
- have informed ideas on inclusive instructional techniques, particularly braille and assistive technology
- apply practical evidence-based tips on including students with visual impairments in general education classrooms.

Box 12.1 Case study: Helen

Helen is a nine-year-old girl who was born with total loss of sight and lives in Athens, Greece. Her family is very supportive, and her parents have adjusted the house to create a safe and pleasant environment for her. Helen currently attends third grade at a public school. Although she gets along well with her classmates, she avoids communication with other students at school. She displays poor orientation and mobility skills, including safe travel around her neighbourhood and tracking objects, and has begun taking formal cane courses. Helen reads braille but experiences comprehension difficulties with longer texts. Moreover, she has satisfactory typing skills but struggles to express her thoughts when writing. Finally, Helen performs poorly on complex maths problems and geometry. In the upcoming school year, Helen will have a new teacher.

Activity
What could be the potential effect on a student with visual impairment of having a new teacher? Consider ways to support Helen's safe travel within and around the school building.

The rationale behind working with individuals with visual impairments

The role of one's social milieu in learning, personality and development has been stressed by many pioneers in the field of psychology, including Bronfenbrenner, Vygotsky and Bowlby (Mitchell and Ziegler 2007). Such a theoretical framework has helped us realise the quality and quantity of one's social relationships are a critical determinant of human development. Beginning from birth, all humans are expected to display certain age-appropriate social behaviours which are, to some extent, shaped by cultural norms and values. A three-month-old is expected to smile back at her caregiver's vocalisations, an eight-year-old to follow classroom rules, and so on. These so-called 'typical' social behaviours almost always result in positive social interactions, which make way for social acceptance and learning.

Eye contact and following non-verbal visual cues are of utmost importance during these interactions; after all, these skills are what the majority of us benefit from in social settings. This process may well be questioned when it comes to individuals with visual impairment, where eye contact and making use of visual cues is absent or significantly limited at best. Individuals with visual impairment, therefore, have different social interaction skills and preferences, which can cause social interaction difficulties beginning, in many cases, at a very early age. Such a potential threat to social interactions may in turn hinder one's learning opportunities (Ferrell 2000; Celeste 2005). For instance, social games require quick reactions among players and these quick reactions almost always require the ability to read visual cues.

According to Warren (1994), individuals with and without visual impairments should be viewed as 'more alike than different' in developmental terms, since both groups learn, albeit in differing ways. Accordingly, the Council for Exceptional Children (CEC 1994) reported that individuals with visual impairment should be supported in ways that match their specific learning patterns. So, there is a need for specialised support that works for these individuals. This framework has been verified by numerous studies beginning in the 1960s (e.g. Fraiberg, Smith and Adelson 1969; Fazzi et al. 2005), showing that psychoeducational programmes help close the developmental gap between individuals with and without visual impairment. It also shows that visual impairment is mostly a biological risk rather than an acquired difference (Warren 1994), in that individuals with visual impairment can develop to their full potential given time with well-tailored support and services (Ferrell 2000).

Pop quiz
1 In what ways might individuals with and without visual impairment may be considered alike?
2 Twelve third graders play hide-and-seek. Would a child with visual impairment be able to keep up their peers? Why/why not?

Definitions and statistics

Visual impairment is a low-incidence condition (Augestad, Klingenberg and Fosse 2012), and this population is characterised by remarkable heterogeneity. For instance, retinopathy of prematurity may result in either total or partial loss of sight, and will have a direct affect on the learning media that will be selected for instruction (Smith and Kelly 2014). Approximately 75 per cent of individuals with visual impairment are 65 or older (Cryer and Home 2011), whereas a very small proportion are under 15 years of age (WHO 2004). In Europe, 1–4/10,000 children are born with a visual impairment (Kocur and Resnikoff 2002), with nearly 85 per cent having residual vision (Holbrook and Koenig 1992). No differences related to gender have been reported in developed countries (Augestad, Klingenberg and Fosse 2012). In contrast, in developing countries such as India, nearly half of children with visual impairment suffer from potentially curable diseases (e.g. cataract) or are deprived of essential ingredients (e.g. vitamin A) in their daily diet, while more females than males have total loss of sight (Dandona and Dandona 2003). Finally, nearly 50 per cent of students with visual impairment have further difficulties requiring additional health and educational support (Hatton, Ivy and Boyer 2013).

Visual impairment may be classified according to age of onset of sight loss (Voss 2013), or as degree of sight loss in relation to visual acuity and visual field (Solebo, Teoh and Rahi 2017) (see Table 12.1).

In individuals with total loss of sight, two prevalent hypotheses are used to explain how the brain reacts. The 'general loss hypothesis' of neuroplasticity, which rests on the deficit model of learning and instruction, supports that loss of vision obstructs certain cognitive and/or sensory functions, such

Table 12.1 Classification of visual impairment

Age of onset		Degree of loss	
Congenital	**Adventitious**	**Total**	**Partial**
(0–12 months)	(>12 months)	Visual acuity <3/60 in the better eye and/or visual field <10 degrees	Visual acuity between 6/60 and 3/60 in the better eye

as the processing of spatial information mostly fed by vision (Occelli, Spence and Zampini 2013). Fortunately, most studies support the 'compensatory hypothesis', which states that total sight loss can induce sensory compensation mostly via sharpening the auditory and haptic senses following the sight loss (Collignon et al. 2013; Voss 2013).

Due to brain plasticity and life experience, each learner displays individual preferences and skills for learning (strengths and challenges). These preferences and skills (strengths) are the essence of selecting appropriate instructional techniques and materials to create bespoke support tailored to each individual learner's needs. According to this individualised approach, students are divided into: (a) those who use tactual and/or auditory channels (e.g. the braille code and/or the aural reading media, a cane for orientation and mobility), and (b) those who use their functional vision (e.g. large print) (Stewart 2014).

Debate
What might the advantages and disadvantages be of congenital vision loss?

Assessment of students with visual impairment

Assessing learners with visual impairment is in many ways similar to assessing their sighted peers. However, there are some important issues. First, few formal assessment instruments for visual impairment exist, and in many countries there are none at all (Celeste 2005). This makes informal assessment necessary, which may be considered a strength rather than a limitation, since it opens the way for individualised assessment and planning. It may, however, become a critical issue if a team prefers to base its educational programme on formal assessment results, which almost always will disregard the nature of visual impairment, resulting in misleading plans and interventions. For instance, children with visual impairment display differences in motor development compared with their sighted peers (Brambring 2006). Children with total sight loss may never crawl in order to avoid head injuries. Formal assessments could misinterpret this tendency as a motor deficit, which would be incorrect.

The second issue to consider is the nature of vision loss, which can significantly impact academic and non-academic performance. Vision is a far sense (that is, sensation of a stimulus that is out of reach of one's body), communicating a rich variety of environmental stimuli to the sighted individual in an instant. In turn, rapid spatial recognition enables that same individual to quickly mobilise and organise cognitive processes and social behaviours. In addition, vision facilitates deductive learning, which saves the learner time. Individuals with visual impairment, on the other hand, generally use inductive reasoning during active exploration and learning (Ferrell 2000). For instance, the teacher may present the class with a wooden cone. All sighted children will encode its properties (shape, size, texture) simultaneously with the teacher's verbal explanation (deductive learning), whereas Helen (see Box 12.1) will have to touch all parts of the cone to form a mental image of the object, which takes time (inductive reasoning). Therefore, a student with visual impairment will need to be given longer response times during assessment as well as instruction (Ferrell 2000).

The third point to consider is the materials to be used during assessment. Younger students with visual impairment generally prefer real-life objects or objects that display very similar sensory characteristics to real-life objects when learning. Therefore, such materials will need to be made available during assessment so that they can display their already acquired skills (Brambring and Troster 1994). For instance, if a student with visual impairment is asked to name a given toy car, its physical characteristics should symbolise the real car's qualities as much as possible. It is possible that a student may well have formed the concept of a real car but still may not have generalised the concept to a tiny model that an assessor will use to measure cognitive and language skills.

There are two major areas of assessment and instruction specific to students with visual impairment: learning media, and orientation and mobility. Unlike what is generally believed, individuals with visual impairment do learn the same knowledge, skills and abilities that the sighted do, but they follow different pathways. For example, from an individual differences perspective (Warren 1994), two students with similar demographics and eye conditions will never select exactly the same learning media. All a teacher will need to do during assessment is use materials that require the use of the five senses. For instance, the teacher may use real fruits to assess the student's taste, olfactory and haptic senses, and use a white or black surface to check simultaneously for residual vision. Thus, extra effort needs to be put into identifying the learning media for building both academic and non-academic goals. A teacher ought to know whether her student will be a braille reader-writer, while an orientation and mobility specialist would have to know her student's auditory and olfactory skills when teaching her to travel around the neighbourhood.

As regards literacy skills, assessment should focus on (a) selecting the appropriate learning and literacy media, and (b) literacy performance, because these skills form the foundation for achievement in various academic and non-academic areas (Koenig and Holbrook 2000). A *learning media assessment* is a systematic process for gathering information on how a student uses visual, tactile and auditory learning channels for reading and writing, and should be conducted on a frequent basis, especially when there are changes either in the student's school life or in their visual, auditory and tactile abilities (McNear and Farrenkopf 2014). For example, in the case of a change in residual vision and/or hearing due to a degenerative eye condition (e.g. Usher's syndrome), a new learning media assessment will be necessary to revise instruction. Moreover, nowadays, children with visual impairment have mixed media preferences, using braille, large print and assistive technology (AT), such as auditory media (e.g. braille displays, screen-reading software), to study and learn in class. Any AT solutions should always meet the ongoing needs of learners with visual impairment, promoting their literacy skills within the mainstream classroom and access to the full curriculum of the grade they are enrolled in, like their sighted peers, but with appropriate modifications (Argyropoulos et al. 2019).

Although formal assessment is an issue in visual impairment, standardised literacy tests may be used for students with visual impairment as long as any necessary modifications do not significantly change the content, validity or reliability of the test (Heinze 2000; Argyropoulos and Papadimitriou 2017). On the other hand, informal procedures can be used daily or periodically to assess a student's progress in acquiring the necessary skills, such as environmental assessments (analysis of the school environment) and a portfolio with samples of the student's work (Layton 2000). Such techniques guide instruction by ensuring that teaching, learning and evaluation are integral parts of a continuous cycle, help document the student's functioning and achievement of the IEP (Individualised Education Plan) goals, based on chapter tests and objectives, while securing the appropriate accommodation (e.g. modifying instructions: Layton 2000).

The second specific area of assessment and instruction for visual impairment is orientation and mobility (O&M). *Orientation* is being aware of one's location in a certain environment and knowing where to go and how to get there with the help of one's senses, while *mobility* is the ability to travel safely from one place to another (Griffin-Shirley, Trusty and Rickard 2000). The two sets of skills combine to support the safe, independent and purposeful movement of someone with visual impairment. Proficiency in O&M is important because it supports active exploration of the environment, cognitive skills and social skills (Jacobson 1993). The skills that are assessed for O&M needs include body image, motor skills, stamina, gait, sensory processing and concept formation (e.g. environmental concepts), together with formal orientation (e.g. using auditory cues effectively in traffic) and formal mobility (e.g. proficiency in the sighted guide technique) skills (Jacobson 1993). The assessment of these skills requires O&M specialists to work in collaboration with general and special educators.

As can be seen, the educational assessment of students with visual impairment is a complex task that requires careful planning and consideration by a truly specialised team, especially since most formal assessment instruments and procedures are not standardised for visual impairment (Heinze 2000). Therefore, all assessments require careful observation by a team of professionals with further information collected through interviews with significant others (e.g. parents, former teachers).

Pop quiz

1. How would you modify reading instruction for a student who is gradually losing their sight and will eventually become blind?
2. Think of three physical modifications that would facilitate Helen's orientation and mobility within the school building (see Box 12.1).

Curriculum and exam modifications

Modifications to the curriculum for students with visual impairment may generally be considered unnecessary because they are mostly able to learn in line with their peers, but the content should be presented using alternative modes of delivery (e.g. the braille code, audiobooks, screen reading software). According to Viljoen (2020a), a decision to modify learning content can generally be linked to three aspects that may require adaptation: abstract content, adaptation to ensure variety, and adaptation due to complexity. More specifically, students are more likely to comprehend using real objects or experiences and content that they can relate either from whole-to-part or part-to-whole. Of course, tactile and other sensory experiences that match individual needs may co-exist with the visual experiences for sighted classmates, while teachers need to adapt complex learning content (e.g. guidance on how to 'read' graphics) (Brown and Glaser 2014).

For exams, students should be provided with alternative test conditions – for example, they should remain close to an activity to maintain tactile control. The teacher may conduct an oral exam and record the student's responses. The teacher can also adapt the questions and provide extra time as well as the necessary equipment, such as computer and geometric instruments (Viljoen 2020a).

Instruction via the combined-medium approach

Inclusive classrooms aim to meet the individual preferences and needs of all students. In the case of students with visual impairment, this involves the physical characteristics of the classroom and the school (e.g. class dimensions, precautions taken for travel around the schoolyard) as well as planning instruction (e.g. long-term lesson planning, accessible learning materials).

Teaching students with visual impairment via a combined-medium approach, involving braille as well as AT (audio and tactile input), is relatively new and constitutes a challenge for educational inclusion because the teacher has to continuously update their knowledge in order to increase their students' independence. For example, students with visual impairment can download, print and submit their homework to their teacher at the same time as their sighted peers without requiring assistance (Smith and Kelly 2014). However, AT should supplement and not replace braille, as this may significantly delay the development of braille skills (Argyropoulos et al. 2020).

The responsibility for teaching braille lies primarily with qualified teachers. Both general educators and assistant teachers should create a positive learning environment that is rich in braille experiences and ensure that all the necessary teaching materials are available (Roe et al. 2014). Reading and writing instruction are fully adapted to individual needs and interests and obviously differ from literacy instruction for sighted students (Swenson 2008).

For this reason, especially in the early grades, students with visual impairment need continuous and organised instruction on a daily basis to improve their literacy skills via direct and explicit instruction (Emerson, Holbrook and D'Andrea 2009). Moreover, students with visual impairment will need additional time to participate holistically in literacy activities alongside their classmates (Swenson 2008).

Access to mathematics and scientific notations is enabled by the Nemeth code, an extension of the braille code. Since visual techniques, such as observation, imitation and modelling, cannot be adapted to teach mathematical and scientific concepts (Jitngernmadan et al. 2017), direct instruction is the most widely used approach (Koenig and Holbrook 2000). Teachers should also offer incidental learning opportunities (Zebehazy, Zigmond and Zimmerman 2012) through multisensory methods. Finally, screen reader software (e.g. ReadHear) is appropriate for science and mathematics (van Leendert et al. 2021), while students with visual impairment can use rulers, set squares and protractors that are embossed as well as talking calculators (McNear and Farrenkopf 2014).

Assistive technology and material modifications

Materials for training students with total loss of sight are distinguished according to aural and tactile features and are subject to transcription, processing and adaptation to specific student needs. This procedure depends on students' previous experience (e.g. braille proficiency), teacher competencies, the teacher's assessment and the available resources in the educational setting where students with visual impairment are enrolled (Argyropoulos et al. 2020).

Teachers can assist students with visual impairment through verbal prompts and descriptions of the activities presented in class (Ondin 2015). They also can be provided with class notes in advance (e.g. a list of tasks, another student's notes, notes on a CD/USB) and a record of the lesson to take notes from afterwards (Viljoen 2020a). In audio lectures, the content should be broken down into chunks. Priority should be given to the main information, followed by details, where necessary. Teachers should provide detailed explanations for a new term/object/subject introduced and access to control over audio files in terms of playing, stopping, rewinding and controlling the speed (Ondin 2015).

Tactile materials, which are necessary for learners with visual impairment to take control of the reading process, also allow connections with theory and curriculum activities. For instance, tactile maps with elevated features can be perceived through tactile exploration (Jehoel et al. 2005). Students with visual impairment usually explore tactile maps inductively. They use the fingers of both hands and execute gentle movements, with the variety of movements resulting in more correct answers compared with an unmoved hand (McLinden and McCall 2016). Additionally, texture is an important factor for the exploration of tactile maps, so teachers should prefer microcapsule paper and paper with rougher surfaces (Jehoel et al. 2009). Moreover, adjustments to braille

Table 12.2 Literacy devices for visually impaired learners

Device	Description	Purpose
Brailler	Device with six keys corresponding to the dots of the braille code and three additional keys	Writing in braille
Laptop with screen reader	Software converting any text into oral speech	Suitable for extensive texts or inexperienced braille readers
Mountbatten brailler	Multi-device and electronic braille typewriter which, among other things, stores and edits texts, translates from print in braille and vice versa without a personal computer, allows sighted readers to read in print what students with visual impairment write in braille	Writing essays
Optical character recognition (OCR) software	Converts printed text into accessible digital text via a scanner	Digital texts are read orally via a screen reader or tactilely through a braille display
Refreshable braille displays	Device for displaying braille characters	Enhances braille skills and communication
Braille embossers	Render print into braille	Printing text

books are essential so that braille readers have direct contact with the source of information, but material in braille takes time to adapt and produce in the correct format (Argyropoulos et al. 2019). Teachers should reduce the amount of information without modifying the level of difficulty, while more time is always essential. If necessary, teachers could use e-books or provide links for extra details (Viljoen 2020b). Similarly, 3D constructions, tactile or textbook maps and diagrams should be simplified, comprehensive and related to the already acquired experience and/or knowledge of the student, so as to improve the formation of permanent mental images (Dulin 2008).

Table 12.2 presents some of the most popular devices that students will need to learn to use.

> *Pop quiz*
> Helen must read a poem from Blake and a three-page passage about Shakespeare for the Literature course. Which reading medium/media would be best for each task and why?

Concluding points and inclusion tips for students with visual impairments

Being a part of one's society is a basic right and individuals with visual impairment are no exception. School is a perfect socialising and learning environment for an individual, which brings us to inclusive education where everyone is educated under one roof. Contrary to traditional models, inclusive education does not stress a developmental disability/at risk/special needs-specific paradigm but rather embraces the individual developmental needs and preferences of all students (Tanrıverdi and Sarıca 2021) (for more information on inclusion, see Chapter 1). When it comes to students with visual impairment, one problem that general educators face is the mismatch between the learning media of the students and their teachers' common preference for using vision-based activities during instruction. Thus, students with visual impairment in general classrooms may be considered at a disadvantage, since they require instruction that triggers the remaining senses to accomplish academic as well as non-academic learning objectives. Again, this calls for a positive attitude on the behalf of teachers to work more willingly on visual impairment-related instructional accommodations (see Table 12.3 for inclusion tips in primary grades).

Table 12.3 Inclusion Tips

Objective	Course	Activity
Peer interaction	Physical education	Pull a guide wire/rope across a gym, track or any safe open area very tightly with a carabiner or handle on the rope. Make sure there is a clear marker at the end of the wire/rope so that the child knows the end of the runway. Assist all students, including the target child, to get in line and run using the wire/rope. Call the name of the child as they take turns. Make sure you verbalise what is going on throughout the activity. You may also tell each child to verbalise their actions, say, 'It's my turn to run. It's …'s turn.'
Reading	All day	Write on small braille papers the names of all class objects and furniture. Glue them on the objects. Help the student touch the objects and read their names. Direct classmates to do the same activity with the target student

> *Resources*
> If you would like to learn more about visual impairment, take a look at the following:
>
> International Council for Education of People with Visual Impairment (ICEVI): https://icevi.org/
>
> Royal National Institute of Blind People (RNIB): https://www.rnib.org.uk/
>
> Perkins School for the Blind: https://www.perkins.org/
>
> American Foundation for the Blind (AFB): https://afb.org
>
> Australian Disability Clearinghouse on Education and Training (ADCET): https://www.adcet.edu.au/inclusive-teaching/specific-disabilities/blind-vision-impaired

References

Argyropoulos, V. and Papadimitriou, V. (2017) Spelling accuracy and students with visual impairments: a quantitative and qualitative approach of spelling errors, *International Journal of Educational Research*, 83: 135–141.

Argyropoulos, V., Padeliadu, S., Avramidis, E., Tsiakali, T. and Nikolaraizi, M. (2019) An investigation of preferences and choices of students with vision impairments on literacy medium for studying, *British Journal of Visual Impairment*, 37 (2): 154–168.

Argyropoulos, V., Sideridis, G., Nikolaraizi, M., Martos, A., Padeliadu, S., Gkyrtis, K. et al. (2020) Refreshable braille displays and reading fluency: a pilot study in individuals with blindness, *Education and Information Technologies*, 25 (5): 3613–3630.

Augestad, L.B., Klingenberg, O. and Fosse, P. (2012) Braille use among Norwegian children from 1967 to 2007: trends in the underlying causes, *Acta Ophthalmologica*, 90 (5): 428–434.

Brambring, M. (2006) Divergent development of gross motor skills in children who are blind or sighted, *Journal of Visual Impairment & Blindness*, 100 (10): 620–634.

Brambring, M. and Troster, H. (1994) The assessment of cognitive development in blind infants and preschoolers, *Journal of Visual Impairment & Blindness*, 88 (1): 9–18.

Brown, L.C. and Glaser, S. (2014) Teaching the expanded core curriculum in general education settings, in C.B. Allman and S. Lewis (eds.), *ECC Essentials: Teaching the Expanded Core Curriculum to Students with Visual Impairments*. New York: AFB Press.

Celeste, M. (2005) Impact of twin-to-twin transfusion syndrome, preterm birth and vision loss on development, *Journal of Visual Impairment & Blindness*, 99 (9): 535–548.

Collignon, O., Dormal, G., Albouy, G., Vandewalle, G., Voss, P., Phillips, C. et al. (2013) Impact of blindness onset on the functional organization and the connectivity of the occipital cortex, *Brain*, 136 (9): 2769–2783.

Council for Exceptional Children (CEC) (1994) Family-focused services for infants and young children with visual handicaps, *RE:view*, 25 (4): 184–189.

Cryer, H. and Home, S. (2011) *Final report: Feasibility of developing a diagnostic touch test to determine braille reading potential*. Birmingham: RNIB Centre for Accessible Information.

Dandona, R. and Dandona, L. (2003) Childhood blindness in India: a population based perspective, *British Journal of Ophthalmology*, 87 (3): 263–265.

Dulin, D. (2008) Effects of prior experience in raised line materials and prior visual experience in length estimations by blind people, *British Journal of Visual Impairment*, 26 (3): 223–237.

Emerson, R.W., Holbrook, M.C. and D'Andrea, F.M. (2009) Acquisition of literacy skills by young children who are blind: results from the ABC braille study, *Journal of Visual Impairment and Blindness*, 103 (10): 610–624.

Fazzi, E., Signorini, S.G., Bova, S.M., Ondei, P. and Bianchi, P.E. (2005) Early intervention in visually impaired children, *International Congress Series*, 1282: 117–121.

Ferrell, K.A. (2000) Growth and development of young children, in M.C. Holbrook and A.J. Koenig (eds.), *Foundations of Education: History and Theory of Teaching Children and Youths with Visual Impairments*. vol. 1, 2nd edition. New York: AFB Press.

Fraiberg, S., Smith, M. and Adelson, E. (1969) An educational program for blind infants, *Journal of Special Education*, 3 (2): 121–139.

Griffin-Shirley, N., Trusty, S. and Rickard, R. (2000) Orientation and mobility, in A. Koenig and M.C. Holbrook (eds.), *Foundations of Education: Instructional Strategies for Teaching Children and Youths with Visual Impairments*, vol. 2, 2nd edition. New York: AFB Press.

Hatton, D.D., Ivy, S.E. and Boyer, C. (2013) Severe visual impairments in infants and toddlers in the United States, *Journal of Visual Impairment and Blindness*, 107 (5): 325–336.

Heinze, T. (2000) Comprehensive assessment, in A. Koenig and M.C. Holbrook (eds.), *Foundations of Education: Instructional Strategies for Teaching Children and Youths with Visual Impairments*, vol. 2, 2nd edition. New York: AFB Press.

Holbrook, M.C. and Koenig, A.J. (1992) Teaching braille reading to students with low vision, *Journal of Visual Impairment and Blindness*, 86 (1): 44–48.

Jacobson, W.H. (1993) *The Art and Science of Teaching Orientation and Mobility to Persons with Visual Impairments*. New York: AFB Press.

Jehoel, S., Ungar, S., McCallum, D. and Rowell, J. (2005) An evaluation of substrates for tactile maps and diagrams: scanning speed and users' preferences, *Journal of Visual Impairment and Blindness*, 99 (2): 85–95.

Jehoel, S., Sowden, P. T., Ungar, S. and Sterr, A. (2009) Tactile elevation perception in blind and sighted participants and its implications for tactile map creation, *Human Factors*, 51 (2): 208–223.

Jitngernmadan, P., Stöger, B., Petz, A. and Klaus, M. (2017) IDMILE: an interactive didactic math inclusion learning environment for blind students, *Technology and Disability*, 29 (1/2): 47–61.

Kocur, I. and Resnikoff, S. (2002) Visual impairment and blindness in Europe and their prevention, *British Journal of Ophthalmology*, 86 (7): 716–722.

Koenig, A.J. and Holbrook, M.C. (2000) Literacy skills, in A. Koenig and M.C. Holbrook (eds.), *Foundation of Education: Instructional Strategies for Teaching Children and Youths with Visual Impairments*, vol. 2, 2nd edition. New York: AFB Press.

Layton, C.A. (2000) Ongoing assessments: informal techniques, in A. Koenig and M.C. Holbrook (eds.), *Foundation of Education: Instructional Strategies for Teaching Children and Youths with Visual Impairments*, vol. 2, 2nd edition. New York: AFB Press.

McLinden, M. and McCall, S. (2016) *Learning through Touch: Supporting Children with Visual Impairments and Additional Difficulties*. New York: David Fulton.

McNear, D. and Farrenkopf, C. (2014) Assistive technology, in C.B. Allman and S. Lewis (eds.), *ECC Essentials: Teaching the Expanded Core Curriculum to Students with Visual Impairments*. New York: AFB Press.

Mitchell, P. and Ziegler, F. (2007) *Fundamentals of Development: The Psychology of Childhood*. Hove: Psychology Press.

Occelli, V., Spence, C. and Zampini, M. (2013) Auditory, tactile, and audiotactile information processing following visual deprivation, *Psychological Bulletin*, 139 (1): 189–212.

Ondin, Z. (2015) *Experiences of the students with blindness and visual impairments in online learning environments with regards to instructional media*. Doctoral dissertation, Virginia Tech.

Roe, J., Rogers, S., Donaldson, M., Gordon, C. and Meager, N. (2014) Teaching literacy through braille in mainstream settings whilst promoting inclusion: reflections on our practice, *International Journal of Disability, Development and Education*, 61 (2): 165–177.

Smith, D.W. and Kelly, S.M. (2014) Assistive technology for students with visual impairments: a research agenda, in D. Hatton (ed.), *International Review of Research in Developmental Disabilities*. Waltham, MA: Academic Press.

Solebo, A.L., Teoh, L. and Rahi, J. (2017) Epidemiology of blindness in children, *Archives of Disease in Childhood*, 102 (9): 853–857.

Stewart, J. (2014) *Visual impairment and educational attainment*. Research and Information Service Briefing Paper. Belfast: Northern Ireland Assembly.

Swenson, A.M. (2008) Reflections on teaching reading in braille, *Perspectives*, 102 (4): 206–209.

Tanrıverdi, A. and Sarıca, A.D. (2021) Inclusive education: Theoretical and practical foundations, in A.D. Sarıca and A. Tanrıverdi (eds.), *Inclusive Education: Creating a School for Everyone*. Ankara: Nobel Akademik Yayıncılık [in Turkish].

van Leendert, A., Doorman, M., Drijvers, P., Pel, J. and van der Steen, J. (2021) Teachers' skills and knowledge in mathematics education for braille readers, *Technology, Knowledge and Learning*, 27: 1171–1192.

Viljoen, H. (2020a) Practical approaches to curriculum differentiation for learners with visual impairment, in M.M. Sefotho and R. Ferreira (eds.), *Teaching Learners with Visual Impairment*. Durbanville: AOSIS.

Viljoen, H. (2020b) Adaptation of learning and teaching support material and assessment of learners with visual impairment, in M.M. Sefotho and R. Ferreira (eds.), *Teaching Learners with Visual Impairment*. Durbanville: AOSIS.

Voss, P. (2013) Sensitive and critical periods in visual sensory deprivation, *Frontiers in Psychology*, 4. Available at: https://doi.org/10.3389/fpsyg.2013.00664

Warren, D.H. (1994) *Blindness and Children: An Individual Differences Approach*. New York: Cambridge University Press.

World Health Organisation (WHO) (2004) *Magnitude and causes of visual impairment*. Geneva: WHO. Available at: http://www.who.int/mediacentre/factsheets/fs282/en

Zebehazy, K.T., Zigmond, N. and Zimmerman, G.J. (2012) Performance measurement and accommodation: students with visual impairments on Pennsylvania's alternate assessment, *Journal of Visual Impairment and Blindness*, 106 (1): 17–30.

13 Auditory processing and its implications for learners: 'My ears work fine, it is the way I process sound'

Carmel Capewell

At the end of the chapter, you should be able to:
- explain the implications for learning for young people with auditory processing difficulties (APD)
- identify the physiological basis of APD
- make links between APD and other neurodivergences (attention deficit hyperactivity disorder, dyspraxia, dyslexia, autism spectrum disorder) and learning in an additional language
- explore minor adjustments that can enhance learning for students with APD.

Auditory processing difficulties: disorder or difficulty

In the first part of this chapter, the focus is on definitions of auditory processing difficulties (APD). A discussion around the difference between a 'disorder' and a 'difficulty' sets the context for interpreting APD. This builds upon the ideas explored in Chapter 1. There is always a balance to be had between the medical model of disability, and its dominance in healthcare, and the social model of disability, which seems more appropriate in educational contexts. However, Moriña and Carnerero (2020) found that in the context of education, the medical model still dominates. I focus on a social model of disability whereby the behaviours associated with the functioning of processing of sound are better described as a 'difficulty', and that with changes in the physical environment and/or the behaviour of others, the difficulty can be minimised. The Cambridge

Dictionary online defines 'difficulty' as 'the fact of not being easy, or of being hard to understand' (https://www.powerthesaurus.org/difficulty/definitions). It provides as an example: 'He has some difficulty hearing people when they speak softly'. In this example, it could be suggested that the difficulty a person experiences arises from the way other people, or the environment, add barriers to their ability to interact and understand what is going on around them, inhibiting their active participation.

> *Activity*
>
> Even with 'normal' hearing, individuals have difficulty processing sound, especially in paying attention to what a particular person is saying. All children under the age of 7–8 years require lower levels of background noise than adults if they are to interpret sound effectively.
>
> Think of a noisy environment (e.g. a restaurant maybe, or classroom with students involved in activities) – what are some of the factors that make understanding speech more difficult. Compare that with a situation where one person is talking to another in a room on their own.

Using the medical model approach, someone with APD could be perceived to be disabled. If children and young people are to be supported socially, emotionally and educationally, then there is a need to consider how minor adjustments can be made to adapt and include people. This is especially so in the case of 'hidden disabilities' such as APD. This can have implications for social interactions/participation as well as performance in educational contexts.

The primary purpose of this chapter is to explore what APD is and the way in which previous research can provide an insight into how people with APD can be better supported in educational contexts. However, there is benefit in exploring APD as a condition and whether it should be categorised as a 'disorder', with the accompanying medical implications of assessment and treatment, or a 'difficulty', so that through adjustments and awareness a more optimal listening and sound processing environment can be created. The argument here is that whereas a 'disorder' is medicalised and educators often do not feel fully acquainted with that condition and its implications, seeing APD as a 'difficulty' can provide educators, children and young people, and parents/carers with agency in how to best support students with APD. Often the first people who become aware of the potential difficulties are parents or teachers.

The ability to listen, process, interpret, comprehend and respond to what a specific person is saying in educational contexts is a key skill in learning. This applies from pre-school to all levels of qualifications, up to and including postgraduate study. However, for the most part, little – if any – effort is made to formally teach and develop listening/speech processing skills. The requirement of a person to interpret sound increases as they move from primary to secondary to tertiary education, with an increasing emphasis on listening being the main way in which people are taught. These abilities come under the general term of 'auditory processing'.

The American Academy of Audiology (AAA, n.d.) provides a behaviourally based definition of APD by listing observable characteristics: 'Children with APD experience difficulties in less-than-ideal (noisy) listening situations and may have difficulties with reading, spelling, attention, and language problems'. The list of characteristics provides those who interact with children who may have APD with some understanding of what they should look out for. The AAA suggests that it is best practice for interventions to be implemented by a cross-disciplinary team that is likely to include audiologists, speech and language therapists, psychologists and teachers.

In the British context, the term 'auditory processing disorder' is used in medical contexts, primarily audiology, whereby there is a focus on assessment for diagnosis and treatment (BSA 2011). In their review of the terms and the evidence around identifying what APD is and how it can be diagnosed, the British Society of Audiology (BSA 2011: 8) uses medicalised language that focuses on a 'deficit' within the individual, including 'neurodevelopmental disorder', 'impaired language', 'impaired top-down, cognitive function', 'sensory disability' and 'disordered listening'.

The key point to consider from the conclusion of the BSA's position statement is that there is no agreed standard for assessing people with APD. However, there is agreement that the condition has an effect on day-to-day life, particularly in terms of responding to what is heard. Elsewhere in the document, the BSA acknowledges that one means of identifying APD is developmental, in children who appear to have normal hearing. There is some understanding that it has a strong cognitive component and is related to poor listening skills. The focus on an evidence-based diagnostic tool for assessment is taken up by Moore (2018). This leads to a spiral of focusing on developing an assessment tool and quantifying the 'disorder'. While this certainly has merit, it misses the importance of finding ways in which learners with the condition can be best supported in social and educational contexts and what are appropriate interventions. Here the focus is on a medical model of interacting with the condition.

Activity

Download the BSA (2011) position statement on APD (https://www.thebsa.org.uk/wp-content/uploads/2011/04/OD104-39-Position-Statement-APD-2011-1.pdf). Look at the points under section 3. Try to develop your own checklist for things that you could use to potentially identify APD in your own practice. How could the behaviours listed here perhaps lead you to reinterpret how you see children who do not always appear to listen and respond appropriately to instructions?

There is a distinction to be made between audiologists (Moore 2018) and psychologists (Witton 2010). While audiologists focus on creating a 'gold standard diagnostic tool' specifically for APD as an isolated condition, psychologists see the diagnosis of APD as related to a person having listening difficulties which are not related to damage in the hearing mechanisms, cognitive impairment or language problems. Witton (2010: 84) considers an operational definition of APD as being multifaceted but having a connection to the auditory processing system, at some level. She identifies this as ranging from the auditory cortex, in the recognition and ordering of sounds as well as issues with a specific system in the brain stem, through to a blockage in the middle ear resulting from glue ear. The observable behaviours associated with the condition include problems with following or paying attention to verbal commands or dialogue. This appear to be exacerbated in less than optimum hearing conditions, which are explored later.

> **Box 13.1   Case study: Eddie**
>
> Eddie is known to have APD and has had recurring glue ear, which results in temporary hearing loss of between six and ten weeks, since two years of age. He often becomes frustrated and shouts at other students when working in a group in the classroom. Other students have started not including them in their group as he shouts over them. His vocabulary is quite limited and he tends to use simple sentences. There are times when he appears to switch off.

> *Activity*
> From what you have read so far, apply this to how you would support Eddie, aged 10 years, in any learning environment. Then as you continue to read the chapter, build on your initial ideas as to how Eddie could be supported.

Rather than dismissing the connection to other neurodevelopmental conditions, Witton (2010) makes explicit that APD is part of an umbrella condition which has connections to dyslexia and attention deficit hyperactivity disorder (ADHD). This line of thought is supported by research into the association between APD and dyslexia (Richardson et al. 2004), dyspraxia and autism spectrum disorder (ASD) (O'Connor 2012). Witton (2010) makes the point that the brain does not consist of unique processing areas and that there are overlaps between the different brain regions. Without going into too much technical detail, an example of the complexity of how sound is processed is when someone hears a spoken word. The word is initially processed in the primary auditory cortex, then passed to Wernicke's area. A search takes place to identify, match and retrieve the signal for that word (or phrase). This needs both matching and interpreting within the given context. Before the word can be pronounced, the signal has to pass to Broca's area for appropriate pronunciation. The signal then transfers to the motor cortex to stimulate the muscles to enable pronunciation. This explanation does not include the roles of synaptic reactions/development, the implications of brain plasticity or the expression of specific genes associated with the processing of sound. Even with this simplified explanation of auditory processing, it is clear to see why it is difficult to identify where exactly the APD occurs.

Not a single condition: links to other neurodivergences

It seems that there is a connection between APD and difficulties associated with memory, attention, speech and language, as well as in learning to read and processing written text (Witton 2010). De Wit et al. (2018) undertook a systematic review of the interaction between APD and other developmental conditions – speech and language difficulties, dyslexia, ADHD, learning disorder and ASD – to try and identify specific characteristics linked to APD. Although the authors failed to provide conclusive results, they attributed this more to the quality of the studies and the lack of robust measurement instruments. De Wit et al. (2018) also cite research that identifies similar behaviours between APD and other neurodivergences. The behavioural characteristics of ADHD, for example, are poor concentration and attention; ASD difficulties include sensitivity to specific noises (hyperacusis), being upset by certain pitched sound and poor ability to understand speech in noisy environments. De Wit et al. (2018) concur with Moore (2018) whether such similarities render APD as a discrete condition. There may be general reading delay and difficulties in deciphering text. APD can also result in dyslexia and speech and language difficulties.

Implications of APD for learners being taught in an additional language

Although the focus of Saito et al. (2022) is the role that APD plays in learning a second language, they also show how it functions in language acquisition in general and the importance of effective auditory processing skills. They identify that, in order to learn a language, all babies need to detect and discriminate patterns in speech/non-speech, along with connections to pitch (Saito et al. 2022: 59). They state that any difficulties in processing sound might not only impact the ability to phonetically analyse it, but also the development of vocabulary and understanding the meaning of individual words in a specific context. Saito et al. also suggest that good auditory processing skills impact the learning of an additional language (EAL: the acronym is usually used to mean 'English as an additional language', but here it refers to any language learned as additional). Potentially, students taught in an additional language with less than optimal auditory processing skills are likely to find understanding what is said to them difficult.

Even those EAL students who have proficient auditory processing skills are likely to require additional time to comprehend what is being said. In addition to general issues around engagement, EAL students need to have opportunities and motivation to develop their skills, which has implications for educators working with students who are using EAL (Saito et al. 2022).

Some of the ways in which APD can impact children and young people's processing of speech (not just in the classroom)

In their position statement on central auditory processing disorders, the American Speech-Language-Hearing Association (ASHA 2005) identified possible behavioural descriptions of how it could impact children and young people. It can be seen from the list below that this is quite broad. Children with APD may have difficulty:

- responding to sounds (discrimination)
- understanding when listening (decoding)
- retaining what is said to be able to process it (tolerance fading)
- concentrating (localisation of sound)
- learning songs (ordering)
- remembering instructions (grouping)
- expressing themselves clearly using speech (ordering and grouping)
- reading and spelling (decoding).

There is insufficient space here to discuss and relate all of these to research but the implications of the two most common (decoding and tolerance-fading memory) provide insight for those working with children and young people with APD in learning environments.

Human hearing is based on binaural (two ears) hearing. This means that information from both ears feeds into the auditory nerve and into the cerebral cortex to be processed (Moore 2007). As sound travels from the source to which a person is attending, it reaches the ears at slightly different instants, so that the tiny time lag can provide information as to where the sound is coming from (location) and from which side of the person (lateralisation), and provide extra information related to meaning when the sound is processed.

Activity
Look at the letters below and see if you can create a sentence – keep moving between the left and right groups of letters:

PU A ZE AP S   –   T DO N PLE I TH CK

The key to decoding this is to consider that each ear takes priority over the other as the syllables are heard at slightly different times. The brain processes the sounds in order, then decodes and interprets the sounds as meaningful words relevant to the context. The sentence should read: 'Put a dozen apples in the sack'.

Decoding

The decoding category is the most common difficulty for APD, encompassing 50 per cent of all weaknesses (Katz and Tillery 2003). There is an impairment or breakdown of auditory processing at the phonemic level. It occurs when someone has difficulty accurately and quickly interpreting sounds, so that they need more time to process what they hear. They demonstrate difficulty with reading and speaking skills that depend upon phonics. Phonics are the basic sound categories of speech (sounds). Some of the processing difficulties arise from not being able to differentiate between sounds that are quite similar, for example p/d/v, s/f or th/ch, and so on (Katz and Tillery 2003). This is especially noticeable when reading aloud. Articulation errors can happen with the 'r' and 'l' sounds. The overlap of these difficulties has suggested a relationship to the posterior temporal lobe, or Wernicke's lobe (Katz and Tillery 2003). Adults have more experience than children and young people of processing language by using context to interpret what they hear, so issues with discrimination of sounds may not be as obvious. However, it is likely that a longer time would be needed to process and make sense of the sounds (decode them).

Activity
Often children with APD will mispronounce words: for example, 'I am putting on my glups' (instead of 'gloves'). Think of some other sentences whereby pronunciation confusion is based on not being able to discriminate between sounds, so leading to decoding problems. What is the likely perception of other students by older children using such language?

Tolerance-fading memory

Tolerance-fading memory (TFM) refers to two skills that are often associated with one another. The word 'tolerance' refers to understanding speech in noise and 'fading memory' refers to auditory short-term or working memory

(Katz and Tillery 2003). Related characteristics such as attention also fit the TFM category. These include difficulty in blocking out noise, short-term/working auditory memory and attention. In a busy classroom, the impact of this can often be seen at the end of a lesson, when the teacher is trying to get a number of things done in a short period of time. There may be a series of instructions given, in quick succession, concurrent to students moving around and making noise with furniture. For example, a teacher could say, 'Write down your homework, put your books away, put your chair on the desk, put your coat on, pick up your bag, stand behind your chair'. There are six instructions, and it is likely that a student with APD may attend to and process perhaps the first one or two, but then not be able to retain the other four as there is insufficient capacity within their short-term memory to both process the meaning and retain the instructions. The background noise of other children is also likely to cause additional difficulties because non-speech noises will have to be ignored and not processed. In behavioural terms, the child can be perceived as being impulsive (perhaps following the first instruction without attending to the full list), easily distracted (as they may start one task, then move to the next without finishing the previous one), appear lost and a bit overwhelmed (as they recognise that there is a list of instructions, but cannot process them), or become cross and/or frustrated (as they can see their peers following and doing a range of things, while they cannot).

Activity
Work with someone else to check your own short-term memory. Choose seven numbers that are single digits and not sequential. Have one of you say them and the other try to remember and repeat them back. Then, choose a second sequence of numbers and have background noise such as a radio playing and compare your performance in both conditions.

What was your performance like? Which situation was better/worse? What are the implications of this for children and young people?

The physical learning environment

Many teachers consider teaching rooms in terms of displays and the layout of tables and chairs, and the acoustic environment is not often taken into consideration. However, being able to understand what a specific person is saying within a classroom can be very difficult and quite complex for students with APD. The reasons why it is important for educators to familiarise themselves and understand specific elements of the listening environment is to provide them with ways in which they can adapt the physical learning environment to make it more accessible to students with APD (Capewell 2014).

> *Activity*
> Take a few minutes to think about the noises that you can hear around you. Note them down. Which ones had you been aware of before being asked to think about them? Which ones had you been blocking out? Would you find it hard to concentrate on what a person was saying if you could not block out non-speech sounds? How do you think that would make you feel?
>
> As you read through the following text, think about the inability to screen out sounds and the potential impact it could have on learning, concentration and emotions.

The ability to identify the precise location of a sound is known as 'localisation'. In a study of people ranging from babies to adults, Freigang et al. (2015) found that this ability develops over time, probably not becoming optimal until a person is 12–14 years old. It is connected to the auditory processing system as well as experience in locating sounds. In practice, this means that younger children may take longer to locate the person who is speaking, before being able to attend to what they are saying. This could lead to a time lag in which the listener is not actively processing what is said. Additionally, in younger people with blockages in their ears (such as glue ear), difficulties with the speed of processing speech (dyslexia, ADHD) and deciphering the meaning of words (ASD and EAL students), as well as less than ideal hearing environments, can result in poorer performance in understanding what is said to them. In behavioural terms, this could mean that a student is perceived as not paying attention, has low cognitive skills or is easily distracted. They may also show signs of frustration.

> *Activity*
> Sit in a chair with your back towards someone who is speaking. Put your finger in your left ear, listen and try to understand what is being said. Now put your finger in your right ear and listen to what is said. Now try it without your fingers in your ears. Finally, face the person without putting your fingers in your ears. Which was the best of the four? Why do you think that is? Use the information in this chapter to apply the science to this.

Research into both classroom acoustics and its impacts on children, due to the development of the hearing processes and the layout of classrooms, provides useful insight into how children and young people with APD can be better supported. For educators, being aware of the potential difficulties there are with processing sound and thus making a room more listening-friendly can be a minor modification that makes a big difference. For example, noisy equipment and a lot of hard surfaces that cause reverberation can make listening difficult (Capewell 2014).

Klatte et al. (2010) reviewed cognitive performance in children, in particular in relation to background noise and when sound levels fluctuate. Their findings suggest that the monitoring of sound levels in classrooms is important for all young children, not just those with APD. This is a consequence both of the development of the hearing system and young children's lack of experience of listening in noisy environments. With background noise, children need lower levels of noise than adults to clearly understand what is being said, what is required of them and to perform a task. This continues until about the age of six years in children with normal hearing development. Additionally, with fluctuating sound differences or more than one speaker, adult performance is not achieved until the age of 10 years. As children lack experience and knowledge of phonemes, performance in young children is poorer than in adults by up to 39 per cent. For all children, it is likely that they have less developed short-term memory, speed of auditory processing and are more severely impacted by irrelevant sound effects than adults.

Classrooms are often not optimum listening environments. For example, Mealings et al. (2015) investigated differences in noise levels and their impact on learning when comparing open-plan and enclosed classrooms. They found that, on average, children spend 45–60 per cent of their time at school listening and comprehending. It is worth remembering that generally children are not taught to listen and understand in the same way that writing, reading and spelling are taught explicitly. Mealings et al. also identified the types of noises that can interfere with listening. These include ongoing external classroom noises, such as road traffic, building construction, aircraft and trains, as well as intermittent noises such as grass cutting. There are also intruding noises such as noise from other classrooms and/or corridors. And there are internal noises, including students talking, general movement and appliance noise (the pumps on fish tanks or projectors). The authors highlighted that even 'silent' classrooms have higher noise levels than empty classrooms because of students moving around, chairs being pushed back, even students writing on paper. They noted that noise levels are reported to be highest in the early years when children have less developed auditory systems and less practice in blocking out interfering noises. Interestingly, they identified that increased noise levels induce 'stress' symptoms – headaches, higher blood pressure – in both children and teachers.

Shield and Dockrell (2003) reviewed students' performance in open-plan classrooms compared to enclosed ones. They concluded that open-plan classrooms are likely to be detrimental to learning and lead to poorer performance than enclosed ones. This is in the context that up to 40 per cent of children in primary school may have hearing issues (even short-term hearing loss can adversely impact cognitive processes). Those taught in their non-first language, or who have attentional or speech/language difficulties are more likely to be impacted by poor classroom acoustics, which are generally in evidence in open-plan classrooms. Extraneous external and internal noise can impact children's ability to learn to read. The children in Shield and Dockrell's study reported that in their perception of noise annoyance they were less able to concentrate, block out interfering noises or understand speech from a targeted speaker.

Activity
Ideally, this activity would be carried out in a classroom but can be undertaken in an office environment. The objective is to consciously pay attention to those noises that you would tend to block out (as this is likely what is happening to most young children and particularly those with APD). What are the external noises that you can hear (such as traffic)? What are the intruding noises that you can identify (such as noise coming from somewhere else in the building)? What are the internal noises that you can hear (these could be human or from equipment within the room)?

In the light of your own findings and those from the research above, how could you help students to have a more optimal, noise-reduced, learning environment?

Conclusion

APD is a complex condition, with some audiologists suggesting it represents a combination of difficulties in the auditory processing system. While this is important in understanding the condition, the focus is on the 'defect' as perceived in the medical model of disability. APD has links to a range of other specific learning difficulties, such as dyslexia, ADHD and ASD, so understanding it is highly relevant in educational contexts. The social model of disability and the Equality Act (2010) provide an appropriate approach to supporting children and young people with APD in education. Understanding the functionality of APD, then making minor adjustments to enable better conditions for processing speech in noisy environments, is most important. Knowledge about APD is especially important for those in early years environments when all children have immature auditory processing skills. Making small adjustments for a few children can lead to better support for all.

Case study review
Now that you have reached the end of this chapter, compare your initial ideas about supporting Eddie (see Box 13.1) with those you have now. What are some of the differences you have noted? How could this impact your future practice?

References

American Academy of Audiology (AAA) (n.d.) *Auditory processing disorders*. Available at: https://www.audiology.org/consumers-and-patients/hearing-and-balance/auditory-processing-disorders/ (accessed 2 May 2022).

American Speech-Language-Hearing Association (ASHA) (2005) *(Central) Auditory processing disorders – the role of the audiologist*. Position statement of the Working Group on Auditory Processing Disorders. Available at: https://www.asha.org/policy/ps2005-00114/ (accessed 1 May 2022).

British Society of Audiology (BSA) (2011) *Position statement: Auditory processing disorder (APD)*. BSA: Bathgate, Scotland. Available at: https://www.thebsa.org.uk/wp-content/uploads/2011/04/OD104-39-Position-Statement-APD-2011-1.pdf (accessed 1 May 2022).

Capewell, C. (2014) The hearing environment, *Support for Learning*, 29 (2): 102–116.

De Wit, E., van Dijk, P., Hanekamp, S., Visser-Bochane, M.I., Steenbergen, B., van der Schans, C.P. et al. (2018) Same or different: the overlap between children with auditory processing disorders and children with other developmental disorders: a systematic review, *Ear and Hearing*, 39 (1): 1–19.

Freigang, C., Richter, N., Rübsamen, R. and Ludwig, A. (2015) Age-related changes in sound localisation ability, *Cell Tissue Research*, 361 (1): 371–386.

Katz, J. and Tillery, K. (2003) Central auditory processing, in L. Verhoeven and H. van Balkom (eds.), *Classification of Developmental Language Disorders: Theoretical Issues and Clinical Implications*. London: Lawrence Erlbaum.

Klatte, M., Hellbruck, J., Seidel, J. and Leistner, P. (2010) Effects of classroom acoustics on performance and well-being in elementary school children: a field study, *Environment and Behavior*, 42 (5): 659–692.

Legislation.Gov.UK (2010) *Equality Act*. Available at: https://www.legislation.gov.uk/ukpga/2010/15/contents (accessed 2 May 2022).

Mealings, K., Buchholz, J., Demuth, K. and Dillon, H. (2015) Investigating the acoustics of a sample of open plan and enclosed kindergarten classrooms in Australia, *Applied Acoustics*, 100: 95–105.

Moore, D.R. (2007) Auditory processing disorders: acquisition and treatment, *Journal of Communication Disorders*, 40 (4): 295–304.

Moore, D.R. (2018) Editorial: Auditory processing disorder, *Ear and Hearing*, 39 (4): 617–620.

Moriña, A. and Carnerero, F. (2020) Conceptions of disability at education: a systematic review, *International Journal of Disability, Development and Education*, 69 (3): 1032–1046.

O'Connor, K. (2012) Auditory processing in autism spectrum disorder: a review, *Neuroscience and Biobehavioural Reviews*, 36 (2): 836–854.

Richardson, U., Thomson, J.M., Scott, S.K. and Goswamy, U. (2004) Auditory processing skills and phonological representation in dyslexic children, *Dyslexia*, 10 (3): 215–233.

Saito, K., Sun, H., Kachlidka, M., Alayo, J.R.C., Nakata, T. and Tierney, A. (2022) Domain-general auditory processing explains multiple dimensions of L2 acquisition in adulthood, *Studies in Second Language Acquisition*, 44 (1): 57–86.

Shield, B. and Dockrell, J. (2003) The effects of noise on children at school: a review, *Building Acoustics*, 10 (2): 97–116.

Witton, C. (2010) Childhood auditory processing disorder as a developmental disorder: the case for a multi-professional approach to diagnosis and management, *International Journal of Audiology*, 49:(2): 83–87.

Part IV

Bilingualism and Exceptional Cognitive Abilities

This final section covers bilingualism and individuals with exceptional cognitive abilities. Although neither may be identified as SEN, special educational needs arise from barriers to learning (see Chapter 1) that bilingual and very able learners may experience.

14 Bilingualism, second language learning and developmental differences

Aris Terzopoulos, Georgia Niolaki and Jackie Masterson

By the end of this chapter, you should be able to:

- define bilingualism and understand the multiple parameters that need to be considered
- be aware of approaches to understanding needs and differences that bilingual individuals have
- be aware of the different types of intervention and able to evaluate them.

The where, what, how and when of bilingualism

While for some children and young adults learning a second language is a choice, sometimes starting from birth, it is a necessity for many others if they wish to study, work, and access the health and welfare system. Crucially, language enables socialisation (Kulick and Schieffelin 2004: 349), which concerns 'ways of being in the world', through a culturally dependent language development practice.

As discussed in Chapter 1, educational inclusion is the removal of barriers to learning for all learners, where learners can access the curriculum and feel a sense of belonging at school. As such, there may be barriers to participation for children who need to learn an additional language to enable them to make friends, learn at school, watch television and use a phone. Imagine a nine-year-old, new to the school, new to the country, who cannot speak, comprehend, read or write fluently in the school's language. Aside from any other challenges the child may face, a language barrier can negatively affect their social and emotional development. While the SEND Code of Practice (DfE/DoH 2015) does not consider bilingualism and second language learning as an identified SEN, you will have noticed from reading Chapter 1 that special educational needs arise from barriers to learning, which bilingual learners may experience.

To support bilinguals, we first need to understand bilingualism: what affects additional language learning or EAL (the acronym is usually used to mean 'English as an additional language', but here it refers to any language learned as additional), what are language developmental difficulties, and how schools and teachers can best support bilinguals by understanding differences and planning interventions.

Activity
Who is considered bilingual? Reflect on your own experiences; think about friends and relatives, school and classmates and consider all the different types of bilingualism. *Tip*: Think of bilingualism as a continuum where, at one extreme, there is competence in one language only and, at the other, the individual can speak, read, write and comprehend in two languages proficiently. Is this competence enough, however, to define bilingualism?

Figure 14.1 A continuum of bilingualism: from one language only to proficiency in two languages

ONE LANGUAGE ONLY   PROFICIENT IN TWO LANGUAGES

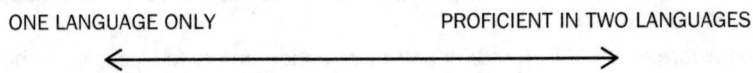

It is not, however, a clear-cut task to define bilingualism. The reason is that bilingualism is intrinsically related to multiple factors (Grosjean 2012), a summary of which now follows.

The *when*

This refers to the age of acquisition (AoA), when bilinguals acquire their languages. Studies have shown that AoA influences reading acquisition (Protopapas 2017), response to intervention (Niolaki, Masterson and Terzopoulos 2014) and ability to name words (Cortese and Khanna 2007), to name but a few. In a study by Bylund et al. (2019), for example, adult bilinguals' lexical differences were attributed to AoA rather than bilingual proficiency. Lexical differences denote when bilinguals have lower levels of, for example, oral vocabulary than monolingual speakers.

Simultaneous bilinguals learn their languages very early in life. Sequential bilinguals learn their additional language after they have learned their first language. There is no consensus about the cut-off criterion for a bilingual to be considered sequential or simultaneous, but most agree that this happens at some point in early childhood, usually in the first 3–5 years (Nicoladis 2018).

One of the critical worries in school is when EAL children's performance will become similar to that of their monolingual peers. The evidence suggests this may take several years, sometimes all the years spent in primary school (Paradis, Genesee and Crago 2011), though sometimes earlier. This is because the language elements, such as phonology (the sounds of the language) and oral vocabulary, have different rates of development. This can be affected by the language spoken at home. Some families prefer to speak only the heritage language at home, while others prefer to speak both the dominant and the heritage language if they can. School plays a crucial role, as does the extent to which the family is involved in the child's education. Some schools have immersion programmes, as in Canada, where children learn both their heritage language and their community's dominant language. Other schools are international, where both languages are taught, while most have no heritage language programmes. Socio-linguistic factors come into play: level and measurement of language proficiency of the child, his or her parent(s)/caregiver(s) and siblings, socio-economic status (SES), type of languages, and child-related factors, such as motivation, phonological awareness (the ability to manipulate the sounds of language) and speed of processing (how fast information can be retrieved from long-term memory).

The *where*

The environment in which children learn a second language is definitive, especially for sequential bilinguals. In a subtractive environment, the focus is placed on learning the second or majority language. For example, when Kostas, a Greek-speaking child, arrived in the UK at the age of eight years as an economic migrant, he attended Year 2 in a school in a small town in the South West, where there were no other Greek-English bilinguals. The school and his parents focused on his learning English, the majority language, as fast as possible to catch up with his monolingual peers. In contrast, Eleni, who came at the same age to live in West London, attended an international school where both languages are taught by bilingual teachers, with an emphasis on the heritage or minority language (60 per cent heritage and 40 per cent majority language). In this area, many Greek-English bilinguals form a community where learning the heritage language is appreciated and encouraged. Arguably, everyone would be in favour of an additive environment, an environment where learning the heritage language, both at school and in the community, is encouraged and systematically taught.

The *what*

The varied profiles of bilinguals are made more complex by what type of languages they learn, what is the level of their knowledge and how this is measured. The first language features (grammar, syntax, phonology, orthography, spelling; for explanations on some of these terms, see Chapter 9) affect second language learning. The influence that one language has on the other language is called cross-language transfer. The degree of transfer effects is related to the type of language and the rate of development in each language. Verhoeven (2007), for example, showed that Turkish-Dutch bilingual children (aged 5–6 years), with Turkish as the dominant and Dutch as the second language, scored higher in phonological awareness tasks in both languages than their monolingual peers, and had higher levels of vocabulary and reading proficiency in these two languages.

In other words, there is an interdependence (Cummins 2000) between the two languages, such that the language repository of the first language can be used to develop the second. This is crucial for teachers and educational psychologists supporting children who are late learners of the second – majority – language because understanding the level of knowledge in children's two languages can enhance understanding and use of the strategies they employ to support bilinguals. Niolaki and Masterson (2012) is an excellent example of this: spelling accuracy in the majority language (English) was accounted for by the strategies 9–11-year-old Greek-English bilingual children used in Greek. The group with weaker Greek language competence, who were second- or third-generation children and for whom Greek was a heritage language, used visual memory to support their English spelling, a skill more aligned to English orthography. The group with stronger Greek competence used predominantly phonological skills in their English spelling, a process more aligned to Greek orthography.

Why was this the case? English is a deep orthography: spelling does not map easily to letter sounds, hence the heavy reliance on visual memory. Greek, in contrast, is a transparent writing system, with much more consistent correspondences between letters and sounds, hence the heavy reliance on phonological skills. Greek and English are alphabetic languages, so such influences of one writing system on the other are more apparent than when the languages differ in their writing code (e.g. as in the case of Chinese and English).

Language proficiency or competence intertwines with transfer effects, type of language, rate of development and environment to create varied profiles in bilinguals. However, there is no agreement what language proficiency entails and how it should be measured. It was common to refer to bilinguals as balanced when they were proficient in both languages, or unbalanced when they were more proficient in one language than the other. However, such terms assume that the bilingual mind is the sum of two languages (Grosjean 1998) and proficiency a simple metric of knowledge, not experience or usage.

Most now agree that the two languages are interconnected and influence each other (Romaine 2010). The term 'dominance' has been proposed to denote that even simultaneous bilinguals may be more proficient in one language than the other (Treffers-Daller 2015). However, this can falsely imply some lack of completeness (e.g. not complete grammatical knowledge) for the non-dominant language. Therefore, language usage should be considered as well. We can be equally proficient in some aspects of one language (e.g. reading, spelling) but not in others (e.g. oral vocabulary) depending on how much we use, are exposed to and converse in that language. From our previous example, Kostas and Eleni are both Greek-dominant; however, Eleni uses Greek often, as she engages with a vibrant community and an international school. She will catch up with English, and at some point, English may become more dominant, but both languages will have their fair share of usage. Kostas's dominance in Greek will gradually shift to English within 1–2 years as he tries to engage with the local non-bilingual community and school. Greek will become less active, as he speaks the heritage language only at home with his parents. If his parents do not speak English well, this may become a burden in their communication with Kostas. The cost of language barriers in bilinguals is nicely presented by Marku et al. (2022) and Mejía (2016).

Now that you have read the above on the different concepts and aspects of bilingualism, perhaps it is better to visualise bilingualism as an overlay of multiple crossing continua (Figure 14.2). A bilingual learner may be at different points on these continua. Consider, for example, Aisha, a refugee from Syria who came to the UK at 15 years of age. Aisha might possibly be placed in the middle of the 'WHEN' continuum (i.e. she learnt the second language halfway between infancy and adulthood). She moved to Birmingham, in the West Midlands, where there is a large Arabic-English bilingual community, so she was somewhat closer to an ADDITIVE environment. The two scripts are more towards the DIFFERENT endpoint, meaning there are not many cross-language transfer effects to support the learning of English. While she learns

Figure 14.2 Crossing continua linked to bilingual AoA, script similarity, language usage and dominance, and bilingual environment

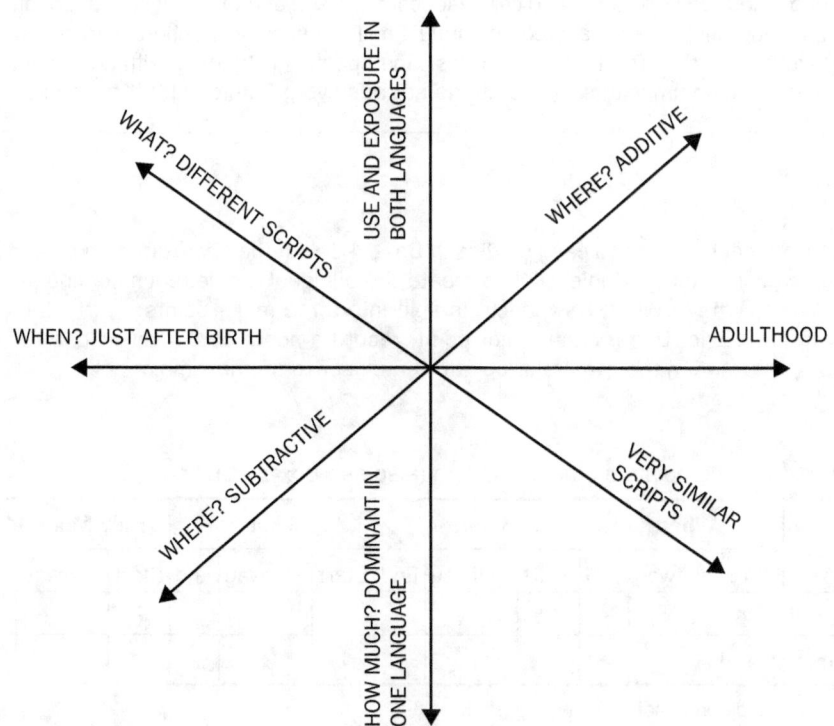

English, she uses mainly Arabic at home and within the community, making her more dominant in her heritage language. Is this valuable information for teachers and educational psychologists? How can teachers and educational psychologists use this information to create inclusive educational experiences for Aisha?

This type of information is probably the first and most important data we need for children who learn English as a majority language.

Box 14.1 Case studies: Zhen and Theresa

Case study 1: Zhen moved to North London with her family from mainland China when she was 18 months old. Her grandparents have a shop in London. She attended nursery for two years, a few hours (state-funded) per day, and now she attends Reception class in her local primary school, where a few Chinese-English bilingual children also attend. Her parents and older brother speak some English but all speak Mandarin Chinese at home. Zhen attends a Chinese community school every Sunday and they have good family connections and engagement with the Chinese community in London. According to her Year 2 teachers, she meets the expected targets for her age in English and Mathematics.

Case study 2: Teresa moved from Portugal to Southampton with her parents and younger sister when she was aged 14. She had learned English as a second language in Portugal and can read, comprehend and write but cannot speak fluently. She attends a predominantly English secondary school with a few bilingual children from other countries. She speaks Portuguese with her family and in the community school that she attends every Saturday for three hours.

Activity
Match each of the two case studies in Box 14.1 with the approximate point on each continuum in Table 14.1 to create the bilingual profile. Each continuum (When, Where, What, How Much) is split into three major points: Start, Halfway and End. Under each major point, record a score of 1 = very close to, 2 = in between the two major points, 3 = closer to the next major point.

Table 14.1 The points on the continuum (also see Box 14.1)

Case	When			Where			What			How Much L2		
	Start	Halfway	End	Start	Halfway	End	Start	Halfway	End	Start	Halfway	End
Zhen												
Teresa												

Note: L2 = additional majority language.

The profiles vary, as you have noticed (see, for example, a recent study of Greek refugee children by Olioumtsevits, Papadopoulou and Marinis 2023). The data you gain are very informative, but are they enough for a teacher to have a complete picture? What can be missing? How can we tell if they are not achieving as we would expect, whether this is because they are still learning the second language or because they have underlying challenges (e.g. dyslexia or other specific learning difficulties (SpLDs))? How can we create a profile of strengths and challenges to implement the appropriate intervention and support the individual reach their potential?

> Activity
> Think back to the social model introduced in Chapter 1 and the idea of 'normalising' a child. What is optimal functioning for EALs? How might this process of normalisation to native/monolingual peers affect them (positively and/or negatively)? How can teachers make sure they feel valued and included, ensuring their cultural norms and language are celebrated?

Understanding the needs and differences

These questions lead nicely to the main challenge set by the recognition of needs and differences process and the primary question one should ask is: how reliable and valid are the tools we currently have to support understanding of the needs and differences of a learning/language difficulty in an EAL learner. There are important implications when measuring language proficiency with tests that have been normalised with monolinguals and then comparing bilinguals' scores to the norms of monolingual peers. One consequence is identifying EALs as 'in deficit' compared with monolinguals, pushing them to learn the majority language and ignore the heritage language, which then becomes a passive language.

Slavkov (2015) reports a case study of an English-Bulgarian bilingual child who acquired both languages from birth with the One Parent/One Language model, where each parent speaks their language to the child. The child at two years and three months old was English-dominant with production in Bulgarian less than 1 per cent. A passive heritage language can negatively affect well-being, as it impedes cultural transmission (Inman et al. 2007), social interaction (Cho 2000) and ethnic identity (Kim and Chao 2009).

Curriculum directives can further instigate this. For example, the National Curriculum for England, for Key Stages 1 and 2 in primary schools (DfE 2015) has only one mention of children learning English as an additional language. This is some general advice on page 8 of the guidance, under 'Inclusion' – mainly that teachers should cater for these children and monitor their progress.

Understanding the needs and differences between EAL and dyslexia or other SpLDs is important. For example, we may think that an EAL who lags behind other children in school subjects will eventually catch up without particular support as they become more proficient in English. In other words, we may think any delay is because of lack of proficiency in the majority language and dismiss worries that there may be underlying language difficulties. Similarly, we may too often think that there is a language difficulty behind any EAL delay, leading to the planning of unnecessary interventions. Occasionally, these interventions require the child to leave the classroom for individual support with negative consequences for their well-being and self-esteem. An overlap between language difficulties and delay because of late learning of the majority language, particularly at the early stages, is expected. Teachers and educational psychologists need training to distinguish between them, so that appropriate support can be organised in a timely manner. Too late, and the EAL might miss learning opportunities. Too early, and the EAL will potentially be labelled and valuable time and resources spent in the wrong direction.

Therefore, recognition of needs has to be carefully considered. The first step is always to collect data about the language and literacy profiles of the children, as suggested above. Then we need to consider what assessments are appropriate.

> **Box 14.2 Case study: Anna**
>
> Ms Davies has in her Year 3 classroom a bilingual child, Anna, who arrived from Slovakia six months ago. She is worried that, as the end of the school year is approaching, Anna will not meet the expected targets in reading and speaking English. She decides to use the Wechsler Individual Achievement Test, Third UK Edition (WIAT-III UK; Wechsler 2017) for teachers. WIAT-III is a standardised test that assesses a variety of language and literacy skills.

Activity
Reflect on the scenario in Box 14.2. What would you advise Ms Davies about the use of a test that has been normalised with English monolinguals? Consider also if it is always feasible to assess a bilingual in their heritage language?

To correctly distinguish, for example, speech, language and communication needs (SLCN) or dyslexia (Chapter 9) from difficulties due to EAL, we first need to understand the similarities and differences between them. Research has shown, for example, that EALs with SLCNs produce less complex sentence structures (e.g. co-ordinate clauses) than EALs with SLCN (Paradis et al. 2022). SLCN EAL children score lower on story generation tasks than EALs without SLCN (Govindarajan and Paradis 2019). Then there may be misidentification of mistakes in the majority language. For example, a dominant Greek Year 2 child might often use the English letter <*p*> in words like <lette*p*> (for <letter>) only because <*p*> in Greek is pronounced as /r/. Such errors tend to disappear over time as the second language becomes gradually dominant, whereas among bilingual children with dyslexia such non-phonologically plausible errors persist (Niolaki, Terzopoulos and Masterson 2017). Focusing on errors is not always the optimal strategy. This is because errors in the majority language can in fact be transfer-effect errors from the dominant heritage language. These errors will tend to decrease in frequency gradually and may disappear depending on age, school instruction and mastering of the second language, but for children with additional needs this might not be the case.

One of the most troubling issues in the history of psychological testing has been the difference in mean scores and distribution of scores (see also Chapter 12) achieved by children from minority groups compared with children from the majority cultural group. Specifically, intelligence and attainment tests have often been considered biased against culturally and linguistically diverse groups and low-income students, and in favour of white and middle-class students (Boyle and Fisher 2007). There have been similar concerns about test bias against children with learning differences (Boyle and Fisher 2007).

There are suggestions to overcome these obstacles. For example, the use of non-verbal assessments that are culture-free (Niolaki et al. 2014, 2017) with tasks that involve symbols, made-up words and numbers. To explore strengths and weaknesses in verbal reasoning, the British Picture Vocabulary Scale (Dunn, Dunn and Styles 2009) has EAL norms, so it is considered to be an effective way to identify these needs. For the recognition of needs in the cognitive area (such as phonological ability, processing and memory), tasks can be conducted in the dominant or heritage language, if this is possible, as there is strong evidence of transfer effects between the two languages. For example, if someone has a difficulty with verbal memory, this will exist in any language the individual is using (Niolaki et al. 2017). It is frequently the case that teachers request a translator or an older sibling or parent for the recognition of needs. Additionally, the use of multiple tasks tapping the same skills can be a useful way to make sure that the result is reliable (cf. Niolaki et al. 2020). Additionally, arrangements to have an interpreter during the exploration of needs can be beneficial for interpreting the administration instructions and generally managing the testing situation for EAL students.

Activity
Referring back to Anna in Box 14.2, what options might you suggest to her teacher to effectively check if she has a language difficulty beyond EAL?

Intervention and support

Supporting bilinguals with language and literacy difficulties is a multifaceted and challenging task. Overall, the support programmes suggested can be summarised as classroom-based, a combination of classroom and small-group-based, and individual case support. We will examine three examples. As we do, consider the case of Anna in Box 14.2.

Classroom-based interventions are typically conducted in the classroom, but children can be taken from the classroom to receive specialist one-to-one or small-group teaching. The idea is first to support all children using specific instruction (e.g. on phonics) and then, using screening tools accessible to classroom teachers – namely, letter recognition, phonological awareness, single-word and prose reading, reading comprehension, simple spelling and grammar test (e.g. filling in a simple sentence a single word) – identify the children that do not respond to the classroom programme and utilise a small-group or individual intervention. Such programmes stem from the response to intervention (RTI) model discussed in Chapter 9 (Jimerson, Burns and VanDerHeyden 2016).

Siegel (2020) describes such a whole-class intervention in a school in Canada with EAL and English monolingual children. Children learn English at the early stages of schooling and French, the majority language, is introduced later. The researchers first screened the children to identify those at risk of dyslexia and found the 50 per cent of EAL and 25 per cent of English monolinguals were at risk. In the first phase, in Reception (Kindergarten) and Year (Grade) 1, teachers implemented an instruction programme (called Firm Foundations) in English. The idea behind early intervention in English is that by providing support as early as possible, this can have beneficial effects for later learning of French as well. The intervention targeted important language and literacy skills, namely phonological awareness (see Chapter 9), letter-sound knowledge and vocabulary (picture-naming). Teachers monitored closely those at risk and identified a small group of students still facing difficulties with a particular skill, despite the classroom intervention, and supported them further. The percentage of EAL and English monolinguals who showed reading difficulties in Kindergarten dropped in Grade 7 to 1.5 per cent. Interestingly, Siegel reports that EAL dyslexics had higher scores on specific language skills like vocabulary and phonology than English monolingual children with dyslexia, which she attributed to cross-language transfer effects from their first language (interdependence).

Another way to support bilingual learners is through smaller group interventions. Proctor et al. (2020) conducted a language intervention with Spanish-English and Portuguese-English Grade 4 and 5 students in the USA delivered by teachers, most of whom were also bilinguals. Importantly, the programme's content had been developed in consultation with bilingual children and consisted of three cycles of instruction on academic vocabulary, reading comprehension and writing. The texts and the content chosen were linked to the themes of nature, rights and immigration. The sessions were enriched with short videos and interactive presentations and activities such as defining words, making maps with word meanings and guided reading. To support reading comprehension, the children were supported to recognise and manipulate morphemes, create complex sentences and connect ideas. There was also small-group discussion based on the text they had to read, which further facilitated comprehension and argumentative speech production. At the end of each instructional cycle there was a writing workshop where the children were encouraged to write in an argumentative way to a certain audience (e.g. the headteacher) about an issue related to the discussions they have had. The overall focus of the intervention was on broader language use, utilising the children's existing knowledge base and experiences, valuing their contribution and their linguistically diverse background.

> *Activity*
> Can you identify the approach to intervention? Is it more special education or inclusive education?

Working inclusively means taking a holistic approach – remember the square peg in the round hole metaphor from Chapter 1? Can you think of anything a teacher could do to work inclusively with bilingual learners with or without SpLD?

As you probably noticed, the intervention discussed above is more special education, targeting and changing the individual difference. That does not mean it cannot be delivered in an inclusive way. Any intervention or support programme needs to consider how the children will feel valued and included. You could think about who will deliver it and how. Taking the child out of the classroom is not optimal and can lead to stigmatisation and a negative effect on self-esteem; and they can miss out on other important learning experiences. Instead, support should be designed to be given in the classroom during the lessons either individually with the teacher or teacher assistant or even better in small groups. In terms of delivery, teachers can critically reflect on their use of language across teaching, learning and assessment material, and make accommodations where possible. For example, does the bilingual child learn and understand best through spoken words or writing? Are there words or syntax they struggle with, and so could be avoided? Will the student perform better through written or spoken assessment?

We can also think as a whole community – inclusion is about everyone. Parents, members of the community or translators can help with translating tasks and instructions. Teachers can explore opportunities to promote and celebrate a bilingual student's cultural background, values and ethnic identities.

Table 14.2 Type of intervention and possible strengths and challenges

Type of intervention	Strengths	Challenges
Classroom based		
Individual case based		
Combination of classroom and smaller group and individual instruction		

EALs with and without language difficulties will feel welcomed and motivated if activities are also organised and initiatives are taken that show their culture and language are valued. Such activities include days of celebrating differences and sharing culture, often involving families (e.g. food tasting, sports, arts and crafts exhibitions). Teachers can also incorporate celebrative diversity aspects in everyday lessons, such as in history lessons where children can share stories and facts from the past about their country of origin, and in geography lessons planning an imaginary trip to their country of origin and learning about its climate, the physical and human environment. With such activities, EALs will thrive, communicate and feel important members of the society, which eventually will make them much more engaged in support programmes.

Activity
In Table 14.2, record three strengths and three challenges for each approach if they were implemented in the case of each intervention presented earlier.

Conclusion

In this chapter, we have seen how bilingualism cannot be defined as simply as one might think. There are many parameters, like when and where an EAL started to learn a second language and what type of languages they are learning, that should be taken into consideration. We have focused in the main on children for whom learning an additional language could be a challenging task and a potential barrier to inclusion, for example economic migrants and refugees. It is important for all those working with these children to understand their needs, the limitations of the available assessments and inclusive ways to support them. Whole-class or small-group programmes tailored to bilingual children's needs can be very beneficial and inclusive if delivered with care and adjusted to their cognitive, social and emotional needs.

> *Resources*
>
> To learn more about the topic of EAL children with literacy difficulties, see the resources below.
>
> NALDIC is the national association for those involved with EAL learners. They have useful resources, links to other organisations, publications and events. You can visit their website: https://naldic.org.uk/ to check what is free and what is offered with paid membership.
>
> Bilingualism Matters is a community of people involved in bilingual research and education. For more information, go to: https://www.bilingualism-matters.org/

References

Boyle, J. and Fisher, S. (2007) *Educational Testing: A Competence-based Approach.* Chichester: Wiley.

Bylund, E., Abrahamsson, N., Hyltenstam, K. and Norrman, G. (2019) Revisiting the bilingual lexical deficit: the impact of age of acquisition, *Cognition*, 182: 45–49.

Cho, G. (2000) The role of heritage language in social interactions and relationships: reflections from a language minority group, *Bilingual Research Journal*, 24 (4): 369–384.

Cortese, M.J. and Khanna, M.M. (2007) Age of acquisition predicts naming and lexical-decision performance above and beyond 22 other predictor variables: an analysis of 2,342 words, *Quarterly Journal of Experimental Psychology*, 60 (8): 1072–1082.

Cummins, J. (2000) *Language, Power, and Pedagogy: Bilingual Children in the Crossfire.* Clevedon: Multilingual Matters.

Department for Education (DfE) (2015) *National Curriculum in England: Primary Curriculum*. Available at: https://www.gov.uk/government/publications/national-curriculum-in-england-primary-curriculum (accessed 23 December 2022).

Department for Education and Department of Health (DfE/DoH) (2015) *Special Educational Needs and Disability Code of Practice: 0 to 25 years*. London: DfE. Available at: https://www.gov.uk/government/uploads/system/uploads/attachment_data/file/398815/SEND_Code_of_Practice_January_2015.pdf

Dunn, L., Dunn, D. and Styles, B. (2009) *The British Picture Vocabulary Scale*, 3rd edition. London: GL Assessment.

Govindarajan, K. and Paradis, J. (2019) Narrative abilities of bilingual children with and without developmental language disorder (SLI): differentiation and the role of age and input factors, *Journal of Communication Disorders*, 77: 1–16.

Grosjean, F. (1998) Living with Two Languages and Two Cultures, in Parasnis, I. (ed.), *Cultural and language diversity and the deaf experience*. Cambridge: Cambridge University Press.

Grosjean, F. (2012) Bilingualism: a short introduction, in F. Grosjean and P. Li (eds.), *The Psycholinguistics of Bilingualism*. Oxford: Wiley-Blackwell.

Inman, A.G., Howard, E.E., Beaumont, R.L. and Walker, J.A. (2007) Cultural transmission: influence of contextual factors in Asian Indian immigrant parents' experiences, *Journal of Counseling Psychology*, 54 (1): 93–100.

Jimerson, S.R., Burns, M.K. and VanDerHeyden, A.M., eds. (2016) *Handbook of Response to Intervention: The Science and Practice of Multi-tiered Systems of Support*, 2nd edition. New York: Springer.

Kim, S.Y. and Chao, R.K. (2009) Heritage language fluency, ethnic identity, and school effort of immigrant Chinese and Mexican adolescents, *Cultural Diversity and Ethnic Minority Psychology*, 15 (1): 27–37.

Kulick, D. and Schieffelin, B.B. (2004) Language socialisation, in A. Duranti (ed.), *A Companion to Linguistic Anthropology*. Oxford: Blackwell.

Marku, B., Niolaki, G., Terzopoulos, A. and Wood, C. (2022) Eastern European parents' experiences of parenting a child with SEN in England, *Educational Psychology in Practice*, 38 (3): 297–316.

Mejía, G. (2016) Language usage and culture maintenance: a study of Spanish-speaking immigrant mothers in Australia, *Journal of Multilingual and Multicultural Development*, 37 (1): 23–39.

Nicoladis, E. (2018) Simultaneous child bilingualism, in D. Miller, F. Bayram, J. Rothman and L. Serratrice (eds.), *Bilingual Cognition and Language: The State of the Science across its Subfields*. Amsterdam: John Benjamins.

Niolaki, G.Z. and Masterson, J. (2012) Transfer effects in spelling from transparent Greek to opaque English in seven-to-ten-year-old children, *Bilingualism: Language and Cognition*, 15 (4): 757–770.

Niolaki, G.Z., Masterson, J. and Terzopoulos, A.R. (2014) Spelling improvement through letter-sound and whole-word training in two multilingual Greek- and English-speaking children, *Multilingual Education*, 4 (1): 1–23.

Niolaki, G.Z., Terzopoulos, A.R. and Masterson, J. (2017) A sublexical training study for spelling in a biliterate Greek- and English-speaking child, *Neuropsychological Rehabilitation*, 27 (4): 540–562.

Niolaki, G.Z., Vousden, J., Terzopoulos, A.R., Taylor, L.M., Sephton, S. and Masterson, J. (2020) Predictors of single word spelling in English speaking children: a cross sectional study, *Journal of Research in Reading*, 43 (4): 577–596.

Olioumtsevits, K., Papadopoulou, D. and Marinis, T. (2023) Vocabulary teaching in refugee children within the context of the Greek formal education, *Languages*, 8: 7. Available at: https://doi.org/10.3390/languages8010007

Paradis, J., Genesee, F. and Crago, M.B. (2011) *Dual Language Development and Disorders: A Handbook on Bilingualism and Second Language Learning*. Baltimore, MD: Paul H. Brookes.

Paradis, J., Sorenson-Duncan, T., Thomlinson, S. and Rusk, B. (2022) Does the use of complex sentences differentiate between bilinguals with and without DLD? Evidence from conversation and narrative tasks, *Frontiers in Education*, 6: 804088. Available at: https://doi.org/10.3389/feduc.2021.804088

Proctor, C.P., Silverman, R.D., Harring, J.R., Jones, R.L. and Hartranft, A.M. (2020) Teaching bilingual learners: effects of a language-based reading intervention on academic language and reading comprehension in grades 4 and 5, *Reading Research Quarterly*, 55 (1): 95–122.

Protopapas, A. (2017) Learning to read Greek, in L.W.T. Verhoeven and C.A. Perfetti (eds.), *Learning to Read across Languages and Writing Systems*. Cambridge: Cambridge University Press.

Romaine, S. (2010) Contact and language death, in R. Hickey (ed.), *The Handbook of Language Contact*. Oxford: Blackwell.

Siegel, L.S. (2020) Early identification and intervention to prevent reading failure: a response to intervention (RTI) initiative, *Educational and Developmental Psychologist*, 37 (2): 140–146.

Slavkov, N. (2015) Language attrition and reactivation in the context of bilingual first language acquisition, *International Journal of Bilingual Education and Bilingualism*, 18 (6): 715–734.
Treffers-Daller, J. (2015) The construct of language dominance, its operationalization and measurement, in C. Silva Corvalan and J. Treffers-Daller (eds.), *Language Dominance in Bilinguals: Issues of Measurement and Operationalization*. Cambridge: Cambridge University Press.
Verhoeven, L. (2007) Early bilingualism, language transfer, and phonological awareness, *Applied Psycholinguistics*, 28 (3): 425–439.
Wechsler, D. (2017) *Wechsler Individual Achievement Test, Third UK Edition* (WIAT-III UK). London: Pearson.

15 Why it is important to give additional support to children and young people of exceptional cognitive ability

Lyn Kendall

By the end of this chapter, you should be able to:

- identify an exceptionally able child in an academic setting
- name six areas where exceptionally able children are likely to experience special educational needs and/or other differences
- develop an understanding and be able to plan for those needs in an educational setting
- develop an understanding of support tools for parents and colleagues in their dealings with such children.

Let us begin by defining the concepts at the very heart of this chapter: first, what is intelligence? And second, how do we identify, acknowledge and support those with exceptional intelligence?

Although rather simplistic (see Lykken 1998) for the purposes of this chapter, intelligence will be considered as raw brainpower: cognitive ability as it applies to problem-solving, speed of processing, attention and working memory (Ness 2010, cited in Kaye 2010). It is innate and an indicator of one's ability to learn.

The formal definition of an exceptionally able individual has changed many times over the years and will doubtlessly continue to do so as we learn more about our brains and ourselves. A few minutes spent online reveals a plethora of different figures, competing terminology and a host of definitions, few if any of which align. Guidance on how schools should accommodate their exceptionally able children has proven to be just as fluid and inconsistent. Ofsted, the government office that inspects schools in the UK, has over the years made 'gifted and talented' provision a focus of its inspections (1992), looked at the prospects for children achieving a level 5 or 6 at the end of Year 6 (2013), and grouped such children as 'high prior attainers' (2019). Clearly, being exceptionally able means many different things to many different people. Some argue that intellectually able children are so bright they will do well anyway, but for reasons we will explore later in this chapter, high intelligence and high attainment do not automatically go hand in hand.

Studies in the US, where there is a gifted programme, have shown that children with high ability tend to be good all-rounders and successful no matter the path they follow (Terman and Oden 1959). However, a more recent study in the UK by Professor Joan Freeman (2010) portrayed a very different picture of the prospects for highly intelligent students educated under the British system. Her conclusions have been supported by more recent research, such as that by Reid and Horváthová (2016), which suggests that students of high cognitive ability should be taught using alternative teaching methods, just as those students who are classed as having difficulties with learning would be taught with more flexibility. This raises the question: what aspects of exceptional cognitive ability imply that such students should be included under the SEN umbrella?

Recognition of needs: what are the challenges?

Activity
Make a few notes now about the sorts of difficulties that exceptionally able children might encounter.

The following difficulties are commonly seen in an educational setting.

Developmental mismatch

The child's physical development will be age-appropriate. They will not be taller or stronger because they have high cognitive ability, but they will have the understanding, knowledge and often aspirations of a much older child. This, if not addressed, can lead to frustration and temper tantrums in younger children and challenging behaviour in older children. Kendall and Allcock (2020) describe how one six-year-old refused to draw in class because he was comparing his efforts to that of Leonardo Da Vinci!

Additionally, a child's emotional development and life experience will most usually reflect their chronological age. When a child is capable of understanding concepts that are beyond their years but does not yet have the emotional maturity to be able to assimilate those ideas, this can result in anxiety, nightmares and a refusal to take risks.

Overthinking

Overthinking is something that affects exceptionally able children and adults alike. When your brain can consider all the possibilities and does so, all the time, there are various consequences. A common one is difficulty falling asleep. Once a 'bright spark' is asleep, they tend to stay asleep but getting there is quite a different matter. It is not easy to switch off a busy brain. ('Bright spark' is another name for exceptionally able children in the cognitive domain.)

Furthermore, making a choice becomes a chore, not a pleasure. Whether it is the flavour of an ice-cream or which subjects/modules to choose, there are so many possibilities that the individual can end up crashing just like a computer that is running too many programs. Overtiredness, anxiety, refusal to work and perfectionism can all be consequences of overthinking.

Social development

When the exceptionally able child is at home, their behaviours and interests seem quite usual as there is nothing to compare them to. Once a young child starts to attend playgroup or nursery, those differences become clear. Here we have a child that has little in common with their peers. Consequently, the child makes fewer, if any, friends, thus limiting the opportunity for practising essential social skills. Additionally, while other children are being rewarded for learning their colours or knowing the words and actions to a song, there are few opportunities to praise individuals that have already achieved those skills. By the time such a child reaches full-time schooling, they are often becoming isolated. It is common for schools to misinterpret the behaviours exhibited by exceptionally able children as a sign that the individual may have an autistic spectrum condition (ASC). The similarities in presentation will be discussed later in this chapter. Kendall and Allcock (2020) describe how in workshops for exceptionally able children aged 8–11 years, run by Lyn Kendall, participants struggled to turn take, share and follow rules set by other children.

Adolescence is another particularly challenging time. Our bright spark might be top of the class, but there's no coming top in adolescence.

Academic underperformance

Exceptionally able students have special educational needs because the very brightest of them will often underperform academically. In 2009, Kendall gave a talk to a group of fifty Mensa members at its annual general meeting in Chester. Following the formal part of the talk, there was discussion. Kendall asked the audience to raise their hands if they had been to university. All raised their hands. Then she asked how many of them had completed their studies coming away with a qualification. Fewer than half raised their hands.

There is no one reason why people with exceptional cognitive ability do not perform to their potential academically, but the huge loss to society should be considered when our potential doctors, scientists, lawyers and academics fall by the wayside. Much of it can be down to individual temperament and resilience. As shown by Freeman (2010), given the same circumstances, everyone will react differently. Parental and family expectations also play a large part in academic achievement.

Schools may assume that bright children will achieve anyway and that if a child is 'top of the class', all is well, but it could be argued that being top of the class is not the same as achieving one's potential.

Developing study skills

High-level skills that occur naturally in people with a high IQ have been described as follows:

- *Problem-solving*: the ability to grasp the nature of an obstacle or dilemma and to think a way through or around the issue (Green and Gilhooly 2010, cited in Kaye 2010).
- *Speed of processing*: how quickly information can be taken in, assimilated and recalled.
- *Attention*: how much input can be usefully taken in at any time, and the level of detail recorded (Naish 2010, cited in Kaye 2010; Ness 2010, cited in Kaye 2010).
- *Working memory*: how much information can be actively retained and manipulated at any one time (Hitch 2010, cited in Kaye 2010).

It can appear that most bright children just soak up information. This can be a particular advantage at primary and secondary school. Taking in, memorising and recalling facts is a mainstay of the exam system. However, universities require that their students can research, provide evidence and show an in-depth understanding of a topic. If an individual has survived thus far without developing those skills and relying entirely on their memory, we have done them a disservice. A child that is continually fed a diet of work that is not challenging will never learn how to study.

Betts and Neihart (1988) developed six profiles of gifted and talented children, based on observation, interviews and literature reviews. They created a matrix to assist parents, teachers and other relevant adults to understand the nature and needs of those six types of young people, and to enable them to identify the different ways in which gifted children present.

Sensory processing sensitivity

Sensory processing sensitivity (SPS) is an innate trait that a highly sensitive person is born with. A highly sensitive person can be empathetic, intelligent, creative, compassionate, kind and caring but become easily overstimulated by loud sounds, bright lights or chaotic environments (Aron 1997). It is also referred to by some as 'overexcitabilities' (Bainbridge 2020). Recent research has shown SPS to be common in exceptionally able children and adults. 'For highly intelligent individuals with overexcitabilities, even normal stimuli such as a clothing tag or a common but unnatural sound can become physically painful' (Karpinski et al. 2018).

Duncan et al. (2018) describe how exceptionally able children can be sensitive to their environment and react with heightened responses. These sensitivities can make a classroom, office or busy environment a difficult place to be for our bright sparks regardless of age.

To summarise the first part of this chapter, there are six main reasons why our brightest individuals should be considered to have SEN: developmental mismatch, overthinking, asynchronous social development, academic underperformance, lack of appropriate study skills and sensory sensitivities. How we ensure that children with high learning potential succeed despite their ability is the next challenge. Having considered the reasons as to why our bright sparks have special educational needs, we must turn our attention to how they can be identified and supported by parents/carers, schools and other professionals. In order to facilitate clarity of thought and purpose, we shall proceed in the same order that the issues appear in the first part of the chapter.

Recognition of needs: how can we support children/young people of exceptional cognitive ability?

While parents and staff in 'early years' settings will often quote examples or relay anecdotes to support their judgement about a child's ability, if more formal action is to be taken to support an individual, more formal identification is needed. An individual assessment by a suitably qualified psychologist or assessor is the ideal. However, these are expensive when undertaken privately and a school educational psychologist's time is like gold dust.

There are assessments available to schools from reputable companies, which can be administered by suitably trained or qualified teachers. In other cases, schools will screen all their students as a matter of course using cognitive abilities tests (CATS) (GL Assessment 2019) or similar.

A word of caution here. Any test or assessment is a snapshot in time and reflects how the individual performed on a particular day. As any of us will attest to, if we have had a late night, poor quality of sleep, are worrying or struggling with a cold or other illness, our performance will not reflect our best efforts. Test results should not be taken as a given, but an indication of potential.

Activity
Psychological and educational tests are given clearance levels. Find out what your clearance level is by looking at a website that supplies such tests.

Developmental mismatch

Intellectually gifted children tend to display asynchronous development – that is to say, as they grow, their physical and emotional advancement does not progress at the same rate as their cognitive ability.

Even when a gifted child's physical development is age-appropriate and there are no additional difficulties or disabilities, they are still an 'old head' in a young body. They may understand life's protocols and how to behave but will be held back from doing so by their age, size, motor skills or cultural expectations. The subsequent frustration can cause meltdowns or defiant behaviour. While it is impossible to alleviate these frustrations entirely, there are some techniques that can help allay them.

At home and school, allow the child to help as much as they are able. Even young children can fetch things, carry messages, take used towels to the laundry basket, lay the table for dinner or give out books. Comment on the things they can do now that they could not do before. Conversely, beginning a sentence with 'I think you are old enough to …' shows that when the time is right you will allow them to do things, and makes it easier for them to swallow a bitter pill when you forbid them to do something for safety reasons.

This can also be approached more formally. Look at videos of very young babies and talk about how the child was once like that – unable to do anything for themselves. Children find it hilarious to see footage of babies learning to feed themselves or to walk. Next, discuss what would have happened if they, having fallen over as infants, had decided that walking was too hard and given up. Finally, talk about how there are things that they still cannot do because of their age, size or maturity, but which they will be able to do as they get older as long as they keep trying. Driving a car is an excellent example.

This 'learning journey' approach works well for all children but is particularly efficacious for children and young people who set themselves overly high or unrealistic standards. Regular reminders of past triumphs and future goals improve self-esteem and encourage resilience.

Emotionally, in their early years, a child's life experience is restricted. Relationships are limited to family, friends and classmates, and the wider world represented by home, school, day trips or holidays.

Most children have never experienced hunger, homelessness or trauma. When an exceptionally able child encounters these concepts, they have no way of reconciling them with their own life experiences and internalising the emotions they cause within them. These ideas can come from anywhere: books the child has been reading, hearing adults or older children talking, movies and television programmes, or even things they have learned at school. Much as we may wish to completely shield children from knowledge that is going to cause them distress in this way, even if it were possible to do so, it can be argued that we should not. Just as when they deal with physical challenges, it is important that we help children learn to face life's misfortunes and develop emotional resilience. Providing a strong adult presence to talk through any worries can help provide some perspective, and there are many ways that adults can take the reins and teach some coping strategies.

Adults are advised to disclose only the minimum amount of information necessary to allay the child's fears. The more detail you give, the more likely it is that you will raise further questions and worries in the child's mind.

Ground a child's worries in the known. Place the fear within the realm of the child's experience and draw parallels. This can help assimilate new concepts within current schema.

> *Activity*
> Make a list of positive comments that you could say to a child that will help to place them on a learning journey rather than being in competition with themselves and others.

Overthinking

The busy brains of bright people think and analyse everything non-stop. Sometimes there does not need to be a particular trigger to send minds down a rabbit hole of concerns and worries. Something as simple as 'The boss wants to see me tomorrow and I don't know why' can cause a spiral, as every possibility is mapped out and investigated before the event.

Single-focus activities are those where the individual undertakes a task from which they cannot easily be distracted, and the brain cannot distract itself. They are excellent at halting the maelstrom of thoughts and ideas which can prevent sleep or cause anxiety, crashing and meltdowns. There are many possibilities. Contrary to popular opinion, certain video or computer games are excellent for producing the required calming effect (Scott 2020). Anything where losing concentration causes you to lose the game is very effective. Audio books, sudoku, yoga and gardening are all helpful because you must focus on the task in hand.

Walking, reading, group activities and video games in which others are involved do not work, as they either over-stimulate or allow the mind to wander.

> *Activity*
> The single-focus activities cited above are just a few of the possibilities. Make a list of some you can think of and add to it when you find something new.

Social development

In any society, a child will be inducted into that culture and learn to interact with others. There are rules for social interaction, many of them unwritten, that all children will learn to varying degrees. Modern cultures tend to socialise their children early with day care or mother and baby groups. Unless the child is atypical, they quickly become used to the process of interacting with other humans.

Before most of our exceptionally able children start preschool, they already know colours and shapes, love to count and many can read. They know the alphabet, nursery rhymes and popular children's songs. When they get to nursery and find that the day is structured around learning those same colours and numbers, they soon get bored. They have little in common with their chronological peers, many of whom will still be learning to talk in sentences let alone manage abstract concepts.

If we are not to risk isolating the child at this early age, two things need to be done. First, their knowledge needs to be treated as normal and not a curiosity. Providing the child with additional intellectual experiences and appropriate learning will normalise the process for them. Second, and just as important, attention needs to be refocused on to other desirable attributes that are common to all children. Praise for being patient, kind, thoughtful and so on helps to develop a child as a whole person. Encourage resilience by teaching physical tasks such as buckles, laces, getting dressed and other self-care skills. These are activities where our 'bright spark' will be on a par with other children and the learning process will help the child to become a member of the group rather than an outlier.

When in school, it is common for the brightest children to present with some atypical behaviours, those that professionals more commonly see as being linked to an ASC. This would be a common error because as Kendall and Allcock (2020) describe, there are six traits that children with exceptional cognitive ability and those on the autistic spectrum can share:

- being prone to anxiety
- experiencing social difficulties when interacting with others
- having special or unusual interests about which they are hugely knowledgeable
- emotional meltdowns
- crashing – that is, a period of unresponsive behaviour
- sensory sensitivities.

While it is possible to have an ASC and exceptionally high cognitive ability, generally the causes underlying the presenting behaviours are quite different.

Adolescence

During adolescence, it is common for bright teens to take even a mild rebuke from an adult authority figure, like a teacher, incredibly seriously – it is confirmation of all their new doubts and fears about themselves.

Individuals with exceptional cognitive ability can often feel pressure to hide or suppress their intellect when they hit their teenage years, pushed more towards defining themselves by behaviour and personality. Suddenly, maybe

Table 15.1 The different causes of similar behaviour comparing an autistic spectrum condition and exceptional intelligence

Symptoms	ASC	Exceptional cognitive ability
Anxiety	Change of routine such as exams or school trips	Overthinking or a fear of failure
Social difficulties	Play is repetitive, object-based, lacking in imagination	Lack of people with whom to socialise; play is more sophisticated and complex
Special or unusual interests	Tend to be long-term and all-consuming	Will do a topic to death, then move on to something else
Meltdowns	Overload – too much going on or too far out of their comfort zone	Frustration; an old head on young shoulders; overstimulation
Crashing	Overload or lack of understanding of what is required	Overthinking or anxiety; emotional understanding cannot keep up with head; ability to 'take in' more information due to working memory and speed of processing can cause overload
Sensitivities	Difficulty integrating information from senses – e.g. lack of awareness of heat, cold, pain, thirst, hunger	Lack of filtering

for the first time in their lives, being the cleverest one in the room feels instinctively like a bad thing.

Many gifted children, even those who have been happy and motivated at school up until this point, will find that this new onslaught of social pressures transforms the classroom into an incredibly stressful place filled with unknown pitfalls. As one young woman described to Kendall: 'I used to be so good in school, the teachers loved me. I don't know where that person is any more' (Kendall and Allcock 2020: 74).

For most teenagers, gifted or not, education drops to the bottom of the priority list in favour of friendships, relationships, social media and their appearance (Madison 2013). Teachers understand this and are very adept at constantly stressing the importance of getting homework done, not being absent from school, studying for mock exams and so on, all to keep their students as focused on their studies as possible. They begin to pile on the pressure at the beginning of Year 10, starting as they mean to go on for the next two years. Our 'bright sparks', however, are already aware of what is expected of them. The additional pressure from teachers to stay on task can be taken too seriously, almost personally, as if their current pace is not good enough.

Barely three or four weeks into the term they will be trying to juggle homework, coursework and their social lives while remaining convinced that their teachers believe they are underperforming. This is when cracks may begin to show.

On top of this, schools will be sending regular letters or e-mails to all Year 10 parents, reminding them of how important studying is and hoping that they will reinforce the message. As conscientious parents who may be gifted themselves, it is natural to follow up thoroughly. For teens, this diligence risks reinforcing the existing misconception that not only do teachers think they are underperforming, but their parents do too.

For those working with any high-ability students in Key Stage 4, it is beneficial to take them aside and have a quiet word, explaining that what is being said to the class does not apply to them. High-ability teens need to be supported in keeping the pressure and their workload manageable so that they make it to exam season and get the best results they can.

Academic underperformance

The disparity between how bright sparks behave at home and at school can often cause conflict between parents and teachers. Kanevsky and Keighley (2003) introduced the five Cs, which they considered would determine whether an exceptionally able older child will engage in school. These were: control, choice, challenge, complexity and caring teachers.

Developing study skills

There are many ways that exceptionally able students can be supported by schools and colleges. In 2016–17 Kendall completed research with a group of 14 Year 9 students. They attended a school where most children came from a background of financial poverty and the overall A* to C grades at GCSE were well below the city average. Students included in the group were identified through a high non-verbal reasoning score, the top 5 per cent, on the CAT. A baseline academic assessment was undertaken. This found that most were not achieving their academic potential across all subjects, with many in the average range and others below average in certain areas. Over a period of six months, the group was seen weekly and underwent a study support and confidence-building programme. They were then reassessed and asked to provide feedback as to any benefits the programme had for them. Student and teacher feedback showed that all felt more confident as learners. Progress in reading ranged between one year and four years over the six-month period. Progress across all subjects was made in all but two cases, and progress was dependent upon attendance at lessons.

The concept of a zone of proximal development (ZPD) was developed by Lev Vygotsky during the late 1920s. In *Mind in Society: The Development of Higher Psychological Processes* (1978), Vygotsky defined the ZPD as 'the distance between the actual development level as determined by independent problem solving and the level of potential development as determined through problem solving under adult guidance or in collaboration with more capable peers' (1978: 86). Learning takes place in the ZPD.

If, in school, a gifted child only ever encounters things they can do on their own, they are not learning. It is essential that if a child is to develop good study habits, they must be provided with tasks that are within their ZPD.

Sensory sensitivities

It is worth mentioning that sensory sensitivities are not classified as a disability. That may change in the future once further research has been undertaken and more proof has been accrued but, for now, sensory sensitivities as we understand them do not meet the criteria that classifies a disability under the 2010 Equality Act.

Visual sensitivities can include an intolerance of bright lights, certain colours or visually busy environments. Dealing with the difficulties of visual sensitivities can be quite straightforward. Wearing dark or tinted glasses can help. If a child finds a situation before them so complex as to be overwhelming, they can close their eyes for a few seconds. Or they can avert their eyes to focus on something small or nearby.

There are a few noises that almost everyone finds intensely grating, but those with sensory sensitivities can be disturbed by far more subtle sounds that go unnoticed by most of us. People chewing, whispering or even breathing can be enough to cause irritation. In school, the normal quiet buzz of a classroom can be a real distraction for those with aural sensitivities and make concentration impossible. Gel earplugs can be helpful. They mute minor, irritating noises and help to lessen the impact of loud, unexpected ones. Additionally, they are almost undetectable.

Everyone experiences uncomfortable clothing at some point. The list of tactile sensitivities can sometimes seem endless – hair accessories, shoes and socks, hair touching the back of your neck, and so on. School uniforms can be so uncomfortable as to affect concentration and mood. Wearing a soft cotton T-shirt under a school shirt, trousers or skirts made from a skin-friendly material, and wearing hair up or away from the face can all help.

Having a highly sensitive sense of smell can cause unwanted physical reactions. Certain food smells – chlorine in swimming pools or an open wheelie bin – can induce intense reactions. Coping with a sensory sensitivity to smells can be hard, but it is not impossible. If the smell is localised, avoidance is usually the best answer. Masking the smell with another, more pleasant one works well. Keeping a handkerchief impregnated with a pleasant smell such as perfume or menthol in the pocket, can be a quick and effective fix.

The type of sensory sensitivity – where food textures or flavours are the problem – can make life difficult not just for the individual but for others too. For safety's sake, should a child gag when eating a particular food, check that there is no accompanying rash, facial swelling or breathing difficulties. For those with sensitivities, teaching the etiquette surrounding food consumption can be invaluable and save embarrassment for all.

> *Activity*
> How could a classroom or other area be adapted to support the inclusion of those individuals with sensory sensitivities?

Boxes 15.1 and 15.2 provide sample Individual Plans, which address various aspects of the child's needs at different ages.

Box 15.1 A sample Individual Plan for an exceptionally able child aged six

Child's Name/Age	Ella (01/01/2013) six years		
Date of Plan	Summer Term 2019		
Area of Focus	**Action**	**Expected Progress**	**Responsibility**
Ella struggles to make friends with her peers	1) School will have organised games at playtime that Ella will watch and learn the rules of	1) Ella will begin to take part in organised games in the playground	1) School
	2) Parents will look at Mensa and Potential Plus for events that are suitable for Ella	2) Ella will attend events so that she can meet other bright children	2) Home
Ella needs help to dress herself following PE	1) Parents will teach Ella to dress and undress herself	Ella will be able to dress herself without adult help and achieve her certificate by the next review meeting	Home and school
	2) School will instigate an 'I can dress myself' certificate for each child that achieves this		
Ella's literacy and numeracy skills are at least two years ahead of her actual age	Ella will work with a Year 3 class for English and maths	Ella will work at a level that reflects her ability in English and maths	School

Date of next meeting: September 2019

> **Box 15.2 A sample Individual Plan for an exceptionally able child aged 12**
>
> | Child's Name/Age | Ella (01/01/2007) 12 years | | |
> |---|---|---|---|
> | Date of Plan | Summer Term 2019 | | |
> | **Area of Focus** | **Action** | **Expected Progress** | **Responsibility** |
> | Ella is taking most of the evening to complete her homework because she thinks that it is not good enough. This has resulted in missing bedtimes and clashing with her parents | Ella will spend no more than 30 minutes on each piece of homework. It will then be handed in regardless of whether it is finished | Ella will get used to being more focused and producing 'good enough' work. This will allow for a good work/rest balance | Ella, with support from home and backed up by school |
> | Ella has not been eating lunch during her break as she wants to practise for the end-of-term concert. This has meant that she has become over-tired and irritable | School will arrange with the canteen for all students taking part in the concert to collect a packed lunch | Ella's mood and performance in the afternoons will improve | Ella, with support from school |
> | Ella is a gifted mathematician | As from September, Ella will join the Year 10 GCSE mathematics group. Work missed will need to be caught up | Ella will take GCSE mathematics two years early | Ella, with support from home and school |
>
> Date of next meeting: September 2019

Conclusion

Looking after the physical, social, emotional and academic needs of an exceptionally able child is essential but does not have to be expensive or time-consuming for the school. It does, however, require flexibility and a positive attitude. As with any other child that has additional needs, collaborating closely with parents is advised and having a written plan helps to keep the relationship manageable for all.

If you want to learn more about the 'bright sparks', see the further reading list below.

Further reading

Fonseca, C. (2015) *Emotional Intensity in Gifted Students: Helping Kids with Explosive Feelings*. Waco, TX: Prufrock Press.

Leyden, S. (1985) *Helping the Child of Exceptional Ability*. London: Routledge.

Madison, L. (2013) *The Feelings Book: The Care & Keeping of Your Emotions*. Middleton, WI: American Girl Publishing.

Orloff, S. (2018) *The Empath's Survival Guide: Life Strategies for Sensitive People*. Louisville, CO: Sounds True.

Painter, F. (1984) *Living with a Gifted Child*. London: Souvenir Press.

Williams, J. (2015) *Understanding the Highly Sensitive Child: Seeing an Overwhelming World through Their Eyes*. CreateSpace Independent Publishing Platform.

References

Aron, E.N. and Aron, A. (1997). Sensory-processing sensitivity and its relation to introversion and emotionality. *Journal of Personality and Social Psychology*, 73(2), 345–368. https://doi.org/10.1037/0022-3514.73.2.345

Bainbridge, C. (2020) *Dabrowski's overexcitabilities in gifted children*. Available at: https://www.verywellfamily.com/dabrowskis-overexcitabilities-in-gifted-children-1449118 (accessed 22 April 2022).

Betts, G.T. and Neihart, M. (1988) Profiles of the gifted and talented, *Gifted Child Quarterly*, 32 (2): 248–253.

Duncan, S., Goodwin. C., Haase, J. and Wislon, S. (2018) *Neuroscience of giftedness: greater sensory sensitivity*. Available at: https://2e-learning.com/about-gifted-and-2e/greater-sensory-sensitivity/ (accessed 15 May 2022).

Equality Act (2010) London: TSO. Available at: https://www.legislation.gov.uk/ukpga/2010/15/pdfs/ukpga_20100015_en.pdf.

Freeman, J., (2010) *Gifted Lives: What Happens When Gifted Children Grow up?* London: Routledge.

GL Assessment (2019) *CAT4*. London: GL Assessment. Available at: https://www.gl-assessment.co.uk/assessments/cat4/ (accessed 8 November 2022).

Kanevsky, L. and Keighley, T. (2003) To produce or not to produce? Understanding boredom and the honour in underachievement, *Roeper Review: A Journal on Gifted Education*, 26 (1): 20–28.

Karpinski, R.I., Kolb, A.M.K., Tetreault, N.A. and Borowski, T.B. (2018) High intelligence: a risk factor for psychological and physiological overexcitabilities, *Intelligence*, 66: 8–23.

Kaye, H. (2010) *Cognitive Psychology*, Maidenhead: Open University Press.

Kendall, L. and Allcock, C. (2020) *A Brilliant IQ Gift or Challenge?* Dunstable: Brilliant Publications.

Lykken, D.T. (1998) The genetics of genius, in A. Steptoe (ed.), *Genius and Mind: Studies of Creativity and Temperament*. Oxford: Oxford University Press.

Madison, L. (2013) *The Feelings Book: The Care & Keeping of Your Emotions*. Middleton, WI: American Girl Publishing.

Ofsted (2019) Education inspection framework Updated 14 July 2023. Available at https://www.gov.uk/government/publications/education-inspection-framework/education-inspection-framework (accessed 5 September 2023).

Ofsted (2013) *The most able students: Are they doing as well as they should in our non-selective secondary schools?* Available at: https://www.bl.uk/collection-items/most-able-students-are-they-doing-as-well-as-they-should-in-our-nonselective-secondary-schools (accessed 9 September 2022).

Ofsted (1992) The Education Acts 1944 to 1992.

Reid, E. and Horváthová, B. (2016) Teacher training programs for gifted education with focus on sustainability, *Journal of Teacher Education for Sustainability*, 18 (2): 66–74.

Scott, E. (2020) *The link between video games and stress relief*. Available at: https://www.verywellmind.com/how-video-games-relieve-stress-4110349 (accessed 9 April 2022).

Terman, L.M. and Oden, M.H. (1959) *The Gifted Group at Mid-Life: Thirty-five Years' Follow-up of the Superior Child*. Genetic Studies of Genius, #5. Stanford, CA: Stanford University Press.

Vygotsky, L.S. (1978) *Mind in Society: The Development of Higher Psychological Processes*. London: Harvard University Press.

Epilogue: A journey at the end! Is it truly the end or the beginning?

The aim of this book was to draw on psychological and educational theories, research and practice to increase students' and practitioners' awareness of issues related to identifying needs and supporting children with SEN in an educational setting. We hope that we have achieved our aim, highlighting the importance of inclusion and the need for inclusive practices to be informed by psychological and educational evidence. We included SEN that can be frequently found in the school, but there are other needs not included in the book.

Sometimes applying psychological theory to inclusive educational situations and scenarios is easier said than done, since there is often a tension within theory and practice in how it is done, when it is done, and what the consequences are. However, we hope the framework we have provided demonstrates needs and educational experiences within and along the special and inclusive continuum. Depending on the presentation (e.g. type and severity) of the needs, at times, a more specialist, individualist approach might be required, but even on these occasions, accommodations and adaptations to the environment are needed so that the individual does not experience exclusion but instead experiences a sense of belonging. Furthermore, the approach (both special and inclusive) should be done in partnership with parents/carers and the children themselves. This recognition of their competencies and autonomy is central to neurodivergence, and the individual learner being and feeling accepted and valued for who they are. Thus, the two approaches (special and inclusive) can co-exist to serve the individual's needs and development.

These two practices can, on the one hand, provide an in-depth awareness and understanding of needs, and on the other, a sense of belonging and being part of the classroom environment. Such an environment provides opportunities for empowerment on the part of the individual learner and works within a strengths-based model. In this way, the challenges experienced by learners with SEN can be minimised, through a combination of the learner's development (e.g. coping strategies) and the barriers they experience being removed. Hence, it is not a question of what is the 'correct' approach (special or educational inclusion) but how both approaches can serve the learner's needs and wishes, and so effectively support and include them. It is a case of the teacher 'picking and mixing' the best elements of each approach based on the uniqueness of the individual learner (e.g. differences, strengths, needs, interests, beliefs).

Teaching children with SEN is challenging for teachers, but they also enrich the tapestry of the classroom, the school and society. We hope that our book, tailored around the recognition of needs and ways to support these unique learners effectively, will be able to serve teachers by giving them strategies to provide opportunities for empowerment of their learners and ways to understand their needs in a 'specialist and inclusive continuum'.

The end! ☺

Index

Page numbers in italics are figures; with 't' are tables.

ABC model 122–3, *122*, 123t
Abidin, R.R. 108
access deficit hypothesis, of
    developmental dyscalculia 159–60
accommodation, and ADHD 126–7
ADHD *see* attention deficit hyperactivity
    disorder (ADHD)
adolescence, and exceptionally able
    children 253–5
adverse childhood experiences (ACEs)
    90
adversity 89–90
affective support, and MLD 166–9, 167–8t
affirmative models 10
age of acquisition (AoA), and
    bilingualism 232–3, *235*
Ager, S. 55
Ainsworth, Mary 34t
Aitken, D. 70
Al Otaiba, S. 144
Allcock, C. 247, 248, 253
American Academy of Audiology 219
American Speech-Language-Hearing
    Association (ASHA) 222
Anderson, A. 48, *49*
Anderson, J. 56
Antecedent-Behaviour-Consequence
    (ABC) model 122–3, *122*, 123t
anxiety
    and exceptionally able children 253,
        254t
    maths 158, 160, 166, 167t
APD *see* auditory processing difficulties
    (APD)
apps, math 166, 168
Arakelyan, S. 55
areas of need (SEND Code of Practice)
    23–4
Armstrong, D. 24–5, 87
ASD *see* autism/autism spectrum
    disorders (ASDs)
Asperger's disorder (Asperger
    syndrome) 64

assistive technology (AT), and visual
    impairment 208–9, 210, 211–12,
    212t
Attachment Theory 34t, 88–9
attention deficit hyperactivity disorder
    (ADHD) 113–18, 115t, *116*, 129
    culture/meaning/stigma 120–1
    difficulties 118–20
    interventions/practices 121–9, *122*,
        123t, 129t
auditory processing difficulties (APD)
    217–21, 227
    and additional languages 221–2
    and neurodivergences 221
    and the physical learning environment
        224–7
autism/autism spectrum disorders
    (ASDs) 63–9, 68t, 69t, 75
    and APD 220
    and exceptionally able children 248,
        254t
    and mental health difficulties 85
    theory and evidence-based framework
        69–75
Ayres, A.J. 182

Ball, S. 25
Bandura, A. 34t, 87
Barkley, R.A. 119
barriers-to-participation 6, 8t
Barton, L. 16
Becker, Howard 11
behavioural management 86–7, 124
behaviourism 86–7
Bellis, M.A. 90
Bešić, E. 54
Betts, G.T. 249
bias, and social inequality 108
bilingualism/second language learning
    231–7, *232*, *235*, 236t, 242
    intervention and support 240–2, 242t
    needs and differences 237–9
bio-ecological approach 33–8, 42–3

bio-medical model 4, 4t
biopsychosocial model 11, 91
Bishop, D. 135
Blume, Harvy 9
Bowlby, J. 34t, 88–9
Boyle, C. 83
Bradley, R.H. 101
braille 210–12, 212t
Braun, A. 25
British Society of Audiology 219
Bronfenbrenner, Urie 23, 33–40, 42–3, 48, 49, 91
Brown, T. 116
Brown's Model of Executive Functions Impaired in ADHD *116*
Bruner, J.S. 161–2
Bunford, N. 126
Bylund, E. 232

Caldin, R. 54
Carnerero, F. 217
CASEL model 87
CAST model of UDL 40
Castles, A. 136, 137, 139
challenging behaviours 80, 85–91
Chan, E.S. 118
child-centred approaches 88
Children and Families Act (2014) 21, 22, 27
chronosystem 35–6, 55
co-morbidity 92
cognition, numerical 158–9
cognitive behaviour therapy (CBT) 87
Cognitive Development Theory 34t
cognitive factors, and MLD 164
Cognitive Orientation to daily Occupational Performance Approach (CO-OP™), and DCD 189–90
Cohen, L. 158
collaboration, and ADHD 127–8
collaborative and proactive solutions (CPS) 128, 129t
combined-medium approach, visual impairment 210–11
Comiskey, C. 35
concrete-pictorial-abstract (CPA) approach 162
conduct disorder (CD) 102, *102*, 107
CONSORT (Consolidated Standards of Reporting Trials) 93
contingency management, and ADHD 124–5

Cooper, P. 89
Corbett, J. 16
Corwen, R.F. 101
Cowan, R. 160
Cox, Beckett 69
Coyne, I. 35
CPS *see* collaborative and proactive solutions (CPS)
Csikszentmihalyi, M. 81
culture, and ADHD 120–1
curriculum and exam modifications, visual impairment 210

Daily Report Cards (DRCs) 124–5
DCD *see* developmental coordination disorder (DCD)
DD *see* developmental dyscalculia (DD)
De Wit, E. 221
decoding, and APD 223
DeFries, J.C. 135
Dehaene, S. 135, 158–9
demand characteristics 37
Dempsey, C. 35
developmental coordination disorder (DCD) 179–80, 201
 background/defined/identification 180–7, 184–6t
 interventions/practices 188–93, 194–8t, 199–200t
 supporting 187–8
developmental dyscalculia (DD) 155–6, 156–7t, 159–60, 168
developmental mismatch, and exceptionally able children 247, 251
Devine, A. 160
diagnostic systems 84–5
difficulties, definition 218
dilemma of difference 12
discovery learning 143
disorders, defined 80, 218
distributed practice 143
Dockrell, J. 226–7
domain-general/specific hypotheses, and developmental dyscalculia 159–60
Done, E.J. 25
Donkin, A. 109
Double Empathy Problem 12, 71
DSM-5 (*Diagnostic and Statistical Manual*) 84
 and ADHD 113, 114–15
 and DCD 183, 194–8t

Dubsky, R. 27
Duncan, S. 250
Dunlap, G. 127
DuPaul, G. 124
DuPaul, G.J. 125–6, 128
Durlak, J.A. 87
Dvorsky, M.R. 118
Dweck, C.S. 34t
dyscalculia *see* developmental dyscalculia (DD)
dyslexia 133–5, 146–7
  aetiologies of unexpected reading difficulties 140–2, 141t
  and APD 220
  debate 135–7
  interventions 142–6, *145*, 146t
  profiles of children with 137–40, 138t, *140*
dyspraxia 182–3

Eckert, T.L. 125–6
ecological systems theory 23, 48–55, *49*
Education Act (1981) 21, 22
educational practices, defined 14
Ekins, A. 25
Elliott, J.G. 136
Engel, G.L. 11, 91
English as an additional language (EAL)
  and APD 221–2
  see also bilingualism/second language learning
Equality Act (2010) 227
Erikson, Erik 34t
Evans, S.W. 126
exams
  and ADHD 14
  and mental health 84
  and visual impairment 210
exceptionally able children 246–7, 258–9
  challenges 247–50
  sample individual plans 257–8
  supporting 250–8, 254t
executive functions 116, *116*, 164
exosystem 35, 51–3

Fabiano, G.A. 92
family *see* home support and parents
Family Stress Model (FSM) 106–7
Felitti, V.J. 90
Fletcher, J.M. 143
Fletcher-Watson, S. 70, 72
force characteristics 37

Foucault, M. 6, 84
Francis, D.A. 11
Freeman, Joan 247, 249
Freigang, C. 225
French, S. 10
Friend, A. 135
Fuchs, D. 5
Fuchs, L.S. 5
functionally based interventions (FIs) 122, *122*, 123t
functioning, high/low 66

Gable, S.L. 81
gender
  and ADHD 116–17
  and dyslexia 136
  and autism 68t
  and visual impairment 206
gifted and talented *see* exceptionally able children
Gillespie, A. 143–4
Glazzard, J. 21, 22
Goodley, D. 10
graduated approach 21, 23, 24, 26–7, 28, 155, 200t
Graham, S. 143–4
Greene, R.W. 128
Griffiths, D. 27
Griffiths, K.M. 83
Grigorenko, E.L. 136

Haidt, J. 81
handwriting, and DCD 190–1
Harrison, J.R. 126
Hartmann, T. 117
Hayes, S.W. 55
hearing *see* auditory processing disorders (ASD)
Hellawell, B. 24
Hickinbotham, L. 83
high-ability children *see* exceptionally able children
high-quality teaching 25–6
history, inclusive education 20–1
Hobfoll, S.E. 90
Hochgatterer, L. 54
Hodkinson, A. 25
holistic approach 11, 23, 33
  and bilingualism 241
  and DCD 188–9
  migrant children 56

and SEMH 90–1
home support and parents
    and ADHD 118–19
    and bilingualism 241
    and DCD 187, 199–200t
    and exceptionally able children 251–2
    and MLD 169–70
Hoover, W.A. 139
Hornby, G. 21
Horváthová, B. 247
humanistic psychology 88
Hummerstone, H. 67
hunter-farmer theory 117
Huppert, F.A. 87
hybrid model 11, 141
hypersensitivity, neurological 191

identity 12
individual model (medical model) of disability 4–5, 4t, 24
interventions, defined 14, 91

Jacobs, B. 89
Jia, M. 125
Jorm, A.F. 83

Kanevsky, L. 255
Keighley, T. 255
Kessler, R.C. 90
Klatte, M. 226
Knowler, H. 25

labels 11–12, 66, 83
Lancet Psychiatry convention 12, 83
Langberg, J.M. 118
language 11–12
    and APD 222–4
        and additional language 221–2
    and autism 66
    mathematical 164–5, 165t
    and migrant children 54
    and social inequality 102–3, *103*, 106
    see also bilingualism
Lauchlan, F. 83
learner voice 27
Learning about Neurodiversity in Schools (LEANS) 75
learning media assessment 208
Lehane, T. 28
Levesque, A.R. 104
Liber, J.M. 92

localisation 225
Loxley, A. 12

Mace, Ron 39
Mackenzie, C. 48
macrosystem 35, *49*, 50
macrotime 38
Maguire, M. 25
Main, Mary 34t
Marmot, M. 109
Maslow, Abraham 88
mathematical learning difficulties (MLD) 151–2, 155, 157
    identifying learners with mathematical learning difficulties/developmental dyscalculia/maths anxiety 155–8, 156–7t
    interventions/practices 160–9, 162t, 163t, 164t, 165t, 167–8t
    mathematical development 152–5, 154t
    psychological models 158–60
mathematics see numeracy
Mealings, K. 226
medical model of disability see individual model
mental health
    and dyslexia 141
    and social inequality 101, *102*, 104, 106, 108–9
    stigma/labelling/diagnosis 82–5
mesosystem 35, 54–5
mesotime 38
metacognition 164
Miciak, J. 143
microsystem 35, 53–4
microtime 38
migrant children 47–8, 56–7
    ecological systems theory 48–55, *49*
    implications for practice 55–6
Mikami, A.Y. 125
Mind in Society (Vygotsky) 255–6
MLD see mathematical learning difficulties (MLD)
models of disability 3–11, 4t, 8t
Moore, D.R. 219–20, 221
Moriña, A. 217
Morris, P.A. 37
Murray, Fergus 69

Na, J.J. 125
Negoita, A. 141

Neihart, M. 249
Nemeth code 211
neuro-affirmative models 7, 9–10, 15
neurobiology, and social inequality 107
neurodivergence 9, 75
neurodivergences, and APD 221
neurodiversity 9
 -affirming supports 73
 and autism 70
 and the curriculum 74–5
Neuromotor Task Training (NTT) 190
Norwich, B. 11, 22
numeracy 151–2
 identifying learners with MLD/DD/
   maths anxiety 155–8, 156–7t
 mathematical development 152–5, 154t
 psychological models 158–60
 supporting learners with MLD 160–9,
   165t, 167–8t
numerical cognition 158–9

Olson, R.K. 135
orientation and mobility (O&M), and
   visual impairment 209
orthography 139
Outhwaite, L. 166, 168
overexcitabilities 249–50, 256
overthinking, and exceptionally able
   children 248, 252
Owens, J.S. 125, 126

Paat, Y. 48
Pan, S.C. 144
Paniagua, A. 54
parents *see* home support and parents
Parsons, S. 67
pedagogy, and MLD 161, 162t
peer modelling 72–3
peer support, autistic 73–4
Pennington, B.F. 141
Perfetti, C. 144
PERMA model 81, *82*
Perry, T. 55
person-environment fit (P-E fit) 7
person-first language 12, 66, 83
personalisation, and MLD 162, 163t
Pfiffner, L.J. 124
phonics 223
phonology 139
physical development, and exceptionally
   able children 247

Piaget, Jean 34t
positive education 81
positive psychology 16, 81
Powell, D. 160
prevention, defined 91
Priestley, M. 4
process-person-context-time (PPCT)
   model 36–7, 38
Proctor, C.P. 240
profiles, children's 92
promotion, defined 91
promotional approaches 87
prosthetic environment 142
proximal processes 36–8
psy-medical model 4, 4t
psychoanalytic theory 88
psychobiology 86
psychology 14
 of inclusive education 15–17
 of special education 15
psychopathology, critical 83–5
Psychosocial Development Theory 34t
Pyle, K. 92

Radford, J. 28
Ready, D.D. 108
Redmond, G. 48
Reid, E. 247
relationships, and ADHD 118–19
resilience, mathematical 166
resource characteristics 37
resources, and MLD 162–3
response to intervention (RTI) model
   142–3, 240
Richards, M. 87
Roberts, J. 109
Robinson, 108
Rogers, Carl 88
Rose, J./Rose review 134, 142
Runswick-Cole, K. 10

Saito, K. 221–2
Sapon-Shevin, M. 32
savantism 68
Schmidt, P. 107
Schwenk, C. 159
self-regulation strategies 125–6
Seligman, M.E.P. 81
SEMH *see* social, emotional and mental
   health (SEMH)
SEN (special educational needs) 4, 17

models of disability 3–11, 4t, 8t
special and inclusive education continuum 13–17, *13*
see also SEND Code of Practice (Special Educational Needs and Disabilities Code of Practice)
SENCOs (special educational needs coordinators) 27–8
SEND Code of Practice (Special Educational Needs and Disabilities Code of Practice) 21
and bilingualism/second language learning 231–2
and Children and Families Act 22
current guidance 23–4
and DCD 181
and enacting SEN 24–5
and high-quality teaching 25–6
and learner voice 27
on SEMH difficulties 80
see also SENCOs
sensitivities, sensory 249–50, 256
sensory integration 182
sensory processing 184–6t, 191
sensory processing sensitivity (SPS), and exceptionally able children 249–50, 256
Shakespeare, T. 11
Sharma, M.C. 162
Sharma, P. 27
Shevlin, M. 12
Shield, B. 226–7
Siegel, L.S. 240
Silberman, Steve, *NeuroTribes* 9
Simple View of Reading (SVoR) formula 137–9, 138t
Singer, Judy 9
Singh, I. 121
skills development, and ADHD 125–6
Skinner, B.F. 86
Slavkov, N. 237
SLCN see speech, language and communication needs (SLCN)
Slee, R. 16
small-group interventions, and dyslexia 143
social development, and exceptionally able children 248, 252–3, 254t
social and emotional learning (SEL) 87
social, emotional and mental health (SEMH) 24, 79–82, *82*, 94
and challenging behaviours 85–91
response to difficulties 91–3
stigma/labelling/diagnosis 82–5
social gradients 101–3, *102–3*
social inequality 99–100, 109–10
causality 104–5, *105*
and child outcomes 100–2
interventions in the classroom 108–9
mechanisms 105–7
social gradients 101–3, *102–3*
Social Learning Theory 34t, 87
social model of disability 5–7, 8t, 24
social skills training 125
socio-economic status (SES) defined 100
and ADHD 118
and bilingualism 233
Sociocultural Theory of Cognitive Development 34t
Soni, A. 83
Soppitt, R. 121
Sosu, E.M. 107
special educational needs see SEN (special educational needs)
special educational needs coordinators (SENCOs) 27–8
Special Educational Needs and Disabilities Code of Practice see SEND Code of Practice (Special Educational Needs and Disabilities Code of Practice)
special and inclusive education continuum 28–9
challenge of enacting 24–5
Children and Families Act (2014) 22
current guidance for applying the definition of SEN 234
first response to provision 25–7
policy and legislation 20–1
supporting children in schools 27–8
specific learning differences (SpLD) see developmental dyscalculia; dyslexia; mathematical learning difficulties
speech, language and communication needs (SLCN) 137–8, 238–9
stigma 8t, 11, 52
and ADHD 120–1
and mental health 83
Stoner, G. 128
Straatmann, V.S. 106
Strange Stories task 71–2

strengths-based approach 9
 and ADHD 117–18
 and dyslexia 142
stress 89–90
study skills, and exceptionally able children 249, 255–6
SVoR *see* Simple View of Reading (SVoR) formula
Swain, J. 10
systems model 35–6

teachers, and autism 67, 68, 69
Theory of Mind (ToM) 70–5
Thomas, C. 6, 7
Thomas, G. 12
time
 and ADHD 127
 and MLD 162–3, 164t
 and visual impairment 212
tolerance-fading memory (TFM) 223–4
Torvik, F.A. 101, 105
trauma 89–90
triple code model (TCM) 158–9
Tunmer, W.E. 139

UN Convention on the Rights of the Child 27
underperformance, academic, and exceptionally able children 248–9, 255
Universal Design for Learning (UDL) 26, 27, 40–2, 42–3
Universal Design (UD) 38–40, 42–3

Verhoeven, L. 234

Vilardo, B. 125–6
Viljoen, H. 210
visual impairment 204–6
 assessment of 207–9
 and assistive technology 208–9, 210, 211–12, 212t
 combined-medium approach 210–11
 curriculum and exam modifications 210
 definitions/statistics 206–7, 206t
 inclusion tips 213, 213t
voice
 children's 93
 and ADHD 128
Vygotsky, L.S. 34t, 255–6

'Wait to Fail Approach' 5
Walker, N. 70
Walton, E. 50–1
Warnes, E. 25
Warnock, M. 16
Warnock Report 21
Warren, D.H. 205
Watson, N. 11
Weakland, M. 143
Webster, R. 28
Williams-Brown, Z. 25
Witton, C. 230
Wright, D.L. 108

Yu, Q. 107

Zizzo, G. 48
zone of proximal development (ZPD) 255–6

www.ingramcontent.com/pod-product-compliance
Lightning Source LLC
Chambersburg PA
CBHW051112230426
43667CB00014B/2539